Introduction to College Accounting

With Working Papers

Fourth Edition

Gregory W. Bischoff
Houston Community College

THOMSON

™

CUSTOM PUBLISHING

Editor: Heather Holtz
Production Manager: Staci Powers
Production Coordinator: Christina Smith
Marketing Coordinator: Sara L. Hinckley

ISBN 003-0464-18-8

Preface

The Fourth Edition of *Introduction to College Accounting* continues to provide a straightforward, practical introduction to accounting. As in previous editions, this textbook is designed to be "user friendly" to help students:

▩ Complete an academic degree.

▩ Complete a technical program.

▩ Acquire accounting skills for employment or advancement.

▩ Maintain accounting records if self-employed.

▩ Prepare for more advanced accounting courses.

Overall, *Introduction to College Accounting* has been revised with both flexibility and price in mind.

Flexibility

Introduction to College Accounting is now published through the Custom Publishing division of the Dryden Press. Instructors can order the sequence of chapters and modules that best meets the needs of their students. New modules can be written by the author (or submitted by the instructor to the publisher) to supplement the textbook. This flexibility allows an instructor to select any number of chapters and modules. Furthermore, student ancillaries can be added to the end of the textbook. For example, for a one-semester course, an adopter could order Chapters 1-14 of the textbook and have the 1-14 Working Papers ancillary bound in, giving students the textbook and working papers under one cover. See your Dryden sales representative for details.

Price

The new format allows Dryden to offer the book at a lower price than comparable textbooks without lowering the quality. Instructors can expect the same quality they saw in the previous three editions.

Integrated Learning System

The author has prepared or assisted in the preparation of all instructor and student aids. These items are integrated or cross-referenced with the Learning Objectives in each chapter of the textbook.

Chapter Organization

Each chapter includes these pedagogical aids:

▩ **Learning Objectives,** are listed at the beginning of each chapter and are noted in the margin where they are discussed in the text; all chapter exercises and problems are also keyed to the objectives. These Learning Objectives serve as an outline for all instructor and student aids, thus contributing to the integrated learning system.

- **Exhibits** detail the procedures used in producing important items and forms in accounting practices.
- **Realistic accounting forms** are used throughout.
- The **Chapter Review** summarizes each Learning Objective.
- The **Glossary** in each chapter defines the important words and concepts discussed.
- Five multiple-choice **Self-Test Questions for Review** give students immediate feedback on their grasp of each chapter. Answers are at the end of each chapter.
- A **Practical Review Problem** (with answer) helps students understand significant concepts or processes.
- **Discussion Questions** focusing on major concepts and terms can be used to stimulate classroom discussion.
- **Exercises and Problems** provide students with a variety of homework assignments. Each exercise and problem is identified by Learning Objective number(s), and each has a short description. Many chapters have Comprehensive Chapter Review Problems covering all the chapter's Learning Objectives.
- Exercises and problems that can be worked using computer spreadsheets are indicated by a **computer logo.**

Special Review Problems

This textbook includes the following special review problems:

- The **Accounting Cycle Review Problem** (after Chapter 6) is a mini-practice set that tests a student's knowledge of the accounting cycle for a service-type company.
- The **Special Journals Review Problem** (after Chapter 9) tests a student's knowledge of special journals.
- The **Payroll Review Problem** (after Chapter 14) tests a student's knowledge of payroll.
- A **Checklist of Key Figures** (for problems) is at the end of each chapter.

For the Instructor

- **INSTRUCTOR'S MANUAL**   This manual is organized in four sections for each chapter in the testbook: (a) Suggested Teaching or Lecture Outline; (b) Homework Analysis; (c) Demonstration Problem (also available as PowerPoint slides); and (d) 2 Ten-Minute Quizzes with answers. The manual also includes a list of the PowerPoint slides and the solutions to Practice Sets A–E.
- **SOLUTIONS MANUAL**   This manual contains answers to all discussion questions, exercises, problems, and special review problems in the textbook.
- **SOLUTIONS TRANSPARENCIES**   Transparencies of problems are available to departments adopting the textbook.
- **POWERPOINT SLIDES**   These teaching slides of selected text material and demonstration problems (from the Instructor's Manual) are also available to adopters upon request to the publisher.
- **TEST BOOK**   The Test Book offers 22 true/false questions, 22 multiple-choice questions, and 6 exercises for each chapter of the textbook (a total of 50 questions and exercises per chapter). Each question and exercise is organized by learning objective(s) and difficulty level (Easy, Average, or Difficult).

- **COMPUTERIZED TEST BOOK**   A computerized version of the Test Book is available to adopters upon request to the publisher. This computerized version of the Test Book enables instructors to vary the order of test items, select items randomly, and modify the tests as needed.
- **ACHIEVEMENT TESTS**   This book consists of four series (A, B, C, and D) that are perforated for easy removal and duplication. Series B is an alternate to Series A (in which tests cover two chapters each) and Series D is an alternate to Series C (in which tests cover four to five chapters each).
- **INSTRUCTIONAL VIDEOS**   A series of instructional videos is available to adopters upon request to the publisher.
- **COMPUTER GUIDE SOLUTIONS**   Solutions disks are available from the publisher on request.

For the Student

- **STUDY GUIDE**   The Study Guide provides a review of the learning objectives, a detailed review of the significant concepts and processes, 40 true/false questions, 20 completion questions, two exercises, and answers for self-scoring for each chapter in the textbook. Also included is a thorough mathematics review.
- **WORKING PAPERS**   This package is provided for all exercises, problems, and special review problems.
- **COMPUTER GUIDE: ELECTRONIC SPREADSHEET TEMPLATES AND PRACTICE SET**   Includes Excel templates for selected exercises and problems. "What If" questions are asked to show the power of the spreadsheet. Practice Set A (The Village Printer) is included along with instructions for Microsoft Excel (Windows version).
- **PRACTICE SET A, "THE VILLAGE PRINTER"**   This practice set covers a sole proprietorship service-type company and can be introduced at any point after Chapter 6.
- **PRACTICE SET E WITH BUSINESS PAPERS, "WALT's WINDOW WASH-ING"**   This practice set, prepared by Thomas Jackson (Cerritos Community College), covers a sole proprietorship service-type company. It covers the basic steps in the accounting cycle (Chapters 1-6) and provides business documents (invoices, checks, receipts, etc.) for students to work with.
- **PRACTICE SET B, "LAKE PLUMBING SUPPLY"**   This practice set covers a sole proprietorship merchandising-type firm and is designed to be used after Chapter 12.

Acknowledgments

As in the previous edition, many fine educators and professionals have made significant contributions to this book. Once again, I would sincerely like to thank my many students for their participation in the classroom testing of this new edition. My colleagues at Houston Community College have been most helpful, and their valuable input is greatly appreciated.

I am deeply indebted to the many perceptive reviewers and questionnaire respondents throughout the country who helped in the development of this and past editions: **Terry G. Aime,** *Delgado Community College;* **James R. Bryce,** *Del Mar College;* **Donald R. Davis,** *Modesto Junior College;* **Tom Dent,** *St. Louis Community College—Florissant Valley;* **Doris Edwards,** *National Education Centers;* **Jacolin P. Eichelberger,** *Hillsborough Community College;* **Tom Jackson,** *Cerritos Community College;* **Edward A.**

Klump, *Knapp Business College;* **Robert J. McCarter,** *Macomb Community College;* **La Verne Vertrees,** *St. Louis Community College—Meramec;* and **Philip Walter,** *Bellevue Community College.*

Other instructors graciously participated in telephone interviews and surveys, and I am grateful for their comments: **Harold Anderson,** *Arizona Western College;* **John Carstens,** *Knapp Business College;* **David Champagne,** *Antelope Valley College;* **John Chestnutt,** *Alan Hancock College;* **Judith Chowen,** *Cerritos Community College;* **Frank Cress,** *Butte College;* **John di Stasio,** *Pikes Peak Community College;* **Karen Durling,** *Beal Business College;* **William M. Evans,** *Cerritos Community College;* **Don Freeman,** *Pikes Peak Community College;* **David Godley,** *Arizona Western College;* **Janet Grant,** *Skyline College;* **Jan Hanson,** *Rancho Santiago College;* **Cynthia Harrison,** *Knapp Business College;* **Jack Heinsius,** *Modesto Junior College;* **Polly Hewes,** *Beal Business College;* **Ed Hinrichs,** *St. Louis Community College—Florissant Valley;* **Gerald Holtke,** *Crafton Hills College;* **Marlene Krause,** *South Puget Sound Community College;* **Carol McCain,** *King's River Community College;* **Pam Melville,** *King's River Community College;* **Albert Motley,** *Arizona Western College;* **Linda Murdock,** *North Harris County Junior College;* **José Ortega,** *Modesto Junior College;* **Kay Pallaviciani,** *North Harris County Junior College;* **Dave Risch,** *St. Louis Community College— Florissant Valley;* **Bonnie Robinson,** *Arizona Western College;* **Francis Sakiey,** *Mercer County Community College;* **Howard Sherman,** *Rancho Santiago College;* **Elaine Simpson,** *St. Louis Community College—Florissant Valley;* **Sharon V. Smith,** *Texas Southmost College;* **Allen Stehle,** *Beal Business College;* and **Penny Westerfield,** *North Harris County Junior College.*

Finally, I would like to thank the members of the book team at The Dryden Press and Custom Publishing—George Provol, publisher; Eddie Dawson, senior production manager; Scott Baker, art director; Laura Miley, project editor; Cathy Spitzenberger, senior electronic publishing coordinator; Nanda Patel, electronic publishing coordinator; Virginia Main, electronic publishing coordinator; Scott Timian, vice president, custom publishing; Mike Beaupré, director of digital publishing; Felix Frazier, custom publisher, and Mary Botello, production manager.

Gregory W. Bischoff

Contents

6 Closing the Accounting Records   6-1

7 The Sales Journal and Accounts Receivable Subsidiary Ledger   7-1

8 The Purchases Journal and Accounts Payable Subsidiary Ledger   8-1

9   The Cash Receipts and Cash Payments Journals   9-1

10   Cash, Petty Cash, and the Change Fund   10-1

11 Adjustments and Worksheets for a Merchandising Firm   11-1

12 Financial Statements and Closing Entries for a Merchandising Firm   12-1

13 Payroll: Employee Earnings and Deductions   13-1

14 Payroll: Employer's Taxes and Reports   14-1

Accounting and Business Transactions

LEARNING OBJECTIVES

After reading this chapter, discussing the questions, and working the exercises and problems, you will be able to do the following:

1. Define accounting and the role of accountants

2. Identify the forms of business organizations

3. Identify the types of business operations

4. Understand the fundamental accounting equation

5. Record business transactions

6. Prepare a balance sheet

Although there are many reasons to study accounting, you will find that the following are among the most important:

1. Accounting is a basic component of business management.
2. Accounting is one means by which managers stay informed of the progress of their companies.
3. Accounting provides a method of recording, evaluating, and interpreting business activities.
4. Government agencies, banks, owners, and investors all require accounting information.

Clearly, accounting is a critical part of any business. In fact, it would be almost impossible for a business to function successfully without accounting information. Consequently, accounting is also an important and dynamic academic discipline. With this in mind, let's begin.

Definition of Accounting

Objective 1
Define accounting and the role of accountants.

Accounting is the "language" of business. It translates and communicates the movement of resources throughout economic systems. Accounting also measures the performance and status of business and economic entities—large, multinational corporations; state, local, and federal governments; schools and universities; and individual small businesses. An economic entity is able to analyze, classify, record, report, and interpret each of its transactions by using acceptable accounting practices and procedures. These procedures are called **generally accepted accounting principles** (GAAP), which represent an informed agreement on the theory and practice of accounting.

Accountants are the professionals in the business or economic entity who analyze, classify, record, and interpret transactions. Most accountants have at least a four-year college degree.

The American Institute of Certified Public Accountants prepares a comprehensive two-and-one-half-day examination in accounting practice, accounting theory, auditing, and business law. An accountant must pass all four parts of the examination to become a certified public accountant (CPA). Thus, the public is assured of the competency and knowledge of the CPA and can rely on the CPA's presentations and recommendations. As with many other professions, such as law and medicine, accountants also specialize in various fields and industries. The three broad professional fields are public accounting, private accounting, and nonprofit accounting. (See Exhibit 1-1 for career paths that a student may pursue.)

EXHIBIT 1-1   Career Path(s) of Accounting Students

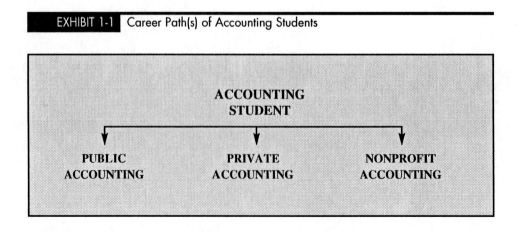

Public Accounting

Many CPAs work in public accounting, specializing in such areas as tax preparation and consultation, auditing, and management information advisory services. The public relies heavily on **auditing,** which is an independent analysis of the financial records of an organization. For this reason, the CPA or public accountant must make sure that he or she has no conflict of interest with a client organization so the public can rely on his or her review of financial records.

Private Accounting

This field includes such diverse industries as oil and gas businesses, steel manufacturing plants, textile businesses, department stores, and so on. Accountants employed in this area prepare financial statements, internal management reports, tax calculations, and internal audits.

Nonprofit Accounting

Accountants who work in universities, city governments, public hospitals, and other governmental or public organizations help to ensure that these nonprofit organizations use their resources wisely and efficiently. Because the nonprofit sector of our economy has grown considerably in recent years, there will be an increasing demand for accountants to perform internal audits, process forms and paperwork, and ensure compliance with laws and regulations.

Forms of Business Organizations

Objective 2
Identify the forms of business organizations.

The three major forms of business organizations in the United States are **sole proprietorships, partnerships,** and **corporations.** All are similar in that they are started and maintained to make a profit and/or distribute services to the public. Accountants perceive a business organization as an economic entity separate from its owners. This separate existence of the owners from the organization is known as the **entity concept.** For example, if you owned three businesses, each one would be considered a separate economic unit, and you would keep separate accounting records for each. You would also keep your personal nonbusiness accounting records (for example, the mortgage papers on your home) separate from each of your businesses.

Sole Proprietorships

A sole proprietorship is a business formed and owned by one individual. This form of organization represents the largest number of businesses in the United States. Because there is only one owner, sole proprietorships are generally the smallest in size and the easiest to create.

Partnerships

A partnership is a business formed and owned by two or more individuals. The partners enter into a contractual agreement, whether written or oral, whereby they share duties and responsibilities, profits and losses.

Corporations

A corporation, unlike a sole proprietorship or partnership, is a business organization that is legally separate from its owners. Remember that accountants treat all business organizations as separate from their owners, but *legally* only the corporation is separate. Corporations represent the smallest number of business organizations, but they are also the largest. Ownership is divided into shares of stock.

Types of Business Operations

Objective 3
Identify the types of business operations.

There are three major types of business operations in the United States: **service, merchandising,** and **manufacturing.**

Service

Most law firms, accounting firms, consulting firms, and medical practices are service oriented, offering services rather than goods to the public.

Merchandising

Merchandising businesses primarily offer resalable goods (or *merchandise*) for sale to the public. The merchandiser does not produce these goods but instead usually purchases them from a manufacturer. Grocery stores, department stores, and hardware stores are examples of this type of business operation.

Manufacturing

A manufacturing business operation is usually *capital intensive,* meaning the business must purchase expensive machinery and equipment. Working materials are also purchased in raw or unprocessed form and are combined with labor to produce a salable product. The manufacturer may either sell directly to the public or to a distributor or merchandising business, who will, in turn, sell to the public.

Assets, Liabilities, and Owner's Equity

Objective 4
Understand the fundamental accounting equation.

Assets, liabilities, and owner's equity are *broad classes of accounts.* Later, you are introduced to two other broad classes of accounts—revenues and expenses.

Assets

Assets are anything of value owned by a business. They are usually recorded in the accounting records or books of the acquiring business at *historical cost* (actual cost). Some examples of assets include Cash, Accounts Receivable, Prepaid Expenses (such as Prepaid Insurance and Prepaid Rent), Land, Buildings, Equipment, Furniture, and Supplies.

Liabilities

A **creditor** is one to whom money is owed. **Liabilities** are the creditor's claims against the assets of a business. A common term for liabilities is *debts,* the amounts owed by a business. Liabilities are recorded *at the amount to be paid in the future.* Accounts Payable, Wages Payable, Notes Payable, and Bonds Payable are some examples of liabilities.

Owner's Equity

Owner's equity or **Capital** is the owner's claims after the creditor's claims against the assets of a business. This represents the owner's original investment plus any additional investments in the business, along with the results of operations. If the owner withdraws any assets from the business, owner's equity (Capital) decreases. Simply defined, owner's equity equals assets minus liabilities.

Fundamental Accounting Equation

The **fundamental accounting equation** is stated as follows:

$$\text{Assets} = \text{Liabilities} + \text{Owner's Equity}$$

As with any equation, the left side (assets) must always equal the right side (liabilities plus owner's equity). You will need this equation to analyze, classify, record, report, and interpret business transactions.

Accounts   An **account** is a separate record for each asset, liability, and owner's equity. A broad class of accounts would include all the accounts within that particular classification. For example, assets comprise a broad class of accounts, whereas Cash is an *individual asset account*. The broad classes of accounts and individual accounts are illustrated in Exhibit 1-2.

Manipulating the Fundamental Accounting Equation

If you know two parts of the fundamental accounting equation, you can always find the third. We look at several examples that follow.

Finding Assets   If liabilities total $10,000 and owner's equity totals $15,000, then total assets can be determined by adding liabilities and owner's equity:

$$\text{Assets} = \text{Liabilities} + \text{Owner's Equity}$$
$$\$\ ? = \$10,000 + \$15,000$$
$$\$25,000 = \$10,000 + \$15,000$$

Finding Liabilities   If assets total $30,500 and owner's equity totals $16,750, then liabilities can be determined as follows:

$$\text{Assets} = \text{Liabilities} + \text{Owner's Equity}$$
$$\$30,500 = \$\ ? + \$16,750$$

Liabilities are isolated by subtracting owner's equity from each side of the equation:

$$\text{Assets} - \text{Owner's Equity} = \text{Liabilities}$$
$$\$30,500 - \$16,750 = \$13,750$$

EXHIBIT 1-2   Broad and Individual Classes of Accounts

	Broad Class of Accounts		
	Assets	**Liabilities**	**Owner's Equity**
Examples of	Cash	Accounts Payable	Kay Loomis, Capital
Individual	Accounts Receivable	Notes Payable	
Accounts	Prepaid Insurance	Bonds Payable	

Finding Owner's Equity If assets total $63,190 and liabilities total $27,380, then owner's equity equals

$$\text{Assets} = \text{Liabilities} + \text{Owner's Equity}$$
$$\$63,190 = \$27,380 + \$\,?$$

Owner's equity is isolated by subtracting liabilities from each side of the equation:

$$\text{Assets} - \text{Liabilities} = \text{Owner's Equity}$$
$$\$63,190 - \$27,380 = \$35,810$$

Business Transactions

Objective 5
Record business transactions.

An economic event can also be called a *business transaction*. A business transaction occurs when resources move through an organization. These movements can be internal or external in nature. An internal movement is self-contained within the organization, whereas an external resource movement occurs between two or more separate business organizations. To simplify the terminology, in future discussions an economic event or business transaction will be called a **transaction** and any type of business organization will be called a **firm.**

Starting a Sole Proprietorship (Firm)

A firm with a single owner is a sole proprietorship and will commonly have many transactions. Suppose that Kay Loomis is the sole owner of Kay Loomis, CPA, and in starting her firm, she has the following transactions:

a. Investment of cash by owner
b. Purchase of office equipment for cash
c. Purchase of office equipment on credit
d. Purchase of office supplies for cash and on account
e. Investment of accounting library by owner
f. Payment of a liability

Transaction (a). January 1, 19XX: Investment of cash by owner.

Kay believes that another accounting service is needed in her town. Therefore, she withdraws $10,000 in cash from her personal savings account and deposits it in a bank in the business name Kay Loomis, CPA. (Remember that the entity concept states that the business organization, or firm, must be kept separate from the owners. All accounting records must be maintained separately.)

The fundamental accounting equation looks like this after the investment (for illustration purposes, dollar signs are not presented):

Assets	=	**Liabilities**	+	**Owner's Equity**
Cash	=			Kay Loomis, Capital
(a) +10,000	=			+10,000

Analysis The owner invested cash in her newly formed accounting service. Assets increased and owner's equity (Capital) increased. There are no liabilities. Assets = Owner's Equity (10,000 = 10,000).

Transaction (b). January 3, 19XX: Purchase of office equipment for cash.

Kay purchases a typewriter from Rogers Office Equipment at a total cost of $1,200. She writes a check (which is considered cash) for the purchase.

The fundamental accounting equation now looks like this:

	Assets		=	Liabilities +	Owner's Equity
	Cash	+ Office Equip.	=		Kay Loomis, Capital
Prev. Bal.	10,000		=		10,000
(b)	− 1,200	+ 1,200	=		
New Bal.	8,800	+ 1,200	=		+10,000
		10,000			10,000

Analysis The firm purchased a typewriter for cash. Assets both increased and decreased. Assets are now 10,000 (8,800 + 1,200). The fundamental accounting equation is still in balance (10,000 = 10,000).

Transaction (c). January 5, 19XX: Purchase of office equipment on credit.

Kay purchases a computer from Chen Computers at a total cost of $8,000. She decides to buy the computer on account (on credit). The full amount is to be paid within twelve months. A liability account entitled **Accounts Payable** is increased for amounts owed to creditors.

After this transaction, the fundamental accounting equation looks like this:

	Assets		=	Liabilities	+	Owner's Equity
	Cash	+ Office Equip. =		Accounts Payable	+	Kay Loomis, Capital
Prev. Bal.	8,800	+ 1,200	=			10,000
(c)		+ 8,000	=	+8,000		
New Bal.	8,800	+ 9,200	=	8,000	+	10,000
		18,000			18,000	

Analysis The firm purchased a computer on account. Assets increased and liabilities increased. Assets are now 18,000 (8,800 + 9,200). Liabilities and owner's equity are also 18,000 (8,000 + 10,000). The fundamental accounting equation is in balance (18,000 = 18,000).

Transaction (d). January 8, 19XX: Purchase of office supplies for cash and on account.

Kay purchases $500 of office supplies from Leon's Office Supply. She pays $100 in cash with the remainder on account ($500 − $100 = $400).

The fundamental accounting equation, after this transaction, looks like this:

	Assets			=	Liabilities	+	Owner's Equity
	Cash +	Office Equip. +	Office Supp. =		Accounts Payable	+	Kay Loomis, Capital
Prev. Bal.	8,800 +	9,200	=		8,000	+	10,000
(d)	−100		+ 500	=	+ 400		
New Bal.	8,700 +	9,200	+ 500	=	8,400	+	10,000
		18,400				18,400	

Analysis The firm purchased office supplies for cash and on account. Assets are both increased and decreased. Liabilities are increased. Assets are now 18,400 (8,700 + 9,200 + 500). Liabilities and owner's equity are 18,400 (8,400 + 10,000). The fundamental accounting equation is in balance (18,400 = 18,400).

Transaction (e). January 10, 19XX: Investment of accounting library by owner.

Kay invests some personal accounting books worth $75. These books increase the owner's Capital account because the assets of the firm are increased.

The fundamental accounting equation, after this transaction, appears as follows:

	Cash +	Office Equip. +	Office Supp. +	Library =	Accounts Payable	+	Kay Loomis, Capital
Prev. Bal.	8,700 +	9,200 +	500	=	8,400	+	10,000
(e)				+ 75 =		+	75
New Bal.	8,700 +	9,200 +	500 +	75 =	8,400	+	10,075

Assets = 18,475   Liabilities + Owner's Equity = 18,475

Analysis The owner invested personal assets in the firm. Assets total 18,475 after this transaction. Liabilities and owner's equity also total 18,475. Because these amounts agree (18,475 = 18,475), the fundamental accounting equation is in balance.

Transaction (f). January 13, 19XX: Payment of a liability.

Kay pays Leon's Office Supply $130 as a partial payment of the $400 owed [see Transaction (d)].

After this transaction, the fundamental accounting equation appears as follows:

	Cash +	Office Equip. +	Office Supp. +	Library =	Accounts Payable	+	Kay Loomis, Capital
Prev. Bal.	8,700 +	9,200 +	500 +	75 =	8,400	+	10,075
(f)	– 130			=	– 130	+	
New Bal.	8,570 +	9,200 +	500 +	75 =	8,270	+	10,075

Assets = 18,345   Liabilities + Owner's Equity = 18,345

Analysis A partial payment is made on an amount owed. Both assets (Cash) and liabilities (Accounts Payable) are decreased. Assets now total 18,345 (8,570 + 9,200 + 500 + 75). Liabilities and owner's equity are 18,345 (8,270 + 10,075). The fundamental accounting equation is in balance (18,345 = 18,345).

Other Transactions Any firm will have many more transactions than the ones described above. But there is one common element for all transactions: *the left side of the fundamental accounting equation must always equal the right side.* Assets must always equal liabilities plus owner's equity (Capital).

Summary of Transactions

An accountant is always very careful while recording transactions, but errors do occur. Therefore, the transactions must be summarized and totaled to ensure that the total account balances of the left side equal the total account balances of the right side.

Although each transaction is recorded separately, it is interrelated to the other transactions. So far, the firm Kay Loomis, CPA, has used four asset accounts: Cash, Office Equipment, Office Supplies, and Library. One liability account has been used, Accounts Payable, and one owner's equity account, Kay Loomis, Capital. The six previous transactions are summarized as follows:

	Assets									=	Liabilities	+	Owner's Equity
										=	**Accounts**		**Kay Loomis,**
	Cash	+	**Office Equip.**	+	**Office Supp.**	+	**Library**			=	**Payable**	+	**Capital**
(a)	+10,000									=		+	10,000
(b)	−1,200	+	1,200							=			
Bal.	8,800	+	1,200							=			10,000
(c)		+	8,000							=	+8,000		
Bal.	8,800	+	9,200							=	8,000	+	10,000
(d)	−100			+	500					=	+400		
Bal.	8,700	+	9,200	+	500					=	8,400	+	10,000
(e)						+	75			=		+	75
Bal.	8,700	+	9,200	+	500	+	75			=	8,400	+	10,075
(f)	−130									=	−130		
Bal.	8,570	+	9,200	+	500	+	75			=	8,270	+	10,075 *

Left Side Equals Right Side

It is imperative that the left side (assets) equals the right side (liabilities plus owner's equity). Therefore, you must add the final balances of all the accounts on the left side and add the final balances of all the accounts on the right side. The right side and the left side must equal.

LEFT SIDE			RIGHT SIDE	
ACCOUNT	**FINAL BALANCE**		**ACCOUNT**	**FINAL BALANCE**
Cash	+8,570		Accounts Payable	+8,270
Office Equipment	+9,200		Kay Loomis, Capital	+10,075
Office Supplies	+500			
Library	+75			
Left Side Totals	18,345		Right Side Totals	18,345

If the account totals are not equal, then the accountant must correct the error(s). Otherwise, the information will be of no use to the firm.

Balance Sheet

Objective 6
Prepare a balance sheet.

The **balance sheet** is a statement of the financial position of a firm at a point in time (a certain date). The balance sheet is usually prepared at the end of an accounting period—one month, three months, twelve months, and so on. It may, however, be prepared at any time. Most firms use a twelve-month business year, which accountants call a **fiscal year.** This twelve-month period can start at any time; for example, a firm may start May 1 and end the following year on April 30. Any financial statements prepared for a period of less than one fiscal year are called **interim statements.**

All asset, liability, and owner's equity accounts that have balances are presented on the balance sheet. The balance sheet, like the fundamental accounting equation, is proof that assets = liabilities + owner's equity (Capital).

---

*Remember that Capital is the owner's claims against the assets of the business. At this time, total assets are 18,345 (8,570 + 9,200 + 500 + 75). Creditors have claims of 8,270, with the remaining 10,075 equaling the owner's claim.

Steps in Preparing the Balance Sheet

A balance sheet, in report form, for Kay Loomis, CPA, is prepared in Exhibit 1-3. The point in time (or date) is January 13, 19XX. The following six steps for preparing the balance sheet are keyed ((a), (b), (c), and so on) to Exhibit 1-3:

EXHIBIT 1-3 Preparation of Balance Sheet in Report Form

	Kay Loomis, CPA	
(a)	**Balance Sheet**	
	January 13, 19XX	

(b) **Assets**			
Cash	$8,570 –		
Office Supplies	500 –		
Office Equipment	9,200 –		
Library	75 –		
Total Assets		$18,345 –	(c)
(d) **Liabilities**			
Accounts Payable		$ 8,270 –	
(e) **Owner's Equity**			
Kay Loomis, Capital		10,075 –	
Total Liabilities and Owner's Equity		$18,345 –	(f)

(a) The balance sheet has a three-part heading that is centered and includes, in this order, (1) the name of the firm, (2) the name of the financial statement, and (3) the date for which the financial statement is prepared. Leave one blank line before "Assets."

(b) The most liquid assets (Cash, Receivables, Supplies, and so on) are listed first, followed by the more permanent assets (Equipment, Library, and Building). A dollar sign appears at the beginning of each column. A line is drawn after the column to indicate that there are no more assets. A dash (—) is used in the cents column to indicate that there are no (zero) cents. For example, $8,570 is written as "$8,570—."

(c) The final total of assets is double-underlined. A double underline means "in balance." The single line above the total means that there are no more assets and calculations can be made. In this example, the calculation is to sum. A dollar sign appears at the final total. Leave one blank line before "Liabilities."

(d) Liabilities are listed in payment order, with Accounts Payable usually listed first. A dollar sign is given at the beginning of the column. Leave one blank line before "Owner's Equity."

(e) For a sole proprietorship, Owner's Equity is designated by Capital only. A line is drawn after Capital.

(f) Total Liabilities and Owner's Equity are added, and the total is double-underlined. This total must equal Total Assets. A dollar sign appears at the final total.

Chapter Review

1. **Define accounting and the role of accountants.**
   Accounting is the "language" of business. Accountants are the professionals who analyze, classify, record, and interpret transactions.

2. **Identify the forms of business organizations.**
   There are three forms of business organizations: sole proprietorships, partnerships, and corporations.

3. **Identify the types of business operations.**
   There are three types of business operations: service, merchandising, and manufacturing.

4. **Understand the fundamental accounting equation.**
   The fundamental accounting equation is:

   $$\text{Assets} = \text{Liabilities} + \text{Owner's Equity}$$

5. **Record business transactions.**
   A business transaction occurs when resources move through a business organization. Six transactions were recorded as examples in the chapter.

6. **Prepare a balance sheet.**
   A balance sheet is a statement of the financial position of the firm at a given point in time. The six steps for preparing a balance sheet were covered.

Glossary

Account Individual or single classification within the broad classes of accounts

Accountant A professional in an organization who analyzes, classifies, records, and interprets business transactions

Accounting The "language" of business; the means of analyzing, classifying, recording, reporting, and interpreting business transactions

Assets Anything of value owned by a business

Auditing Independent analysis of financial records

Balance Sheet Statement of the financial position of a firm at a point in time

Corporation Form of business organization that is legally separate from its owner(s); ownership is divided into shares of stock

Creditor One to whom money is owed

Entity Concept The owner is perceived as being separate from the business organization

Firm Any type of business organization

Fiscal Year Twelve-month business period

Fundamental Accounting Equation Assets = Liabilities + Owner's Equity

Generally Accepted Accounting Principles Informed agreement on the theory and practice of accounting; abbreviated as GAAP

Interim Statements Financial statements prepared for a period of less than one fiscal year

Liabilities Creditor's claims against the assets of a business

Owner's Equity Owner's claims against the assets of the business

Partnership Business formed and owned by two or more individuals

Sole Proprietorship Business formed and owned by one individual

Transaction An economic event

Self-Test Questions for Review

(Answers are at the end of Chapter 1.)

1. Sole proprietorships are the _____ in size and the _____ to create.
   a. smallest; easiest
   b. largest; most difficult
   c. smallest; most difficult
   d. largest; easiest

2. An example of an asset is _____
   a. Accounts Payable.
   b. Notes Payable.
   c. Accounts Receivable.
   d. Bonds Payable.

3. Assets are $70,000 and owner's equity is $50,000. Liabilities are _____
   a. $120,000.
   b. $70,000.
   c. $50,000.
   d. $20,000.

4. An owner invests a library in her accounting firm. Which of the following is increased?
   a. Cash
   b. Owner, Capital
   c. Accounts Payable
   d. Office Supplies

5. Find total assets given these accounts and account balances: Library, $1,000; Accounts Payable, $2,000; Cash, $5,000; Office Supplies, $3,000; and Office Equipment, $10,000.
   a. $19,000
   b. $21,000
   c. $18,000
   d. $20,000

Practical Review Problem

Objective 6

Preparing a Balance Sheet   Juan Tovar owns Tovar's Consulting Service. Juan lists his accounts in alphabetical order. He had the following accounts and account balances as of September 15, 19XX:

Accounts Payable	$ 2,710
Bonds Payable	21,000
Building	73,440
Cash	9,380
Equipment	7,930
Land	52,070
Notes Payable	12,360
Office Supplies	1,850
Juan Tovar, Capital	107,790
Wages Payable	810

REQUIRED
Prepare a balance sheet.

Answer to Practical Review Problem

Tovar's Consulting Service

Balance Sheet

September 15, 19XX

Assets			
Cash	$ 9 3 8 0 –		
Office Supplies	1 8 5 0 –		
Equipment	7 9 3 0 –		
Land	52 0 7 0 –		
Building	73 4 4 0 –		
Total Assets		$144 6 7 0 –	
Liabilities			
Accounts Payable	$ 2 7 1 0 –		
Wages Payable	8 1 0 –		
Notes Payable	12 3 6 0 –		
Bonds Payable	21 0 0 0 –		
Total Liabilities		$ 36 8 8 0 –	
Owner's Equity			
Juan Tovar, Capital		107 7 9 0 –	
Total Liabilities and Owner's Equity		$144 6 7 0 –	

Discussion Questions

Q 1-1 Define accounting. What is GAAP?

Q 1-2 What are the three broad professional accounting fields? Explain the three.

Q 1-3 What are the three forms of business organization? Explain the three.

Q 1-4 What are the three types of business operations? Explain the three.

Q 1-5 State the fundamental accounting equation. Define assets, liabilities, and owner's equity.

Q 1-6 Explain how assets can be determined if you know liabilities and owner's equity. Also, explain how owner's equity can be found if you know assets and liabilities.

Q 1-7 What account is increased and what account is decreased for each of the following transactions: (a) investment of cash by owner; (b) purchase of office equipment on account; and (c) payment of cash to a creditor?

Q 1-8 What accounts are increased and/or decreased for each of the following transactions: (a) purchase of office equipment for cash; (b) purchase of office supplies for cash and on account; and (c) investment of a law library by the owner?

Q 1-9 Define the following: (a) balance sheet; (b) fiscal period; and (c) interim statements.

Q 1-10 Briefly list the six steps in preparing the balance sheet.

Exercises

Objective 4	**E 1-1**	**Identifying Accounts** Paul Morgan is planning to open and operate a travel agency.

a. Name at least three asset accounts that he may use.

b. Name at least three liability accounts that he may use.

c. Name at least one owner's equity account that he may use.

Objective 5	**E 1-2**	**Recording Transactions** Complete the following transactions:

a. Owner invests cash in the firm. The account(s) increased are _____ and _____.

b. A liability is paid. The account(s) decreased are _____ and _____.

Objective 4	**E 1-3**	**Manipulating the Equation** Fill in the missing amounts:

ASSETS	LIABILITIES	OWNER'S EQUITY
10,000	6,000	(a)
(b)	4,000	9,000
15,000	(c)	12,000

Objective 6	**E 1-4**	**Completing a Balance Sheet** Fill in the missing amounts:

ASSETS

Cash	$ (a)
Office Supplies	1,000
Equipment	8,000
Land	10,000
Building	80,000
Total Assets	$ (b)

LIABILITIES

Accounts Payable	$ 3,000
Wages Payable	2,000
Total Liabilities	$ (c)

OWNER'S EQUITY

Erin Wade, Capital	(d)
Total Liabilities and Owner's Equity	$110,000

Objective 5	**E 1-5**	**Identifying Transactions** Determine what happened to cause the following account changes:

a. Cash increased $15,000 and Owner, Capital increased $15,000.

b. Equipment increased $5,000 and Cash decreased $5,000.

c. Accounts Payable decreased $200 and Cash decreased $200.

d. Office Supplies increased $300 and Accounts Payable increased $300.

Objective 6	**E 1-6**	**Using Balance Sheet Amounts** Thomas Freight has the following accounts and account balances (not including Capital): Cash, $10,000; Accounts Payable, $4,000; Office Supplies, $2,000; Wages Payable, $1,000; Office Equipment, $5,000.

a. What is the amount of total assets?

b. What is the amount of total liabilities?

c. What is the amount of owner's equity?

Objective 5   **E 1-7**   **Finding Missing Amounts**   Fill in the missing amounts:

CASH	SUPPLIES	EQUIPMENT	ACCOUNTS PAYABLE	WAGES PAYABLE	CAPITAL
5,000	2,000	10,000	3,000	1,000	(a)
(b)	1,000	20,000	5,000	2,000	15,000
7,000	3,000	30,000	(c)	4,000	34,000

Objective 6   **E 1-8**   **Preparing a Balance Sheet**   Prepare a balance sheet for Linda Nu, Attorney at Law, in report form, using the following information:

Cash, $26,000; Office Supplies, $3,000; Equipment, $10,000; Library, $4,000; Accounts Payable, $5,000; Linda Nu, Capital, $38,000. The date is April 15, 19XX.

Problems

Objective 5   **P 1-1**   **Identifying Accounts**   Ray's Market is owned by Ray Sawyer. He had the following transactions:

a. He started Ray's Market by investing $20,000.

b. Paid $3,000 for furniture.

c. Purchased $2,000 of office supplies on account.

d. Purchased $6,000 of furniture on account.

e. Paid $1,000 to apply to the amount owed in (c).

REQUIRED

List the accounts that are increased and/or decreased for each transaction. First, write the account(s) increased, if any, and then write the account(s) decreased, if any.

Objective 5   **P 1-2**   **Recording Transactions**   Maria Garcia is the sole owner of Garcia's Consulting Service. She had the following transactions:

a. Investment of $30,000 by the owner.

b. Purchased office equipment for cash, $10,000.

c. Purchased $4,000 of office supplies. Paid $1,000 in cash with the remainder on account.

d. Purchased office equipment on account, $8,000.

e. Paid $2,000 to apply to the purchase of office supplies in (c).

f. Owner invested a personal library valued at $3,000.

REQUIRED

1. Write the owner's name in the working papers for Capital.

2. Record the transactions in account columns, using plus and minus signs.

3. Prove the equality of Assets = Liabilities + Owner's Equity.

Objective 6   **P 1-3**   **Preparing a Balance Sheet**   Frank Longia started an accounting service, Frank Longia, CPA. Frank lists his accounts in alphabetical order. He had the following accounts and account balances as of October 19, 19XX:

Accounts Payable	$ 6,500
Bonds Payable	12,300
Building	70,000
Cash	15,600
Equipment	20,400
Land	43,700
Frank Longia, Capital	124,500
Notes Payable	11,200
Office Supplies	5,900
Wages Payable	1,100

REQUIRED
Prepare a balance sheet.

Objective 5 and 6

P 1-4 **Comprehensive Chapter Review Problem** Helen Kendall is an attorney. She started her own firm, Helen Kendall, Attorney at Law. She had the following transactions:
a. Investment of $50,000 by the owner.
b. Purchased office furniture for cash, $13,670.
c. Purchased $5,790 of office supplies. Paid $2,000 in cash with the remainder on account.
d. Purchased office furniture on account, $9,410.
e. Paid $1,000 to apply to the purchase of office supplies in (c).
f. Owner invested a personal library valued at $6,320.

REQUIRED
1. Write the owner's name in the working papers for Capital.
2. Record the transactions in account columns, using plus and minus signs.
3. Prove the equality of Assets = Liabilities + Owner's Equity.
4. Prepare a balance sheet (dated March 31, 19XX).

Checklist of Key Figures

P 1-1	No key figure
P 1-2	(3) Owner Capital, $33,000
P 1-3	Total Assets, $155,600
P 1-4	(4) Total Assets, $68,520

Answers to Self-Test Questions

1. a   **2.** c   **3.** d   **4.** b   **5.** a

The Double-Entry System

Earlier, we analyzed transactions and prepared a balance sheet by using the fundamental accounting equation:

$$Assets = Liabilities + Owner's\ Equity$$

This equation must, however, be expanded to apply to all possible transactions. In this chapter, we expand the equation and also present a new method for recording transactions that is both easy and efficient.

Because it is crucial that you thoroughly understand *owner's equity* and *Capital,* we begin this chapter with a discussion of these terms.

Broad Classes of Accounts

Drawing

Objective 1
Identify and discuss the broad classes of accounts.

A **Drawing** account is increased whenever the owner of a firm withdraws cash or other assets from the firm for his or her personal use. Drawing may thus be viewed as the opposite of Capital. It would be included in the owner's equity broad class of accounts as a reduction from Capital.

Owner's Equity versus Capital

Sometimes, the terms *owner's equity* and *Capital* are used synonymously. But you should remember that owner's equity is a broad class of accounts that includes both Capital and Drawing (see Exhibit 2-1). Capital represents the equity or ownership balance for a single owner of a firm (sole proprietorship). Equity is the owner's claims against the assets of the firm. The balance in the Drawing account would be subtracted from Capital to arrive at a final Capital balance.

Two other broad classes of accounts affect owner's equity and the final Capital balance. These are **revenues** and **expenses.**

Revenues

A firm is established to produce and distribute goods and/or services. These goods and services, when sold to another firm or individual, are called revenues. *Revenues increase Capital.* A firm generates revenues and thus increases Capital through selling goods and services. A firm that is operating without a clear set of ideas as to what goods and/or services to sell and deliver will soon go out of business.

Some examples of revenues include legal fees, auditing fees, management advisory services, tax services, interest income, and advertising income. Revenues are earned during a specific period of time—a month, three months, twelve months, and so on; but this period is generally not longer than one year.

EXHIBIT 2-1 | Owner's Equity Is a Broad Class of Accounts That Includes Capital and Drawing

Broad Class of Accounts	Accounts
Owner's Equity	Kay Loomis, Capital
	Kay Loomis, Drawing

Expenses

The final broad class of accounts is expenses. *Expenses reduce Capital.* They are the goods and services that are purchased and consumed to support the revenues. Wages Expense, Advertising Expense, Rent Expense, and Utilities Expense are some examples of expenses. *Do not confuse these expenses with prepaid expenses such as prepaid rent or prepaid insurance, which are assets.*

A firm cannot generate revenues without expenses. Imagine a business operating without a place to conduct business (Rent Expense) or without employees to do the necessary work (Wages Expense). This, of course, would be impossible.

Like revenues, expenses are also time-related. They too are measured for one month, three months, twelve months, and so on but usually not longer than twelve months, which is the normal fiscal year.

Expanded Fundamental Accounting Equation

Objective 2
Use the expanded fundamental accounting equation.

To include revenues and expenses, the fundamental accounting equation must be expanded as follows:

Assets = Liabilities + Owner's Equity + Revenues – Expenses

As before, the left side of the equation must always equal the right side. You will use this revised equation to analyze, classify, record, and interpret transactions.

Let's examine the fundamental accounting equation in more detail. To begin, on the right side, liabilities represent the creditors' claims against the assets of the firm. Owner's equity is the owner's claims against the assets of the firm. Revenues are generated through selling goods and services. And expenses represent assets that are used to support the revenues. For example, Cash, which is an asset, is used to pay wages to employees (Wages Expense). The employees work for the firm and, in turn, generate revenues by selling the firm's product or service, billing customers for amounts owed, manufacturing the product, and so on. Exhibit 2-2 illustrates the flow of assets to support revenues.

Double-Entry System

Every transaction uses two or more accounts for recording purposes. The **double-entry system** is a method of recording a transaction using at least two accounts, or a double entry. A transaction that uses more than two accounts is called a **compound entry.** The double-entry system is a system of checks and balances. In accounting, for every resource (asset) that enters the firm, another departs. For example, when the firm purchased office equipment for cash, the equipment received represented the inflow of resources (assets). You can probably guess what the outflow is. You are right—the payment of cash. Thus, the balance of inflows and outflows prevails.

EXHIBIT 2-2 | Flow of Assets to Support Revenues

ASSET →	(flow to) →	EXPENSE →	(flow to) →	REVENUES
Cash →	(payment of cash for) →	Wages Expense → for Employees	(perform → work)	(generate → revenues) → Increase Cash and/or Accounts Receivable (assets)

T Accounts

A **T account** derives its name from its resemblance to a T and is often used to record transactions. It is a tool that will eventually show you how to keep a set of books. A T account should be presented as follows:

The account name is placed at the top of the T:

Account Name

Debit

Debit, in accounting, means *left side only* and is abbreviated "Dr." In a T account, a debit would always appear on the left side. If you were using the account Cash, you would place "Cash" at the top of the T:

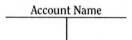

Cash	
Debit (or Dr.)	

Credit

In accounting, **credit** means *right side only* and is abbreviated "Cr." In a T account, a credit would always be on the right side. If you were using the account Accounts Payable, you would place "Accounts Payable" at the top of the T, just as you did with Cash before:

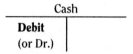

Accounts Payable	
	Credit (or Cr.)

Applications of Debits and Credits

Debits and credits, along with T accounts, can be used to record transactions. To illustrate, we will apply debits and credits to the broad classes of accounts in T account form:

Rule Assets are increased (+) by debits. Credits decrease (−) assets.

Assets	
Debit	Credit
+	−

Rule Liabilities are decreased (−) by debits. Credits increase (+) liabilities.

Liabilities	
Debit	Credit
−	+

Rule   Owner's equity is decreased (–) by debits. Credits increase (+) owner's equity.

Owner's Equity	
Debit	Credit
–	+

There is, however, an exception to these rules. The Drawing account is increased by debits and decreased by credits. It is a reduction to owner's equity. Drawing is a **contra** account, which means that its normal balance is contrary or "contra" to the normal balance within that broad class of accounts. Owner's equity or Capital normally has a *credit* balance. However, Drawing has a normal *debit* balance (see Exhibit 2-3).

Rule   Revenues are decreased (–) by debits. Credits increase (+) revenues.

Revenues	
Debit	Credit
–	+

Rule   Expenses are increased (+) by debits. Credits decrease (–) expenses.

Expenses	
Debit	Credit
+	–

Note that expenses decrease the equity of the firm, as they use up or consume assets to support revenues. Thus, we see that expenses are increased by debits and decreased by credits.

Rules for Using T Accounts to Record Transactions

1. Analyze the transaction—mentally review the accounts to be used.
2. Record the transaction's debit(s) first.
3. Record the transaction's credit(s) next.
4. Check to see that the total debit(s) monetary amount equals the total credit(s) monetary amount for the transaction.

EXHIBIT 2-3   Drawing Account Reduces Owner's Equity

Owner's Equity	
Debit	Credit
–	+

Drawing	
Debit	Credit
+	–

Objective 3
Apply debits and credits to business transactions using the T account format.

Transaction (a). January 1, 19XX: Investment of cash by owner[1]

Cash			Kay Loomis, Capital	
Dr.	Cr.		Dr.	Cr.
+	–		–	+
(a) 10,000				(a) 10,000

Transaction (b). January 3, 19XX: Purchase of office equipment for cash

Office Equipment			Cash	
Dr.	Cr.		Dr.	Cr.
+	–		+	–
(b) 1,200				(b) 1,200

Transaction (c). January 5, 19XX: Purchase of office equipment on credit

Office Equipment			Accounts Payable	
Dr.	Cr.		Dr.	Cr.
+	–		–	+
(c) 8,000				(c) 8,000

Transaction (d). January 8, 19XX: Purchase of office supplies for cash and on account

Office Supplies		Cash		Accounts Payable	
Dr.	Cr.	Dr.	Cr.	Dr.	Cr.
+	–	+	–	–	+
(d) 500			(d) 100		(d) 400

Transaction (e). January 10, 19XX: Investment of accounting library by owner

Library			Kay Loomis, Capital	
Dr.	Cr.		Dr.	Cr.
+	–		–	+
(e) 75				(e) 75

Transaction (f). January 13, 19XX: Payment of a liability

Accounts Payable			Cash	
Dr.	Cr.		Dr.	Cr.
–	+		+	–
(f) 130				(f) 130

---

[1]The first six transactions (a–f) were introduced earlier.

Transaction (g). January 14, 19XX: Cash revenues

Kay Loomis, CPA, bills Rey Foods $1,820 for tax services. Rey Foods pays immediately. Assume that this is a cash revenue because the bill was paid on receipt. Tax Services is a revenue account and is credited.

Cash			Tax Services	
Dr.	Cr.		Dr.	Cr.
+	–		–	+
(g) 1,820				(g) 1,820

Transaction (h). January 15, 19XX: Payment of wages

Kay pays her secretary $600 for two weeks of work. Wages Expense is an expense account and is debited.

Wages Expense			Cash	
Dr.	Cr.		Dr.	Cr.
+	–		+	–
(h) 600				(h) 600

Transaction (i). January 17, 19XX: Credit revenues

Kay Loomis, CPA, bills James Kowalski $2,010 for management advisory services. **Accounts Receivable** is used to record the future receipt of the $2,010 and is debited. Management Advisory Services is a revenue account and is credited. Accounts Receivable is an asset account that represents money due to the firm. This money due is usually from the sale of services and goods on credit (on account).

Accounts Receivable			Management Advisory Services	
Dr.	Cr.		Dr.	Cr.
+	–		–	+
(i) 2,010				(i) 2,010

Transaction (j). January 20, 19XX: Payment of advertising

Kay advertises the services of her firm in a local newspaper. She pays $85 for the advertising. Advertising Expense is an expense account and is debited.

Advertising Expense			Cash	
Dr.	Cr.		Dr.	Cr.
+	–		+	–
(j) 85				(j) 85

Transaction (k). January 21, 19XX: Cash revenues

Kay Loomis, CPA, bills and collects $990 from Feng Li, Attorney at Law, for auditing fees. Like transaction (g), assume that this is a cash revenue because the bill was paid on receipt. Auditing Fees is a revenue account and is credited.

Cash			Auditing Fees	
Dr.	Cr.		Dr.	Cr.
+	–		–	+
(k) 990				(k) 990

Transaction (l). January 23, 19XX: Withdrawal by owner

Kay withdraws $395 in cash for her personal use. Kay Loomis, Drawing, is a contra account that reduces owner's equity and is debited.

Kay Loomis, Drawing			Cash	
Dr.	Cr.		Dr.	Cr.
+	–		+	–
(l) 395				(l) 395

Transaction (m). January 26, 19XX: Receipt of utilities bill

The firm receives but does not pay a utilities bill for $65. Utilities Expense is an expense account and is debited. Accounts Payable is credited to record the liability that will be paid at a future date.

Utilities Expense			Accounts Payable	
Dr.	Cr.		Dr.	Cr.
+	–		–	+
(m) 65				(m) 65

Transaction (n). January 28, 19XX: Partial collection

The firm receives $1,005 from James Kowalski as partial payment of the January 17 billing. The revenue has been previously recorded [see transaction (i)], so the account, Management Advisory Services, is not used. Cash is debited for the amount received. Accounts Receivable is credited because the firm has received money for an amount previously owed to the firm.

Cash			Accounts Receivable	
Dr.	Cr.		Dr.	Cr.
+	–		+	–
(n) 1,005				(n) 1,005

Transaction (o). January 31, 19XX: Payment of wages

Kay pays her secretary $600 for two weeks of work. The Wages Expense account is debited, and Cash is credited.

Wages Expense			Cash	
Dr.	Cr.		Dr.	Cr.
+	–		+	–
(o) 600				(o) 600

Footings and the Final Account Balance

The debit and credit totals of each account are called **footings,** which are recorded in pencil. The debit footings and the credit footings must be subtracted to arrive at the final account balance. The one with the largest balance becomes the new account balance. The final account balance is written in pencil below the footings. By writing the footings and final balance in pencil, any addition or subtraction errors can be easily erased and corrected. For example, assume that Cash had the following transaction amounts:

	Cash	
	Dr.	Cr.
	1,000	100
	500	200
	300	400
Footing (in pencil)	1,800	700 Footing (in pencil)
Final balance (in pencil)	1,100	

Writing Transactions

Transactions should be written in ink and never erased. If an error is made and needs to be corrected, you should draw a line through the incorrect transaction. The correct entry should be written above the incorrect entry in ink. Otherwise, it may appear that you are trying to hide something.

Summarizing Transactions and Preparing the Trial Balance

Summarizing Transactions

Objective 4
Summarize transactions and prepare a trial balance.

Let's prepare financial statements for the previous fifteen transactions. First, the transactions have to be summarized by account. In Exhibit 2-4, (a) refers to the first transaction, (b) to the second, and so on.

Note that in Exhibit 2-4, whenever a T account has only one amount, that amount is the final account balance. A T account that has only one debit and one credit amount does not need footings. The two amounts are subtracted and the difference is the final account balance.

Preparing the Trial Balance

Earlier, we said that it is important that the left side of the accounting equation equals the right side of the accounting equation.

Exhibit 2-5 lists the accounts and account balances of Kay Loomis, CPA, to make sure that the total debits equal the total credits before preparing financial statements. This procedure, called the **trial balance,** is examined in more detail in later chapters.

Preparing Financial Statements

Objective 5
Prepare financial statements.

When preparing financial statements, the income statement is always prepared first. Next is the statement of owner's equity, followed by the balance sheet.

Income Statements

An **income statement** measures a firm's performance for a stated (or defined) period of time.

Steps in Preparing the Income Statement An income statement for Kay Loomis, CPA, is prepared in Exhibit 2-6 on January 31, 19XX. The following steps in preparing an income statement are keyed (ⓐ, ⓑ, ⓒ, and ⓓ) to Exhibit 2-6:

EXHIBIT 2-4 | Transactions Summarized in T Account Form

| | ASSETS | = | LIABILITIES | + | OWNER's EQUITY | + | REVENUES | – | EXPENSES |

ASSETS

Cash

(a) 10,000	(b) 1,200
(g) 1,820	(d) 100
(k) 990	(f) 130
(n) 1,005	(h) 600
	(j) 85
	(l) 395
	(o) 600
13,815	**3,110**
10,705	

Accounts Receivable

(i) 2,010	(n) 1,005
1,005	

Office Supplies

(d) 500	

Office Equipment

(b) 1,200	
(c) 8,000	
9,200	

Library

(e) 75	

LIABILITIES

Accounts Payable

(f) 130	(c) 8,000
	(d) 400
	(m) 65
130	**8,465**
	8,335

OWNER's EQUITY

Kay Loomis, Capital

	(a) 10,000
	(e) 75
	10,075

Kay Loomis, Drawing

(l) 395	

REVENUES

Tax Services

	(g) 1,820

Management Advisory Services

	(i) 2,010

Auditing Fees

	(k) 990

EXPENSES

Wages Expenses

(h) 600	
(o) 600	
1,200	

Advertising Expense

(j) 85	

Utilities Expense

(m) 65	

EXHIBIT 2-5 Preparation of a Trial Balance

Kay Loomis, CPA
Trial Balance
January 31, 19XX

Accounts	Debit	Credit
Cash	10 7 0 5 –	
Accounts Receivable	1 0 0 5 –	
Office Supplies	5 0 0 –	
Office Equipment	9 2 0 0 –	
Library	7 5 –	
Accounts Payable		8 3 3 5 –
Kay Loomis, Capital		10 0 7 5 –
Kay Loomis, Drawing	3 9 5 –	
Tax Services		1 8 2 0 –
Management Advisory Services		2 0 1 0 –
Auditing Fees		9 9 0 –
Wages Expense	1 2 0 0 –	
Advertising Expense	8 5 –	
Utilities Expense	6 5 –	
Totals	23 2 3 0 –	23 2 3 0 –

EXHIBIT 2-6 Preparation of an Income Statement (Net Income)

(a) **Kay Loomis, CPA**
Income Statement
For the Month Ended January 31, 19XX

Revenues (b)		
Tax Services	$1 8 2 0 –	
Management Advisory Services	2 0 1 0 –	
Auditing Fees	9 9 0 –	
Total Revenues		$4 8 2 0 –
Expenses (c)		
Wages Expense	$1 2 0 0 –	
Advertising Expense	8 5 –	
Utilities Expense	6 5 –	
Total Expenses		1 3 5 0 –
Net Income (d)		$3 4 7 0 –

(a) The income statement has a three-part heading that is centered and includes, in this order, the name of the firm, the name of the financial statement, and the period of time for which the financial statement is prepared. Leave one blank line before "Revenues."

(b) List the revenues. A dollar sign appears at the beginning of the Revenue column. A line is drawn after the column. Revenues are totaled with a dollar sign. Leave one blank line before "Expenses."

(c) List the expenses. A dollar sign appears at the beginning of the Expense column. Expenses are totaled and underlined. Leave one blank line before "Net Income" or "Net Loss."

(d) **Net Income** or **Net Loss** is determined by subtracting Total Expenses from Total Revenues. When Total Revenues exceed Total Expenses, there is Net Income. Net Loss occurs when Total Expenses are greater than Total Revenues. The net income or net loss amount is preceded by a dollar sign and double-underlined.

Income Statement with a Net Loss   An income statement with a net loss is illustrated in Exhibit 2-7. Assume the accounts and amounts for Williams Advisory Service.

Statement of Owner's Equity

The second financial statement usually prepared is the **statement of owner's equity.** Generally accepted accounting principles (GAAP) do not require that this financial statement be prepared. However, the statement of owner's equity is usually prepared because it summarizes the changes in the owner's Capital account for a stated (or defined) period of time. This financial statement is prepared after the income statement, as net income or net loss must first be determined.

Steps in Preparing the Statement of Owner's Equity

In Exhibit 2-8, a statement of owner's equity is prepared for Kay Loomis, CPA, for the month ended January 31, 19XX. The following steps in preparing the statement of owner's equity are keyed ((a), (b), (c), and so on) to Exhibit 2-8:

EXHIBIT 2-7   Preparation of an Income Statement (Net Loss)

Williams Advisory Service
Income Statement
For the Year Ended December 31, 19XX

Revenue		
Advisory Services		$2 0 0 0 –
Expense		
Wages Expense	$1 0 0 0 –	
Advertising Expense	9 0 0 –	
Utilities Expense	3 0 0 –	
Total Expenses		2 2 0 0 –
Net Loss		($ 2 0 0 –)

EXHIBIT 2-8 | Preparation of a Statement of Owner's Equity (with Net Income)

Kay Loomis, CPA
(a)   **Statement of Owner's Equity**
For the Month Ended January 31, 19XX

Kay Loomis, Capital, January 1, 19XX (b)		$10 0 0 –
Add: Net Income for January (c)		3 4 7 0 –
Additional Investment		7 5 –
Subtotal (d)		$13 5 4 5 –
Deduct: Kay Loomis, Drawing (e)		3 9 5 –
Kay Loomis, Capital, January 31, 19XX (f)		$13 1 5 0 –

(a)   The statement of owner's equity has a three-part heading that is centered and includes, in this order, the name of the firm, the name of the financial statement, and the period of time for which the statement of owner's equity is prepared. Leave one blank line before "Capital."

(b)   List the owner's beginning Capital balance with a dollar sign.

(c)   Net Income and Additional Investments, if any, are listed.

(d)   Net Income and Additional Investment(s) are added to the beginning Capital for a subtotal, with a dollar sign. A line is drawn after the amount of the Additional Investment(s).

(e)   The owner's Drawing account is listed. A line is drawn after the Drawing account amount.

(f)   The final Capital balance is determined by subtracting Drawing from Subtotal. Kay Loomis, Capital, January 31, 19XX, is double-underlined with a dollar sign.

Statement of Owner's Equity with a Net Loss   A statement of owner's equity with a net loss is illustrated in Exhibit 2-9.

EXHIBIT 2-9 | Preparation of a Statement of Owner's Equity (with Net Loss)

Sean O'Malley, Computer Consultant
Statement of Owner's Equity
For the Month Ended August 31, 19XX

Sean O'Malley, Capital, August 1, 19XX		$47 6 0 0 –
Add: Additional Investment		4 2 0 0 –
Subtotal		$51 8 0 0 –
Deduct: Net Loss for August	$3 9 0 0 –	
Sean O'Malley, Drawing	1 3 0 0 –	
Total Deductions		5 2 0 0 –
Sean O'Malley, Capital, August 31, 19XX		$46 6 0 0 –

Balance Sheet

The third financial statement for Kay Loomis, CPA, is the balance sheet (as shown in Exhibit 2-10). This financial statement is usually prepared after the statement of owner's equity, as the owner's Capital account balance must first be determined.

EXHIBIT 2-10 Preparation of a Balance Sheet in Report Form

Kay Loomis, CPA
Balance Sheet
January 31, 19XX

Assets		
Cash	$10 705 –	
Accounts Receivable	1 005 –	
Office Supplies	500 –	
Office Equipment	9 200 –	
Library	75 –	
Total Assets		$21 485 –
Liabilities		
Accounts Payable		$ 8 335 –
Owner's Equity		
Kay Loomis, Capital		13 150 –
Total Liabilities and Owner's Equity		$21 485 –

Chapter Review

1. **Identify and discuss the broad classes of accounts.**
   The broad classes of accounts include assets, liabilities, owner's equity, revenues, and expenses.

2. **Use the expanded fundamental accounting equation.**
   The expanded accounting equation is

   $$\text{Assets} = \text{Liabilities} + \text{Owner's Equity} + \text{Revenues} - \text{Expenses}$$

3. **Apply debits and credits to business transactions by using the T account format.**
   Fifteen transactions were examined.

4. **Summarize transactions and prepare a trial balance.**
   To prepare financial statements, the transactions must be summarized by account, and then a trial balance is prepared.

5. **Prepare financial statements.**
   The financial statements are prepared in this order: (a) income statement, (b) statement of owner's equity, and (c) balance sheet.

Glossary

Compound Entry Transaction that uses more than two accounts

Contra Account Account whose balance is different (contra) than the normal balances within that broad class of accounts

Credit Right side only

Debit Left side only

Double-Entry System Recording of a transaction by using two or more accounts

Drawing Withdrawals of cash or other assets by the owner for his or her personal use

Expanded Fundamental Accounting Equation Assets = Liabilities + Owner's Equity + Revenues – Expenses)

Expenses Goods and/or services purchased and consumed by a firm to support revenues

Footing Debit and credit totals of an account

Income Statement Financial statement that measures a firm's performance for a stated (or defined) period of time

Net Income Revenues are greater than expenses for a stated (or defined) period of time

Net Loss Expenses exceed revenues for a stated (or defined) period of time

Revenues Sale of goods and/or services

Statement of Owner's Equity Financial statement that summarizes changes in the owner's Capital account for a stated (or defined) period of time

T Account Resembles a T and is often used to record transactions

Trial Balance Listing of accounts and account balances

Self-Test Questions for Review

(Answers are at the end of Chapter 2.)

1. Revenues _____ Capital and expenses_____ Capital.
   a. decrease; increase
   b. decrease; decrease
   c. increase; decrease
   d. increase; increase

2. Which of the following is subtracted on the right side of the expanded fundamental accounting equation?
   a. Revenues
   b. Liabilities
   c. Owner's Equity
   d. Expenses

3. An owner invests cash in his business. He would
   a. debit Accounts Payable.
   b. debit Cash.
   c. debit Owner, Capital.
   d. debit Accounts Receivable.

4. Tax Services is included under _____ and Auditing Fees is included under _____ on an income statement.
   a. Revenues; Revenues
   b. Revenues; Expenses
   c. Expenses; Expenses
   d. Expenses; Revenues

5. Which account does a firm bill for management advisory services and debits?
   a. Accounts Receivable
   b. Cash
   c. Accounts Payable
   d. Management Advisory Services

Practical Review Problem

Objective 5

Preparing Financial Statements Martha Wheel owns Wheel's Decorating Service. Martha had the following trial balance for the month:

Wheel's Decorating Service
Trial Balance
May 31, 19XX

Accounts	Debit	Credit
Cash	11200 –	
Accounts Receivable	1000 –	
Store Supplies	1000 –	
Accounts Payable		750 –
Wages Payable		800 –
Martha Wheel, Capital		13000 –
Martha Wheel, Drawing	750 –	
Decorating Services		1000 –
Wages Expense	1600 –	
Totals	15550 –	15550 –

REQUIRED
Prepare an income statement, a statement of owner's equity, and a balance sheet.

Answer to Practical Review Problem

Wheel's Decorating Service
Income Statement
For the Month Ended May 31, 19XX

Revenue		
Decorator Services		$1000 –
Expense		
Wages Expense		1600 –
Net Loss		($ 600 –)

Wheel's Decorating Service
Statement of Owner's Equity
For the Month Ended May 31, 19XX

Martha Wheel, Capital, May 1, 19XX		$13 0 0 0 –
Deduct: Net Loss for May	$6 0 0 –	
Martha Wheel, Drawing	7 5 0 –	
Total Deductions		1 3 5 0 –
Martha Wheel, Capital, May 31, 19XX		$11 6 5 0 –

Wheel's Decorating Service
Balance Sheet
May 31, 19XX

Assets		
Cash	$11 2 0 0 –	
Accounts Receivable	1 0 0 0 –	
Store Supplies	1 0 0 0 –	
Total Assets		$13 2 0 0 –
Liabilities		
Accounts Payable	$ 7 5 0 –	
Wages Payable	8 0 0 –	
Total Liabilities		$ 1 5 5 0 –
Owner's Equity		
Martha Wheel, Capital		11 6 5 0 –
Total Liabilities and Owner's Equity		$13 2 0 0 –

Discussion Questions

Q 2-1 What is the difference between owner's equity and Capital?

Q 2-2 Define revenues and expenses. What effect do revenues have on Capital? What effect do expenses have on Capital?

Q 2-3 State the expanded fundamental accounting equation.

Q 2-4 Describe the double-entry system.

Q 2-5 What is a T account? What does a debit mean in accounting? What does a credit mean?

Q 2-6 Explain how debits and credits increase or decrease each of the following broad classes of accounts: assets, liabilities, owner's equity, drawing, revenues, and expenses.

Q 2-7   Describe the four rules for using T accounts to record transactions.

Q 2-8   Which financial statement is prepared first? Which is usually prepared second? Third? Why are financial statements prepared in this order?

Q 2-9   Briefly list the four steps in preparing the income statement.

Q 2-10   Briefly list the six steps in preparing the statement of owner's equity.

Exercises

Objective 3   **E 2-1**   **Identifying Accounts**   Write the account debited and the account credited for each of the following transactions:

a. The owner, Lupe Rodriguez, invested $20,000.

     Account debited: _____

     Account credited: _____

b. Paid a secretary $1,000 for two weeks of work.

     Account debited: _____

     Account credited: _____

Objective 3   **E 2-2**   **Recording Transactions**   Record the following transactions in T account form:

a. Purchased $2,200 of office equipment with $900 cash and the remainder on account.

b. The owner, Ike Owens, withdrew $400 for his personal use.

c. Billed a customer $700 for advertising services.

d. Owner invested a library valued at $800.

e. Received a utilities bill for $100.

Objective 5   **E 2-3**   **Completing an Income Statement**   Complete the following income statement for Cheng Wu, Attorney at Law, for the month ended April 19XX:

(a)		
(b)		
(c)		
(d)		
Legal Fees		$2,900
Guardian Fees		1,200
Total Revenues		(e)
(f)		
Wages Expense		$1,500
Advertising Expense		600
Utilities Expense		200
Total Expenses		(g)
(h)		(i)

Objective 5 **E 2-4** **Completing a Statement of Owner's Equity** Complete the following statement of owner's equity for Albert Conner, Medical Doctor, for the month ended November 19XX:

	(a)
	(b)
	(c)

___(d)___, Capital, November 1, 19XX	$21,400
Add: Net Income for November	5,700
Additional Investment	2,300
Subtotal	(e)
Deduct: ___(f)___, Drawing	1,600
___(g)___, Capital, November 30, 19XX	(h)

Objective 5 **E 2-5** **Completing a Balance Sheet** Complete the following balance sheet for Paula Lyski, CPA, for the month ended December 19XX:

	(a)
	(b)
	(c)

(d)			
Cash	$17,300		
Accounts Receivable	6,900		
Store Supplies	7,500		
(e)			(f)

(g)			
Accounts Payable	$ 4,400		
Wages Payable	1,200		
(h)			(i)
(j)			
(k)___, Capital			(l)
(m)			(n)

Objective 3 **E 2-6** **Recording Transactions** Record the following transactions in T account form:
  a. The owner, Unis Singh, invested $35,000 cash in a new firm named Camino Design Services.
  b. Purchased furniture for cash, $11,000.
  c. Billed customer $6,000 for design services.
  d. Owner invested a library valued at $2,000.
  e. Purchased office supplies on account, $4,000.
  f. Paid employees for work performed, $3,000.

Objective 4 **E 2-7** **Summarizing Transactions** Summarize the transactions in E 2-6 by using the format presented in Exhibit 2-4.

Objective 5

E 2-8 **Preparing Financial Statements** For the month ended August 31, 19XX, prepare (a) an income statement and (b) a statement of owner's equity given the following account balances: Norma Lewis, Capital, August 1, 19XX, $45,000 (credit); Norma Lewis, Drawing, $2,000 (debit); Weather Services, $8,000 (credit); Wages Expense, $4,000 (debit); Advertising Expense, $2,000 (debit); and Utilities Expense, $1,000 (debit). The firm is Lewis Weather Service.

Problems

Objective 3

P 2-1 **Identifying Accounts** Grady Kennedy owns Kennedy Door Repair. He had the following transactions for April 19XX:

April 1   He started Kennedy Door Repair by investing $55,000.

April 4   Paid $6,000 for furniture.

April 8   Purchased $2,000 of office supplies on account.

April 14 Paid wages of $3,000.

April 19 Owner invested an additional $5,000 cash.

April 23 Billed a customer $9,000 for repair services.

April 29 Received a utilities bill for $1,000.

REQUIRED
1. Write the date for each transaction.
2. List the account debited and the account credited for each transaction. First, write the account debited, and then write the account credited.

Objective 3

P 2-2 **Recording Transactions** Laura McFalls is the sole owner of McFalls Consulting Service. She had the following transactions:

a. Owner invested $60,000 cash.

b. Purchased office furniture for cash, $13,000.

c. Purchased $7,000 of office supplies. Paid $4,000 in cash with the remainder on account.

d. Purchased office equipment on account, $9,000.

e. Paid $2,000 to apply to the purchase of office supplies in (c).

f. Owner invested a personal library valued at $5,000.

g. Paid wages of $6,000.

h. Billed a customer $12,000 for consulting services.

i. Received an advertising bill, $1,000.

REQUIRED
Record the transactions in T account form.

Objective 5

P 2-3 **Preparing Financial Statements** Howard Potter owns Potter's Catering Service. He had the following trial balance for the month:

Potter's Catering Service
Trial Balance
March 31, 19XX

Accounts	Debit	Credit
Cash	25 9 0 0 —	
Accounts Receivable	3 6 0 0 —	
Office Supplies	1 2 0 0 —	
Accounts Payable		1 8 0 0 —
Wages Payable		9 0 0 —
Howard Potter, Capital		27 4 0 0 —
Howard Potter, Drawing	6 0 0 —	
Catering Services		4 1 0 0 —
Wages Expense	2 9 0 0 —	
Totals	34 2 0 0 —	34 2 0 0 —

REQUIRED

Prepare an income statement, a statement of owner's equity, and a balance sheet (Capital is from March 1 investment).

Objective 3, 4, and 5

P 2-4

Comprehensive Chapter Review Problem   Teresa Galindo owns the firm called Teresa Galindo, CPA. She had the following transactions:

a. Galindo invested $37,520 cash (November 1—beginning capital).

b. Billed and collected $8,290 for auditing fees (remember that this is a cash revenue).

c. Purchased office equipment for cash, $18,610.

d. Purchased $11,340 of office supplies. Paid $6,150 in cash with the remainder on account.

e. Purchased office furniture on account, $23,730.

f. Paid wages, $5,960.

g. Teresa invested a personal library valued at $2,280.

h. Received an advertising bill, $4,840.

i. Billed a customer $7,430 for tax services.

j. Paid $1,160 to apply to the purchase of office supplies in (d).

k. Received $2,620 to apply to the billing in (i).

l. Billed a customer $3,870 for advisory services.

m. Owner withdrew $1,910 in cash for her personal use.

REQUIRED

1. Record the transactions in T account form.

2. Summarize the transactions using the format presented in Exhibit 2-4.

3. Prepare a trial balance (list accounts and account balances) to make sure that total debits equal total credits.

4. Prepare financial statements (income statement, statement of owner's equity, and balance sheet) for the month ended November 30, 19XX.

Checklist of Key Figures

P 2-1	No key figure
P 2-2	No key figure
P 2-3	Net Income, $1,200
P 2-4(4)	Net Income, $8,790

Answers to Self-Test Questions

1. c   **2.** d   **3.** b   **4.** a   **5.** a

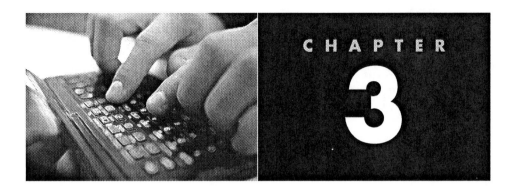

CHAPTER
3

Posting and the Trial Balance

LEARNING OBJECTIVES

After reading this chapter, discussing the questions, and working the exercises and problems, you will be able to do the following:

1. Record transactions in the general journal

2. Post from the general journal to the general ledger

3. Prepare a trial balance from the general ledger

Earlier, we presented the fundamental accounting equation and the expanded fundamental accounting equation, respectively. The expanded accounting equation is

$$\text{Assets} = \text{Liabilities} + \text{Owner's Equity} + \text{Revenues} - \text{Expenses}$$

T accounts were used to illustrate how various transactions are recorded. The double-entry system, where two or more accounts are used to record each transaction, was also examined.

In this chapter, the general journal method of recording transactions, as well as the posting process and preparation of a trial balance, is presented.

Chart of Accounts

Objective 1
Record transactions in the general journal.

Every business operation—sole proprietorship, partnership, or corporation—must have a **chart of accounts.** A chart of accounts is a detailed listing of all the accounts that the firm uses for recording transactions. The chart of accounts for Kevin Young, Attorney at Law, is as follows:

Kevin Young, Attorney at Law
Chart of Accounts

ASSETS (100–199)		OWNER'S EQUITY (300–399)	
101	Cash	301	Kevin Young, Capital
111	Accounts Receivable	311	Kevin Young, Drawing
121	Office Supplies		
131	Prepaid Insurance	**REVENUES (400–499)**	
141	Furniture	401	Legal Fees
LIABILITIES (200–299)		**EXPENSES (500–599)**	
201	Accounts Payable	501	Wages Expense
		511	Advertising Expense
		521	Rent Expense
		531	Utilities Expense

The chart-of-accounts numbers precede the account titles and indicate the classification of accounts. Assets usually start with a 1, liabilities with a 2, owner's equity with a 3, revenues with a 4, and expenses with a 5. The second and third digits are used to place the accounts within their particular classification.

The chart of accounts is never static because a firm is always conducting business. The firm should allow for the addition of new accounts as necessary.

General Journal

T Accounts Reviewed

A T account is one of the most useful tools for recording transactions. With T accounts, you can easily see if an account is increased or decreased depending on whether there is a debit or credit. The T account method can be extended so that transactions can be *tracked* (audited) more easily and recorded more systematically, using less space.

T Accounts and the General Journal

The **general journal** is a book of original entry. Making transaction entries in a general journal is called **journalizing.** The general journal looks somewhat like a T account in that there are debit and credit columns. A T account, you'll remember, looks like this:

Account Name	
Debit	Credit

A journal entry looks like this:

GENERAL JOURNAL   Page _____

Date	Description	Post Ref.	Debit	Credit
Date of				
Trans-	Account Name		Amount	
action	Account Name			Amount
	Description of Transaction			

Rules for Recording Transactions in the General Journal

There are eight rules for recording transactions (journalizing) in the general journal:

(a) Each page for the period (month, year, and so on) must be in consecutive order.

(b) The date of the transaction must be placed in the Date column. The year and month are only written once on each page.

(c) The transactions are recorded daily or as they occur. There will be some days during the accounting period when transactions may not occur (for example, holidays and weekends).

(d) The debit account(s) and amount(s) are listed first. Once all the debit(s) have been recorded, the credit account(s) and amount(s) are listed. Note that the credit account is commonly indented three spaces to make observation easier. Some accountants may elect to indent using a fraction of an inch. This could be one-fourth inch, one-half inch, and so on. For consistency in presentation, this book indents three spaces.

(e) The Posting Reference (Post. Ref.) column is described later in this chapter.

(f) All debit(s) must equal all credit(s) for each transaction.

(g) A brief description of the transaction is made below the last account credited. This description is not indented in this book.

(h) Skip one line between entries.

To illustrate journalizing, assume that Kevin Young, attorney at law, started a law practice. He invested $25,000 cash in the firm on April 1, 19XX. The eight rules are keyed ((a), (b), (c), and so on) to this general journal entry as follows:

GENERAL JOURNAL
Page ___ 1 ⓐ

	Date		Description	Post Ref.	Debit	Credit
	19XX ⓑ					
ⓒ	*Apr.*	*1*	*Cash* ⓓ	ⓔ	25 0 0 0 – ⓕ	
			Kevin Young, Capital			25 0 0 0 –
		ⓖ	*Investment by Owner to Start a New Firm*			
			Kevin Young, Attorney at Law			
		ⓗ				

The general journal is the accounting record into which transactions are first recorded. In future chapters, we use other journals. But for now, the general journal will be the only one used.

Recording Transactions Using the General Journal

Kevin Young, Attorney at Law, had sixteen transactions during April 19XX. These transactions are recorded in the general journal in Exhibits 3-1 and 3-2. The transactions are as follows (assume that cash is paid or received unless otherwise stated):

April 1   The owner, Kevin Young, started the firm by investing $25,000.

April 1   Paid the rent for the month, $800.

April 1   Paid for a two-year liability insurance policy, $1,200. Prepaid Insurance is debited and Cash is credited. **Prepaid Insurance** is an asset as it benefits future time periods.

April 2   Billed and collected $1,900 in legal fees (cash revenue).

April 3   Purchased furniture, $6,400.

April 4   Purchased $600 of office supplies on account.

April 6   Hired a secretary. No entry is required.

April 7   Received and paid a utilities bill, $100.

April 11 Received a bill for newspaper advertising, $300. Accounts Payable is credited because the bill is not yet paid.

April 14 Owner invested an additional $1,000 in the firm.

April 17 Paid a secretary for wages, $700.

April 19 Billed a customer $1,800 for legal fees.

April 22 Paid $400 to apply to the April 4 purchase.

April 24 Billed a customer $1,500 for legal fees.

April 26 Received $900 from a customer to apply to the April 19 billing.

April 29 Owner withdrew $200 for his personal use.

April 30 Paid a bill received April 11, $300. Accounts Payable is debited because the bill (a liability) is paid.

EXHIBIT 3-1 Transactions (April 1–11, 19XX): Page 1

GENERAL JOURNAL

Page ___1___

Date		Description	Post Ref.	Debit	Credit
19XX					
Apr.	1	Cash		25 000 –	
		Kevin Young, Capital			25 000 –
		Investment by Owner to Start a New Firm			
		Kevin Young, Attorney at Law			
	1	Rent Expense		800 –	
		Cash			800 –
		For Month Ended April 30			
	1	Prepaid Insurance		1 200 –	
		Cash			1 200 –
		Two-Year Insurance Policy			
	2	Cash		1 900 –	
		Legal Fees			1 900 –
		For Services Provided			
	3	Furniture		6 400 –	
		Cash			6 400 –
		Purchased Furniture for Cash			
	4	Office Supplies		600 –	
		Accounts Payable			600 –
		Purchased Office Supplies on Account			
	7	Utilities Expense		100 –	
		Cash			100 –
		Paid Bill for Utilities			
	11	Advertising Expense		300 –	
		Accounts Payable			300 –
		Received Advertising Bill			

EXHIBIT 3-2 Transactions (April 14–30, 19XX): Page 2

GENERAL JOURNAL

Page ___2___

Date		Description	Post Ref.	Debit	Credit
19XX					
Apr.	14	Cash		1000 –	
		Kevin Young, Capital			1000 –
		Additional Investment by Owner			
	17	Wages Expense		700 –	
		Cash			700 –
		Paid Wages April 6–17			
	19	Accounts Receivable		1800 –	
		Legal Fees			1800 –
		For Services Provided			
	22	Accounts Payable		400 –	
		Cash			400 –
		Partial Payment for April 4 Purchase			
	24	Accounts Receivable		1500 –	
		Legal Fees			1500 –
		For Services Provided			
	26	Cash		900 –	
		Accounts Receivable			900 –
		To Apply to April 19 Billing			
	29	Kevin Young, Drawing		200 –	
		Cash			200 –
		Withdrawal for Personal Use			
	30	Accounts Payable		300 –	
		Cash			300 –
		Paid April 11 Advertising Bill			

General Ledger

The **general ledger** is the book that contains all the accounts of the firm. The accounts are listed numerically with Cash (101) first and Utilities Expense (531) last. Of course, other accounts can be added as they are needed or anticipated. These new accounts would also be added to the chart of accounts. A typical general ledger page is presented below:

GENERAL LEDGER ACCOUNT						
Account:					Account No.	
		Post			Balance	
Date	Item	Ref.	Debit	Credit	Debit	Credit

An account page in the general ledger usually has four amount columns, one each for the debit or credit transaction entry and one each for the debit or credit balance. Also included is the Posting Reference (Post Ref.), which is used to reference the general journal to the general ledger. The Post. Ref. column is also used to reference the general ledger to the general journal. The Item column is used to explain or identify unusual transactions. Generally, there is a separate page for each account in the general ledger.

Posting

Objective 2
Post from the general journal to the general ledger.

Posting is the process of transferring debit and credit amounts from the general journal to the general ledger. The general journal will have at a minimum one debit and one credit for each transaction. The general ledger will have either a debit or a credit for each account used in the general journal. The full transaction will appear in the general ledger but will be on separate account pages depending on the accounts used.

The posting process is illustrated in Exhibit 3-3. The first transaction, Investment of Cash by Owner, is journalized and posted to the general ledger. The rules of posting are keyed (ⓐ, ⓑ, ⓒ, and so on) to Exhibit 3-3.

Rules of Posting

1. The transaction must be properly recorded in the general journal.

2. Post one line at a time from the general journal to the general ledger starting with the first debit. In Exhibit 3-3, the first debit is Cash.

3. You then ⓐ turn to the proper account in the general ledger. You enter the ⓑ transaction date, ⓒ amount, and ⓓ journal and page number in the Post. Ref. column. "J" is used to signify the general journal. "1" means page 1 of the journal. Thus, J1 would identify page 1 of the general journal.

4. You then ⓔ calculate the new balance in the account. For now, do not use the Item column.

5. On completion of 3 and 4, go back to the general journal and enter the ⓕ general ledger account number in the Post. Ref. column of the general journal.

EXHIBIT 3-3 | Posting to the General Ledger

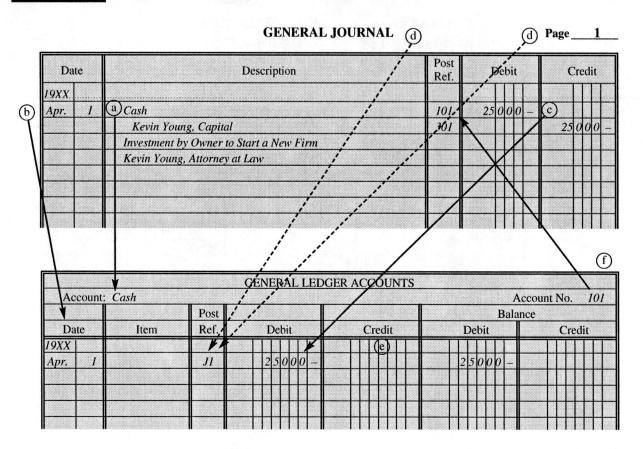

6. Then go back to the next line in the general journal and repeat the process for all the additional accounts that are recorded. In Exhibit 3-3, you would repeat the process for Kevin Young, Capital.

Review and Use of the Posting Process

Once the posting is complete, you can determine where amounts and accounts originated. Let's say that you looked at the general ledger account, Kevin Young, Capital, and you wanted to find the complete general journal entry for April 1, 19XX. The J1 in the Post. Ref. column and the Apr. 1 in the Date column would indicate a transaction on page 1 (J1) of the general journal for April 1, 19XX, (Apr. 1). The opposite would also be true.

An examination of page 1 of the general journal on April 1 might lead you to inquire about Cash. The 101 in the Post. Ref. Column and Apr. 1 in the Date column would designate that a 25,000 debit was posted to the Cash account on April 1, 19XX, in the general ledger.

The general ledger for Kevin Young, Attorney at Law, is illustrated in Exhibit 3-4. This general ledger shows the account balances after the April 19XX transactions have been posted.

EXHIBIT 3-4 General Ledger Accounts

GENERAL LEDGER ACCOUNTS

Account: *Cash* — Account No. *101*

Date		Item	Post Ref.	Debit	Credit	Balance Debit	Balance Credit
19XX							
Apr.	1		J1	25000 —		25000 —	
	1		J1		800 —	24200 —	
	1		J1		1200 —	23000 —	
	2		J1	1900 —		24900 —	
	3		J1		6400 —	18500 —	
	7		J1		100 —	18400 —	
	14		J2	1000 —		19400 —	
	17		J2		700 —	18700 —	
	22		J2		400 —	18300 —	
	26		J2	900 —		19200 —	
	29		J2		200 —	19000 —	
	30		J2		300 —	18700 —	

Account: *Accounts Receivable* — Account No. *111*

Date		Item	Post Ref.	Debit	Credit	Balance Debit	Balance Credit
19XX							
Apr.	19		J2	1800 —		1800 —	
	24		J2	1500 —		3300 —	
	26		J2		900 —	2400 —	

Account: *Office Supplies* — Account No. *121*

Date		Item	Post Ref.	Debit	Credit	Balance Debit	Balance Credit
19XX							
Apr.	4		J1	600 —		600 —	

(continued)

(Ex. 3-4 continued)

Account: *Prepaid Insurance*							Account No. *131*
		Post				Balance	
Date	Item	Ref.	Debit	Credit	Debit	Credit	
19XX							
Apr. 1		J1	1200 –		1200 –		

Account: *Furniture*							Account No. *141*
		Post				Balance	
Date	Item	Ref.	Debit	Credit	Debit	Credit	
19XX							
Apr. 3		J1	6400 –		6400 –		

Account: *Accounts Payable*							Account No. *201*
		Post				Balance	
Date	Item	Ref.	Debit	Credit	Debit	Credit	
19XX							
Apr. 4		J1		600 –		600 –	
11		J1		300 –		900 –	
22		J2	400 –			500 –	
30		J2	300 –			200 –	

Account: *Kevin Young, Capital*							Account No. *301*
		Post				Balance	
Date	Item	Ref.	Debit	Credit	Debit	Credit	
19XX							
Apr. 1		J1		25000 –		25000 –	
14		J2		1000 –		26000 –	

(continued)

(Ex. 3-4 continued)

Account: *Kevin Young, Drawing*						Account No. 311	
		Post				Balance	
Date	Item	Ref.	Debit	Credit		Debit	Credit
19XX							
Apr. 29		J2	200 –			200 –	

Account: *Legal Fees*						Account No. 401	
		Post				Balance	
Date	Item	Ref.	Debit	Credit		Debit	Credit
19XX							
Apr. 2		J1		1900 –			1900 –
19		J2		1800 –			3700 –
24		J2		1500 –			5200 –

Account: *Wages Expense*						Account No. 501	
		Post				Balance	
Date	Item	Ref.	Debit	Credit		Debit	Credit
19XX							
Apr. 17		J2	700 –			700 –	

Account: *Advertising Expense*						Account No. 511	
		Post				Balance	
Date	Item	Ref.	Debit	Credit		Debit	Credit
19XX							
Apr. 11		J1	300 –			300 –	

(continued)

(Ex. 3-4 continued)

Account: *Rent Expense*							Account No. 521	
			Post				Balance	
Date	Item	Ref.	Debit		Credit		Debit	Credit
19XX								
Apr. 1		J1	8 0 0 –				8 0 0 –	

Account: *Utilities Expense*							Account No. 531	
			Post				Balance	
Date	Item	Ref.	Debit		Credit		Debit	Credit
19XX								
Apr. 7		J1	1 0 0 –				1 0 0 –	

Common Errors

The accountant should not be misled by debits and credits alone. Account balances should also be *normal*. Assets normally have debit balances; liabilities and Capital, credit balances; Drawing, debit balance; revenues, credit balances; and expenses, debit balances. If the final balance of an account has other than a normal balance, a variety of errors could have taken place. Some of these errors include

1. *Reversal of the original entry.* For example, a transaction that should have been recorded as a debit of 100 to Cash and a credit of 100 to Service Fees may have been reversed. This, of course, is incorrect; but debits do equal credits.

   Correction of this error. The entry was journalized incorrectly as follows:

	Debit	Credit
Service Fees	100	
Cash		100

   The correct entry was the opposite. Therefore, you would correct this by the following entry:

	Debit	Credit
Cash	200	
Service Fees		200

   The resulting account balances would be a debit of 100 for Cash (100 credit and 200 debit equals a 100 debit) and a credit of 100 for Service Fees (100 debit and 200 credit equals a 100 credit).

2. *Transposition or slide error.* A **transposition** error occurs whenever the order of digits is reversed. A transposition always results in an error divisible by 9. For example, 85 is written as 58. 85 minus 58 equals 27. 27 is divisible by 9. 27

divided by 9 equals 3. Any error divisible by 9 is a transposition error. A **slide** is when a decimal is incorrectly moved (for example, 9.08 is written as 90.80).

Correction of this error. Whenever a transposition or slide error occurs, the erroneous entry should be reversed and the correct entry then entered. For example, assume that Supplies should have been debited for 7.65 and Cash should have been credited for 7.65. Instead, the following incorrect entry was made:

	Debit	Credit
Supplies	76.50	
Cash		76.50

To correct this error, the original incorrect entry is reversed as follows:

	Debit	Credit
Cash	76.50	
Supplies		76.50

And then correctly entered as follows:

	Debit	Credit
Supplies	7.65	
Cash		7.65

3. *The proper account is not used.* Suppose an entry should have been made as follows: debit Accounts Payable 200 and credit Cash 200. However, the entry was actually recorded as debit Telephone Expense 200 and credit Cash 200. This is not correct, but debits do equal credits.

Correction of this error. The entry was journalized incorrectly as follows:

	Debit	Credit
Telephone Expense	200	
Cash		200

The correct entry was a debit to Accounts Payable for 200 and a credit to Cash for 200. Because Cash is correct, only Accounts Payable is corrected, as follows:

	Debit	Credit
Accounts Payable	200	
Telephone Expense		200

The resulting account balances would be a credit of 200 for Cash, a 200 debit to Accounts Payable, and Telephone Expense would be eliminated (200 debit and 200 credit equals 0).

There are many ways to make errors when recording and posting transactions. But the best way to avoid such errors is to be careful while you work.

Trial Balance

Objective 3
Prepare a trial balance from the general ledger.

We briefly examined the **trial balance** in an earlier chapter. Let's now examine this topic in more detail. The trial balance is prepared from the final account balances in the general ledger at a certain date. A trial balance can be prepared at any time, but most often it is done at the end of the accounting period.

The purpose of the trial balance is twofold: first, to make sure that total debits equal total credits. Financial statements cannot be prepared unless total debits equal total credits. If debits do not equal credits, then any error(s) must be found and corrected. Second, we use the trial balance to ensure that account balances are "normal." Sometimes an entry or entries are made to incorrect accounts but are in balance (debits equal credits). If this happens, the accounts must be analyzed to see if an error or errors were made. Then the error(s) must be corrected. The normal balances are as follows:

ACCOUNT	NORMAL BALANCE
Assets	Debits
Liabilities	Credits
Capital	Credit
Drawing	Debit
Revenues	Credits
Expenses	Debits

Preparing the Trial Balance

The trial balance is prepared by listing the accounts in chart-of-accounts number order, the same sequence we used in the general ledger. Any account that has a zero balance is not listed. The trial balance is prepared after all transactions are posted to the general ledger. The trial balance for Kevin Young, Attorney at Law, is illustrated in Exhibit 3-5.

EXHIBIT 3-5 Preparation of a Trial Balance

Kevin Young, Attorney at Law
Trial Balance
April 30, 19XX

Accounts	Debit	Credit
Cash	18 700 —	
Accounts Receivable	2 400 —	
Office Supplies	600 —	
Prepaid Insurance	1 200 —	
Furniture	6 400 —	
Accounts Payable		200 —
Kevin Young, Capital		26 000 —
Kevin Young, Drawing	200 —	
Legal Fees		5 200 —
Wages Expense	700 —	
Advertising Expense	300 —	
Rent Expense	800 —	
Utilities Expense	100 —	
Totals	31 400 —	31 400 —

Chapter Review

1. **Record transactions in the general journal.**
   The general journal is a book of original entry. Making transaction entries in a general journal is called journalizing. There are eight rules for recording transactions in the general journal.

2. **Post from the general journal to the general ledger.**
   Posting is the process of transferring debit and credit amounts from the general journal to the general ledger. There are six rules of posting.

3. **Prepare a trial balance from the general ledger.**
   The trial balance is prepared from the final account balances in the general ledger at a certain date. Although a trial balance can be prepared at any time during the accounting period, this is usually done at the end of the accounting period.

Glossary

Chart of Accounts Detailed listing of all the accounts a firm uses for recording transactions

General Journal Book of original entry

General Ledger Book that contains all the accounts of the firm

Journalizing Process of recording transactions in a journal

Posting Process of transferring amounts from a journal to the general ledger

Prepaid Expense Prepayment of an expense that is classified as an asset; benefits future time periods

Slide When a decimal is incorrectly moved

Transposition Order of the digits is reversed in a number; this error is divisible by 9

Trial Balance Listing of the final balances of the general ledger accounts in chart-of-accounts number order

Self-Test Questions for Review

(Answers are at the end of Chapter 3.)

1. In a chart of accounts, number 521 would most likely refer to
   a. Accounts Payable.
   b. Homer Smith, Drawing.
   c. Legal Fees.
   d. Rent Expense.

2. A description for a transaction reads: For Services Provided. Which of the following accounts could be debited?
   a. Accounts Receivable
   b. Legal Fees
   c. Accounts Payable
   d. Advertising Expense

3. Which of the following accounts could be listed in the debit column of a trial balance?
   a. Accounts Payable
   b. Bill O'Malley, Capital
   c. Yolanda Vega, Drawing
   d. Legal Fees

4. A. K. Lim invests a library in his law firm. Which of the following is correct?
   a. Credit Library
   b. Credit A. K. Lim, Capital
   c. Credit A. K. Lim, Drawing
   d. Credit Accounts Payable

5. A firm debits Accounts Payable. Which of the following transactions could be correct?
   a. Paid wages.
   b. Received utilities bill.
   c. Withdrawal by owner.
   d. Paid previous advertising bill.

Practical Review Problem

Objective 3

Preparing a Trial Balance   Doris Newly, CPA, lists her general ledger accounts in alphabetical order. The accounts and account balances (all balances are normal) for October 31, 19XX, are as follows:

Accounts Payable	$ 1,020
Accounts Receivable	2,310
Advertising Expense	630
Auditing Fees	5,480
Cash	18,690
Equipment	5,430
Furniture	3,900
Doris Newly, Capital	29,260
Doris Newly, Drawing	380
Office Supplies	540
Prepaid Insurance	1,500
Rent Expense	930
Utilities Expense	140
Wages Expense	1,310

REQUIRED
Prepare a trial balance in proper account order (assets listed first, followed by liabilities, and so on).

Answer to Practical Review Problem

Doris Newly, CPA
Trial Balance
October 31, 19XX

Accounts	Debit	Credit
Cash	18 6 9 0 –	
Accounts Receivable	2 3 1 0 –	
Office Supplies	5 4 0 –	
Prepaid Insurance	1 5 0 0 –	
Furniture	3 9 0 0 –	
Equipment	5 4 3 0 –	
Accounts Payable		1 0 2 0 –
Doris Newly, Capital		29 2 6 0 –
Doris Newly, Drawing	3 8 0 –	
Auditing Fees		5 4 8 0 –
Wages Expense	1 3 1 0 –	
Advertising Expense	6 3 0 –	
Rent Expense	9 3 0 –	
Utilities Expense	1 4 0 –	
Totals	35 7 6 0 –	35 7 6 0 –

Discussion Questions

Q 3-1 How is a general journal somewhat like a T account? Define general journal and journalizing.

Q 3-2 Name the eight rules for recording transactions in the general journal.

Q 3-3 Give the debit(s) and credit(s) for each of the following transactions: (a) owner started firm by investing cash; (b) paid rent for the month; (c) paid for a three-year insurance policy; and (d) purchased office supplies for cash and on account.

Q 3-4 Give the debit(s) and credit(s) for each of the following transactions: (a) received a utilities bill; (b) paid for a previously received advertising bill; (c) owner invested additional cash in the firm; and (d) purchased office equipment for cash and on account.

Q 3-5 What is a chart of accounts? What do the account numbers indicate? Why is the chart of accounts never static?

Q 3-6 What is the general ledger? How are accounts listed in the general ledger?

Q 3-7 Name the seven columns for a general ledger account page.

Q 3-8 What is posting? Name the six rules for posting.

Q 3-9 Briefly explain how the following errors could have taken place and explain how the errors are corrected: (a) reversal of the original entry; (b) transposition or slide error; and (c) use of wrong account.

Q 3-10 Name the two purposes of the trial balance. How is the trial balance prepared?

Exercises

Objective 1

E 3-1 Completing Transactions Complete the following transactions:

	Debit	Credit
a. Cash	10,000	
_____(a)_____		10,000
Investment by Owner to Start a New Firm, Eddie Greer, Attorney at Law		
b._____(b)_____	4,000	
Accounts Payable		4,000
Received Advertising Bill		
c. Cash	6,000	
Legal Fees		6,000
_____(c)_____		

Objective 1

E 3-2 Designing Chart of Accounts J. G. Patel is starting a law firm. She is in the process of designing a chart of accounts.

a. Name at least five asset accounts that she could use.

b. Name at least one liability account that she could use.

c. Name two owner's equity accounts that she could use.

d. Name at least one revenue account that she could use.

e. Name at least four expense accounts that she could use.

Objective 1

E 3-3 Reviewing T Accounts Record the following transactions in T account form:

a. The owner, John Tipton, invested $17,000.

b. Purchased office supplies on account, $4,000.

    c. Paid creditor, $3,000.

    d. Paid a secretary $1,000 for two weeks of work.

Objective 1

E 3-4 **Recording Transactions** Record the following transactions in the general journal for 19XX, page 1:

March 1	The owner Gene Roark, invested $15,000 to start his new business called Gene Roark, Graphics Designer.
March 5	Purchased office furniture for $9,000 on account.
March 7	Hired a secretary.
March 11	Owner withdrew $1,000 for his personal use.
March 15	Billed customer $6,000 for design fees.
March 20	Paid for a four-year insurance policy, $3,000.
March 26	Paid rent for the month, $4,000.
March 31	Owner invested an additional $5,000.

Objective 2

E 3-5 **Posting Transactions** Post the transactions in E 3-4 to the general ledger using the following chart-of-accounts numbers:

Cash 101; Accounts Receivable 111; Prepaid Insurance 121; Office Furniture 131; Accounts Payable 201; Gene Roark, Capital 301; Gene Roark, Drawing 311; Design Fees 401; Rent Expense 501.

Objective 3

E 3-6 **Completing a Trial Balance** Complete the following trial balance for Kimberly Green, Computer Consultant (June 30, 19XX):

	(a)	
	(b)	
	(c)	
_____(d)_____	Debit	__(e)__
Cash	34,000	
Accounts Receivable	4,000	
Office Supplies	2,000	
Accounts Payable		5,000
_____(f)_____, Capital		(g)
_____(h)_____, Drawing	1,000	
Consulting Fees		12,000
Wages Expense	8,000	
_____(i)_____	(j)	(k)

Objective 2

E 3-7 **Correcting Errors** Use a general journal to correct the following errors:

a. A transaction that should have been recorded as a debit of 569 to Cash and a credit of 569 to Service Fees was reversed.

b. Office Supplies should have been debited for 9.63. Cash should have been credited for 9.63. Instead, the following incorrect entry was made:

	Debit	Credit
Office Supplies	96.30	
Cash		96.30

c. This entry was incorrectly journalized:

	Debit	Credit
Advertising Expense	783	
Cash		783

The correct entry was a debit to Accounts Payable for 783 and a credit to Cash for 783.

Objective 3

E 3-8 **Preparing a Trial Balance** Prepare a trial balance for Ralph Polinski, Tennis Instructor. He had the following general ledger account balances at October 31, 19XX. All account balances are normal (assets are debits, liabilities are credits, and so on):

Cash, $71,000; Accounts Receivable, $16,000; Store Supplies, $11,000; Office Furniture, $21,000; Library, $3,000; Accounts Payable, $18,000; Ralph Polinski, Capital, $100,000; Ralph Polinski, Drawing, $2,000; Tennis Fees, $26,000; Wages Expense, $12,000; Advertising Expense, $7,000; Rent Expense, $1,000.

Problems

Objective 1

P 3-1 **Recording Transactions** Cheng Lui owns Lui Advertising Service. She had the following transactions for March 19XX:

March 1	The owner started the firm by investing $98,000.
March 1	Paid the rent for the month, $10,000.
March 1	Paid for a two-year liability insurance policy, $6,000.
March 3	Billed and collected $12,000 in advertising fees (cash revenue).
March 4	Purchased furniture, $31,000.
March 5	Purchased $9,000 of office supplies on account.
March 7	Hired a secretary.
March 8	Received and paid a utilities bill, $2,000.
March 12	Received a bill for newspaper advertising, $13,000.
March 15	Owner invested an additional $5,000 in the firm.
March 20	Billed a customer $8,000 for advertising fees.
March 23	Paid $3,000 to apply to the March 5 purchase.
March 24	Paid a secretary for wages, $1,000 (March 7–24).
March 25	Received $4,000 from a customer to apply to the March 20 billing.
March 28	Owner withdrew $10,000 for her personal use.
March 31	Paid a bill received March 12.

REQUIRED
Record the March transactions in a general journal, pages 1 and 2.

Objective 2

P 3-2 **Posting Transactions** You are hired as the accountant for Foteh Investment Advisors. The accountant you replaced recorded transactions in the general journal and included the proper general ledger account numbers in the Post. Ref. column of the general journal. However, he did not post to the general ledger. These transactions are shown on page 3-20.

REQUIRED
1. Using the general ledger account numbers in the Post. Ref. column, write the account names and account numbers in the general ledger. List Cash (101) first, followed by Accounts Receivable (111), and so on.
2. Post the week's transactions to the general ledger; include all posting references in the general ledger.

GENERAL JOURNAL   Page ___1___

Date		Description	Post Ref.	Debit	Credit
19XX					
Nov.	1	Cash	101	18600 –	
		A. J. Foteh, Capital	301		18600 –
		Investment by Owner to Start a New Firm			
		Foteh Investment Advisors			
	1	Rent Expense	521	2400 –	
		Cash	101		2400 –
		For Month Ended November 30			
	2	Prepaid Insurance	131	1200 –	
		Cash	101		1200 –
		Four-Year Insurance Policy			
	4	Accounts Receivable	111	6800 –	
		Advisement Fees	401		6800 –
		For Services Provided			
	7	Advertising Expense	511	3700 –	
		Accounts Payable	201		3700 –
		Received Advertising Bill			

Objective 3

P 3-3 **Preparing a Trial Balance** Alvin Teng, Graphics Consultant, lists his general ledger accounts in alphabetical order. The accounts and account balances (all balances are normal) for December 31, 19XX, are as follows:

Accounts Payable	$ 23,890	Office Supplies	$ 3,900
Accounts Receivable	78,090	Prepaid Insurance	2,640
Advertising Expense	10,560	Rent Expense	1,560
Cash	54,120	Alvin Teng, Capital	166,180
Equipment	34,890	Alvin Teng, Drawing	4,560
Furniture	11,780	Utilities Expense	980
Graphics Fees	18,900	Wages Expense	5,890

REQUIRED
Prepare a trial balance in proper account order (assets listed first, followed by liabilities, and so on).

Objective 1, 2, and 3

P 3-4 **Comprehensive Chapter Review Problem** Powers Syms owns Syms Advertising Service. The firm's chart of accounts is as follows:

**Syms Advertising Service
Chart of Accounts**

ASSETS (10–19)

11 Cash
12 Accounts Receivable
13 Office Supplies
14 Prepaid Insurance
15 Equipment

LIABILITIES (20–29)

21 Accounts Payable

OWNER'S EQUITY (30–39)

31 Powers Syms, Capital
32 Powers Syms, Drawing

REVENUES (40–49)

41 Advertising Fees

EXPENSES (50–59)

51 Wages Expense
52 Advertising Expense
53 Rent Expense
54 Utilities Expense

Syms had the following transactions for March 19XX:

March 1   Powers started Syms Advertising Service by investing $74,920.
March 1   Paid for a two-year insurance policy, $960.
March 1   Paid rent for the month, $1,230.
March 2   Received a utilities bill, $630.
March 3   Hired an advertising assistant.
March 4   Billed and collected $2,980 in advertising fees (cash revenue).
March 6   Purchased equipment on account, $6,900.
March 11   Purchased $850 of office supplies. Paid $340 in cash with the remainder on account.
March 12   Paid the March 2 utilities bill.
March 12   Billed a customer $2,780 for advertising fees.
March 13   Received a bill for advertising, $780.
March 16   Owner invested an additional $1,090 in the firm.
March 19   Paid $200 to apply to the March 11 purchase.
March 23   Received $2,000 to apply to the March 12 billing.
March 26   Received an advertising bill, $510.
March 28   Paid wages, $820 (March 3–28).
March 30   Paid $250 to apply to the March 26 advertising bill.
March 31   Owner withdrew $1,900 for his personal use.

REQUIRED

1. Record the March transactions in a general journal, pages 1 and 2.

2. Post the March transactions to the general ledger (use the chart of accounts to first write the accounts and account numbers in the general ledger).

3. Prepare a trial balance.

Checklist of Key Figures

P 3-1   No key figure

P 3-2   Cash, $15,000

P 3-3   Totals, 208,970

P 3-4(2) Cash, $74,660; (3) Totals, 90,020

Answers to Self-Test Questions

1. d   2. a   3. c   4. b   5. d

Calculating Adjustments and Completing the Worksheet

LEARNING OBJECTIVES

After reading this chapter, discussing the questions, and working the exercises and problems, you will be able to do the following:

1. Explain the matching concept
2. Calculate adjustments
3. Complete the worksheet

Earlier, we recorded the April 19XX transactions for Kevin Young, Attorney at Law, in a general journal. We then posted the transactions from the general journal to the general ledger and prepared a trial balance. In this chapter, we examine the matching concept, calculate adjustments, and complete a worksheet. Let's begin with a discussion of the accounting cycle.

The **accounting cycle** contains the basic steps that must be followed in specific order for each accounting period. The following steps (in order) represent the accounting cycle:

1. Analyze transactions from source documents.
2. Record the transactions in a journal.
3. Post to the general ledger accounts.
4. Prepare a trial balance.
5. Adjust the general ledger accounts.
6. Complete the worksheet.
7. Prepare financial statements.
8. Journalize and post-adjusting entries.
9. Journalize and post-closing entries.
10. Prepare a post-closing trial balance.

We concentrate on steps 5 and 6 in this chapter—adjusting the general ledger accounts and completing the worksheet.

Matching Concept

Objective 1
Explain the matching concept.

Many individuals and small businesses operate on a **cash basis** of accounting, in which revenues are recorded only when cash is received and expenses are recorded only when cash is paid. Tax laws require that many individuals and some small businesses function on the cash basis. However, the cash basis is not one of the generally accepted accounting principles (GAAP). GAAP *and* the **matching concept** require a proper matching of revenues and expenses in a given time period (accounting period). Therefore, GAAP dictate that revenues must be recognized when earned and expenses must be recognized when incurred. This recognition of revenues and expenses is the basis for the matching concept.

Cash Basis

Not all revenues and expenses are realized into cash for an accounting period. How many times have you heard, "The check is in the mail"? Even though you have earned the money, you have not received it.

When using the cash basis, revenues earned but not yet received in cash would not be recorded. Expenses incurred but not yet paid would also not be recorded. For example, suppose that employees are always paid on Fridays. If the end of the accounting period falls on Thursday, then the next accounting period will receive a portion of this period's expense. The expense will only be acknowledged if cash is paid.

Accrual Basis

The **accrual basis** of accounting solves the problems caused by the cash basis and is according to GAAP. Revenues are recorded when earned. A revenue can be recorded without the actual receipt of cash, which may be received in future periods. One example would be the billing of a customer for services performed.

Expenses are also recorded when incurred. Whenever an asset is consumed or used up to support a revenue, an expense exists. Like a revenue, the expense does not have to be paid in that particular period to be considered an expense. One example would be the receipt of a utilities bill that will be paid later.

The accrual basis of accounting is used throughout this book, unless stated otherwise. Accrual accounting requires that general ledger accounts be brought to their proper balances at the end of an accounting period. This process is known as *calculating adjustments* or *adjusting entries.*

Adjusting Entries

Objective 2
Calculate adjustments.

Adjusting entries are necessary to ensure that there is a proper matching of revenues and expenses for an accounting period. Sometimes, a revenue or expense is not known or may not be determinable in the normal course of business for an accounting period. That is, the transaction has not been journalized and posted with the other transactions of the accounting period. Adjustments provide a means of placing assets, liabilities, owner's equity, revenue, and expense accounts at their proper balances for the accounting period.

Certain correcting entries are sometimes made during the adjustment process. Correcting entries are transactions that rectify or correct errors that have been made. In the case of adjusting entries, no errors were made. The necessary information was not available to prepare a journal entry until after the accounting period was closed. An accounting period is opened on a particular day and closed on a particular day. For example, if you prepared the accounting records for the month of May, then the accounting records would be opened May 1 and closed May 31. Any transactions that were not entered in the accounting records during this period but that apply to the month of May would be entered as adjusting entries.

Types of Adjusting Entries

Remember that the accrual basis of accounting requires that revenues be recorded when earned and expenses be recorded when incurred. Adjusting entries allow you to apply the accrual basis of accounting to transactions that cover two or more accounting periods.

There are two types of adjusting entries: **deferrals** and **accruals.** The deferral type of adjusting entry is used to postpone the recognition of a revenue already received or an expense already paid. An accrual type of adjusting entry is used to recognize an *unrecorded* revenue that has been earned or an *unrecorded* expense that has been incurred.

Adjustments for Kevin Young, Attorney at Law

Four adjusting entries are necessary to place the general ledger accounts at their proper balances for the accounting period April 1–30, 19XX. The adjustments and types of adjustments are as follows (the adjustments are keyed a, b, c, and d):

ADJUSTMENT	TYPE OF ADJUSTMENT
a. Adjust Office Supplies	Deferral-Expense
b. Adjust Prepaid Insurance	Deferral-Expense
c. Adjust Furniture	Deferral-Expense
d. Adjust Wages Expense	Accrual-Expense

Adjust Office Supplies (a)   On April 4, 19XX, Kevin Young purchased $600 of office supplies, but not all were to be used in the month of April. Kevin wanted a certain amount of supplies on hand so no one would have to spend productive time buying supplies one item at a time as they were needed. On April 30, 19XX, a physical count was made. The actual office supplies on hand totaled $390. But, because this balance was not available until after the accounting records were closed, an adjustment was necessary. A brief illustration to show the accounting treatment follows:

April 1, 19XX, Beginning Balance	$ 0
Add: April 4, 19XX, Purchase	600
Office Supplies Available to be Used	$600
Less: April 30, 19XX, Ending Balance	390
Office Supplies Used or Expensed	$210

Remember, these office supplies were used or consumed to support revenues. Without pencils, pens, paper, staples, and so on, the firm would not be able to provide services (revenues) to its customers. Adjustments are not journalized and posted until the worksheet is complete so the accounts can be reviewed, so preparing T accounts is a good method for organizing this adjusting entry. Let's examine the adjustment using T accounts:

Office Supplies Expense			Office Supplies			
(a) adjusting	210		bal.	600	(a) adjusting	210
			new bal.	390		

Office Supplies Expense is an expense account that represents the office supplies used during April. The $390 debit balance in Office Supplies is the amount of supplies on hand and ready to be used.

Adjust Prepaid Insurance (b)   On April 1, 19XX, Kevin paid $1,200 for a two-year liability insurance policy. The payment of the insurance policy was originally recorded as a debit to Prepaid Insurance and a credit to Cash. Prepaid Insurance is classified as an asset account because it benefits future accounting periods. The benefits are allocated to the future accounting periods by adjusting entries. At the end of the month (or accounting period), the Prepaid Insurance adjustment is calculated by dividing the cost of the asset by the total number of accounting periods:

$$\$1,200 \div 24 \text{ months (2 years)} = \$50 \text{ per month}$$

Let's organize the adjusting entry with T accounts:

Insurance Expense			Prepaid Insurance			
(b) adjusting	50		bal.	1,200	(b) adjusting	50
			new bal.	1,150		

Insurance Expense is an expense account that represents the amount of prepaid insurance that was used during April 19XX. The $1,150 debit balance in Prepaid Insurance is the amount of prepaid insurance that remains to be used (expensed).

Adjust Furniture (c)   Fixed material assets, such as furniture, automobiles, and computers that benefit more than one accounting period are usually depreciated. **Depreciation** is the systematic and rational allocation of the cost of certain tangible assets over their useful lives. A *fixed material asset* is an asset that is tangible (can be seen or felt). To be classified as a fixed asset, the asset will have benefitted more than one accounting period and will meet certain cost levels set by the firm. For example, a small firm may set a cost level of $100. That small firm will classify all assets benefitting more than one accounting period and costing more than $100 as fixed assets. A larger firm may decide that $1,000 is the minimum for classifying assets benefitting more than one period as fixed. These two criteria, cost and time-benefitted, must both be met to classify an asset as fixed. The firm Kevin Young, Attorney at Law, depreciates all fixed material assets that cost more than $200. Thus, any fixed material assets that cost less than $200 will be expensed in the accounting period in which the asset is purchased.

There are many methods of depreciating assets. The one used in this chapter is called the **straight-line method.** The straight-line method allocates the same amount of depreciation to each accounting period. The formula is as follows:

$$\text{Depreciation per Accounting Period} = \frac{\text{Cost} - \text{Salvage Value}}{\text{Useful Life}}$$

Cost is the total amount paid to acquire and prepare an asset for use. **Salvage value** is an estimate of the amount that an asset can be sold for after a firm is done using it. **Useful life** is an estimate of the time that the asset can be productively and economically used.

On April 3, 19XX, Kevin Young purchased furniture at a cost of $6,400. He estimates that the furniture will have a salvage value of $1,000 after three years (thirty-six months) of useful life. The calculation for one month of depreciation expense is as follows:

$$\text{Depreciation Expense for One Month} = \frac{\$6,400 - \$1,000}{36 \text{ months}} = \frac{\$5,400}{36}$$

$$= \$150 \text{ per Month}$$

By using T accounts, the adjusting entry is organized as follows:

Depreciation Expense, Furniture	Accumulated Depreciation, Furniture
(c) adjusting 150	(c) adjusting 150

Depreciation Expense, Furniture is an expense account that represents the decline in the useful life of the furniture. Accumulated Depreciation, Furniture is a contra asset account—an account whose normal balance is contrary or "contra" to the debit balance of furniture. **Accumulated depreciation** is the total depreciation that the firm has taken (expensed) since the purchase of the asset. Accumulated depreciation is subtracted from the cost of the asset to arrive at its **book value.** Book value is what the asset is worth on the books, which is not necessarily what it can be sold for. In Exhibit 4-1, Furniture and Accumulated Depreciation, Furniture is shown on a partial balance sheet for Kevin Young, Attorney at Law. Book value is $6,250 ($6,400 - $150 = $6,250).

EXHIBIT 4-1 Book Value of Assets

Kevin Young, Attorney at Law
Balance Sheet (partial)
April 30, 19XX

Assets		
Furniture	$6,400 –	
Less: Accumulated Depreciation	150 –	$6,250 –

Adjust Wages Expense (d) Kevin Young pays his secretary every two weeks on Friday. The secretary was hired April 6, 19XX, and was paid April 17, 19XX. A calendar for the month of April is as follows:

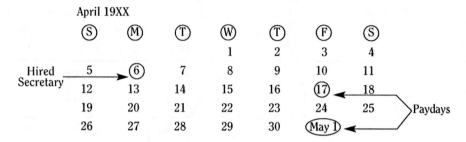

The next payday is Friday, May 1, 19XX. Wages Expense of $630 has not been recorded for the second pay period in April (April 18–30). This expense has been incurred in April 19XX, so it must be recorded in April 19XX by using adjusting entries. Let's organize this adjusting entry with T accounts:

Wages Expense			Wages Payable	
bal.	700			
(d) adjusting	630		(d) adjusting	630
new bal.	1,330			

Wages Expense is debited $630 to record wages expense incurred in April 19XX. A liability account, Wages Payable, is credited $630 to record the obligation to pay wages expense in the future (Friday, May 1, 19XX, is the next payday).

Ten-Column Worksheet

Objective 3
Complete the worksheet.

The **worksheet** is a tool used by accountants to compile the information needed for the preparation of financial statements. It is not part of the firm's formal accounting records but instead is an internal document. A ten-column worksheet has ten columns. There are

EXHIBIT 4-2 Heading of a Ten-Column Worksheet

Kevin Young,
Work
For the Month Ended

Account	Trial Balance		Adjustments	
	Debit	Credit	Debit	Credit

debit and credit columns for the Trial Balance (unadjusted), Adjustments, Adjusted Trial Balance, Income Statement, and Balance Sheet.

Steps in Completing the Worksheet

Step 1: Heading   In Exhibit 4-2, the worksheet has a three-part heading that includes (in this order) the name of the firm, the term *Worksheet,* and the period of time for which the worksheet is prepared.

Step 2: Trial Balance (Unadjusted)   In Exhibit 4-3, the unadjusted trial balance is entered in the Trial Balance columns. The trial balance accounts and amounts are taken from the trial balance. This is step 4 of the accounting cycle. The columns are underlined and added. If they are equal, the columns are double-underlined. Once you are sure that total debits equal total credits, you can go on to the next step.

Step 3: Adjustments   The adjusting entries (as calculated earlier in this chapter) are entered in the Adjustments columns as shown in Exhibit 4-4. The adjustments are keyed (a), (b), (c), and (d) to make it easier to identify all amounts relating to a particular adjustment. If any accounts not appearing in the unadjusted Trial Balance columns require adjustment, their titles are listed as needed below the accounts already recorded. The debit and credit columns are underlined and added. The totals are calculated and double-underlined if equal. Once you have verified that total debits equal total credits, you can go on to the next step.

Step 4: Adjusted Trial Balance   The Trial Balance amounts, plus or minus the Adjustment amounts, are extended to the Adjusted Trial Balance in Exhibit 4-5. The amounts in the Adjusted Trial Balance columns are the account balances reflecting the combination of the Trial Balance and the Adjustments. These amounts are determined by combining horizontally, line by line, the amounts in the first four amount (debit and credit) columns.

To illustrate this process, let's review the first three lines of Exhibit 4-5. The first line shows Cash with a debit of $18,700 in the Trial Balance. There is no adjustment for Cash, so the $18,700 debit is extended to the debit column of the Adjusted Trial Balance. The same is true for the second line, Accounts Receivable. Office Supplies (line 3) begins with a debit of $600 in the Trial Balance. A $210 adjustment appears in the credit column of

Attorney at Law

sheet

April 30, 19XX

Adjusted Trial Balance		Income Statement		Balance Sheet	
Debit	Credit	Debit	Credit	Debit	Credit

EXHIBIT 4-3 Trial Balance Columns of a Worksheet

Kevin Young,
Work
For the Month Ended

	Trial Balance		Adjustments	
Account	Debit	Credit	Debit	Credit
Cash	18 7 0 0 –			
Accounts Receivable	2 4 0 0 –			
Office Supplies	6 0 0 –			
Prepaid Insurance	1 2 0 0 –			
Furniture	6 4 0 0 –			
Accounts Payable		2 0 0 –		
Kevin Young, Capital		26 0 0 0 –		
Kevin Young, Drawing	2 0 0 –			
Legal Fees		5 2 0 0 –		
Wages Expense	7 0 0 –			
Advertising Expense	3 0 0 –			
Rent Expense	8 0 0 –			
Utilities Expense	1 0 0 –			
Totals	31 4 0 0 –	31 4 0 0 –		

the Adjustments. The $210 credit is subtracted from the $600 debit. The $390 debit difference ($600 debit – $210 credit = $390 debit) is extended to the debit column in the Adjusted Trial Balance.

After all amounts are extended to the Adjusted Trial Balance, the debit and credit columns are underlined and added. The totals are double-underlined. Total debits must equal total credits before you can go on to the next step.

Step 5: Extensions to Income Statement and Balance Sheet Columns

The amounts in the Adjusted Trial Balance columns are "extended" as follows:

Assets with Debit Balances	⟶ Debit Column of Balance Sheet
Assets with Credit Balances (Accumulated Depreciation)	⟶ Credit Column of Balance Sheet
Liabilities	⟶ Credit Column of Balance Sheet
Owner's Capital	⟶ Credit Column of Balance Sheet
Owner's Drawing	⟶ Debit Column of Balance Sheet
Revenues	⟶ Credit Column of Income Statement
Expenses	⟶ Debit Column of Income Statement

In Exhibit 4-6, the account balances in the Adjusted Trial Balance are extended to the proper Income Statement and Balance Sheet columns.

Attorney at Law
sheet
April 30, 19XX

Adjusted Trial Balance		Income Statement		Balance Sheet	
Debit	Credit	Debit	Credit	Debit	Credit

Step 6: Balancing the Worksheet   In Exhibit 4-7, the Income Statement and Balance Sheet columns are underlined and added. The column totals are recorded on the same line as the totals of the Adjusted Trial Balance columns. In the Income Statement columns, the difference between the total debits and the total credits is the net income (or net loss) for the accounting period. The Balance Sheet columns should also differ by the same amount of net income (or net loss). After the net income (or net loss) is added to the proper columns, the columns are totaled and double-underlined. "Net Income" (or "Net Loss") is placed in the Account column on the same line as the net income (or net loss) amount. The rules for the placement of net income (or net loss) amounts are as follows:

1. Place Net Income on the worksheet when the Credit column is greater than the Debit column of the Income Statement and the Debit column of the Balance Sheet is greater than the Credit column. This indicates that the net income amount has not been transferred to the owner's Capital account, which has a credit balance.

2. Place Net Loss on the worksheet when the Debit column is greater than the Credit column of the Income Statement and the Credit column of the Balance Sheet is greater than the Debit column. This indicates that the net loss amount has not been transferred to the owner's Capital account, which will reduce the normal credit balance.

(A worksheet with a net loss is completed in the Practical Review Problem at the end of this chapter.)

| EXHIBIT 4-4 | Adjustments Columns of the Worksheet |

Kevin Young,
Work
For the Month Ended

Account	Trial Balance		Adjustments	
	Debit	Credit	Debit	Credit
Cash	18 7 0 0 –			
Accounts Receivable	2 4 0 0 –			
Office Supplies	6 0 0 –			(a) 2 1 0 –
Prepaid Insurance	1 2 0 0 –			(b) 5 0 –
Furniture	6 4 0 0 –			
Accounts Payable		2 0 0 –		
Kevin Young, Capital		26 0 0 0 –		
Kevin Young, Drawing	2 0 0 –			
Legal Fees		5 2 0 0 –		
Wages Expense	7 0 0 –		(d) 6 3 0 –	
Advertising Expense	3 0 0 –			
Rent Expense	8 0 0 –			
Utilities Expense	1 0 0 –			
Totals	31 4 0 0 –	31 4 0 0 –		
Office Supplies Expense			(a) 2 1 0 –	
Insurance Expense			(b) 5 0 –	
Depreciation Expense, Furniture			(c) 1 5 0 –	
Accumulated Depreciation, Furniture				(c) 1 5 0 –
Wages Payable				(d) 6 3 0 –
			1 0 4 0 –	1 0 4 0 –

The worksheet is now complete. Financial statements can be prepared by using the account data on the worksheet. We prepare the financial statements and journalize and post the adjusting entries later. But before we leave this section on completing the worksheet, let's look at how to correct worksheet errors.

Correcting Worksheet Errors

Procedures

Follow these quick and simple procedures if your worksheet does not balance:

1. Read and total all columns vertically.
2. If the worksheet still does not balance, then verify that the net income (or net loss) amounts are correct.

Attorney at Law
sheet
April 30, 19XX

Adjusted Trial Balance		Income Statement		Balance Sheet	
Debit	Credit	Debit	Credit	Debit	Credit

3. Visually examine all accounts and amounts to make sure that the account balances are in the correct columns.

4. If you still have not discovered the error, then read or subtract all accounts horizontally.

Usually, one of these procedures will detect the error.

Common Worksheet Errors

As you follow the four previous procedures, you will see that there are a variety of errors that can occur when you are completing a worksheet. Let's examine two common errors. Remember that with a little practice you will soon be proficient at completing a worksheet.

1. *An amount is placed in the wrong income statement or balance sheet column.* For example, assume that the Furniture amount of $6,400 is placed in the Debit column of the Income Statement rather than the Debit column of the Balance Sheet. If this occurred, the worksheet would have the following totals:

EXHIBIT 4-5	Adjusted Trial Balance Columns

Kevin Young,
Work
For the Month Ended

Account	Trial Balance Debit	Trial Balance Credit	Adjustments Debit	Adjustments Credit
Cash	18,700 –			
Accounts Receivable	2,400 –			
Office Supplies	600 –			(a) 210 –
Prepaid Insurance	1,200 –			(b) 50 –
Furniture	6,400 –			
Accounts Payable		200 –		
Kevin Young, Capital		26,000 –		
Kevin Young, Drawing	200 –			
Legal Fees		5,200 –		
Wages Expense	700 –		(d) 630 –	
Advertising Expense	300 –			
Rent Expense	800 –			
Utilities Expense	100 –			
Totals	31,400 –	31,400 –		
Office Supplies Expense			(a) 210 –	
Insurance Expense			(b) 50 –	
Depreciation Expense, Furniture			(c) 150 –	
Accumulated Depreciation, Furniture				(c) 150 –
Wages Payable				(d) 630 –
			1,040 –	1,040 –

	INCOME STATEMENT		BALANCE SHEET	
	DEBIT	CREDIT	DEBIT	CREDIT
	9,340	5,200	22,840	26,980
Net Loss		4,140	4,140	
	9,340	9,340	26,980	26,980

As we saw earlier in this chapter, the difference between the two sets of columns should agree, which they do. This indicates that a net loss has occurred, which of course is incorrect. Because most firms are in business to generate a profit (net income), you should be very cautious whenever a net loss occurs. In this case, a second glance would quickly point out that the Furniture amount is in the wrong column.

Attorney at Law
sheet
April 30, 19XX

Adjusted Trial Balance		Income Statement		Balance Sheet	
Debit	Credit	Debit	Credit	Debit	Credit
18 700 –					
2 400 –					
390 –					
1 150 –					
6 400 –					
	200 –				
	26 000 –				
200 –					
	5 200 –				
1 330 –					
300 –					
800 –					
100 –					
210 –					
50 –					
150 –					
	150 –				
	630 –				
32 180 –	32 180 –				

2. *An amount is placed in the wrong debit or credit column.* Let's use the Furniture example again and assume that the $6,400 is placed in the Credit column of the Balance Sheet rather than the Debit column. If this occurred, the worksheet would have totals of:

INCOME STATEMENT		BALANCE SHEET	
DEBIT	CREDIT	DEBIT	CREDIT
2,940	5,200	22,840	33,380
2,260 ◄—(CANNOT OCCUR)—►		10,540	
5,200	5,200	33,380	33,380

This error is easier to see because the differences do not agree. The best way to avoid errors is to take your time and be careful. When an error does occur, follow the procedures above to correct the worksheet error.

EXHIBIT 4-6 Extensions to Income Statement and Balance Sheet Columns of the Worksheet

Kevin Young,
Work
For the Month Ended

Account	Trial Balance		Adjustments	
	Debit	Credit	Debit	Credit
Cash	18 7 0 0 –			
Accounts Receivable	2 4 0 0 –			
Office Supplies	6 0 0 –			(a) 2 1 0 –
Prepaid Insurance	1 2 0 0 –			(b) 5 0 –
Furniture	6 4 0 0 –			
Accounts Payable		2 0 0 –		
Kevin Young, Capital		26 0 0 0 –		
Kevin Young, Drawing	2 0 0 –			
Legal Fees		5 2 0 0 –		
Wages Expense	7 0 0 –		(d) 6 3 0 –	
Advertising Expense	3 0 0 –			
Rent Expense	8 0 0 –			
Utilities Expense	1 0 0 –			
Totals	31 4 0 0 –	31 4 0 0 –		
Office Supplies Expense			(a) 2 1 0 –	
Insurance Expense			(b) 5 0 –	
Depreciation Expense, Furniture			(c) 1 5 0 –	
Accumulated Depreciation, Furniture				(c) 1 5 0 –
Wages Payable				(d) 6 3 0 –
			1 0 4 0 –	1 0 4 0 –

Chapter Review

1. **Explain the matching concept.**
    Many individuals and small businesses operate on a cash basis of accounting, in which revenues are recorded only when cash is received and expenses are recorded only when cash is paid. But the cash basis is not GAAP. GAAP and the matching concept require a proper matching of revenues and expenses in a specific time period (accounting period). Therefore, revenues must be recognized when earned and expenses must be recognized when incurred.

2. **Calculate adjustments.**
    Adjusting entries are necessary to ensure that there is a proper matching of revenues and expenses for an accounting period. Adjustments provide a means for placing assets, liabilities, owner's equity, revenue, and expense accounts at their proper balances for the accounting period.

Attorney at Law
sheet
April 30, 19XX

Adjusted Trial Balance		Income Statement		Balance Sheet	
Debit	Credit	Debit	Credit	Debit	Credit
18700 –				18700 –	
2400 –				2400 –	
390 –				390 –	
1150 –				1150 –	
6400 –				6400 –	
	200 –				200 –
	26000 –				26000 –
200 –				200 –	
	5200 –		5200 –		
1330 –		1330 –			
300 –		300 –			
800 –		800 –			
100 –		100 –			
210 –		210 –			
50 –		50 –			
150 –		150 –			
	150 –				150 –
	630 –				630 –
32180 –	32180 –				

3. **Complete the worksheet.**

   The worksheet is a tool used by accountants to compile the information necessary for the preparation of financial statements. It is not part of the firm's formal accounting records; the worksheet is an internal document. A ten-column worksheet has Debit and Credit columns for Trial Balance (Unadjusted), Adjustments, Adjusted Trial Balance, Income Statement, and Balance Sheet.

Glossary

Accounting Cycle Basic steps that are followed in a specific order for each accounting period

Accrual Type of adjusting entry used to recognize an unrecorded revenue that has already been earned or an unrecorded expense that has already been incurred

Accrual Basis Revenues are recorded when earned; expenses are recorded when incurred

EXHIBIT 4-7 Balancing the Worksheet

Kevin Young,
Work
For the Month Ended

Account	Trial Balance		Adjustments	
	Debit	Credit	Debit	Credit
Cash	18 7 0 0 –			
Accounts Receivable	2 4 0 0 –			
Office Supplies	6 0 0 –			(a) 2 1 0 –
Prepaid Insurance	1 2 0 0 –			(b) 5 0 –
Furniture	6 4 0 0 –			
Accounts Payable		2 0 0 –		
Kevin Young, Capital		26 0 0 0 –		
Kevin Young, Drawing	2 0 0 –			
Legal Fees		5 2 0 0 –		
Wages Expense	7 0 0 –		(d) 6 3 0 –	
Advertising Expense	3 0 0 –			
Rent Expense	8 0 0 –			
Utilities Expense	1 0 0 –			
Totals	31 4 0 0 –	31 4 0 0 –		
Office Supplies Expense			(a) 2 1 0 –	
Insurance Expense			(b) 5 0 –	
Depreciation Expense, Furniture			(c) 1 5 0 –	
Accumulated Depreciation, Furniture				(c) 1 5 0 –
Wages Payable				(d) 6 3 0 –
			1 0 4 0 –	1 0 4 0 –
Net Income				

Accumulated Depreciation Total depreciation expense since the purchase (acquisition) of the asset

Adjustments (Adjusting Entries) Necessary to ensure that there is a proper matching of revenues and expenses for an accounting period

Book Value Cost of an asset less accumulated depreciation

Cash Basis Revenues are recognized when cash is received; expenses are recognized when cash is paid

Cost Total amount paid to acquire an asset

Deferral Type of adjusting entry that is used to postpone the recognition of a revenue already received or an expense already paid

Depreciation Systematic and rational allocation of the cost of certain tangible assets over their useful lives

Matching Concept Proper matching of revenues and expenses in an accounting period

Attorney at Law
sheet
April 30, 19XX

	Adjusted Trial Balance		Income Statement		Balance Sheet	
	Debit	Credit	Debit	Credit	Debit	Credit
	18700 –				18700 –	
	2400 –				2400 –	
	390 –				390 –	
	1150 –				1150 –	
	6400 –				6400 –	
		200 –				200 –
		26000 –				26000 –
	200 –				200 –	
		5200 –		5200 –		
	1330 –		1330 –			
	300 –		300 –			
	800 –		800 –			
	100 –		100 –			
	210 –		210 –			
	50 –		50 –			
	150 –		150 –			
		150 –				150 –
		630 –				630 –
	32180 –	32180 –	2940 –	5200 –	29240 –	26980 –
			2260 –			2260 –
			5200 –	5200 –	29240 –	29240 –

Salvage Value Estimate of the amount an asset can be sold for after a firm is done using it

Straight-line Method Depreciation method that allocates the same amount of depreciation to each accounting period

Useful Life Estimate of the time the asset can be productively and economically used

Worksheet Tool used by accountants to compile the information necessary for the preparation of financial statements

Self-Test Questions for Review

(Answers are at the end of Chapter 4.)

1. Using the accrual basis of accounting, expenses are recorded when _____ and revenues are recorded when _____.
   a. earned; incurred
   b. incurred; incurred
   c. incurred; earned
   d. earned; earned

2. You would adjust Wages Expense by crediting
   a. Wages Payable.   b. Wages Expense.
   c. Accounts Payable.   d. Prepaid Insurance.

3. Which of the following accounts could be listed in the debit column of the balance sheet on a completed worksheet?
   a. Accounts Payable   b. Owen Davis, Capital
   c. Wages Expense   d. Vera Howard, Drawing

4. Calculate monthly depreciation given these data: furniture costs $30,000 and has a useful life of five years; the salvage value is $6,000.
   a. $500   b. $400
   c. $600   d. $100

5. A firm paid $3,000 for a two-year insurance policy. In the monthly adjusting entry, _____ is credited for _____.
   a. Prepaid Insurance; $125.   b. Insurance Expense; $125.
   c. Accounts Payable; $1,500.   d. Depreciation Expense, Insurance; $1,500.

Practical Review Problem

Objectives 2 and 3

Calculating Adjustments and Completing the Worksheet   Louis Moyer is the owner of Northside Advertising Service. He had the following trial balance and adjustments at the end of August 19XX:

The following accounts (all balances are normal) were taken from the trial balance: Cash, 18,370; Accounts Receivable, 9,840; Office Supplies, 11,720; Prepaid Insurance, 5,400; Automobile, 15,440; Accounts Payable, 12,730; Louis Moyer, Capital, 51,760; Louis Moyer, Drawing, 5,580; Advertising Fees, 11,890; Consulting Fees, 6,270; Wages Expense, 8,450; Advertising Expense, 4,720; Rent Expense, 2,600; Utilities Expense, 530.

Adjustments:

a. Office Supplies had a beginning balance of $860. During the month, $10,860 of office supplies were purchased. A count was made at the end of the month and $9,560 of office supplies were on hand.

b. On August 1, 19XX, the firm paid $5,400 for a three-year liability insurance policy.

c. An automobile was purchased August 5, 19XX, at a cost of $15,440. Moyer estimates that the automobile will have a $2,000 salvage value after seven years of useful life.

d. At August 31, 19XX, $6,340 of wages expense is incurred but unrecorded.

REQUIRED
1. Calculate the adjusting entries in T account form.
2. Complete the worksheet.

Answer to Practical Review Problem

1. Calculate Adjusting Entries
   a. Office Supplies:

August 1, 19XX, Beginning Balance	$ 860
Add: August Purchases	10,860
Office Supplies Available to Be Used	$11,720
Less: August 31, 19XX, Ending Balance	9,560
Office Supplies Used or Expensed	$ 2,160

Office Supplies Expense		Office Supplies	
(a) adjusting 2,160		bal. 11,720	(a) adjusting 2,160
		new bal. 9,560	

b. Prepaid Insurance:

$$\$5,400 \div 36 \text{ months (3 years)} = \$150 \text{ per month}$$

Insurance Expense		Prepaid Insurance	
(b) adjusting 150		bal. 5,400	(b) adjusting 150
		new bal. 5,250	

c. Depreciation:

$$\text{Depreciation Expense} = \frac{\$15,440 - \$2,000}{84 \text{ months}} = \frac{\$13,440}{84} = \$160$$

Depreciation Expense, Automobile		Accumulated Depreciation, Automobile	
(c) adjusting 160			(c) adjusting 160

d. Wages Expense:

Wages Expense		Wages Payable	
bal. 8,450			(d) adjusting 6,340
(d) adjusting 6,340			
new bal. 14,790			

2. Complete the Worksheet (see p. 4-20).

Discussion Questions

Q 4-1   What is the accounting cycle?

Q 4-2   Name the ten steps that represent the accounting cycle.

Q 4-3   Briefly explain the matching concept.

Q 4-4   Briefly describe the cash basis and the accrual basis of accounting.

Q 4-5   Name the two types of adjusting entries. When are adjusting entries prepared? Why are adjusting entries prepared?

Q 4-6   Name the accounts that are debited and credited for each of the following adjusting entries: (a) adjust Office Supplies; (b) adjust Prepaid Insurance; (c) adjust Furniture; and (d) adjust Wages Expense.

Q 4-7   Define depreciation. Describe and give the formula for the straight-line method of depreciation.

Q 4-8   What is a worksheet? What columns would you find on a ten-column worksheet?

Q 4-9   List the six steps in preparing a worksheet in their proper order.

Q 4-10   What are the four procedures that should be followed if your worksheet does not balance? Identify two common worksheet errors.

Exercises

Objective 2   **E 4-1**   **Calculating and Organizing Adjustments**   Calculate and organize the following adjustments for Office Supplies in T account form:

FIRM	MONTH	BEGINNING BALANCE	PURCHASES DURING THE MONTH	ENDING COUNT
Logan Service	June 19XX	$ 0	$ 1,000	$ 500
A. Wong, CPA	July 19XX	2,890	3,860	2,230

Objective 2   **E 4-2**   **Calculating and Organizing Adjustments**   Calculate and organize the following adjusting entries in T account form for Prepaid Insurance per accounting period:

FIRM	COST	TOTAL NUMBER OF MONTHS	MONTH ENDED
Ruiz Service	$1,920	24	October 19XX
Smith Consulting	3,360	48	August 19XX

Northside

Work

For the Month Ended

Account	Trial Balance Debit	Trial Balance Credit	Adjustments Debit	Adjustments Credit
Cash	18 3 7 0 –			
Accounts Receivable	9 8 4 0 –			
Office Supplies	11 7 2 0 –			(a) 2 1 6 0 –
Prepaid Insurance	5 4 0 0 –			(b) 1 5 0 –
Automobile	15 4 4 0 –			
Accounts Payable		12 7 3 0 –		
Louis Moyer, Capital		51 7 6 0 –		
Louis Moyer, Drawing	5 5 8 0 –			
Advertising Fees		11 8 9 0 –		
Consulting Expense		6 2 7 0 –		
Wages Expense	8 4 5 0 –		(d) 6 3 4 0 –	
Advertising Expense	4 7 2 0 –			
Rent Expense	2 6 0 0 –			
Utilities Expense	5 3 0 –			
Totals	82 6 5 0 –	82 6 5 0 –		
Office Supplies Expense			(a) 2 1 6 0 –	
Insurance Expense			(b) 1 5 0 –	
Depreciation Expense, Automobile			(c) 1 6 0 –	
Accumulated Depreciation, Automobile				(c) 1 6 0 –
Wages Payable				(d) 6 3 4 0 –
			8 8 1 0 –	8 8 1 0 –
Net Loss				

Objective 2 **E 4-3** **Calculating and Organizing Adjustments** Calculate and organize the following adjustments for Depreciation Expense in T account form by using the straight-line method (*Hint:* Convert the useful life into months):

ASSET	MONTH ENDED	COST	USEFUL LIFE	SALVAGE VALUE
Furniture	July 19XX	$10,000	3 years	$1,000
Computer	June 19XX	12,200	5 years	2,000

Objective 2 **E 4-4** **Finding Book Values** Find the book value of each of the following assets:

ASSET	COST	ACCUMULATED DEPRECIATION
a. Automobile	$19,000	$ 200
b. Equipment	26,500	1,300
c. Machinery	79,430	8,850

Advertising Service

sheet

August 31, 19XX

Adjusted Trial Balance Debit	Adjusted Trial Balance Credit	Income Statement Debit	Income Statement Credit	Balance Sheet Debit	Balance Sheet Credit
18370 –				18370 –	
9840 –				9840 –	
9560 –				9560 –	
5250 –				5250 –	
15440 –				15440 –	
	12730 –				12730 –
	51760 –				51760 –
5580 –				5580 –	
	11890 –		11890 –		
	6270 –		6270 –		
14790 –		14790 –			
4720 –		4720 –			
2600 –		2600 –			
530 –		530 –			
2160 –		2160 –			
150 –		150 –			
160 –		160 –			
	160 –				160 –
	6340 –				6340 –
89150 –	89150 –	25110 –	18160 –	64040 –	70990 –
			6950 –	6950 –	
		25110 –	25110 –	70990 –	70990 –

Objective 2

E 4-5 **Organizing Adjustments** Organize the following adjusting entries in T accounts for wages expense incurred but not paid:

FIRM	END OF ACCOUNTING PERIOD	AMOUNT OF WAGES EXPENSE INCURRED
Lopez Consulting	December 31, 19XX	$ 600
Molsky Service	February 28, 19XX	920
Li & Wu Consulting	August 31, 19XX	2,540

Objective 2

E 4-6 **Organizing Adjustments** Organize the following adjustments in T accounts for the month ended October 31, 19XX:

ADJUSTING ENTRY FOR	ADJUSTMENT AMOUNT
(a) Office Supplies	$2
(b) Prepaid Insurance	3
(c) Furniture	4
(d) Wages Expense	1

Objective 3

E 4-7 **Completing a Worksheet** Cornerstone Services had the following trial balance (all account balances are normal) for the month ended October 31, 19XX: Cash, 10; Office Supplies, 8; Prepaid Insurance, 6; Furniture, 24; Lois Emery, Capital, 37; Lois Emery, Drawing, 2; Consulting Fees, 18; Wages Expense, 5. Use the adjustments from E4-6 to complete the worksheet.

Objective 3

E 4-8 **Completing a Worksheet** Complete the following partial worksheet (*Hint:* This worksheet has a net loss):

Florida Services
Worksheet (partial)
For the Month Ended January 31, 19XX

Account	Trial Balance Debit	Trial Balance Credit	Adjustments Debit	Adjustments Credit
Cash	6 9 3 0 –			
Office Supplies	1 2 0 0 –			(a) 3 6 0 –
Prepaid Insurance	1 5 6 0 –			(b) 6 0 –
Equipment	3 8 7 0 –			
Cheng Lu, Capital		13 5 0 0 –		
Cheng Lu, Drawing	2 1 0 –			
Service Fees		2 9 0 0 –		
Wages Expense	2 6 3 0 –		(d) 6 5 0 –	
Totals	16 4 0 0 –	16 4 0 0 –		
Office Supplies Expense			(a) 3 6 0 –	
Insurance Expense			(b) 6 0 –	
Depreciation Expense, Equipment			(c) 1 0 0 –	
Accumulated Depreciation, Equipment				(c) 1 0 0 –
Wages Payable				(d) 6 5 0 –

Problems

Objective 2

P 4-1 **Calculating Adjustments** Dora Jaynes is the accountant for Peterson Computer Repair. Jaynes accumulated the following information concerning adjustments at the end of November 19XX:

a. A count of office supplies was made at the end of the month, and $7,200 of office supplies were on hand. Office supplies had a beginning balance of $4,600 and on November 6, 19XX, $3,300 of office supplies were purchased.

b. On November 1, 19XX, the firm paid $5,400 for a five-year (sixty months) liability insurance policy.

c. The firm uses the straight-line method to depreciate assets. A copier was purchased November 3, 19XX, and will have a useful life of four years. The cost was $29,400. The salvage value is $3,000.

d. On November 30, 19XX, $2,400 of wages expense is incurred but unrecorded.

REQUIRED
1. Calculate the adjusting entries in T account form.
2. Find the book value of the copier.

Objective 2 and 3 **P 4-2**

Calculating Adjustments and Completing the Worksheet Elvira Dixon, CPA, had the following adjustments and trial balance at the end of January 19XX:

Adjustments:

a. Furniture was purchased January 2, 19XX, at a cost of $10,000. Dixon estimates that the furniture will have a $1,000 salvage value after three years of useful life. Use the straight-line method.

b. At January 31, 19XX, $800 of wages expense is incurred but unrecorded.

Elvira Dixon, CPA

Trial Balance

January 31, 19XX

Accounts	Debit	Credit
Cash	16 900 –	
Accounts Receivable	2 800 –	
Furniture	10 000 –	
Accounts Payable		3 400 –
Elvira Dixon, Capital		25 300 –
Elvira Dixon, Drawing	4 500 –	
Auditing Fees		2 800 –
Tax Services		1 700 –
Management Advisory Services		3 800 –
Wages Expense	900 –	
Advertising Expense	1 000 –	
Rent Expense	800 –	
Utilities Expense	100 –	
Totals	37 000 –	37 000 –

REQUIRED

1. Calculate the adjusting entries in T account form.
2. Complete the worksheet.

Objective 2 and 3   P 4-3

Calculating Adjustments and Completing a Worksheet Lawanda Knapp is the owner of Kansas Design Service. She had the following adjustments and trial balance at the end of March 19XX:

Adjustments:

a. Office Supplies had a beginning balance of $0. During the month, $3,900 of office supplies were purchased. A count was made at the end of the month, and $3,000 of office supplies were on hand.

b. On March 1, 19XX, the firm paid $16,200 for a three-year liability insurance policy.

c. An automobile was purchased March 4, 19XX, at a cost of $19,600. Knapp estimates that the automobile will have a $4,000 salvage value after five years of useful life. Use the straight-line method.

d. On March 31, 19XX, $800 of wages expense is incurred but unrecorded.

   The following accounts (all balances are normal) were taken from the trial balance: Cash, 31,600; Accounts Receivable, 8,900; Office Supplies, 3,900; Prepaid Insurance, 16,200; Automobile, 19,600; Accounts Payable, 11,600; Lawanda Knapp, Capital, 64,800; Lawanda Knapp, Drawing, 1,500; Design Fees, 9,700; Wages Expense, 1,200; Advertising Expense, 1,900; Rent Expense, 1,100; Utilities Expense, 200.

REQUIRED

1. Calculate the adjusting entries in T account form.
2. Complete the worksheet.

Objective 2 and 3   P 4-4

Comprehensive Chapter Review Problem Anthony Cruz is the owner of Cruz Advertising Agency. He had the following adjustments and trial balance at the end of January 19XX:

Adjustments:

a. Office Supplies had a beginning balance of $430. During the month, $12,300 of office supplies were purchased. A count was made at the end of the month, and $9,560 of office supplies were on hand.

b. On January 1, 19XX, the firm paid $5,760 for a four-year liability insurance policy.

c. A computer was purchased January 5, 19XX, at a cost of $16,680. Cruz estimates that the computer will have a $3,000 salvage value after six years of useful life. Use the straight-line method.

d. On January 31, 19XX, $3,880 of wages expense is incurred but unrecorded.

REQUIRED

1. Calculate the adjusting entries in T account form.
2. Complete the worksheet (see the Practical Review Problem if you need help).

Cruz Advertising Agency
Trial Balance
January 31, 19XX

Accounts	Debit	Credit
Cash	21 4 1 0 –	
Accounts Receivable	19 3 4 0 –	
Office Supplies	12 7 3 0 –	
Prepaid Insurance	5 7 6 0 –	
Computer	16 6 8 0 –	
Accounts Payable		15 7 8 0 –
Anthony Cruz, Capital		67 2 8 0 –
Anthony Cruz, Drawing	5 9 6 0 –	
Advertising Fees		9 9 5 0 –
Consulting Fees		6 9 6 0 –
Wages Expense	8 7 8 0 –	
Advertising Expense	6 8 2 0 –	
Rent Expense	2 1 0 0 –	
Utilities Expense	3 9 0 –	
Totals	99 9 7 0 –	99 9 7 0 –

Checklist of Key Figures

P 4-1	Depreciation, $550
P 4-2(2)	Net Income, $4,450
P 4-3(2)	Net Income, $2,890
P 4-4(2)	Net Loss, $8,540

Answers to Self-Test Questions

1. c   **2.** a   **3.** d   **4.** b   **5.** a

CHAPTER

5

Preparing Financial Statements; Journalizing and Posting Adjustments

In previous chapters the matching concept was explained along with the accrual basis of accounting. Steps 5 and 6 of the accounting cycle—adjusting the general ledger accounts and completing a worksheet—were also introduced. In this chapter we will concentrate on steps 7 and 8—preparing financial statements and journalizing and posting adjusting entries.

Financial Statements

Objective 1
Prepare financial statements.

Financial statements are usually prepared from the worksheet. Remember that the worksheet is a tool used by accountants to compile the information necessary for the preparation of financial statements. It is not part of a firm's formal accounting records, but is, instead, an internal document.

Kevin Young, Attorney at Law, had the following four adjustments in April 19XX:

EXHIBIT 5-1 Completed Worksheet

Kevin Young,
Work
For the Month Ended

Account	Trial Balance		Adjustments	
	Debit	Credit	Debit	Credit
Cash	18 7 0 0 –			
Accounts Receivable	2 4 0 0 –			
Office Supplies	6 0 0 –			(a) 2 1 0 –
Prepaid Insurance	1 2 0 0 –			(b) 5 0 –
Furniture	6 4 0 0 –			
Accounts Payable		2 0 0 –		
Kevin Young, Capital		26 0 0 0 –		
Kevin Young, Drawing	2 0 0 –			
Legal Fees		5 2 0 0 –		
Wages Expense	7 0 0 –		(d) 6 3 0 –	
Advertising Expense	3 0 0 –			
Rent Expense	8 0 0 –			
Utilities Expense	1 0 0 –			
Totals	31 4 0 0 –	31 4 0 0 –		
Office Supplies Expense			(a) 2 1 0 –	
Insurance Expense			(b) 5 0 –	
Depreciation Expense, Furniture			(c) 1 5 0 –	
Accumulated Depreciation, Furniture				(c) 1 5 0 –
Wages Payable				(d) 6 3 0 –
			1 0 4 0 –	1 0 4 0 –
Net Income				

a. Adjust Office Supplies.

b. Adjust Prepaid Insurance.

c. Adjust Furniture.

d. Adjust Wages Expense.

These four adjustments were entered on the worksheet along with the Unadjusted Trial Balance. A worksheet for the month ended April 30, 19XX, was completed as shown in Exhibit 5-1.

The Chart of Accounts

Remember that a chart of accounts is a detailed listing of all the accounts the firm uses for recording transactions. Kevin expanded his chart of accounts to include the accounts necessary to record the adjusting entries as follows:

Attorney at Law

sheet

April 30, 19XX

Adjusted Trial Balance		Income Statement		Balance Sheet	
Debit	Credit	Debit	Credit	Debit	Credit
18 7 0 0 –				18 7 0 0 –	
2 4 0 0 –				2 4 0 0 –	
3 9 0 –				3 9 0 –	
1 1 5 0 –				1 1 5 0 –	
6 4 0 0 –				6 4 0 0 –	
	2 0 0 –				2 0 0 –
	26 0 0 0 –				26 0 0 0 –
2 0 0 –				2 0 0 –	
	5 2 0 0 –		5 2 0 0 –		
1 3 3 0 –		1 3 3 0 –			
3 0 0 –		3 0 0 –			
8 0 0 –		8 0 0 –			
1 0 0 –		1 0 0 –			
2 1 0 –		2 1 0 –			
5 0 –		5 0 –			
1 5 0 –		1 5 0 –			
	1 5 0 –				1 5 0 –
	6 3 0 –				6 3 0 –
32 1 8 0 –	32 1 8 0 –	2 9 4 0 –	5 2 0 0 –	29 2 4 0 –	26 9 8 0 –
		2 2 6 0 –			2 2 6 0 –
		5 2 0 0 –	5 2 0 0 –	29 2 4 0 –	29 2 4 0 –

Kevin Young, Attorney at Law

Chart of Accounts

ASSETS (100–199)		OWNER'S EQUITY (300–399)	
101	Cash	301	Kevin Young, Capital
111	Accounts Receivable	311	Kevin Young, Drawing
121	Office Supplies		
131	Prepaid Insurance		**REVENUES (400–499)**
141	Furniture	401	Legal Fees
142	*Accumulated Depreciation, Furniture		
			EXPENSES (500–599)
	LIABILITIES (200–299)	501	Wages Expense
201	Accounts Payable	511	Advertising Expense
211	*Wages Payable	521	Rent Expense
		531	Utilities Expense
		541	*Office Supplies Expense
		551	*Insurance Expense
		561	*Depreciation Expense, Furniture

Financial statements are prepared from the completed worksheet in this order: the income statement, the statement of owner's equity, and the balance sheet.

The Income Statement

The income statement measures the performance of a firm over a period of time. This financial statement is prepared from the account data on the worksheet in a series of steps. These steps are keyed (①, ②, ③, and so on) in Exhibit 5-2. We will only use the Income Statement columns of the worksheet to prepare the income statement.

The steps to preparing an income statement are as follows:

① The heading for the income statement includes the name of the firm, "Income Statement," and the period of time. Leave one blank line before "Revenue."

② Revenues are taken from the income statement Credit column of the worksheet and are listed in chart-of-accounts number order. Kevin Young, Attorney at Law, has only one revenue account, Legal Fees. Since there is only one revenue account it is not necessary to total revenues. The Legal Fees amount carries a dollar sign. Leave one blank line before "Expenses."

③ Expenses are taken from the income statement Debit column of the worksheet and are listed in chart-of-accounts number order. A dollar sign appears at the beginning of the expense column. Expenses are totaled and underlined. Leave one blank line before "Net Income" or "Net Loss."

④ The amount of net income is taken from the Income Statement Debit column of the worksheet. A debit indicates that revenues are greater than expenses. A net loss would appear on the Credit column of the worksheet. A credit indicates that expenses exceed revenues. You should subtract the total expenses from the total revenues to check that the net income or net loss amount is correct. The net income or net loss amount is double-underlined and includes a dollar sign.

*Added accounts.

EXHIBIT 5-2 Preparation of an Income Statement from the Worksheet

Kevin Young, Attorney at Law
Worksheet
For the Month Ended April 30, 19XX

Account	Income Statement Debit	Income Statement Credit
Cash		
Accounts Receivable		
Office Supplies		
Prepaid Insurance		
Furniture		
Accounts Payable		
Kevin Young, Capital		
Kevin Young, Drawing		
Legal Fees		5200 –
Wages Expense	1330 –	
Advertising Expense	300 –	
Rent Expense	800 –	
Utilities Expense	100 –	
Totals		31400 –
Office Supplies Expense	210 –	
Insurance Expense	50 –	
Depreciation Expense, Furniture	150 –	
Accumulated Depreciation, Furniture		
Wages Payable		
	2940 –	5200 –
Net Income	2260 –	
	5200 –	5200 –

Kevin Young, Attorney at Law
Income Statement
For the Month Ended April 30, 19XX

Revenue		
Legal Fees		$5200 –
Expenses		
Wages Expense	$1330 –	
Advertising Expense	300 –	
Rent Expense	800 –	
Utilities Expense	100 –	
Office Supplies Expense	210 –	
Insurance Expense	50 –	
Depreciation Expense, Furniture	150 –	
Total Expenses		2940 –
Net Income		$2260 –

The Statement of Owner's Equity

The statement of owner's equity is prepared after the income statement. This financial statement summarizes the changes in the owner's Capital account for a definite period of time. The statement of owner's equity serves as a "bridge." It covers the space between the income statement and balance sheet. This space is the ending balance of owner's equity (Capital). The steps in preparing the statement of owner's equity are keyed (①,②,③, and so on) in Exhibit 5-3. We will use the Balance Sheet columns of the worksheet and the owner's Capital account in the general ledger to prepare the statement of owner's equity. The steps in preparing the statement of owner's equity from the worksheet and Capital account are as follows:

① The heading for the statement of owner's equity includes the name of the firm, "Statement of Owner's Equity," and the period of time. Leave one blank line before "Capital."

EXHIBIT 5-3 Preparation of the Statement of Owner's Equity from the Worksheet

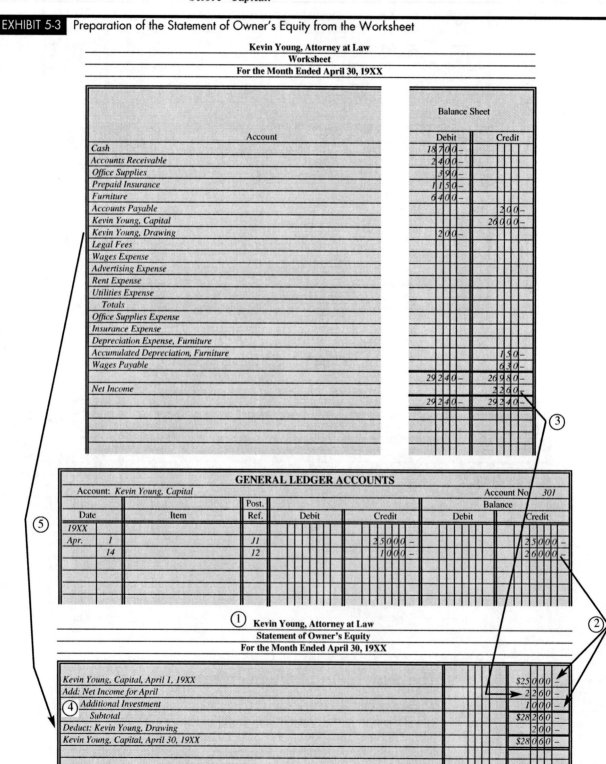

Kevin Young, Attorney at Law
Worksheet
For the Month Ended April 30, 19XX

Account	Balance Sheet Debit	Balance Sheet Credit
Cash	18700 –	
Accounts Receivable	2400 –	
Office Supplies	390 –	
Prepaid Insurance	1150 –	
Furniture	6400 –	
Accounts Payable		200 –
Kevin Young, Capital		26000 –
Kevin Young, Drawing	200 –	
Legal Fees		
Wages Expense		
Advertising Expense		
Rent Expense		
Utilities Expense		
Totals		
Office Supplies Expense		
Insurance Expense		
Depreciation Expense, Furniture		
Accumulated Depreciation, Furniture		150 –
Wages Payable		630 –
	29240 –	26980 –
Net Income		2260 –
	29240 –	29240 –

GENERAL LEDGER ACCOUNTS

Account: *Kevin Young, Capital*   Account No. *301*

Date	Item	Post. Ref.	Debit	Credit	Balance Debit	Balance Credit
19XX						
Apr. 1		J1		25000 –		25000 –
14		12		1000 –		26000 –

① **Kevin Young, Attorney at Law**
Statement of Owner's Equity
For the Month Ended April 30, 19XX

Kevin Young, Capital, April 1, 19XX		$25000 –
Add: Net Income for April		2260 –
④ Additional Investment		1000 –
Subtotal		$28260 –
Deduct: Kevin Young, Drawing		200 –
Kevin Young, Capital, April 30, 19XX		$28060 –

② The owner's Capital balance is taken from the beginning balance in the owner's Capital account in the general ledger. Additional Investments are also found in the Capital account in the general ledger.

③ Net Income is transferred from the Credit column of the Balance Sheet on the worksheet. You should verify this balance to the net income (or net loss) amount on the income statement. A credit balance indicates an increase in the owner's Capital account (net income). A net loss would be taken from the Debit column of the Balance Sheet on the worksheet. A debit balance indicates a decrease in the owner's Capital account (net loss).

④ Net Income and Additional Investment(s) are added to beginning Capital for a subtotal (include a dollar sign). A line is drawn after the amount of Additional Investment(s).

⑤ Owner's Drawing is taken from the Debit column of the Balance Sheet on the worksheet. This amount is subtracted from the subtotal for the final Capital balance. Kevin Young, Capital, April 30, 19XX, is double-underlined with a dollar sign.

The Balance Sheet

The balance sheet is prepared after the income statement and statement of owner's equity. Remember that the balance sheet is a statement of the financial position of the firm at a point in time. The steps in preparing the balance sheet are keyed (①, ②, ③, and so on) in Exhibit 5-4. We will use the Balance Sheet columns of the worksheet and the statement of owner's equity to prepare the balance sheet. The steps for preparing the balance sheet from the worksheet and statement of owner's equity are as follows:

① The heading for the balance sheet includes the name of the firm, "Balance Sheet," and the date. The date is April 30, 19XX. Leave one blank line before "Assets."

② Assets are taken from the Debit and Credit Balance Sheet columns of the worksheet. Most assets will have debit balances but contra assets; for example, Accumulated Depreciation will have credit balances. Assets are listed in chart-of-accounts number order. A dollar sign appears at the beginning of each column. A line is drawn after the column. The final total of Assets is double-underlined with a dollar sign. Leave one blank line before "Liabilities."

③ Liabilities are transferred from the Balance Sheet Credit column of the worksheet. They are listed in chart-of-accounts number order. A dollar sign is placed at the beginning of the column. Since there is more than one liability, Liabilities are totaled. The first column is underlined, and the total carries a dollar sign. Leave one blank line before "Owner's Equity."

④ Kevin Young, Capital, is taken from the statement of owner's equity. A line is drawn after Capital.

⑤ Total Liabilities and Owner's Equity are added and the total is double-underlined. This amount must equal Total Assets. A dollar sign appears at the final total.

Journalizing and Posting Adjustments

Objective 2
Journalize and post adjustments.

Adjustments provide a means of placing assets, liabilities, owner's equity, revenue, and expense accounts at their proper balances for the accounting period. Adjusting entries are not journalized and posted until the worksheet is complete. This way you can see the "full picture" of how the financial statements will look. By examining the completed

EXHIBIT 5-4 | Preparation of a Balance Sheet from the Worksheet

Kevin Young, Attorney at Law
Worksheet
For the Month Ended April 30, 19XX

Account	Balance Sheet Debit	Credit
Cash	18 700 –	
Accounts Receivable	2 400 –	
Office Supplies	390 –	
Prepaid Insurance	1 150 –	
Furniture	6 400 –	
Accounts Payable		200 –
Kevin Young, Capital		26 000 –
Kevin Young, Drawing	200 –	
Legal Fees		
Wages Expense		
Advertising Expense		
Rent Expense		
Utilities Expense		
Totals		
Office Supplies Expense		
Insurance Expense		
Depreciation Expense, Furniture		
Accumulated Depreciation, Furniture		150 –
Wages Payable		630 –
	29 240 –	26 980 –
Net Income		2 260 –
	29 240 –	29 240 –

Kevin Young, Attorney at Law
Statement of Owner's Equity (partial)
For the Month Ended April 30, 19XX

Kevin Young, Capital, April 30, 19XX		$28 060 –

① **Kevin Young, Attorney at Law**
Balance Sheet
April 30, 19XX

Assets			
② Cash		$18 700 –	
Accounts Receivable		2 400 –	
Office Supplies		390 –	
Prepaid Insurance		1 150 –	
Furniture	$6 400 –		
Less Accumulated Depreciation	150 –	6 250 –	
Total Assets			$28 890 –
Liabilities			
③ Accounts Payable		$200 –	
Wages Payable		630 –	
Total Liabilities			$830 –
Owner's Equity			
Keving Young, Capital			$28 060 – ⑤
Total Liabilities and Owner's Equity			$28 890 –

④

worksheet, you can determine if any additional accounts are to be adjusted. Once you are satisfied with the account balances on the worksheet, you can journalize and post adjusting entries. The adjusting entries are taken directly from the Adjustments columns of the worksheet.

The adjusting entries are as follows:

a. Adjust Office Supplies.

b. Adjust Prepaid Insurance.

c. Adjust Furniture.

d. Adjust Wages Expense.

These four adjusting entries are journalized in the general journal in Exhibit 5-5 and posted to the general ledger in Exhibit 5-6. You should indicate in the general journal and general ledger that these entries and postings are from adjusting entries. In the general journal you would write "Adjusting Entries" in the Description column before the first adjustment is entered. You would not need to write a description for each adjusting entry since you have indicated that they are adjusting entries. When you post the adjusting entry to the general ledger you would write "Adjusting" in the Item column. You would then be able to distinguish adjusting entries from other entries.

These adjusting entries are posted to the general ledger in Exhibit 5-6, which shows a partial general ledger for Kevin Young, Attorney at Law. Only those general ledger accounts that are used for this posting process are listed.

Chapter Review

1. **Prepare financial statements.**

   The worksheet is a tool used by accountants to compile the information necessary for the preparation of financial statements. Financial statements are prepared from the completed worksheet in this order: the income statement, the statement of owner's equity, and the balance sheet.

2. **Journalize and post adjustments.**

   Adjusting entries are not journalized and posted until the worksheet is complete. This way you can see the "full picture" of how the financial statements will look.

EXHIBIT 5-5 Journalizing Adjusting Entries

GENERAL JOURNAL Page ___3___

Date		Description	Post Ref.	Debit	Credit
		Adjusting Entries			
19XX					
Apr.	*30*	*Office Supplies Expense*	541	2 1 0 –	
		Office Supplies	121		2 1 0 –
	30	*Insurance Expense*	551	5 0 –	
		Prepaid Insurance	131		5 0 –
	30	*Depreciation Expense, Furniture*	561	1 5 0 –	
		Accumulated Depreciation, Furniture	142		1 5 0 –
	30	*Wages Expense*	501	6 3 0 –	
		Wages Payable	211		6 3 0 –

EXHIBIT 5-6 | General Ledger Accounts Used to Post Adjusting Entries

GENERAL LEDGER ACCOUNTS

Account: *Office Supplies*   Account No. *121*

Date		Item	Post Ref.	Debit	Credit	Balance Debit	Balance Credit
19XX							
Apr.	4		J1	600 –		600 –	
	30	Adjusting	J3		210 –	390 –	

Account: *Prepaid Insurance*   Account No. *131*

Date		Item	Post Ref.	Debit	Credit	Balance Debit	Balance Credit
19XX							
Apr.	1		J1	1200 –		1200 –	
	30	Adjusting	J3		50 –	1150 –	

Account: *Accumulated Depreciation, Furniture*   Account No. *142*

Date		Item	Post Ref.	Debit	Credit	Balance Debit	Balance Credit
19XX							
Apr.	30	Adjusting	J3		150 –		150 –

Account: *Wages Payable*   Account No. *211*

Date		Item	Post Ref.	Debit	Credit	Balance Debit	Balance Credit
19XX							
Apr.	30	Adjusting	J3		630 –		630 –

(continued)

By examining the completed worksheet, you can determine if any additional accounts are to be adjusted. Once you are satisfied with the account balances on the worksheet, you can then journalize and post adjusting entries. The adjusting entries are taken directly from the Adjustments columns of the worksheet.

Ex. 5-6 (concluded)

Account: Wages Expense						Account No. 501
Date	Item	Post Ref.	Debit	Credit	Balance Debit	Balance Credit
19XX						
Apr. 17		J2	700 –		700 –	
30	Adjusting	J3	630 –		1330 –	

Account: Office Supplies Expense						Account No. 541
Date	Item	Post Ref.	Debit	Credit	Balance Debit	Balance Credit
19XX						
Apr. 30	Adjusting	J3	210 –		210 –	

Account: Insurance Expense						Account No. 551
Date	Item	Post Ref.	Debit	Credit	Balance Debit	Balance Credit
19XX						
Apr. 30	Adjusting	J3	50 –		50 –	

Account: Depreciation Expense, Furniture						Account No. 561
Date	Item	Post Ref.	Debit	Credit	Balance Debit	Balance Credit
19XX						
Apr. 30	Adjusting	J3	150 –		150 –	

Self-Test Questions for Review

(Answers are at the end of Chapter 5.)

1. In a chart of accounts for a legal firm, account number 301 would probably be
    a. Owner, Capital.   **b.** Legal Fees.
    c. Wages Expense.   **d.** Wages Payable.

2. To prepare an income statement, the revenues are taken from the _____ column of the worksheet.
   a. balance sheet Debit
   b. income statement Credit
   c. balance sheet Credit
   d. income statement Debit

3. To adjust Office Supplies, the account _____ is credited.
   a. Office Supplies Expense
   b. Accounts Payable
   c. Prepaid Insurance
   d. Office Supplies

4. Which of the following accounts will probably have a credit balance after adjustments have been posted (assume adjustments for office supplies, insurance, and wages)?
   a. Prepaid Insurance
   b. Office Supplies
   c. Wages Payable
   d. Insurance Expense

5. To complete a balance sheet, liabilities are transferred from the _____ column of the worksheet.
   a. balance sheet Debit
   b. income statement Debit
   c. balance sheet Credit
   d. income statement Credit

Practical Review Problem

Objectives 1 and 2

Preparing an Income Statement and Journalizing Adjustments   Pedro Ramos is the owner of Ramos Truck Service. The following accounts and account balances (all are normal) are from the credit "Adjustments" column of a worksheet: (a) Truck Supplies, 1,290; (b) Prepaid Insurance, 540; (c) Accumulated Depreciation, Equipment, 150; and (d) Wages Payable, 1,580. The following accounts and account balances (all are normal) are from the "Income Statement" columns of a worksheet: Truck Service Fees, 7,890; Wages Expense, 4,070; Advertising Expense, 560; Rent Expense, 2,170; Utilities Expense, 260; Truck Supplies Expense, 1,290; Insurance Expense, 540; and Depreciation Expense, Equipment, 150. The time period is the month of June 19XX. The firm had a net loss for the month.

REQUIRED
1. Prepare an income statement. (See next page.)
2. Record adjusting entries in a general journal, page 4. (See next page.)

Answer to Practical Review Problem

1. Prepare an income statement. (See next page.)
2. Record adjusting entries. (See next page.)

Discussion Questions

Q 5-1   Which of the ten steps of the accounting cycle were covered in this chapter?

Q 5-2   Name the ten steps that represent the accounting cycle.

Q 5-3   Name at least four accounts that were added to the chart of accounts for journalizing and posting adjusting entries in this chapter.

Q 5-4   In what order are financial statements prepared from the worksheet?

Q 5-5   Name and describe the four steps to prepare an income statement from the worksheet.

Q 5-6   When is the statement of owner's equity prepared? What items (columns, financial statements, and so on) are used to prepare the statement of owner's equity?

Ramos Truck Service
Income Statement
For the Month Ended June 30, 19XX

Revenue		
Truck Service Fees		$7890 –
Expenses		
Wages	$4070 –	
Advertising Expense	560 –	
Rent Expense	2170 –	
Utilities Expense	260 –	
Truck Supplies Expense	1290 –	
Insurance Expense	540 –	
Depreciation Expense, Equipment	150 –	
Total Expenses		9040 –
Net Loss		($1150 –)

GENERAL JOURNAL   Page ____4____

Date		Description	Post Ref.	Debit	Credit
		Adjusting Entries			
19XX					
June	30	Truck Supplies Expense		1290 –	
		Truck Supplies			1290 –
	30	Insurance Expense		540 –	
		Prepaid Insurance			540 –
	30	Depreciation Expense, Equipment		150 –	
		Accumulated Depreciation, Equipment			150 –
	30	Wages Expense		1580 –	
		Wages Payable			1580 –

Q 5-7 Name and describe the five steps to prepare a statement of owner's equity from the worksheet.

Q 5-8 Name and describe the five steps to prepare a balance sheet from the worksheet.

Q 5-9 What do adjustments provide? When are adjusting entries journalized and posted and why?

Q 5-10 Where and what do you write in the general journal to indicate that the entries are from adjusting entries? Where and what do you write in the general ledger to indicate that the postings are from adjusting entries?

Exercises

Objective 1

E 5-1 **Selecting a Chart of Accounts** Melanie Conyers is starting a law firm.

a. Name at least six asset accounts that she could use.

b. Name two liability accounts that she could use.

c. Name two owner's equity accounts that she could use.

d. Name one revenue account that she could use.

e. Name at least six expense accounts that she could use.

Objective 1

E 5-2 **Completing an Income Statement** Complete the following income statement for Ramon Herrera, Attorney at Law, for the month ended May 19XX:

(a)		
(b)		
(c)		
(d)		
Legal Fees		$5,000
(e)		
Wages Expense	$2,000	
Rent Expense	1,000	
Utilities Expense	200	
Insurance Expense	100	
(f)		(g)
(h)		$ (i)

Objective 1

E 5-3 **Completing a Statement of Owner's Equity** Complete the following statement of owner's equity for Laura McKinnon, Medical Doctor, for the month ended October 19XX:

(a)		
(b)		
(c)		
(d)		$12,000
Add: (e)		2,000
(f)		3,000
Subtotal		$ (g)
Deduct: (h)		4,000
(i)		$ (j)

Objective 2

E 5-4 **Completing Adjusting Entries** Complete the following adjusting entries:

	Debit	Credit
Office Supplies Expense	300	
(a)		300
(b)	200	
Prepaid Insurance		200
Depreciation Expense, Equipment	100	
(c)		100
(d)	600	
Wages Payable		600

Objective 1

E 5-5   Completing a Balance Sheet   Complete the following balance sheet for Stuart Nelson, Computer Consultant (the accounting period ends April 30, 19XX):

	(a)		
	(b)		
	(c)		
(d)			
Cash			$3,000
Accounts Receivable			2,000
Office Supplies			1,000
Equipment		$8,000	
Less: Accumulated Depreciation		(e)	3,000
(f)			$ (g)
(h)			
Accounts Payable			$2,000
Wages Payable			1,000
(i)			$ (j)
(k)			
Stuart Nelson, Capital			(l)
(m)			$ (n)

Use the following partial worksheet for E 5-6:

Norman Tool Design
Worksheet (partial)
For the Month Ended September 30, 19XX

Account	Adjustments	
	Debit	Credit
Cash		
Accounts Receivable		
Tool Supplies		(a) 3600 –
Prepaid Insurance		(b) 700 –
Design Equipment		
Accounts Payable		
L.T. Quan, Capital		
L.T. Quan, Drawing		
Tool Design Fees		
Wages Expense	(d) 4900 –	
Advertising Expense		
Rent Expense		
Utilities Expense		
Totals		
Tool Supplies Expense	(a) 3600 –	
Insurance Expense	(b) 700 –	
Depreciation Expense, Design Equipment	(c) 800 –	
Accumulated Depreciation, Design Equipment		(c) 800 –
Wages Payable		(d) 4900 –
	10000 –	10000 –

Objective 2   **E 5-6** **Journalizing Adjusting Entries** Journalize (page 3) the adjusting entries for Norman Tool Design from the partial worksheet.

Objective 1   **E 5-7** **Preparing an Income Statement** Prepare an income statement for D. H. Yothers (use the Income Statement columns of the following partial worksheet):

D.H. Yothers Landscaping Services

Worksheet (partial)

For the Month Ended December 31, 19XX

	Income Statment	
Account	**Debit**	**Credit**
Cash		
Accounts Receivable		
Store Supplies		
Prepaid Insurance		
Office Furniture		
Accounts Payable		
D.H. Yothers, Capital		
D.H. Yothers, Drawing		
Landscaping Services		12 8 0 0 —
Wages Expense	5 1 0 0 —	
Advertising Expense	2 7 0 0 —	
Rent Expense	1 5 0 0 —	
Utilities Expense	3 0 0 —	
Totals		
Store Supplies Expense	4 0 0 —	
Insurance Expense	1 0 0 —	
Depreciation Expense, Office Furniture	2 0 0 —	
Accumulated Depreciation, Office Furniture		
Wages Payable		

Objective 2   **E 5-8** **Journalizing and Posting Adjusting Entries** The following data was taken from the worksheet of Mills Auto Service.

1. The adjustments are as follows:

(a) adjust Store Supplies, $190; (b) adjust Prepaid Insurance, $50; (c) adjust Depreciation Expense, Computer, $100; and (d) adjust Wages Expense, $970.

2. The chart-of-accounts numbers are as follows:

Store Supplies, 131; Prepaid Insurance, 141; Accumulated Depreciation, Computer, 152; Wages Payable, 221; Wages Expense, 511; Store Supplies Expense, 551; Insurance Expense, 561; Depreciation Expense, Computer, 571.

Journalize the adjusting entries in a general journal, page 5. The date is October 31, 19XX. Also, post the adjusting entries to the general ledger.

Problems

P 5-1 **Preparing Financial Statements** The accountant for Poston Consulting Service completed a worksheet for the month ended August 31, 19XX. The Income Statement and Balance Sheet columns and Capital account are as follows:

Poston Consulting Service
Worksheet (partial)
For the Month Ended August 31, 19XX

Account	Income Statement Debit	Income Statement Credit	Balance Sheet Debit	Balance Sheet Credit
Cash			28 600 –	
Accounts Receivable			13 700 –	
Office Supplies			10 400 –	
Prepaid Insurance			6 900 –	
Machinery			19 000 –	
Accounts Payable				12 400 –
Oliver Poston, Capital				64 500 –
Oliver Poston, Drawing			2 600 –	
Consulting Fees		8 600 –		
Wages Expense	2 700 –			
Advertising Expense	300 –			
Rent Expense	2 100 –			
Utilities Expense	100 –			
Totals				
Office Supplies Expense	300 –			
Insurance Expense	100 –			
Depreciation Expense, Machinery	400 –			
Accumulated Depreciation, Machinery				400 –
Wages Payable				1 300 –
	6 000 –	8 600 –	81 200 –	78 600 –
Net Income	2 600 –			2 600 –
	8 600 –	8 600 –	81 200 –	81 200 –

GENERAL LEDGER ACCOUNT							
Account: *Oliver Poston, Capital*						Account No. *301*	
		Post			Balance		
Date	Item	Ref.	Debit	Credit	Debit	Credit	
19XX							
Aug. *1*		*J1*		6 3 600 –		6 3 600 –	
9		*J3*		900 –		6 4 500 –	

REQUIRED

Prepare financial statements from the worksheet and Capital account.

Objective 2

P 5-2 **Recording and Posting Adjusting Entries** Delagarza Kitchen Designers has the following chart-of-account numbers:

Store Supplies, 141; Prepaid Insurance, 151; Accumulated Depreciation, Copier, 162; Wages Payable, 231; Wages Expense, 521; Store Supplies Expense, 561; Insurance Expense, 571; Depreciation Expense, Copier, 581.

The firm's accountant finds the adjusting entries from the Adjustments columns of a completed worksheet (month ended April 30, 19XX):

a. Adjust Store Supplies, $340.

b. Adjust Prepaid Insurance, $120.

c. Adjust Copier, $260.

d. Adjust Wages Expense, $1,370.

REQUIRED

1. Enter the accounts and account numbers in the general ledger in chart-of-accounts number order.

2. Record the adjusting entries in a general journal, page 9.

3. Post the adjusting entries to the general ledger.

Objectives 1 and 2

P 5-3 **Preparing an Income Statement and Journalizing and Posting Adjustments** Cecil Hargis is the owner of Hargis Hat Repair. The following accounts and account balances (all are normal) are from the credit "Adjustments" column of a worksheet:

(a) Hat Supplies, 3,780; (b) Prepaid Insurance, 620; (c) Accumulated Depreciation, Repair Equipment, 540; and (d) Wages Payable, 5,890.

The following accounts and account balances (all are normal) are from the "Income Statement" columns of a worksheet: Hat Repair Fees, 12,780; Wages Expense, 7,890; Advertising Expense, 1,030; Rent Expense, 1,290; Utilities Expense, 150; Hat Supplies Expense, 3,780; Insurance Expense, 620; and Depreciation Expense, Repair Equipment, 540. The time period is the month of April 19XX. The firm had a net loss for the month.

The chart-of-accounts numbers that apply to the adjusting entries are as follows:

Hat Supplies, 13; Prepaid Insurance, 14; Accumulated Depreciation, Repair Equipment, 16; Wages Payable, 22; Wages Expense, 51; Hat Supplies Expense, 55; Insurance Expense, 56; Depreciation Expense, Repair Equipment, 57.

REQUIRED (See the Practical Review Problem if you need help.)

1. Prepare an income statement.

2. Enter the accounts and account numbers in the general ledger in chart-of-accounts number order.

3. Record adjusting entries in a general journal, page 3.

4. Post only the adjusting entries to the general ledger.

Objectives 1 and 2

P 5-4 **Comprehensive Review Problem** Yong Suh is the owner of Southwest Insurance Agency. Yong had the following trial balance, Capital account, and adjustments at the end of July 19XX:

Southwest Insurance Agency

Trial Balance

July 31, 19XX

Accounts	Debit	Credit
Cash	25 2 4 0 –	
Accounts Receivable	14 7 3 0 –	
Office Supplies	22 8 9 0 –	
Prepaid Insurance	8 1 6 0 –	
Automobile	15 8 0 0 –	
Accounts Payable		12 7 8 0 –
Yong Suh, Capital		66 5 3 0 –
Yong Suh, Drawing	5 6 5 0 –	
Auto Insurance Fees		9 7 9 0 –
Life Insurance Fees		11 6 4 0 –
Wages Expense	4 3 2 0 –	
Advertising Expense	1 7 8 0 –	
Rent Expense	2 0 0 0 –	
Utilities Expense	1 7 0 –	
Totals	100 7 4 0 –	100 7 4 0 –

GENERAL LEDGER ACCOUNT

Account: *Yong Suh, Capital* Account No. *308*

Date	Item	Post Ref.	Debit	Credit	Balance Debit	Balance Credit
19XX						
July 1		J1		6 2 6 4 0 –		6 2 6 4 0 –
22		J3		3 8 9 0 –		6 6 5 3 0 –

Adjustments:

a. Office Supplies had a beginning balance of $15,450. During the month, $7,440 of office supplies were purchased. A count was made at the end of the month and $19,560 of supplies were on hand.

b. On July 1, 19XX, the firm paid $8,160 for a four-year liability insurance policy.

c. An automobile was purchased July 3, 19XX, at a cost of $15,800. Yong estimates that the automobile will have a $2,000 salvage value after five years of useful life.

d. On July 31, 19XX, $1,990 of wages expense is incurred but unrecorded.

The chart-of-accounts numbers that apply to the adjusting entries are as follows:

Office Supplies, 131; Prepaid Insurance, 141; Accumulated Depreciation, Automobile, 152; Wages Payable, 221; Wages Expense, 511; Office Supplies Expense, 551; Insurance Expense, 561; Depreciation Expense, Automobile, 571.

REQUIRED
1. Calculate and organize adjustments using T accounts.
2. Complete the worksheet.
3. Prepare financial statements from the worksheet and Capital account.
4. Record adjusting entries in a general journal, page 5.
5. Post only the adjusting entries to the general ledger (include accounts, account numbers, and previous balances).

Checklist of Key Figures

P 5-1   Net Income, $2,600
P 5-2   No key figure
P 5-3   (1) Net Loss, $2,520
P 5-4   (2) Net Income, $7,440

Answers to Self-Test Questions

1. a   2. b   3. d   4. c   5. c

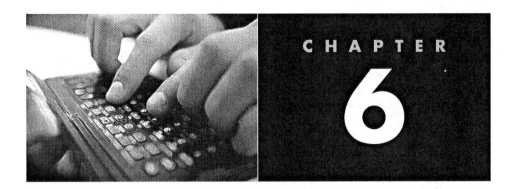

Closing the Accounting Records

LEARNING OBJECTIVES

After reading this chapter, discussing the questions, and working the exercises and problems, you will be able to do the following:

1. Journalize and post closing entries

2. Prepare a post-closing trial balance

By now, you are familiar with the worksheet for a service-type organization or firm. The worksheet is a tool that is used to help prepare financial statements. Since adjustments are prepared as they are needed without regard to chart-of-accounts numbers, you needed a tool, like the worksheet, to account for the haphazard account listings. Then we saw that net income or net loss placed the worksheet in debits-equal-credits balance.

The balance sheet represents the financial position of the firm for a *point* in time. The statement of owner's equity and the income statement measured performance for a definite *period* of time. Once the measured period of time is over, you must set those applicable accounts to zero to begin the new accounting period. In this chapter we will prepare **closing entries** that will clear the appropriate accounts. By the end of this chapter we will have completed the accounting cycle for a service-type firm.

Journalizing and Posting Closing Entries

Objective 1
Journalize and post closing entries.

Those accounts that measure performance and affect capital (that is, revenues, expenses, and Drawing) must be closed or cleared at the end of one accounting period for the start of the next accounting period. Remember that revenues increase Capital while expenses decrease Capital. Drawing is included here because the use of this account indicates that the owner has taken valuable assets, such as Cash, Office Supplies, and so on out of the firm, thus reducing owner's equity or Capital.

Revenues, expenses, and Drawing are called **nominal** or **temporary** accounts. These accounts start at zero at the beginning of the accounting period, accumulate a balance, and then are reduced to zero again for the start of the next accounting period. Thus their balances are temporary or nominal. To illustrate the nominal accounts used for Kevin Young, Attorney at Law, the income statement, statement of owner's equity, and balance sheet are listed in Exhibit 6-1. The nominal or temporary accounts are noted by the term, "Nominal," at the left side.

All balance sheet accounts, with the exception of Drawing, are **real** or **permanent** accounts. These accounts may start with a balance other than zero, and accumulate more or less during the accounting period, but their balances are not closed or cleared at the end of the period. Thus the ending balances of real or permanent accounts for one accounting period will be the beginning balances for the next period. In Exhibit 6-1 the real or permanent accounts used by Kevin Young, Attorney at Law, so far are noted by "Real" at the left side.

In Exhibit 6-1, Net Income is not an account. Remember that net income is the difference between the revenue and expense accounts for an accounting period. Beginning Capital and Additional Investments are part of the ending balance of Capital.

At this time, before closing entries are made, the balance of the account Kevin Young, Capital, is a $26,000 credit. However, both the statement of owner's equity and balance sheet show $28,060. We will bring this account balance up to date by using closing entries.

Let's use a T account to review the activity in the owner's Capital account in April 19XX, which corresponds to the statement of owner's equity in Exhibit 6-1. Remember that net income increases Capital.

	Kevin Young, Capital		
	−	+	
(4/29) Owner withdrew cash	200	25,000	(4/1) Initial investment by owner
		1,000	(4/14) Additional investment by owner
		2,260	(4/14/30) Net income for April 19XX
		28,060	Ending Capital balance

EXHIBIT 6-1   Real and Nominal Accounts Identified

Kevin Young, Attorney at Law
Income Statement
For the Month Ended April 30, 19XX

	Revenue		
Nominal	Legal Fees		$5,200
	Expenses		
	Wages Expense	$1,330	
	Advertising Expense	300	
	Rent Expense	800	
Nominal	Utilities Expense	100	
	Office Supplies Expense	210	
	Insurance Expense	50	
	Depreciation Expense, Furniture	150	
	Total Expenses		2,940
	Net Income		$2,260

Kevin Young, Attorney at Law
Statement of Owner's Equity
For the Month Ended April 30, 19XX

Real	Kevin Young, Capital April 1, 19XX	$25,000
	Add: Net Income for April	2,260
Real	Additional Investment	1,000
	Subtotal	$28,260
Nominal	Deduct: Kevin Young, Drawing	200
	Kevin Young, Capital, April 30, 19XX	$28,060

(continued)

We can see that closing entries have the following purposes:

1. To set the nominal or temporary accounts to zero at the end of an accounting period.

2. To bring the owner's Capital account balance up to date to reflect the balance as shown on the statement of owner's equity and balance sheet.

Income Summary

To facilitate the closing process, a new account—**Income Summary**—must be introduced. The chart-of-accounts number will be 321. Income Summary is a nominal account that will only be used during the closing process. It has a zero balance before and after the closing process.

Ex. 6-1 (continued)

Kevin Young, Attorney at Law
Balance Sheet
April 30, 19XX

Assets

Cash		$18,700	
Accounts Receivable		2,400	
Office Supplies		390	
Prepaid Insurance		1,150	
Furniture	$6,400		
Less: Accumulated Depreciation	150	6,250	
Total Assets			$28,890

Real (bracket spanning Cash through Less: Accumulated Depreciation)

Liabilities

Accounts Payable	$200	
Wages Payable	630	
Total Liabilities		$830

Real (bracket spanning Accounts Payable and Wages Payable)

Owner's Equity

Kevin Young, Capital	28,060
Total Liabilities and Owner's Equity	$28,890

Real

Closing Entries

There are four closing entries to clear the nominal accounts, which consist of revenues, expenses, Income Summary, and Drawing. The closing entries occur in this order: (1) close revenues to Income Summary; (2) close expenses to Income Summary; (3) close Income Summary to Capital, and (4) close Drawing to Capital.

Closing Revenues

To clear the revenue accounts of Kevin Young, Attorney at Law, a general journal entry would be made. This entry would then be posted to the general ledger. The term "Closing Entries" is written after the end of the adjusting entries in the general journal. A description is not needed after each general journal entry because the term "Closing Entries" signifies that the nominal accounts are being cleared. In the general ledger, the term "Closing" is written in the Item column to indicate that the posting is from a closing entry.

Since the revenue accounts have credit balances they must be debited to have a resulting zero balance. The first closing entry is journalized and posted as follows:

GENERAL JOURNAL   Page ___3___

Date	Description	Post Ref.	Debit	Credit
	(after the last adjusting entry)			
	Closing Entries			
Apr. 30	Legal Fees	401	5200 –	
	Income Summary	321		5200 –

GENERAL LEDGER ACCOUNTS

Account: *Income Summary*   Account No.   321

Date	Item	Post Ref.	Debit	Credit	Balance Debit	Balance Credit
19XX						
Apr. 30	Closing	J3		5200 –		5200 –

Account: *Legal Fees*   Account No.   401

Date	Item	Post Ref.	Debit	Credit	Balance Debit	Balance Credit
19XX						
Apr. 2		J1		1900 –		1900 –
19		J2		1800 –		3700 –
24		J2		1500 –		5200 –
30	Closing	J3	5200 –			– 0 –

At this time, the revenue account is closed to Income Summary. Now let's clear the expense accounts.

Closing Expenses

Expenses normally have a debit balance. Thus, to clear expenses, a credit is applied to each expense account. The total of the expenses is debited to Income Summary. The second closing entry is journalized and posted as follows:

GENERAL JOURNAL   Page ___3___

Date	Description	Post Ref.	Debit	Credit
30	Income Summary	321	2940 –	
	Wages Expense	501		1330 –
	Advertising Expense	511		300 –
	Rent Expense	521		800 –
	Utilities Expense	531		100 –
	Office Supplies Expense	541		210 –
	Insurance Expense	551		50 –
	Depreciation Expense, Furniture	561		150 –

GENERAL LEDGER ACCOUNTS

Account: *Income Summary*   Account No.   321

Date	Item	Post Ref.	Debit	Credit	Balance Debit	Balance Credit
19XX						
Apr. 30	Closing	J3		5200 –		5200 –
30	Closing	J3	2940 –			2260 –

Account: *Wage Expense*   Account No.   501

Date	Item	Post Ref.	Debit	Credit	Balance Debit	Balance Credit
19XX						
Apr. 17		J2	700 –		700 –	
30	Adjusting	J3	630 –		1330 –	
30	Closing	J3		1330 –	–0–	

Account: *Advertising Expense*   Account No.   511

Date	Item	Post Ref.	Debit	Credit	Balance Debit	Balance Credit
19XX						
Apr. 11		J1	300 –		300 –	
30	Closing	J3		300 –	–0–	

Account: *Rent Expense*   Account No.   521

Date	Item	Post Ref.	Debit	Credit	Balance Debit	Balance Credit
19XX						
Apr. 1		J1	800 –		800 –	
30	Closing	J3		800 –	–0–	

(continued)

General Journal (continued)

Account: *Utilities Expense*							Account No. *531*
		Post	Debit	Credit	Balance		
Date	Item	Ref.	Debit	Credit	Debit	Credit	
19XX							
Apr. 7		*J1*	1 0 0 —		1 0 0 —		
30	*Closing*	*J3*		1 0 0 —	— 0 —		

Account: *Office Supplies Expense*							Account No. *541*
		Post	Debit	Credit	Balance		
Date	Item	Ref.	Debit	Credit	Debit	Credit	
19XX							
Apr. 30	*Adjusting*	*J3*	2 1 0 —		2 1 0 —		
30	*Closing*	*J3*		2 1 0 —	— 0 —		

Account: *Insurance Expense*							Account No. *551*
		Post	Debit	Credit	Balance		
Date	Item	Ref.	Debit	Credit	Debit	Credit	
19XX							
Apr. 30	*Adjusting*	*J3*	5 0 —		5 0 —		
30	*Closing*	*J3*		5 0 —	— 0 —		

Account: *Depreciation Expense, Furniture*							Account No. *561*
		Post	Debit	Credit	Balance		
Date	Item	Ref.	Debit	Credit	Debit	Credit	
19XX							
Apr. 30	*Adjusting*	*J3*	1 5 0 —		1 5 0 —		
30	*Closing*	*J3*		1 5 0 —	— 0 —		

Now all the expense accounts have been cleared to Income Summary. The next step is to close Income Summary to Capital.

Closing Income Summary

Income Summary is a nominal or temporary account. It must have a zero balance at the start of the next accounting period. The balance of Income Summary, after all revenues and expenses have been cleared, is equal to net income or net loss. Remember that Kevin Young, Attorney at Law, had a net income of $2,260 for April 19XX (see Exhibit 6-1). This corresponds to the Income Summary balance after total revenues and total expenses have been posted. Let's use a T account to illustrate the Income Summary balance:

Income Summary			
Beginning balance (4/1)	–0–	–0–	
		5,200	Credit balance after revenues are posted
Posting of total expenses	2,940		
		2,260	*Credit balance after revenues and expenses are posted (Net Income)

The third closing entry clears the Income Summary balance to the owner's Capital account as follows:

GENERAL JOURNAL   Page ___3___

Date		Description	Post Ref.	Debit	Credit
	30	Income Summary	321	2 2 6 0 –	
		Kevin Young, Capital	301		2 2 6 0 –

GENERAL LEDGER ACCOUNTS

Account: *Kevin Young, Capital*   Account No. *301*

Date		Item	Post Ref.	Debit	Credit	Balance Debit	Balance Credit
19XX							
Apr.	*1*		J1		2 5 0 0 0 –		2 5 0 0 0 –
	14		J2		1 0 0 0 –		2 6 0 0 0 –
	30	*Closing*	J3		2 2 6 0 –		2 8 2 6 0 –

Account: *Income Summary*							Account No. *321*	
Date		Item	Post Ref.	Debit	Credit	Balance Debit	Balance Credit	
19XX								
Apr.	30	*Closing*	J3		5 2 0 0 –		5 2 0 0 –	
	30	*Closing*	J3	2 9 4 0 –			2 2 6 0 –	
	30	*Closing*	J3	2 2 6 0 –			– 0 –	

Let's use a T account again to illustrate the Income Summary balance after the third closing entry is made:

---

*If there is a credit balance, then revenues (5,200) are greater than expenses (2,940) and the difference is net income (5,200 credit – 2,940 debit = 2,260 credit).

	Income Summary		
Beginning balance (4/1)	–0–	–0–	
		5,200	Credit balance after revenues are posted
Posting of total expenses	2,940		
		2,260	Credit balance after revenues and expenses are posted (Net Income)
Third closing entry to clear Income Summary	2,260		
	–0–	–0–	(4/30) Ending balance

Closing Drawing

Drawing is the only nominal account that appears in a Balance Sheet column on the worksheet. As we have previously seen, whenever the owner removes an asset from the firm (Cash, Furniture, and so on) the asset is credited and Drawing is debited. To reflect this decrease in the owner's equity of the firm, the fourth closing entry is made to reduce owner's equity and clear Drawing.

The closing process for the Drawing account is as follows:

GENERAL JOURNAL   Page ___3___

Date	Description	Post Ref.	Debit	Credit
30	Kevin Young, Capital	301	200 –	
	Kevin Young, Drawing	311		200 –

GENERAL LEDGER ACCOUNTS

Account: *Kevin Young, Capital*   Account No. 301

Date		Item	Post Ref.	Debit	Credit	Balance Debit	Balance Credit
19XX							
Apr.	1		J1		25000 –		25000 –
	14		J2		1000 –		26000 –
	30	Closing	J3		2260 –		28260 –
	30	Closing	J3	200 –			*28060 –

Account: *Kevin Young, Drawing*   Account No. 311

Date		Item	Post Ref.	Debit	Credit	Balance Debit	Balance Credit
19XX							
Apr.	29		J2	200 –		200 –	
	30	Closing	J3		200 –	–0–	

Upon completion of these postings, Drawing has a zero balance.

---

*This 28,060 balance in Capital is the ending balance of Kevin Young, Capital, on the statement of owner's equity and the balance sheet (see Exhibit 6-1).

Journalizing Closing Entries

So far we have journalized the closing entries separately. However, they would be journalized in the general journal in order, with revenues first, expenses second, and so on. The four closing entries are illustrated in Exhibit 6-2.

EXHIBIT 6-2 Four Closing Entries Journalized in the General Journal

GENERAL JOURNAL   Page ____3____

Date		Description	Post Ref.	Debit	Credit
		(after the last adjusting entry)			
		Closing Entries			
Apr	30	Legal Fees	401	5 2 0 0 —	
		Income Summary	321		5 2 0 0 —
	30	Income Summary	321	2 9 4 0 —	
		Wages Expense	501		1 3 3 0 —
		Advertising Expense	511		3 0 0 —
		Rent Expense	521		8 0 0 —
		Utilities Expense	531		1 0 0 —
		Office Supplies Expense	541		2 1 0 —
		Insurance Expense	551		5 0 —
		Depreciation Expense, Furniture	561		1 5 0 —
	30	Income Summary	321	2 2 6 0 —	
		Kevin Young, Capital	301		2 2 6 0 —
	30	Kevin Young, Capital	301	2 0 0 —	
		Kevin Young, Drawing	311		2 0 0 —

The General Ledger (after Closing Entries)

Let's bring ourselves up to date on the account balances in the general ledger at the close of the accounting period. The general ledger accounts for Kevin Young, Attorney at Law, are illustrated in Exhibit 6-3. (Notice that Income Summary, account number 321, is included.)

EXHIBIT 6-3   General Ledger Accounts at Close of Accounting Period

GENERAL LEDGER ACCOUNTS

Account: *Cash*   Account No. 101

Date		Item	Post Ref.	Debit	Credit	Balance Debit	Balance Credit
19XX							
Apr.	1		J1	25000 –		25000 –	
	1		J1		800 –	24200 –	
	1		J1		1200 –	23000 –	
	2		J1	1900 –		24900 –	
	3		J1		6400 –	18500 –	
	7		J1		100 –	18400 –	
	14		J2	1000 –		19400 –	
	17		J2		700 –	18700 –	
	22		J2		400 –	18300 –	
	26		J2	900 –		19200 –	
	29		J2		200 –	19000 –	
	30		J2		300 –	18700 –	

Account: *Accounts Receivable*   Account No. 111

Date		Item	Post Ref.	Debit	Credit	Balance Debit	Balance Credit
19XX							
Apr.	19		J2	1800 –		1800 –	
	24		J2	1500 –		3300 –	
	26		J2		900 –	2400 –	

Account: *Office Supplies*   Account No. 121

Date		Item	Post Ref.	Debit	Credit	Balance Debit	Balance Credit
19XX							
Apr.	4		J1	600 –		600 –	
	30	Adjusting	J3		210 –	390 –	

Account: *Prepaid Insurance*   Account No. 131

Date		Item	Post Ref.	Debit	Credit	Balance Debit	Balance Credit
19XX							
Apr.	1		J1	1200 –		1200 –	
	30	Adjusting	J3		50 –	1150 –	

(continued)

Ex. 6-3 (continued)

Account: *Furniture*						Account No. *141*
Date	Item	Post Ref.	Debit	Credit	Balance Debit	Balance Credit
19XX						
Apr. 3		J1	6400 –		6400 –	

Account: *Accumulated Depreciation, Furniture*						Account No. *142*
Date	Item	Post Ref.	Debit	Credit	Balance Debit	Balance Credit
19XX						
Apr. 30	Adjusting	J3		150 –		150 –

Account: *Accounts Payable*						Account No. *201*
Date	Item	Post Ref.	Debit	Credit	Balance Debit	Balance Credit
19XX						
Apr. 4		J1		600 –		600 –
11		J1		300 –		900 –
22		J2	400 –			500 –
30		J2	300 –			200 –

Account: *Wages Payable*						Account No. *211*
Date	Item	Post Ref.	Debit	Credit	Balance Debit	Balance Credit
19XX						
Apr. 30	Adjusting	J3		630 –		630 –

Account: *Kevin Young, Capital*						Account No. *301*
Date	Item	Post Ref.	Debit	Credit	Balance Debit	Balance Credit
19XX						
Apr. 1		J1		25000 –		25000 –
14		J2		1000 –		26000 –
30	Closing	J3		2260 –		28260 –
30	Closing	J3	200 –			28060 –

Account: *Kevin Young, Drawing*						Account No. *311*
Date	Item	Post Ref.	Debit	Credit	Balance Debit	Balance Credit
19XX						
Apr. 29		J2	200 –		200 –	
30	Closing	J3		200 –	–0–	

(continued)

Ex. 6-3 (continued)

Account: *Income Summary*							Account No. 321	
		Post				Balance		
Date	Item	Ref.	Debit	Credit		Debit	Credit	
19XX								
Apr. 30	*Closing*	*J3*		5200 —			5200 —	
30	*Closing*	*J3*	2940 —				2260 —	
30	*Closing*	*J3*	2260 —				—0—	

Account: *Legal Fees*							Account No. 401	
		Post				Balance		
Date	Item	Ref.	Debit	Credit		Debit	Credit	
19XX								
Apr. 2		*J1*		1900 —			1900 —	
19		*J2*		1800 —			3700 —	
24		*J2*		1500 —			5200 —	
30	*Closing*	*J3*	5200 —				—0—	

Account: *Wage Expense*							Account No. 501	
		Post				Balance		
Date	Item	Ref.	Debit	Credit		Debit	Credit	
19XX								
Apr. 17		*J2*	700 —			700 —		
30	*Adjusting*	*J3*	630 —			1330 —		
30	*Closing*	*J3*		1330 —		—0—		

Account: *Advertising Expense*							Account No. 511	
		Post				Balance		
Date	Item	Ref.	Debit	Credit		Debit	Credit	
19XX								
Apr. 11		*J1*	300 —			300 —		
30	*Closing*	*J3*		300 —		—0—		

Account: *Rent Expense*							Account No. 521	
		Post				Balance		
Date	Item	Ref.	Debit	Credit		Debit	Credit	
19XX								
Apr. 1		*J1*	800 —			800 —		
30	*Closing*	*J3*		800 —		—0—		

(continued)

Ex. 6-3 (concluded)

Account: Utilities Expense — Account No. 531

Date	Item	Post Ref.	Debit	Credit	Balance Debit	Balance Credit
19XX						
Apr. 7		J1	100 —		100 —	
30	Closing	J3		100 —	-0-	

Account: Office Supplies Expense — Account No. 541

Date	Item	Post Ref.	Debit	Credit	Balance Debit	Balance Credit
19XX						
Apr. 30	Adjusting	J3	210 —		210 —	
30	Closing	J3		210 —	-0-	

Account: Insurance Expense — Account No. 551

Date	Item	Post Ref.	Debit	Credit	Balance Debit	Balance Credit
19XX						
Apr. 30	Adjusting	J3	50 —		50 —	
30	Closing	J3		50 —	-0-	

Account: Depreciation Expense, Furniture — Account No. 561

Date	Item	Post Ref.	Debit	Credit	Balance Debit	Balance Credit
19XX						
Apr. 30	Adjusting	J3	150 —		150 —	
30	Closing	J3		150 —	-0-	

Preparing a Post-Closing Trial Balance

Objective 2

Prepare a post-closing trial balance.

An accountant may be very confident that all appropriate closing entries have been properly journalized and posted. However, if by chance an error is made, the accountant may not find it until the next accounting period is under way. Thus valuable time could be spent correcting error(s) that occurred in a previous accounting period. To ensure that the accounting records, in particular the general ledger, are ready for the start of the next accounting period a **post-closing trial balance** is prepared. The post-closing trial balance has the following purposes:

1. To assure that all nominal accounts are closed.
2. To assure that total debits equal total credits.
3. To assure that all account balances are normal.

The post-closing trial balance is very similar to the beginning trial balance. The general ledger accounts are listed in chart-of-accounts order. Any account that has a zero balance is not listed. The post-closing trial balance for Kevin Young, Attorney at Law, at the end of the accounting period, April 19XX is as follows:

Kevin Young, Attorney at Law
Post-Closing Trial Balance
April 30, 19XX

Accounts	Debit	Credit
Cash	18 7 0 0 —	
Accounts Receivable	2 4 0 0 —	
Office Supplies	3 9 0 —	
Prepaid Insurance	1 1 5 0 —	
Furniture	6 4 0 0 —	
Accumulated Depreciation, Furniture		1 5 0 —
Accounts Payable		2 0 0 —
Wages Payable		6 3 0 —
Kevin Young, Capital		28 0 6 0 —
Totals	29 0 4 0 —	29 0 4 0 —

Now that the post-closing trial balance is prepared, let's see if the three purposes are met. First we can see that no nominal accounts are listed. This indicates that all nominal accounts have zero balances. Next we see that total debits equal total credits. Then, looking at the accounts and account balances, we see that all account balances are normal; that is, Cash has a debit balance, Accounts Payable a credit balance, and so on. Therefore, the accounting records are properly set for the next accounting period. You should always thoroughly examine the accounting records to make sure that all journal entries, postings, descriptions, and so on are correct before you go on to the next accounting period.

Review of the Accounting Cycle

We have now completed the accounting cycle for a service-type firm. The steps to the accounting cycle are as follows:

1. Analyze transactions from source documents.
2. Record the transactions in a journal.
3. Post to the general ledger accounts.
4. Prepare a trial balance.
5. Adjust the general ledger accounts.
6. Complete the worksheet.
7. Prepare financial statements.
8. Journalize and post adjusting entries.
9. Journalize and post closing entries.
10. Prepare a post-closing trial balance.

Chapter Review

1. **Journalize and post closing entries.**
   Those accounts that measure performance and affect capital (revenues, expenses, and Drawing) must be closed or cleared at the end of one accounting period for the start of the next accounting period. There are four closing entries to clear the nominal accounts: revenues, expenses, Income Summary, and Drawing. The closing entries occur in this order: (a) close revenues to Income Summary; (b) close

expenses to Income Summary; (c) close Income Summary to Capital; and (d) close Drawing to Capital.

2. **Prepare a post-closing trial balance.**
   To ensure that the accounting records, in particular the general ledger, are ready for the start of the next accounting period, a post-closing trial balance is prepared. The post-closing trial balance has the following purposes: (a) to assure that all nominal accounts are closed; (b) to assure that total debits equal total credits; and (c) to assure that all account balances are normal.

Glossary

Closing Entry Entry made to clear the balance of a nominal account.

Income Summary Nominal account used during the closing process.

Nominal Account Account that is cleared at the end of an accounting period.

Permanent Account Another term for real account.

Post-Closing Trial Balance Trial balance prepared after closing entries have been journalized and posted.

Real Account Account that is not cleared at the end of an accounting period. The account balance remains open from one accounting period to the next.

Temporary Account Another term for nominal account.

Self-Test Questions for Review

(Answers are at the end of Chapter 6.)

1. Legal Fees is a _____ account and H. L. Jones, Drawing is a _____ account.
   a. nominal; real
   b. real; nominal
   c. real; real
   d. nominal; nominal

2. Closing expenses is the _____ closing entry and closing drawing is the _____ closing entry.
   a. first; second
   b. third; fourth
   c. second; fourth
   d. first; third

3. Which of the following accounts would probably have a credit balance after all closing entries are posted?
   a. Income Summary
   b. Mary Conners, Drawing
   c. Accounts Receivable
   d. Fred Moore, Capital

4. The account _____ could be listed in the debit column of a post-closing trial balance.
   a. Prepaid Insurance
   b. Accounts Payable
   c. Wages Payable
   d. J. Nguyen, Drawing

5. Preparing a post-closing trial balance is step _____ of the accounting cycle.
   a. 8
   b. 7
   c. 10
   d. 9

Practical Review Problem

Objectives 1 and 2

Journalizing Closing Entries and Preparing a Post-Closing Trial Balance

Lydia Flores owns and operates The Flores Repair Shop. She had the following accounts, chart-of-accounts numbers, and account balances as of March 31, 19XX. All account balances are normal. The firm had a net loss for the month.

ACCOUNT	ACCOUNT NUMBER	ACCOUNT BALANCE
Cash	103	9,620
Accounts Receivable	108	7,810
Store Supplies	131	1,630
Prepaid Insurance	141	2,900
Office Equipment	151	72,270
Accumulated Depreciation, Office Equipment	152	2,050
Accounts Payable	211	41,890
Wages Payable	221	3,600
Lydia Flores, Capital	301	54,620
Lydia Flores, Drawing	311	2,770
Income Summary	321	0
Service Fees	401	1,910
Consulting Fees	411	2,500
Wages Expense	501	3,600
Advertising Expense	511	1,490
Rent Expense	521	1,670
Utilities Expense	531	100
Store Supplies Expense	541	540
Insurance Expense	551	120
Depreciation Expense, Office Equipment	561	2,050

REQUIRED

1. Journalize the four closing entries in the general journal, page 6. DO NOT post to the general ledger.

2. Prepare a post-closing trial balance.

Answer to the Practical Review Problem

1.   **GENERAL JOURNAL**   Page 6

Date		Description	Post Ref.	Debit	Credit
		Closing Entries			
Mar.	31	Service Fees		1910 –	
		Consulting Fees		2500 –	
		Income Summary			4410 –
	31	Income Summary		9570 –	
		Wages Expense			3600 –
		Advertising Expense			1490 –
		Rent Expense			1670 –
		Utilities Expense			100 –
		Store Supplies Expense			540 –
		Insurance Expense			120 –
		Depreciation Expense, Office Equipment			2050 –
	31	Lydia Flores, Capital		5160 –	
		Income Summary			5160 –
	31	Lydia Flores, Capital		2770 –	
		Lydia Flores, Drawing			2770 –

2.

The Flores Repair Shop
Post-Closing Trial Balance
March 31, 19XX

Accounts	Debit	Credit
Cash	9 6 2 0 –	
Accounts Receivable	7 8 1 0 –	
Store Supplies	1 6 3 0 –	
Prepaid Insurance	2 9 0 0 –	
Office Equipment	72 2 7 0 –	
Accumulated Depreciation, Office Equipment		2 0 5 0 –
Accounts Payable		41 8 9 0 –
Wages Payable		3 6 0 0 –
Lydia Flores, Capital		*46 6 9 0 –
Totals	94 2 3 0 –	94 2 3 0 –

Discussion Questions

Q 6-1 What are the two purposes of closing entries?

Q 6-2 Define and describe nominal accounts. Name the financial statement(s) where you would find nominal accounts.

Q 6-3 Define and describe real accounts. Name the financial statement(s) where you would find real accounts.

Q 6-4 What is the purpose of the Income Summary account? How and when is it used?

Q 6-5 List the four closing entries in their proper sequence.

Q 6-6 Record the following activity for owner's Capital in a T account: May 1, initial investment by owner, $19,341; May 11, additional investment by owner, $3,987; May 31, net income for May 19XX, $7,099. Determine the balance.

Q 6-7 Record the following activity for Income Summary in a T account: June 1, beginning balance, $0; closing of revenues, $3,076; closing of expenses, $2,012. Determine the balance.

Q 6-8 Why must a post-closing trial balance be prepared?

Q 6-9 What are the three purposes of a post-closing trial balance?

Q 6-10 Name the ten steps in the accounting cycle. Which of the steps were covered in this chapter?

Exercises

Objective 1 **E 6-1** **Listing Accounts** List at least ten nominal accounts. List at least ten real accounts.

Objective 2 **E 6-2** **Listing Accounts** You are the accountant for the firm Greta Weiss, Attorney at Law. List at least nine accounts that could possibly appear on a post-closing trial balance.

Objective 1 **E 6-3** **Identifying Accounts** Indicate whether the following accounts are nominal or real:

---

*54,620 beginning balance – 5,160 net loss – 2,770 drawing = 46,690 ending Capital balance.

a. Cash	**b.** Ed Gold, Capital
c. Accounts Receivable	**d.** Prepaid Insurance
e. Rent Expense	**f.** Ed Gold, Drawing
g. Income Summary	**h.** Wages Expense
i. Furniture	**j.** Store Supplies
k. Legal Fees	**l.** Advertising Expense
m. Depreciation Expense, Truck	**n.** Accumulated Depreciation, Truck

Objective 1

E 6-4 Finding Revenues, Expenses, and Net Income A firm had the following T account after the second closing entry:

Income Summary	
12,800	13,900

From the T account find: (a) total revenues; (b) total expenses; and (c) net income.

Objective 1

E 6-5 Finding Net Income, Drawing, and Ending Capital Ruben Mata is the owner of a CPA firm. His capital account appears as follows after all closing entries have been journalized and posted:

GENERAL LEDGER ACCOUNTS							
Account: *Ruben Mata, Capital*						Account No. *301*	
		Post				Balance	
Date	Item	Ref.	Debit	Credit	Debit	Credit	
19XX	*Aug. 31 Balance*					*12 0 9 0 0* –	
Aug. *31*	*Closing*	*J13*		*6 4 0 0* –			
31	*Closing*	*J13*	*1 8 0 0* –				

From the capital account find: (a) net income, (b) drawing, and (c) the ending capital balance.

Objective 1

E 6-6 Determining Net Income and Journalizing Closing Entries After the first two closing entries have been journalized and posted, the Income Summary account of a dental firm (Randi Martin, owner) is as follows:

Income Summary	
35,890	38,120

From the T account: (a) determine net income, and (b) journalize the entry necessary to close the Income Summary account (October 31, 19XX).

Objective 1

E 6-7 Journalizing Closing Entries A firm has the following selected accounts and account balances (all account balances are normal) at March 31, 19XX:

Jay Puhlman, Drawing	$ 1,100		Rent Expense	$ 2,500
Income Summary	–0–		Utilities Expense	700
Medical Fees	10,500		Medical Supplies Expense	200
Wages Expense	3,600		Insurance Expense	300
Advertising Expense	1,300			

Journalize the four closing entries in the general journal, page 6.

Objective 2   **E 6-8**   **Preparing a Post-Closing Trial Balance**   Keystone Consulting Service has the following accounts and account balances at August 31, 19XX, after all closing entries are journalized and posted:

Cash	$ 27,190	Accounts Receivable	$ 13,460
Office Supplies	8,950	Prepaid Insurance	2,770
Computer	19,840	Accumulated Depreciation, Computer	4,850
Accounts Payable	10,620	Wages Payable	360
Enid Garrison, Capital	56,380		

Prepare a post-closing trial balance. (Note: All account balances are normal.)

Problems

Objective 1   **P 6-1**   **Journalizing Closing Entries**   Deng Recording Service is owned by Kim Deng. The firm had the following accounts and account balances as of September 30, 19XX. All account balances are normal.

ACCOUNT	ACCOUNT BALANCE
Cash	9,700
Accounts Receivable	3,200
Office Supplies	1,600
Prepaid Insurance	2,800
Truck	17,300
Accumulated Depreciation, Truck	600
Accounts Payable	4,100
Wages Payable	1,200
Kim Deng, Capital	22,300
Kim Deng, Drawing	2,200
Income Summary	0
Recording Fees	6,700
Consulting Fees	8,500
Wages Expense	4,400
Rent Expense	1,100
Office Supplies Expense	300
Insurance Expense	200
Depreciation Expense, Truck	600

REQUIRED
Journalize the four closing entries in the general journal, page 3.

Objective 1   **P 6-2**   **Posting Closing Entries**   You are hired as the accountant for Callahan Design Studio. You find the following closing entries:

GENERAL JOURNAL   Page ___5___

Date		Description	Post Ref.	Debit	Credit
		Closing Entries			
Dec.	31	Design Fees	401	13 4 0 0 –	
		Income Summary	321		13 4 0 0 –
	31	Income Summary	321	11 8 0 0 –	
		Wages Expense	501		6 2 0 0 –
		Advertising Expense	511		2 3 0 0 –
		Rent Expense	521		1 9 0 0 –
		Utilities Expense	531		2 0 0 –
		Design Supplies Expense	541		8 0 0 –
		Insurance Expense	551		1 0 0 –
		Depreciation Expense, Furniture	561		3 0 0 –
	31	Income Summary	321	1 6 0 0 –	
		Tom Callahan, Capital	301		1 6 0 0 –
	31	Tom Callahan, Capital	301	7 0 0 –	
		Tom Callahan, Drawing	311		7 0 0 –

The accountant you replaced recorded the closing entries in the general journal and included the proper general ledger account numbers in the Post. Ref. column of the general journal. However, he did not post to the general ledger.

REQUIRED
1. Using the general ledger account numbers in the Post. Ref. column, write the account names, account numbers, and previous balances (the owner's Capital account has a $26,800 credit balance before closing entries; Income Summary has a zero balance before closing entries; all other account balances from closing entries) in the general ledger. List Owner, Capital (301) first; followed by Owner, Drawing (311), and so on.
2. Post the closing entries to the general ledger. Include all posting references in the general ledger.

Objectives 1 and 2

P 6-3

Journalizing Closing Entries and Preparing a Post-Closing Trial Balance
Lemke Wrecker Service is owned by Nancy Lemke. She had the following accounts, chart-of-accounts numbers, and account balances as of January 31, 19XX. All account balances are normal. The firm had a net loss for the month.

ACCOUNT	ACCOUNT NUMBER	ACCOUNT BALANCE
Cash	101	36,140
Accounts Receivable	110	11,230
Wrecker Supplies	121	4,890
Prepaid Insurance	135	3,780
Wrecker	141	17,900
Accumulated Depreciation, Wrecker	142	300
Accounts Payable	201	5,900
Wages Payable	211	1,450
Nancy Lemke, Capital	301	70,310
Nancy Lemke, Drawing	311	2,650
Income Summary	321	0
Wrecker Fees	401	6,890
Storage Fees	411	5,820
Wages Expense	501	9,910
Rent Expense	511	2,990
Wrecker Supplies Expense	531	320
Insurance Expense	541	560
Depreciation Expense, Wrecker	561	300

REQUIRED

1. Journalize the four closing entries in the general journal, page 8. DO NOT post to the general ledger.

2. Prepare a post-closing trial balance (see Practical Review Problem).

Objectives 1 and 2

P 6-4

Comprehensive Chapter Review Problem   P. K. Lam owns Lam's Financial Services. P. K. had the following accounts, chart-of-accounts numbers, and account balances as of August 31, 19XX. All account balances are normal.

ACCOUNT	ACCOUNT NUMBER	ACCOUNT BALANCE
Cash	101	45,902
Accounts Receivable	110	27,912
Office Supplies	121	12,673
Prepaid Insurance	132	8,674
Automobile	151	15,892
Accumulated Depreciation, Automobile	152	356
Computer	161	11,878
Accumulated Depreciation, Computer	162	234
Accounts Payable	201	19,784
Wages Payable	211	4,891
P. K. Lam, Capital	301	108,218
P. K. Lam, Drawing	311	12,346
Income Summary	321	0
Financial Services	401	17,564
Consulting Fees	411	7,899
Wages Expense	501	12,655
Rent Expense	511	4,892
Advertising Expense	521	1,909
Utilities Expense	531	347
Office Supplies Expense	535	2,734
Insurance Expense	541	542
Depreciation Expense, Automobile	552	356
Depreciation Expense, Computer	553	234

REQUIRED
1. Journalize the four closing entries in the general journal, page 13.
2. Post the closing entries to the general ledger (include accounts, account numbers, and previous balances).
3. Prepare a post-closing trial balance.

Checklist of Key Figures

P 6-1 Net Income, $8,600
P 6-2 Owner, Capital, $27,700
P 6-3 (2) Owner, Capital, $66,290
P 6-4 (2) Owner, Capital, $97,666

Answers to Self-Test Questions

1. d   2. c   3. d   4. a   5. c

Accounting Cycle Review Problem

To test your knowledge of the accounting cycle, complete the following review problem. The working papers are in your Working Papers manual. The answer to this review problem will be provided by your instructor.

Paula Stone is the sole owner of Northwest Insurance Agency. She established the following chart of accounts:

Northwest Insurance Agency

Chart of Accounts

ASSETS (100–199)

101	Cash
111	Accounts Receivable
121	Office Supplies
131	Prepaid Insurance
141	Office Equipment
142	Accumulated Depreciation, Office Equipment
151	Office Furniture
152	Accumulated Depreciation, Office Furniture

LIABILITIES (200–299)

| 201 | Accounts Payable |
| 211 | Wages Payable |

OWNER'S EQUITY (300–399)

301	Paula Stone, Capital
311	Paula Stone, Drawing
321	Income Summary

REVENUES (400–499)

401	Automobile Insurance Fees
411	Life Insurance Fees
421	Health Insurance Fees

EXPENSES (500–599)

501	Wages Expense
511	Advertising Expense
521	Rent Expense
531	Utilities Expense
541	Office Supplies Expense
551	Insurance Expense
561	Depreciation Expense, Office Equipment
571	Depreciation Expense, Office Furniture

Northwest Insurance Agency had thirty transactions during April 19XX. These transactions are to be recorded in the general journal. The transactions are as follows (assume that cash is paid or received unless otherwise stated):

April 1   The owner, Paula Stone, started the firm by investing $54,075.

April 1   Paid the rent for the month, $2,866.

April 1   Paid for a three-year liability insurance policy, $7,272.

April 2   Billed and collected $3,459 in automobile insurance fees (cash revenue).

April 2   Purchased office equipment, $6,907, paying $2,000 cash with the remainder due within 30 days.

April 3   Purchased $984 of office supplies on account.

April 3   Hired a receptionist.

April 3   Received and paid a utilities bill, $103.

April 4   Billed a customer for health insurance fees, $1,378.

April 4   Received a bill for newspaper advertising, $672.

April 4   Purchased office furniture, $6,899, paying $1,595 cash with the remainder due within 30 days.

April 5   Owner invested an additional $4,000 in the firm.

April 5   Billed a customer for life insurance fees, $3,846.

April 7   Paid the receptionist for wages, $495.

April 10   Received a utilities bill, $238.

April 11   Paid $458 to apply to the April 3 purchase of office supplies.

April 12   Billed a customer $5,878 for life insurance fees.

April 12   Received $1,378 from a customer to apply to the April 4 billing.

April 13   Owner withdrew $975 for her personal use.

April 14   Paid the April 4 advertising bill.

April 14   Paid the receptionist for wages, $495.

April 17   Paid $1,054 to apply to the April 2 purchase of office equipment.

April 18   Paid $2,895 to apply to the April 4 purchase of office furniture.

April 20   Owner withdrew $1,023 for her personal use.

April 21   Paid the receptionist for wages, $495.

April 24   Received $2,038 from a customer to apply to the April 5 billing.

April 25   Received an advertising bill, $5,789.

April 26   Billed a customer $1,673 for automobile insurance fees.

April 28   Paid the receptionist for wages, $495.

April 28   Received and paid an advertising bill, $2,192.

April 30   Paid $3,045 to apply to the April 25 advertising bill.

REQUIRED

1. Journalize the transactions in a general journal, starting on page 1.

2. Post the transactions to the general ledger.

3. Prepare a trial balance, using the first two columns of the worksheet.

4. Adjustments are calculated as follows:

    a. Office Supplies Expense, $670.

    b. Insurance Expense, $202.

    c. Depreciation of Office Equipment, $150.

        d. Depreciation of Office Furniture, $140.

        e. Wages incurred but unrecorded at April 30, $297.

5. Complete the worksheet.

6. Prepare financial statements.

7. Journalize and post adjusting entries.

8. Journalize and post closing entries.

9. Prepare a post-closing trial balance.

Checklist of Key Figures

    (2)   Cash, 36,820

    (5)   Net Income, $935

CHAPTER

7

The Sales Journal and Accounts Receivable Subsidiary Ledger

LEARNING OBJECTIVES

After reading this chapter, discussing the questions, and working the exercises and problems, you will be able to do the following:

1. Understand and use the sales journal

2. Understand and use the accounts receivable subsidiary ledger

3. Account for sales returns and allowances

4. Record the sale of assets other than merchandise on account

Remember that there are three types of businesses: service, merchandising, and manufacturing. Service-type businesses offer services rather than goods to the public. Merchandising firms offer resalable goods or merchandise for sale to the public. Manufacturers purchase materials in raw form and use labor to produce or manufacture a salable product. We will continue our discussion by looking at merchandising firms.

Merchandising Firms

Let's look now at United Auto Supply for an example of a merchandising firm. United Auto Supply sells discount auto parts (which we call merchandise.) **Merchandise inventory** represents goods (in this case, auto parts) that a firm buys to resell to its customers *in the same form*. The accounting cycle of a merchandising firm is the same as the accounting cycle of a service firm. Let's begin with steps 1 and 2 of the accounting cycle—analyzing transactions and recording the transactions in a journal.

Sales and Sales Invoice

On October 4, 19XX, United Auto Supply sold nine automobile transmissions to one of its customers, Emma's Auto Repair, on account. The transmissions are considered merchandise inventory. United Auto Supply filled out a sales ticket as shown in Exhibit 7-1.

EXHIBIT 7-1   Sales Ticket

Customer Sales Ticket			**Invoice No.** _831_

Charge Sale __X__   **Cash Sale**_____

United Auto Supply
100 Main Street, Houston, Texas 77001

Account Nos.: *111/401*   **Sold by:** *Frank Rylski*
Sale Date: *10/4/XX*   **Terms:** *2/10, n30*
Invoice (billing) Date: *10/4/XX*

Sold to: *Emma's Auto Repair*
Address: *101 Pinemont Houston, TX 77006*
Ship to: *same*

Quantity	Merchandise	Amount (each)	Total Amount
9	*Transmissions*	*200*	*1,800*
Total			*1,800*

If United Auto Supply recorded the credit sale in a general journal, the sale would be journalized as follows:

GENERAL JOURNAL   Page ___19___

Date		Description	Post Ref.	Debit	Credit
19XX					
Oct.	*4*	*Accounts Receivable*		*1 8 0 0 —*	
		Sales			*1 8 0 0 —*
		Invoice Number 831, Emma's Auto Repair			

Accounts Receivable is debited for the credit sale, and the corresponding credit is to **Sales**. Sales is a revenue account used to record the sale of merchandise inventory. United Auto Supply does not use a general journal for the following reasons:

1. For each credit sale, the terms "Accounts Receivable" and "Sales" must be written.

2. For each credit sale, both Accounts Receivable and Sales must be posted to the general ledger.

Thus, to save time and effort, and to increase efficiency, the firm uses special journals.

Introduction to Special Journals

Objective 1
Understand and use the sales journal.

Many merchandising firms use special journals to record transactions. A **special journal** is a book of original entry that groups together similar transactions. The special journals that we will use are as follows:

TYPE OF SPECIAL JOURNAL	POSTING REFERENCE DESIGNATION	USED TO
Sales Journal	S	Record all sales of merchandise on account only.
Purchases Journal	P	Record all purchases of merchandise on account only.
Cash Receipts Journal	CR	Record cash received from any source.
Cash Payments Journal	CP	Record cash paid for any purpose.

Where "J" was used as the posting reference for the general journal, "S" is used as the posting reference for sales journal, "P" is used for the purchases journal, and so on. Any transaction that cannot be recorded in a special journal is recorded using a general journal. In this chapter we will examine the sales journal.

Purposes of the Sales Journal   A sales journal has the following purposes:

1. To record all credit sales of merchandise in one journal, thus saving space.

2. To save journalizing time by recording each sale amount only once on one line.

3. Customer names, invoice numbers, and terms can be identified easily.

4. Individual credit sales are added and posted as one total to the general ledger at the end of the accounting period. This total is posted as a debit to Accounts Receivable and a credit to Sales.

Structure of the Sales Journal

The sales journal is used to record the sale of merchandise on account (credit) only. The October 4, 19XX, credit sale to Emma's Auto Repair is recorded in a single-column sales journal as illustrated in Exhibit 7-2:

EXHIBIT 7-2 Single-Column Sales Journal

SALES JOURNAL   Page ____**10**____

Date		Customer	Invoice Number	Terms	Post Ref.	Amount A/R (Dr.) Sales (Cr.)
19XX						
Oct.	4	*Emma's Auto Repair*	831	2/10, n30		1 8 0 0 —

In the Amount column of the sales journal, "A/R" is an abbreviation for Accounts Receivable. (The Post. Ref. column will be used later.)

Credit Terms

Many firms offer a discount to encourage their customers to pay their bills (amounts owed) early. Referring to Exhibits 7-1 and 7-2, the term **2/10, n30** indicates that if the invoice or bill is paid within ten days there is a 2 percent discount. If not, the total amount is due within thirty days. The term **1/10, n20** says that the total amount is due within twenty days but a 1 percent discount will be given if paid within ten days. The term **n30** by itself means that no discount is offered and the total is due within thirty days. We will assume that United Auto Supply calculates the discount from the invoice date, which is counted as the first day. (Some firms start the discount period the day after the invoice date. In this book we will start with the invoice date.) Therefore the ten-day discount period for Emma's Auto Repair would start on October 4 and end on October 13 as follows:

Month of October

Days: Oct. 4   5   6   7   8   9   10   11   12   13

Counted: 1 + 1 + 1 + 1 + 1 + 1 + 1 + 1 + 1 + 1 = 10 days

Any payment received October 14 or later would not be subject to a discount.

Posting from the Sales Journal

The sales of merchandise on account for the month of October for United Auto Supply are recorded and posted in Exhibit 7-3.

EXHIBIT 7-3 Recording and Posting Credit Merchandise Sales

SALES JOURNAL   Page ___10___

Date		Customer	Invoice Number	Terms	Post Ref.	Amount A/R (Dr.) Sales (Cr.)	
19XX							
Oct.	*4*	*Emma's Auto Repair*	*831*	*2/10, n30*		*1 8 0 0 –*	
	6	*Montana Company*	*832*	*2/10, n30*		*2 8 0 0 –*	
	6	*Jane's Fine Cars*	*833*	*2/10, n30*		*3 1 0 0 –*	
	11	*Lucky's Auto Repair*	*834*	*2/10, n30*		*9 0 0 –*	
	15	*Atlanta Company*	*835*	*2/10, n30*		*2 2 0 0 –*	
	22	*Montana Company*	*836*	*2/10, n30*		*1 9 0 0 –*	
	25	*Zumwalt Company*	*837*	*2/10, n30*		*1 5 0 0 –*	
	28	*Lai Auto Repair*	*838*	*2/10, n30*		*7 0 0 –*	
	30	*Jane's Fine Cars*	*839*	*2/10, n30*		*2 1 0 0 –*	
	31	*Tamborello Motors*	*840*	*2/10, n30*		*2 4 0 0 –*	
					③	*19 4 0 0 –*	①
						(111) (401)	

GENERAL LEDGER ACCOUNTS								
Account: *Accounts Receivable*							Account No. *111*	
		Post					Balance	
Date	Item	Ref.	Debit		Credit		Debit	Credit
19XX					②			
Oct. 31		*S10*	*1 9 4 0 0 –*				*1 9 4 0 0 –*	

Account: *Sales*							Account No. *401*	
		Post					Balance ④	
Date	Item	Ref.	Debit		Credit		Debit	Credit
19XX								
Oct. 31		*S10*			*1 9 4 0 0 –*			*1 9 4 0 0 –*

There are four steps for posting from the sales journal to the general ledger. These steps are keyed ①, ②, ③, and ④ in Exhibit 7-3. The steps are as follows:

①   The Amount column in the sales journal is underlined after the final sale is entered. The sales are totaled and double-underlined.

②   The total is posted as a debit to Accounts Receivable in the general ledger. "S10" is written in the Post. Ref. column of the general ledger to indicate that the posting is from page 10 of the sales journal.

③ After posting the debit to Accounts Receivable, you would go back to the amount column in the sales journal and write "111" in parentheses below the total. This shows that a posting was made to the accounts receivable general ledger account.

④ Repeat steps 2 and 3 for the credit posting to sales.

Recording Sales Tax Payable Many merchandising firms collect sales taxes from their customers. Usually the *final user* pays the sales tax. By final user we mean the person or firm who will use the goods; these same goods or merchandise will not be sold to another person or firm. Once collected, the sales tax (or taxes) is later paid to the taxing authority, such as the state, county, city, and so on.

For example, on January 9, 19XX, a firm sells merchandise on account to Parr, Inc., for $200. The sales tax is 5 percent. This transaction may be illustrated using T accounts as follows:

Accounts Receivable		Sales		Sales Tax Payable	
+	−	−	+	−	+
210			200		10

The sales tax is calculated as follows:

$$\$200 \times 5 \text{ percent} = \$200 \times .05 = \$10$$

Parr, Inc. owes the firm the sale amount plus the sales tax ($200 + $10 = $210). The firm uses a three-column sales journal to record this transaction (see Exhibit 7-4).

The accountant debits Sales Tax Payable and credits Cash when the tax is paid to the taxing authority. For our purposes, we will assume that United Auto Supply is not required to collect sales tax from its customers.

The Accounts Receivable Subsidiary Ledger

Objective 2
Understand and use the accounts receivable subsidiary ledger.

An **accounts receivable subsidiary ledger** is used in conjunction with the sales journal to identify and accumulate amounts owed by individual customers (as shown in Exhibit 7-5). Most firms need to maintain individual customer information. Imagine asking a large department store how much you owed them today. If the store did not have an accounts receivable subsidiary ledger, you would have to wait while a store employee searched through all the sales journal entries until your name was found.

There is usually a separate page in this ledger for each customer. The customers' names in the accounts receivable subsidiary ledger are often arranged alphabetically, and

EXHIBIT 7-4 Three-Column Sales Journal

SALES JOURNAL Page 1

Date		Customer	Invoice Number	Terms	Post Ref.	Debit Accounts Receivable	Credits Sales Tax Payable	Sales
19XX								
Jan.	9	Parr, Inc	A342	n30		2 1 0 −	1 0 −	2 0 0 −

EXHIBIT 7-5 Customer's Card in Accounts Receivable Subsidiary Ledger

Customer: *Montana Company*

Date		Inv. No.	Item	Post Ref.	Debit	Credit	Balance
19XX							
Oct.	*6*	*832*		*S10*	*2 8 0 0* –		*2 8 0 0* –
	22	*836*		*S10*	*1 9 0 0* –		*4 7 0 0* –

most accountants use a loose-leaf binder so they can add new customers or remove ex-customers as needed. Exhibit 7-5 shows the accounts receivable subsidiary ledger card for the customer Montana Company.

The Control Account

The Accounts Receivable account in the general ledger is called a **control account** because the Accounts Receivable balance in the general ledger provides a check or "control" over the accounts receivable subsidiary ledger. The total of all the customer's balances, which are kept in the accounts receivable subsidiary ledger, must equal the Accounts Receivable account balance in the general ledger when all postings are up to date.

Posting to the Accounts Receivable Subsidiary Ledger

There are three steps to follow when posting from the sales journal to the accounts receivable subsidiary ledger, keyed ①, ②, and ③ in Exhibit 7-6. The posting process is shown for Atlanta Company. The credit sales for the other customers are posted in the same manner. The steps for posting are as follows:

① As sales of merchandise on account are entered in the sales journal, they are posted daily or as they occur to the accounts receivable subsidiary ledger. When a customer buys merchandise on account, the total sale amount, including any tax, is entered into the debit column of the accounts receivable subsidiary ledger. A credit is made whenever the customer pays on his or her account. The Balance column has either a debit or zero balance. (A credit balance would indicate that the customer has paid too much.)

② "S10" for sales journal (S), page 10, is entered in the Post. Ref. column of the customer's accounts receivable subsidiary ledger page after the amount owed has been posted from the sales journal.

③ Once the posting has been entered into the customer's accounts receivable subsidiary ledger page, a check mark (✓) is placed in the Post. Ref. column of the sales journal. This signifies that the credit sale amount, including any sales tax, has been posted to the accounts receivable subsidiary ledger for that customer.

In Exhibit 7-6, we see the postings to the general ledger and the accounts receivable subsidiary ledger. The accounts receivable subsidiary ledger is not posted to the general ledger. A subsidiary ledger (such as the accounts receivable subsidiary ledger) *supports* a book of original entry or journal, which in this case is the sales journal. By utilizing an accounts receivable subsidiary ledger, a firm is able to keep track of the

EXHIBIT 7-6 Posting to the Accounts Receivable Subsidiary Ledger

Date		Customer	Invoice Number	Terms	Post Ref.	Amount A/R (Dr.) Sales (Cr.)
19XX						
Oct.	4	Emma's Auto Repair	831	2/10, n30	✓	1 8 0 0 –
	6	Montana Company	832	2/10, n30	✓	2 8 0 0 –
	8	Jane's Fine Cars	833	2/10, n30	✓	3 1 0 0 –
	11	Lucky's Auto Repair	834	2/10, n30	✓	9 0 0 –
	15	Atlanta Company	835	2/10, n30	✓	③ 2 2 0 0 –
	22	Montana Company	836	2/10, n30	✓	1 9 0 0 –
	25	Zumwalt Company	837	2/10, n30	✓	1 5 0 0 –
	28	Lai Auto Repair	838	2/10, n30	✓	7 0 0 –
	30	Jane's Fine Cars	839	2/10, n30	✓	2 1 0 0 –
	31	Tamborello Motors	840	2/10, n30	✓	2 4 0 0 –
						19 4 0 0 –
						(111) (401)

GENERAL LEDGER ACCOUNTS

Account: *Accounts Receivable*　　Account No. 111

Date		Item	Post Ref.	Debit	Credit	Balance Debit	Credit
19XX							
Oct.	31		S10	1 9 4 0 0 –		1 9 4 0 0 –	

Account: *Sales*　　Account No. 401

Date		Item	Post Ref.	Debit	Credit	Balance Debit	Credit
19XX							
Oct.	31		S10		1 9 4 0 0 –		1 9 4 0 0 –

ACCOUNTS RECEIVABLE SUBSIDIARY LEDGER

Customer: *Atlanta Company*

Date		Inv. No.	Item	Post Ref.	Debit	Credit	Balance
19XX							
Oct.	15	835	②	S10	2 2 0 0 –		2 2 0 0 –

(continued)

Ex. 7-6 continued

Customer: *Emma's Auto Repair*

Date		Inv. No.	Item	Post Ref.	Debit	Credit	Balance
19XX							
Oct.	4	831		S10	1 8 0 0 –		1 8 0 0 –

Customer: *Jane's Fine Cars*

Date		Inv. No.	Item	Post Ref.	Debit	Credit	Balance
19XX							
Oct.	8	833		S10	3 1 0 0 –		3 1 0 0 –
	30	839		S10	2 1 0 0 –		5 2 0 0 –

Customer: *Lai Auto Repair*

Date		Inv. No.	Item	Post Ref.	Debit	Credit	Balance
19XX							
Oct.	28	838		S10	7 0 0 –		7 0 0 –

Customer: *Lucky's Auto Repair*

Date		Inv. No.	Item	Post Ref.	Debit	Credit	Balance
19XX							
Oct.	11	834		S10	9 0 0 –		9 0 0 –

(continued)

Ex. 7-6 continued

Customer: *Montana Company*

Date		Inv. No.	Item	Post Ref.	Debit	Credit	Balance
19XX							
Oct.	6	832		S10	2800 –		2800 –
	22	836		S10	1900 –		4700 –

Customer: *Tamborello Motors*

Date		Inv. No.	Item	Post Ref.	Debit	Credit	Balance
19XX							
Oct.	31	840		S10	2400 –		2400 –

Customer: *Zumwalt Company*

Date		Inv. No.	Item	Post Ref.	Debit	Credit	Balance
19XX							
Oct.	25	837		S10	1500 –		1500 –

account balances (amounts owed) of its customers. When a customer inquires about his or her balance, you can quickly reference that customer's page in the accounts receivable subsidiary ledger and supply the customer with the requested information.

The Schedule of Accounts Receivable

A **schedule of accounts receivable** is normally prepared directly from the accounts receivable subsidiary ledger at the end of the accounting period. As we see in Exhibit 7-7, each customer and the balance owed is listed on the schedule of accounts receivable. The control account, Accounts Receivable, in the general ledger is also shown. The total of the schedule of accounts receivable must equal the control account, Accounts Receivable, in the general ledger. If the two totals do not agree, then a mistake has been made and must be corrected.

EXHIBIT 7-7 Schedule of Accounts Receivable

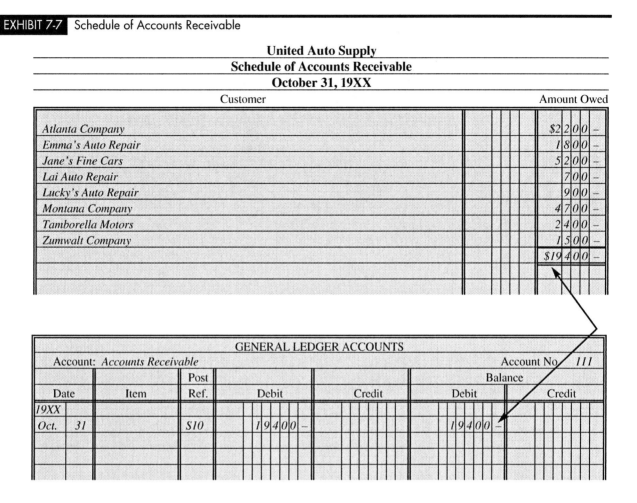

United Auto Supply
Schedule of Accounts Receivable
October 31, 19XX

Customer	Amount Owed
Atlanta Company	$2 2 0 0 –
Emma's Auto Repair	1 8 0 0 –
Jane's Fine Cars	5 2 0 0 –
Lai Auto Repair	7 0 0 –
Lucky's Auto Repair	9 0 0 –
Montana Company	4 7 0 0 –
Tamborella Motors	2 4 0 0 –
Zumwalt Company	1 5 0 0 –
	$19 4 0 0 –

GENERAL LEDGER ACCOUNTS

Account: *Accounts Receivable*   Account No. *111*

Date	Item	Post Ref.	Debit	Credit	Balance Debit	Balance Credit
19XX						
Oct. 31		*S10*	1 9 4 0 0 –		1 9 4 0 0 –	

Sales Returns and Allowances Account

Objective 3
Account for sales returns and allowances.

The **Sales Returns and Allowances** account is used to record two types of transactions that apply to previously sold merchandise. A **return** is the physical return of merchandise by the customer to the seller. An **allowance** is granted by the seller to the customer for inferior, defective, or damaged merchandise. A prenumbered **credit memorandum** is given to the customer by the seller whenever such returns and allowances occur (called a credit memorandum because the customer's account is credited for the return or allowance). A general journal is used to record the return or allowance of merchandise previously purchased on account. Remember that the sales journal is only used to record merchandise sold on account.

The Sales Returns and Allowances account is a contra revenues account; that is, it reduces sales and has a normal debit balance. Sales Returns and Allowances is included in the revenues' broad class of accounts, along with Sales, on the chart of accounts.

Assume that on October 27, 19XX, a customer of United Auto Supply—Montana Company—returns $78 of defective merchandise previously purchased on account. Credit memorandum number CM29 is issued to Montana Company as shown in Exhibit 7-8. (The sale transaction was originally recorded in the sales journal, as shown in Exhibit 7-3.)

EXHIBIT 7-8 | Prenumbered Credit Memorandum

Credit Memorandum   No. *CM 29*

Charge Return   X   Cash Return _____

United Auto Supply
100 Main Street, Houston, Texas 77001

Account Nos.: *111/402*   Sold by: *Frank Rylski*
Sale Date: *10/6/XX*   Terms: *2/10, n30*
Invoice (billing) Date: *10/6/XX*   Return Date: *10/27/XX*

Sold to: *Montana Company*
Address: *P.O. Box 87641 Houston, TX 77001*

Return Information

Quantity	Merchandise	Amount (each)	Total Amount
6	*Water Pump*	$13	$78

Total Amount to Be Credited $78

Journalizing and Posting Sales Returns and Allowances

To record a return of merchandise previously sold on credit, Sales Returns and Allowances is debited and Accounts Receivable is credited. In Exhibit 7-9 the return is journalized and posted to the general ledger and accounts receivable subsidiary ledger. The journalizing and posting steps are keyed ①, ②, and ③. These steps are as follows:

① The return or allowance of a previous credit sale of merchandise must be recorded in the general journal.

② The debit is posted to Sales Returns and Allowances in the general ledger. "J26" is entered in the Post. Ref. column of the general ledger and then "402" is entered in the Post. Ref. column of the general journal.

③ A $78 credit is posted to both the Accounts Receivable account in the general ledger and the customer's account in the accounts receivable subsidiary ledger. "J26" is entered in the Post. Ref. columns. Once the posting is complete, "111/✓" is entered in the Post. Ref. column of the general journal. The term "111" indicates a posting to Accounts Receivable in the general ledger. The "✓" indicates a posting to the customer's account in the accounts receivable subsidiary ledger. The slash "/" is used to keep the two references separate.

EXHIBIT 7-9 Recording and Posting Sales Returns and Allowances

① **GENERAL JOURNAL**   Page ___26___

Date		Description	Post Ref.	Debit	Credit
19XX					
Oct.	27	Sales Returns and Allowances	402	78 – ②	
		Accounts Receivable–Montana Company	111/✓ ③		78 –
		Return of Defective Merchandise, Credit Memorandum CM29			

GENERAL LEDGER ACCOUNTS

Account: *Accounts Receivable*   Account No. *111*

Date		Item	Post Ref.	Debit	Credit	Balance Debit	Balance Credit
Oct.	27	③	J26		78 –		

Account: *Sales Returns and Allowances*   Account No. *402*

Date		Item	Post Ref.	Debit	Credit	Balance Debit	Balance Credit
19XX							
Oct.	27		J26	78 – ②			

ACCOUNTS RECEIVABLE SUBSIDIARY LEDGER

Customer: *Montana Company*

Date		Inv. No.	Item	Post Ref.	Debit	Credit	Balance
19XX							
Oct.	6	832		S10	2800 –		2800 –
	22	836		S10	1900 –		4700 –
	27			J26		③ 78 –	4622 –

Recording Other Transactions

Objective 4
Record the sale of assets other than merchandise on account.

There are other transactions that cannot be recorded in a special journal. Any asset (other than merchandise inventory sold on account) must be recorded using a general journal. For example, let's assume that on October 20, 19XX, United Auto Supply sold $2,000 of office equipment (beginning balance $15,000), which is not merchandise inventory, to Paul Henley on account. The terms are 2/10, EOM, n30. We will also assume that this transaction is not taxable. The terms 2/10, EOM, n30 mean that a 2 percent discount will be given if paid within ten days after the end of the month. Otherwise the full amount is due within thirty days of the invoice date. This transaction would be recorded in the general journal as follows:

GENERAL JOURNAL   Page ___26___

Date		Description	Post Ref.	Debit	Credit
19XX					
Oct.	20	Accounts Receivable – Paul Henley	111/✓	2 0 0 0 –	
		Office Equipment	141		2 0 0 0 –
		Terms 2/10, EOM, n30			

For illustration purposes, let's also record this transaction using T accounts:

Accounts Receivable	Office Equipment
(10/20) 2,000	2,000 (10/20)

This general journal entry would be posted to the general ledger and accounts receivable subsidiary ledger as follows:

GENERAL LEDGER ACCOUNTS

Account: *Accounts Receivable*   Account No. *111*

Date		Item	Post Ref.	Debit	Credit	Balance Debit	Balance Credit
19XX							
Oct.	20		J26	2 0 0 0 –		2 0 0 0 –	
	27		J26		7 8 –	1 9 2 2 –	
	31		S10	1 9 4 0 0 –		2 1 3 2 2 –	

Account: *Office Equipment*   Account No. *141*

Date		Item	Post Ref.	Debit	Credit	Balance Debit	Balance Credit
19XX		Previous balance				1 5 0 0 0 –	
Oct.	20		J26		2 0 0 0 –	1 3 0 0 0 –	

(continued)

ACCOUNTS RECEIVABLE SUBSIDIARY LEDGER

Customer: *Paul Henley*

Date	Inv. No.	Item	Post Ref.	Debit	Credit	Balance
19XX						
Oct. 20			J26	2000 –		2000 –

Chapter Review

1. **Understand and use the sales journal.**
   Many merchandising firms use special journals to record transactions. A special journal is a book of original entry that groups similar transactions together. The sales journal is used to record the sale of merchandise on account (credit) only.

2. **Understand and use the accounts receivable subsidiary ledger.**
   An accounts receivable subsidiary ledger is used in conjunction with the sales journal to identify and accumulate amounts owed by individual customers. There is usually a separate page for each customer in this ledger. The customers' names are often arranged alphabetically.

3. **Account for sales returns and allowances.**
   The Sales Returns and Allowances account is used to record two types of transactions that apply to previously sold merchandise. A return is the physical return of merchandise by the customer to the seller. An allowance is granted by the seller to the customer for inferior, defective, or damaged merchandise. A general journal is used to record the return or allowance of merchandise previously purchased on account.

4. **Record the sale of assets other than merchandise on account.**
   When using special journals, any asset (other than merchandise inventory) sold on account must be recorded using a general journal.

Glossary

Accounts Receivable Subsidiary Ledger Used in conjunction with the sales journal to identify and accumulate amounts owed by individual customers. Supports a book of original entry.

Allowance Granted by the seller to the customer (buyer) for inferior, defective, or damaged merchandise.

Cash Payments Journal Special journal used to record cash paid for any purpose.

Cash Receipts Journal Special journal used to record cash received from any source.

Control Account Account that provides a check or control over a subsidiary ledger.

Credit Memorandum Prenumbered document issued to the customer by the seller whenever returns and allowances occur.

Merchandise (Merchandise Inventory) Goods that a firm buys to resell to its customers in identical form.

Purchases Journal Special journal used to record all purchases of merchandise on account only.

Return Physical return of merchandise by the customer to the seller.

Sales Revenue account that is used to record the sale of merchandise inventory.

Sales Journal Special journal used to record all sales of merchandise on account only.

Sales Returns and Allowances Contra revenues account used to record transactions that apply to previously sold merchandise.

Schedule of Accounts Receivable Listing of each customer and the balance the customer owes.

Special Journal Book of original entry that groups together similar transactions.

Self-Test Questions for Review

(Answers are at the end of Chapter 7.)

1. Sales is a _____ account used to record the sale of _____.
   a. revenue; services
   b. asset; services
   c. liability; merchandise inventory
   d. revenue; merchandise inventory

2. The discount period for "2/10, n30" is
   a. thirty days.
   b. exactly one month.
   c. ten days.
   d. two days.

3. The debit column in a three-column sales journal is posted to
   a. Sales Tax Payable.
   b. Accounts Receivable
   c. Sales.
   d. Cash.

4. Credit memorandum CM781 is listed in the description of a transaction in a general journal. The account debited in this transaction is
   a. Cash.
   b. Sales.
   c. Sales Returns and Allowances.
   d. Accounts Receivable.

5. Office Equipment (not merchandise inventory) is sold on account. The account credited is
   a. Office Equipment.
   b. Sales.
   c. Accounts Receivable.
   d. Sales Returns and Allowances.

Practical Review Problem

Objectives 1, 3, and 4

Recording Sales, Returns and Allowances Alice Copier Supply had the following credit transactions during the month of October 19XX:

October 3	Sold $1,500 of merchandise on credit to Tellez Company, invoice number T204. Terms are n30.
October 5	Sold to McCree Company $1,300 of office supplies, on credit; terms are 1/10, EOM, n30.
October 8	Tellez Company returned $200 of damaged merchandise previously purchased October 3. Credit memorandum CM17 is issued.
October 16	Sold $2,300 of merchandise on credit to Edwards Company, invoice number T205. Terms are n30.
October 27	Sold $1,900 of merchandise on account to Tellez Company, invoice number T206. Terms are 1/10, n30.
October 31	Edwards Company returned $400 of inferior merchandise previously purchased October 16. Credit memorandum CM18 is issued.

REQUIRED
1. Record the sale of merchandise in a sales journal, page 1.
2. Record the return of merchandise and the sale of assets other than merchandise in a general journal, page 22.

Answer to Practical Review Problem

1. **SALES JOURNAL** Page ___1___

Date		Customer	Invoice Number	Terms	Post Ref.	Amount A/R (Dr.) Sales (Cr.)
19XX						
Oct.	3	Tellez Company	T204	n30		1500 –
	16	Edward's Company	T205	n30		2300 –
	27	Tellez Company	T206	1/10, n30		1900 –
						5700 –

2. **GENERAL JOURNAL** Page ___22___

Date		Description	Post Ref.	Debit	Credit
19XX					
Oct.	5	Accounts Receivable – McCree Company		1300 –	
		Office Supplies			1300 –
		Terms 1/10, EOM, n30			
	8	Sales Returns and Allowances		200 –	
		Accounts Receivable – Tellez Company			200 –
		Return of Damaged Merchandise, Credit Memorandum CM17			
	31	Sales Returns and Allowances		400 –	
		Accounts Receivable – Edwards Company			400 –
		Return of Inferior Merchandise, Credit Memorandum CM18			

Discussion Questions

Q 7-1 Briefly explain the difference between a service-type firm and a merchandising-type firm.

Q 7-2 Briefly describe the following credit terms: (a) n30; (b) 2/10, n30; (c) 1/10, n20; and (d) 2/10, EOM, n30.

Q 7-3 Name the two reasons why a merchandising firm would not use a general journal if a special journal could be used.

Q 7-4 Name the four special journals. State the Posting Reference symbol for each. Also, briefly describe what each special journal is used for.

Q 7-5 Name the four purposes of a sales journal.

Q 7-6 Name the four steps for posting from the sales journal to the general ledger.

Q 7-7 What is the accounts receivable subsidiary ledger used for? Name the three steps to follow when posting to the accounts receivable subsidiary ledger.

Q 7-8 Briefly describe the Sales Returns and Allowances account. What is a return? An allowance? A credit memorandum?

Q 7-9 Name the three steps in journalizing and posting the return of merchandise previously sold on account.

Q 7-10 Which journal and ledgers would the following transaction be recorded in: sold equipment, which is not merchandise inventory, on account, for $165 to Quinn Company? Also, give the appropriate accounts that would be debited and credited.

Exercises

Objective 1

E 7-1 Recording Sales Record this transaction in (a) a general journal, page 7; and then (b) a sales journal, page 7:

June 9   Sold $1,200 of merchandise on account to Robin Haws, terms 2/10, n30. Invoice number 765. The year is 19XX.

Objective 2

E 7-2 Completing Customer's Card Complete a customer's card in the accounts receivable subsidiary ledger given the following information for 19XX:

May 14   Sold to Hawthorne Service, $400 of merchandise on account, invoice number 098. The entry was made in page 5 of the sales journal.

May 20   Sold to Hawthorne Service, $300 of merchandise on account, invoice number 103 (page 5 of the sales journal).

Objective 3

E 7-3 Recording Sales Returns and Allowances Record this transaction in a general journal, page 13: On August 19, 19XX, Logan Company returned $800 of inferior merchandise previously sold on account. Credit memorandum CM15 is issued.

Objective 4

E 7-4 Recording Other Transactions On April 19, 19XX, Smith Grocery Supply sold $2,800 of office equipment (not merchandise inventory) to Pham Company on account. Record this transaction using T accounts.

Objectives 1, 3, and 4

E 7-5 Describing Transactions Describe the three transactions recorded in the following T accounts:

Accounts Receivable		Machinery	
(a) 1,280	(b) 860	(c) 2,540	
(c) 2,540			

Sales		Sales Returns and Allowances	
	(a) 1,280	(b) 860	

Objective 1

E 7-6 Recording Sales Record this transaction (a) using T accounts and then (b) using a three-column sales journal, page 2: On April 12, 19XX, a firm sold $500 of merchandise on account to Jay Brown, terms n30. The invoice number is C390. The sales tax is 6 percent.

Objective 2

E 7-7 Completing a Schedule of Accounts Receivable Complete the following schedule of accounts receivable for Oklahoma Gasket Supply (June 30, 19XX):

(a)	
(b)	
(c)	

(d)	(e)
Benson Company	3,000
Gantley Repair	4,000
Petrovich Enterprises	2,000
Smallwood Manufacturing	6,000
	$ (f)

Objective 4

E 7-8 Recording and Posting Other Transactions On December 19, 19XX, a firm sold a $5,000 computer (not merchandise inventory) to Alvin Computer Service, terms 2/10, EOM, n30. The balance in the computer account (151) was $10,000 before this transaction. In your answer, open the previous balance in the computer account. Also, record this transaction in a general journal, page 8, and post to the accounts receivable subsidiary ledger and the general ledger. Accounts Receivable is account number 111.

Problems

Objectives 1 and 2

P 7-1 Recording and Posting Sales Jones Plumbing Supply is owned by Lisa Jones. The firm had the following credit sales of merchandise during the first half of October 19XX:

DATE	AMOUNT	TERMS	INVOICE NUMBER	CUSTOMER
October 1	$300	2/10, n30	M452	Alvaro Rojas
October 5	$600	2/10, n30	M453	Terri Gray
October 8	$800	2/10, n30	M454	Alvaro Rojas
October 12	$100	2/10, n30	M455	John Satori
October 13	$500	2/10, n30	M456	Terri Gray
October 15	$900	2/10, n30	M457	John Satori

REQUIRED
1. Record the sale of merchandise in a sales journal, page 8.
2. Post to the accounts receivable subsidiary ledger. List the customers alphabetically.

Objectives 1 and 2

P 7-2 Posting Sales Transactions You are hired as the accountant for Green Office Supply. You find the following sales journal (top of next page).

The accountant you replaced recorded the sales transactions in the sales journal and included the proper posting references. However, she did not post to the accounts receivable subsidiary ledger and the general ledger.

REQUIRED
1. Using the general ledger account numbers below the Amount column, write the account names and account numbers in the general ledger. List Accounts Receivable first, followed by Sales.
2. Post to the accounts receivable subsidiary ledger. List the customers alphabetically.
3. Post to the general ledger.
4. Prepare a schedule of accounts receivable.

SALES JOURNAL Page ___11___

Date		Customer	Invoice Number	Terms	Post Ref.	Amount A/R (Dr.) Sales (Cr.)
19XX						
Aug.	2	Bronson Company	V071	1/10, n30	✓	900 –
	6	Mathisen Company	V072	1/10, n30	✓	500 –
	9	Ellison Company	V073	1/10, n30	✓	400 –
	12	Bronson Company	V074	1/10, n30	✓	1900 –
	16	Ellison Company	V075	1/10, n30	✓	1200 –
	18	Mathisen Company	V076	1/10, n30	✓	200 –
	24	Ellison Company	V077	1/10, n30	✓	700 –
	31	Bronson Company	V078	1/10, n30	✓	1700 –
						7500 –
						(110) (411)

Objectives 1, 3, and 4

P 7-3

Recording Sales Returns and Allowances Huan Paper Supply had the following credit transactions during the month of March 19XX:

March 1   Sold $1,800 of merchandise on account to Elroy Company, invoice number S563. Terms are n30.

March 4   Sold $3,700 of merchandise on credit to Kossman Company, invoice number S564. Terms are n30.

March 6   Sold to Steen Company $4,000 of machinery, on account. Terms are n30.

March 8   Elroy Company returned $1,000 of inferior merchandise previously purchased March 1. Credit memorandum CM13 is issued.

March 11   Sold $5,400 of merchandise on account to Pruski Company, invoice number S565. Terms are n30.

March 17   Sold $6,900 of merchandise on account to Kossman Company, invoice number S566. Terms are n30.

March 20   Sold $7,100 of merchandise on credit to Lerma Company, invoice number S567. Terms are n30.

March 24   Pruski Company returned $1,500 of damaged merchandise previously purchased March 11. Credit memorandum CM14 is issued.

March 27   Sold $2,800 of merchandise on account to Elroy Company, invoice number S568. Terms are n30.

March 29   Sold to Philip Company $9,700 of equipment on account. Terms are n30.

March 31   Sold $5,000 of merchandise to Evans, Inc. Terms are n30. Invoice number is S569.

REQUIRED

1. Record the sale of merchandise in a sales journal, page 10.

2. Record the return of merchandise and the sale of assets other than merchandise in a general journal, page 19.

**Objectives 1
through 4**

P 7-4

Comprehensive Chapter Review Problem Lomas Medical Supply had the following credit transactions during the month of August 19XX:

August 1   Sold $3,700 of merchandise on credit to Slatten Company, invoice number P786. Terms are 1/10, n30.

August 3   Sold $8,400 of merchandise on account to Waller Company, invoice number P787. Terms are 1/10, n30.

August 6   Sold to Johns Company $3,800 of merchandise on credit. Terms are 1/10, n30. The invoice number is P788.

August 8   Sold to Diman Company $8,900 of furniture, account number 151, on credit. Terms are n30. Furniture had a $23,700 balance before this sale.

August 10 Slatten Company returned $2,900 of damaged merchandise previously purchased August 1. Credit memorandum CM96 is issued.

August 13 Sold $1,800 of merchandise on credit to Bonner Company, invoice number P789. Terms are 1/10, n30.

August 16 Sold $5,800 of merchandise on account to Johns Company, invoice number P790. Terms are 1/10, n30.

August 19 Sold $2,700 of merchandise on credit to Slatten Company, invoice number P791. Terms are 1/10, n30.

August 21 Sold to Franklin Company $2,700 of equipment, account number 161, on account. Terms are n30. Equipment had a $4,700 balance before this sale.

August 24 Bonner Company returned $600 of inferior merchandise previously purchased August 13. Credit memorandum CM97 is issued.

August 25 Sold $4,800 of merchandise on account to Waller Company, invoice number P792. Terms are 1/10, n30.

August 27 Sold to Rogers Company a $10,600 automobile, account number 171, on account. Terms are n30. The automobile had a $10,600 balance before this sale.

August 28 Sold $3,600 of merchandise to Abbot, Inc. Terms are 1/10, n30. Invoice number is P793.

August 30 Waller Company was allowed a $1,100 credit for defective merchandise previously purchased August 3. Credit memorandum CM98 is issued.

August 31 Sold $9,700 of merchandise on credit to Xeno Company. Terms are 1/10, n30. The invoice number is P794.

REQUIRED
1. Open the previous balances in the Furniture, Equipment, and Automobile accounts. Record the sale of merchandise in a sales journal, page 12.
2. Record the return of merchandise and the sale of assets, other than merchandise, in a general journal, page 18. Sales Returns and Allowances is account number 432.
3. Post to the accounts receivable subsidiary ledger. List the customers alphabetically.
4. Post to the general ledger. Accounts Receivable is account number 109, and Sales is 431.
5. Prepare a schedule of accounts receivable.

Checklist of Key Figures

P 7-1 No key figure

P 7-2 (3) Accounts Receivable, $7,500

P 7-3 (1) Total Sales, $32,700
P 7-4 (4) Accounts Receivable, $61,900

Answers to Self-Test Questions

1. d   **2.** c   **3.** b   **4.** c   **5.** a

CHAPTER 8

The Purchases Journal and Accounts Payable Subsidiary Ledger

LEARNING OBJECTIVES

After reading this chapter, discussing the questions, and working the exercises and problems, you will be able to do the following:

1. Understand and use the purchases journal

2. Understand and use the accounts payable subsidiary ledger

3. Account for purchases returns and allowances

4. Record the purchase of assets other than merchandise on account

In this chapter we will look at the purchases of merchandise on account. Let's begin with a discussion of internal control.

Internal Control

Internal control is the system of policies and procedures adopted by a firm to safeguard assets and promote operational efficiency. In this chapter we are concerned with the internal control over purchases.

Internal Control and Purchases

Most firms will use the following procedures when making purchases:

1. **Purchase Requisition:** a request by a department to purchase certain goods. For example, a department of United Auto Supply has requested the purchase of twenty-five water pumps, which are merchandise inventory. The manager, or another official of the department, approves the purchase requisition and forwards it to the purchasing department. An approved purchase requisition is shown in Exhibit 8-1.

2. **Purchase Order:** a written order for merchandise or other items. Once the purchase has been approved, the firm issues a purchase order to Boyle Manufacturing, requesting that the seller (Boyle Manufacturing) sell the merchandise or other items specified to the buyer (United Auto Supply). The approved purchase order (see Exhibit 8-2) is sent to Boyle Manufacturing, requesting that they sell United Auto Supply twenty-five water pumps at $20 each.

3. **Purchase Invoice:** If Boyle Manufacturing accepts the terms of the purchase order, they will sell the merchandise as specified and issue the buyer (United Auto Supply) a purchase invoice, as shown in Exhibit 8-3. The buyer then compares the purchase invoice to the purchase order to see if the order was properly filled. The buyer also makes sure that the merchandise (or other items received) is correct as ordered and in good working order. This purchase invoice is kept in an unpaid-invoice file until it is paid.

Recording the Purchase in a General Journal

If United Auto Supply recorded the credit sale in a general journal, the purchase would be journalized as shown below.

Purchases is debited for the purchase of merchandise. The corresponding credit is to Accounts Payable. Purchases is part of the cost of goods sold broad classification of accounts used to record the purchase of merchandise inventory. **Cost of goods sold** represents the cost of merchandise inventory sold during an accounting period. However, United Auto Supply would not use a general journal for these reasons.

GENERAL JOURNAL   Page ____1____

Date		Description	Post Ref.	Debit	Credit
19XX					
Oct.	*1*	*Purchases*		5 0 0 –	
		Accounts Payable – Boyle Manufacturing			5 0 0 –
		Invoice Number B6661, Terms 2/10, n30			

EXHIBIT 8-1 Purchase Requisition

Purchase Requisition		**No.**	_W1278_

United Auto Supply
100 Main Street
Houston, Texas 77001

Date Issued: _10/1/XX_   **Order From:** _Boyle Manufacturing_
Date Requested: _10/2/XX_   _P.O. Box 11001_
                                                      New York, NY 10001

Quantity	Description	Amount(each)	Total
25	_Water Pump_	$20	$500

Ordered by: _Frank Rylski_   **Date:** _10/1/XX_

Approved by: _Hu Le_

Purchase Order Number Issued: _1037_

EXHIBIT 8-2 Purchase Order

Purchase Order		**No.**	_W1037_

From: _United Auto Supply_
          100 Main Street
          Houston, Texas 77001

To: _Boyle Manufacturing_
        P.O. Box 11001
        New York, NY 10001

Purchase Requisition Date: _10/1/XX_   **Ship To:** _above address_
Purchase Order Date: _10/1/XX_
Terms: _2/10, n30_
Ship By: _Rogers Freight_

Quantity	Description	Amount (each)	Total
25	_Water Pump_	$20	$500

Anita Torres
Purchasing Department Manager

EXHIBIT 8-3	Purchase Invoice

Invoice No. **_B6661_**

Boyle Manufacturing
P.O. Box 11001
New York, NY 10001

Sold To: *United Auto Supply*
100 Main Street
Houston, Texas 77001

Order Received: *10/2/XX*   **Ship To:** *above address*
Order Sent: *10/2/XX*
Terms: *2/10, n30*
Purchase Order No.: *1037*
Shipped By: *Rogers Freight*

Quantity	Description	Amount (each)	Total
25	*Water Pump*	$20	$500
Tax			0
Total			$500

---

1. For each credit purchase, the words Purchases and Accounts Payable must be written.

2. For each credit purchase, both Purchases and Accounts Payable must be posted to the general ledger.

To save time and effort, and to increase efficiency, the firm would use special journals.

The Purchases Journal

Objective 1
Understand and use the purchases journal.

The single-column purchases journal in Exhibit 8-4 is used for credit purchases of merchandise only. The credit purchase from Boyle Manufacturing is recorded.

The single-column purchases journal includes a column for the Date, Vendor, Invoice Number, Terms, Post. Ref., and Amount. (The Post. Ref. column will be used later.) "A/P" is an abbreviation for accounts payable. In this chapter we will distinguish the buyer from the seller by using the term **"vendor,"** indicating who the firm "purchased from."

A single-column purchases journal is normally used because sales tax charged and paid is considered a cost of acquiring an asset, in this case, merchandise inventory. The final user or consumer normally pays the sales tax. United Auto Supply is buying the merchandise to sell to the final user, therefore no tax is charged. Any acquisition that is not merchandise inventory, such as office supplies, telephone service, and so on, may have a charge for sales tax. Most firms include this sales tax in the cost of the asset or expense. A few firms may actually establish a Sales Tax Expense account. But, in order to simplify this procedure, we will assume that any sales tax is included in the cost.

EXHIBIT 8-4 Single-Column Purchases Journal

PURCHASES JOURNAL   Page ___10___

Date		Vendor	Invoice Number	Terms	Post Ref.	Amount Purch. (Dr.) A/P (Cr.)
19XX						
Oct.	*1*	*Boyle Manufacturing*	*B6661*	*2/10, n30*		5 0 0 –

Purposes of the Purchases Journal

The purchases journal has the following purposes:

1. To record all credit purchases of merchandise in one journal, thus saving space.
2. To save journalizing time by recording each purchase amount only once on one line.
3. Vendor names, invoice numbers, and terms can be identified easily.
4. The individual credit purchases are added and posted as one total to the general ledger at the end of the accounting period. This total is posted as a debit to Purchases and a credit to Accounts Payable.

Posting from the Purchases Journal

Two of the purposes of the purchases journal are to save space and time. We can see this illustrated in Exhibit 8-5 where the purchases of merchandise on account for October for United Auto Supply are recorded and posted.

There are four steps for posting from the purchases journal to the general ledger, keyed as ①, ②, ③, and ④ in Exhibit 8-5. The steps are as follows:

① The Amount column in the purchases journal is underlined after the final purchase is entered. The purchases are totaled and double-underlined.

② The total is posted as a debit to Purchases in the general ledger. "P10" is written in the Post. Ref. column of the general ledger to indicate that the posting is from page 10 of the purchases journal.

③ After posting the debit to Purchases, you would go back to the Amount column in the purchases journal and write "501" in parentheses below the total.

④ Steps 2 and 3 are repeated for the credit posting to Accounts Payable.

The Accounts Payable Subsidiary Ledger

Objective 2
Understand and use the accounts payable subsidiary ledger.

An **accounts payable subsidiary ledger** (as shown in Exhibit 8-6) is used in conjunction with the purchases journal to identify and accumulate amounts owed to individual vendors. There is usually a separate page in this ledger for each vendor. The vendors' names in the accounts payable subsidiary ledger are often arranged alphabetically, and most accountants use a loose-leaf binder so they can add or remove vendors as needed. Exhibit 8-6 shows the accounts payable subsidiary ledger page for Boyle Manufacturing.

EXHIBIT 8-5 | Recording and Posting Credit Merchandise Purchases

PURCHASES JOURNAL
Page ___10___

Date		Vendor	Invoice Number	Terms	Post Ref.	Amount Purch.(Dr.) A/P (Cr.)
19XX						
Oct..	1	Boyle Manufacturing	B6661	2/10, n30		500 –
	5	Hakala Enterprises	X095	n30		2100 –
	10	Zamora Warehouse	21087	1/25, n60		1700 –
	14	Boyle Manufacturing	B7348	2/10, n30		1800 –
	19	Anderson Inc.	IA566	n30		400 –
	23	Nguyen Distributors	00982	3/10, n30		1500 –
	28	Mehta Manufacturing	786M	4/10, n30		1900 –
	31	Anderson Inc.	IA612	n30		900 –
					③ ①	10800 –
						(501) (201)

GENERAL LEDGER ACCOUNTS ④

Account: *Accounts Payable*   Account No. 201

Date		Item	Post Ref.	Debit	Credit	Balance Debit	Credit
19XX							
Oct.	31		P10		10800 –		10800 –

③

Account: *Purchases*   Account No. 501

Date		Item	Post Ref.	Debit	Credit	Balance Debit	Credit
19XX							
Oct.	31	②	P10	10800 –		10800 –	

The Control Account

In this chapter the Accounts Payable account in the general ledger is called a control account. The Accounts Payable balance in the general ledger provides a check or control over the accounts payable subsidiary ledger. The total of all the vendor's balances kept in the accounts payable subsidiary ledger must equal the Accounts Payable account balance in the general ledger when all postings are up to date.

EXHIBIT 8-6 Vendor's Page in Accounts Payable Subsidiary Ledger

ACCOUNTS PAYABLE SUBSIDIARY LEDGER

Vendor: *Boyle Manufacturing*

Date		Item	Post Ref.	Debit	Credit	Balance
19XX						
Oct.	1		P10		500 –	500 –
	14		P10		1 800 –	2 300 –

Posting to the Accounts Payable Subsidiary Ledger

There are three steps to follow when posting from the purchases journal to the accounts payable subsidiary ledger, keyed as ①, ②, and ③ in Exhibit 8-7. The posting process is shown for Anderson, Inc. The credit purchases for the other vendors are posted in the same manner. The steps are as follows:

① As purchases of merchandise on account are entered in the purchases journal, they are posted daily or as they occur to the accounts payable subsidiary ledger. When a firm buys merchandise on account, the total purchase amount, including any tax, is entered into the Credit column of the accounts payable subsidiary ledger. A debit is made whenever the firm pays on the account. The Balance column has either a credit or zero balance. (A debit balance would indicate that the firm has paid too much.)

② "P10" for purchases journal (P) page 10 is entered in the Post. Ref. column of the vendor's accounts payable subsidiary ledger page after the amount owed has been posted from the purchases journal.

③ Once the posting has been entered into the vendor's accounts payable subsidiary ledger page, a check mark (✓) is placed in the Post. Ref. column of the purchases journal. This signifies that the credit purchase amount, including any tax, has been posted to the accounts payable subsidiary ledger for that vendor.

Exhibit 8-7 shows the postings to the accounts payable subsidiary ledger. The accounts payable subsidiary ledger is not, however, posted to the general ledger. A subsidiary ledger (such as the accounts payable subsidiary ledger) supports a book of original entry or journal, which in this case is the purchases journal. By utilizing an accounts payable subsidiary ledger, a firm is able to keep track of the account balances (amounts owed) to its vendors. When a vendor inquires about the balance owed, you can quickly reference that vendor's page in the accounts payable subsidiary ledger and supply the requested information.

Freight In

The merchandise purchased from Boyle Manufacturing is to be delivered by Rogers Freight, terms n30. We will assume that the goods are shipped **FOB shipping point**, which means that the buyer pays the transportation cost from the selling point to the place of delivery. The seller does not pay the transportation cost. FOB is an abbreviation for *free-on-board*. When the buyer pays the transportation cost, an account called **Freight In** is debited. Freight In is a cost of goods sold account that is used to record the transportation cost of merchandise paid for by the buyer.

EXHIBIT 8-7 | Posting to the Accounts Payable Subsidiary Ledger

PURCHASES JOURNAL

Page ___10___

Date		Vendor	Invoice Number	Terms	Post Ref.	Amount Purch. (Dr.) A/P (Cr.)
19XX						
Oct.	1	Boyle Manufacturing	B6661	2/10, n30	✓	500 –
	5	Hakala Enterprises	X095	n30	✓	2100 –
	10	Zamora Warehouse	21087	1/25, n60	✓	1700 –
	14	Boyle Manufacturing	B7348	2/10, n30	✓	1800 –
	19	Anderson, Inc.	LA566	n30	✓	③ 400 –
	23	Nguyen Distributors	00982	3/10, n30	✓	1500 –
	28	Mehta Manufacturing	786M	4/10, n30	✓	1900 –
	31	Anderson, Inc.	IA612	n30	✓	900 –
						10800 –
						(501) (201)

ACCOUNTS PAYABLE SUBSIDIARY LEDGER

Vendor: *Anderson, Inc.*

Date		Item	Post Ref.	Debit	Credit	Balance
19XX						
Oct.	19	②	P10		① 400 –	400 –
	31		P10		900 –	1300 –

Vendor: *Boyle Manufacturing*

Date		Item	Post Ref.	Debit	Credit	Balance
19XX						
Oct.	1		P10		500 –	500 –
	14		P10		1800 –	2300 –

Vendor: *Hakala Enterprises*

Date		Item	Post Ref.	Debit	Credit	Balance
19XX						
Oct.	5		P10		2100 –	2100 –

(continued)

Ex. 8-7 (concluded)

Vendor: *Mehta Manufacturing*

Date		Item	Post Ref.	Debit	Credit	Balance
19XX						
Oct.	*28*		*P10*		*1 9 0 0 –*	*1 9 0 0 –*

Vendor: *Nguyen Distributors*

Date		Item	Post Ref.	Debit	Credit	Balance
19XX						
Oct.	*23*		*P10*		*1 5 0 0 –*	*1 5 0 0 –*

Vendor: *Zamora Warehouse*

Date		Item	Post Ref.	Debit	Credit	Balance
19XX						
Oct.	*10*		*P10*		*1 7 0 0 –*	*1 7 0 0 –*

United Auto Supply's general journal entry to record the transportation charge on the October 1, 19XX, shipment from Boyle Manufacturing is as follows:

GENERAL JOURNAL   Page ____**26**____

Date		Description	Post Ref.	Debit	Credit
19XX					
Oct.	*1*	*Freight In*	*516*	*3 0 0 –*	
		Accounts Payable – Rogers Freight	*201/✓*		*3 0 0 –*
		Terms n30			

This general journal entry is then posted to the general ledger and accounts payable subsidiary ledger as follows:

GENERAL LEDGER ACCOUNTS

Account: *Accounts Payable*   Account No.   201

Date		Item	Post Ref.	Debit	Credit	Balance Debit	Balance Credit
19XX							
Oct.	1	*	J26		3 0 0 –		3 0 0 –
	31		P10		1 0 8 0 0 –		1 1 1 0 0 –

Account: *Freight In*   Account No.   516

Date		Item	Post Ref.	Debit	Credit	Balance Debit	Balance Credit
19XX							
Oct.	1		J26	3 0 0 –		3 0 0 –	

ACCOUNTS PAYABLE SUBSIDIARY LEDGER

Vendor: *Rogers Freight*

Date		Item	Post Ref.	Debit	Credit	Balance
19XX						
Oct.	1		J26		3 0 0 –	3 0 0 –

Goods are frequently shipped another way—**FOB destination**, where the seller pays the transportation cost from the shipping point to the place of destination. In this book we will assume that all merchandise is shipped FOB shipping point unless stated otherwise.

The Schedule of Accounts Payable

A **schedule of accounts payable** is normally prepared at the end of the accounting period directly from the accounts payable subsidiary ledger. As we see in Exhibit 8-8, each vendor and the balance owed is listed on the schedule. Also shown is the control account, Accounts Payable, in the general ledger. The total of the schedule of accounts payable must equal the total of the control account, Accounts Payable, in the general ledger. If the two do not agree, then a mistake has been made and must be corrected. (Notice that Rogers Freight is included.)

---

*Note: Entries are made in date order.

EXHIBIT 8-8 | Schedule of Accounts Payable

United Auto Supply
Schedule of Accounts Payable
October 31, 19XX

Vendor	Amount Owed
Anderson, Inc.	$1 300 –
Boyle Manufacturing	2 300 –
Hakala Enterprises	2 100 –
Mehta Manufacturing	1 900 –
Nguyen Distributors	1 500 –
Rogers Freight	300 –
Zamora Warehouse	1 700 –
	$11 100 –

must equal

GENERAL LEDGER ACCOUNTS

Account: *Accounts Payable*   Account No. *201*

Date	Item	Post Ref.	Debit	Credit	Balance Debit	Balance Credit
19XX						
Oct. 1		J26		300 –		300 –
31		P10		10 800 –		11 100 –

The Purchases Returns and Allowances Account

Objective 3
Account for purchases returns and allowances.

The Purchases Returns and Allowances account is used to record two types of transactions that apply to merchandise previously purchased. A **return** is a physical return of merchandise by the purchaser to the vendor. An **allowance** is granted by the vendor to the purchaser for inferior, defective, or damaged merchandise. Whenever a return or allowance occurs, the purchaser will notify the vendor by sending a prenumbered debit memorandum. It is called a **debit memorandum** because the vendor's account will be debited for the return or allowance. A general journal is used to record the return or allowance of merchandise previously purchased on account. Remember that the purchases journal is only used to record merchandise purchased on account.

The Purchases Returns and Allowances account is a *contra* cost of goods sold account. That is, it reduces cost of goods sold and has a normal credit balance. Purchases Returns and Allowances is included in the cost of goods sold classification of accounts, along with purchases, on the chart of accounts.

Assume that on October 29, 19XX, United Auto Supply returns $400 of defective merchandise previously purchased on account to Zamora Warehouse. Debit memorandum number DM782 is issued to Zamora Warehouse (as shown in Exhibit 8-9). The purchase transaction was originally recorded in the purchases journal (see Exhibit 8-5). On receipt of the debit memorandum, Zamora Warehouse will issue United Auto Supply a credit memorandum (discussed in the previous chapter).

EXHIBIT 8-9 | Prenumbered Debit Memorandum

Debit Memorandum	**No.** _782_

Charge Return _X_   **Cash Return** _____

United Auto Supply
100 Main Street, Houston, Texas 77001

Prepared By: *Carl Moore*
Purchase Date: *10/10/XX*   **Terms:** *1/25, n60*
Invoice (billing) Date: *10/10/XX*   **Return Date:** *10/29/XX*

Vendor: *Zamora Warehouse*
            300 Travis Road, San Antonio, TX 78201

Return Information

Quantity	Merchandise	Amount (each)	Total Amount
16	*Fuel Pumps*	*$25*	*$400*
Total Amount to Be Debited			*$400*

Journalizing and Posting Purchases Returns and Allowances

To record a return of merchandise, Accounts Payable is debited, and Purchases Returns and Allowances is credited. In Exhibit 8-10, the return is journalized and posted to the general ledger and accounts payable subsidiary ledger. The journalizing and posting steps are keyed as ①, ②, and ③. These three steps are as follows:

① The return or allowance of a previous credit purchase of merchandise must be recorded in the general journal.

② The debit is posted to both the Accounts Payable account in the general ledger and the vendor's page in the accounts payable subsidiary ledger. "J26" is entered in the Post. Ref. column of the general ledger and accounts payable subsidiary ledger. Once the posting is complete, "201/✓" is entered in the Post. Ref. column of the general journal. The term "201" indicates a posting to Accounts Payable in the general ledger. The "✓" indicates a posting to the vendor's account in the accounts payable subsidiary ledger. The slash (/) is used to keep the two references separate.

③ The credit is posted to Purchases Returns and Allowances in the general ledger. "J26" is entered in the Post. Ref. column. Once the posting is complete, "502" is entered in the Post. Ref. column of the general journal.

EXHIBIT 8-10 | Recording and Posting Purchases Returns and Allowances

① **GENERAL JOURNAL**   Page __26__

Date		Description	Post Ref.	Debit	Credit
19XX					
Oct.	*29*	Accounts Payable – Zamora Warehouse	201/✓	400 ②	
		Purchase Returns and Allowances	502 ③		400
		Return of Defective Merchandise, Debit Memorandum DM782			

GENERAL LEDGER ACCOUNTS

Account: *Accounts Receivable*   Account No. __201__

Date		Item	Post Ref.	Debit	Credit	Balance Debit	Credit
Oct.	*29*		J26	400			

Account: *Purchase Returns and Allowances*   Account No. __502__

Date		Item	Post Ref.	Debit	Credit	Balance Debit	Credit
19XX							
Oct.	*29*		J26		400		400

ACCOUNTS PAYABLE SUBSIDIARY LEDGER

Vendor: *Zamora Warehouse*

Date		Item	Post Ref.	Debit	Credit	Balance
19XX						
Oct.	*10*		P10		1700	1700
	29		J26	400		1300

Recording Other Transactions

Objective 4
Record the purchase of assets other than merchandise on account.

There are other purchase transactions that cannot be recorded in a one-column purchases journal. Any asset (other than merchandise inventory) purchased on account must be recorded using a general journal. For example, let's assume that on October 9, 19XX, United Auto Supply purchased $3,300 of office supplies, which is not merchandise inventory, from County Office Supplies on account. The terms are **COD**. We will also assume that this transaction is not taxable. COD means that the invoice must be paid when the office supplies are delivered. COD is an abbreviation for *cash-on-delivery*. This transaction would be recorded in the general journal as follows:

GENERAL JOURNAL Page ___26___

Date		Description	Post Ref.	Debit	Credit
19XX					
Oct.	9	Office Supplies	131	3 3 0 0 –	
		Accounts Payable – County Office Supplies	201/✓		3 3 0 0 –
		Terms COD			

Some accountants do not use Accounts Payable to record a COD (purchase) transaction. Since cash will be paid on delivery and the period of time is usually short, the previous transaction could be recorded, using T accounts, as follows:

Office Supplies		Cash	
(10/9) 3,300			(10/9) 3,300

Notice that Office Supplies is still debited. Only the account credited will change (in this case Cash is credited instead of Accounts Payable). In this textbook we will use Accounts Payable to record COD purchases. Ask your instructor how she or he wants you to record COD transactions. Using Accounts Payable as a credit, the general journal entry would then be posted to the general ledger and accounts payable subsidiary ledger as follows:

GENERAL LEDGER ACCOUNTS

Account: *Office Supplies*   Account No.   *131*

Date		Item	Post Ref.	Debit	Credit	Balance Debit	Balance Credit
Oct.	9		J26	3 3 0 0 –		3 3 0 0 –	

GENERAL LEDGER ACCOUNTS

Account: *Accounts Payable*   Account No.   *201*

Date		Item	Post Ref.	Debit	Credit	Balance Debit	Balance Credit
19XX							
Oct.	1		J26		3 0 0 –		3 0 0 –
	9		J26		3 3 0 0 –		3 6 0 0 –
	29		J26	4 0 0 –			3 2 0 0 –
	31		P10		1 0 8 0 0 –		1 4 0 0 0 –

ACCOUNTS PAYABLE SUBSIDIARY LEDGER

Vendor: *County Office Supplies*

Date		Item	Post Ref.	Debit	Credit	Balance
19XX						
Oct.	*9*		*J26*		3 3 0 0 –	3 3 0 0 –

Chapter Review

1. **Understand and use the purchases journal**
   A single-column purchases journal is used to record the purchase of merchandise on account.

2. **Understand and use the accounts payable subsidiary ledger**
   An accounts payable subsidiary ledger is used in conjunction with the purchases journal to identify and accumulate amounts owed to individual vendors.

3. **Account for purchases returns and allowances**
   The Purchases Returns and Allowances account is used to record a return or an allowance that applies to merchandise previously purchased. A return is a physical return of merchandise by the purchaser to the vendor. An allowance is granted by the vendor to the purchaser for inferior, defective, or damaged merchandise. A prenumbered debit memorandum is issued to the vendor by the purchaser for purchases returns and allowances.

4. **Record the purchase of assets other than merchandise on account**
   Any asset (other than merchandise inventory) purchased on account must be recorded using a general journal.

Glossary

Accounts Payable Subsidiary Ledger Used in conjunction with the purchases journal to identify and accumulate amounts owed to individual vendors. Supports a book of original entry

COD Abbreviation for cash-on-delivery. Goods must be paid for when delivered

Cost of Goods Sold Represents the cost of merchandise inventory that is sold during an accounting period

Debit Memorandum Prenumbered document issued to the vendor by the purchaser for purchases returns and allowances

FOB Abbreviation for free-on-board

FOB Destination Used when the seller pays the transportation cost from the shipping point to the place of destination

FOB Shipping Point Used when the buyer, not the seller, pays the transportation cost from the selling point to the place of delivery

Freight In Cost of goods sold account that is used to record the transportation cost of merchandise paid for by the buyer

Internal Control System of policies and procedures adopted by a firm to safeguard assets and promote operational efficiency

Purchase Invoice Issued by the seller to the buyer for payment upon acceptance of a purchase order

Purchase Order Written order for merchandise or other items

Purchase Requisition Request by a department to purchase merchandise or other items

Purchases Cost of goods sold account that is used to record the purchase of merchandise inventory

Purchases Returns and Allowances Account used to record the return or allowance on previously purchased merchandise

Schedule of Accounts Payable Listing of each vendor and the amount owed

Vendor Used to indicate from whom the firm made its purchase

Self-Test Questions for Review

(Answers are at the end of Chapter 8.)

1. A request by a department to purchase certain goods is a
   a. purchase requisition.
   b. purchase invoice.
   c. purchase order.
   d. debit memorandum.

2. Which of the following accounts will probably have a credit balance after the purchases journal is posted to the general ledger?
   a. Purchases
   b. Accounts Payable
   c. Cash
   d. Accounts Receivable

3. Which of the following is NOT an asset account?
   a. Prepaid Insurance
   b. Accounts Receivable
   c. Freight In
   d. Cash

4. Which of the following is a contra cost of goods sold account?
   a. Purchases
   b. Accounts Payable
   c. Freight In
   d. Purchases Returns and Allowances

5. "DM109" is listed in the description of a transaction. Which of the following accounts is credited for this transaction?
   a. Freight In
   b. Purchases
   c. Accounts Payable
   d. Purchases Returns and Allowances

Practical Review Problem

Objectives 1, 3, and 4

Recording Purchases Returns and Allowances Mid-Atlantic Sports Supply had the following credit transactions during the month of November 19XX:

November 2   Purchased $400 of merchandise on credit from Babino Company, invoice number B340. Terms are n30.

November 10   Purchased $900 of office supplies on credit. Terms are COD. The vendor is Talmadge, Inc.

November 17   Returned $100 of damaged merchandise previously purchased November 2 from Babino Company. Debit memorandum DM32 is issued.

November 22   Received a freight invoice from Loadstar Freight for the November 2 delivery from Babino Company. Terms are 2/10, n30. The amount is $50.

November 30   Purchased $500 of merchandise on credit from Phu Manufacturing, invoice number L7829. Terms are 1/10, n30.

REQUIRED
1. Record the purchase of merchandise in a purchases journal, page 1.

2. Record the return of merchandise, purchase of assets other than merchandise, and freight in a general journal, page 13.

Answer to Practical Review Problem

1.   **PURCHASES JOURNAL**   Page ___1___

Date		Vendor	Invoice Number	Terms	Post. Ref.	Amount Purch. (Dr.) A/P (Cr.)
19XX						
Oct.	*2*	*Babino Company*	*B340*	*n30*		*400 –*
	30	*Phu Manufacturing*	*L7829*	*1/10, n30*		*500 –*
						900 –

2.   **GENERAL JOURNAL**   Page ___13___

Date		Description	Post Ref.	Debit	Credit
19XX					
Nov.	*10*	*Office Supplies*		*900 –*	
		Accounts Payable – Talmadge, Inc.			*900 –*
		Terms COD			
	17	*Accounts Payable – Babino Company*		*100 –*	
		Purchases Returns and Allowances			*100 –*
		Return of Damaged Merchandise, Debit Memorandum DM32			
	22	*Freight In*		*50 –*	
		Accounts Payable – Loadstar Freight			*50 –*
		Terms 2/10, n30			

Discussion Questions

Q 8-1 What is internal control? Name the procedures that should be followed when making purchases.

Q 8-2 Briefly describe the following: (a) COD, (b) FOB shipping point, and (c) FOB destination.

Q 8-3 Name the two reasons why a merchandising firm would NOT use a general journal if a purchases journal could be used.

Q 8-4 Define Purchases and Cost of Goods Sold. Also, name the six columns in a purchases journal.

Q 8-5 Name the four purposes of a purchases journal.

Q 8-6 Name the four steps for posting from the purchases journal to the general ledger.

Q 8-7 For what is the accounts payable subsidiary ledger used? Name the three steps to follow when posting to the accounts payable subsidiary ledger.

Q 8-8 Briefly describe the Purchases Returns and Allowances account. What is a debit memorandum? Why is it called a debit memorandum?

Q 8-9 Name the three steps in journalizing and posting the return of merchandise previously purchased on account.

Q 8-10 Which journal and ledgers would the following transaction be recorded in: purchased machinery, which is not merchandise inventory, on account for $790 from Chen Company? Also, give the appropriate accounts that would be debited and credited.

Exercises

Objective 1

E 8-1 **Recording Purchases**   Record this transaction in (a) a general journal, page 9; and then (b) a purchases journal, page 9:

May 4, 19XX   Purchased $700 of merchandise on account from Hauser Enterprises, terms 1/10, n30. Invoice number 197.

Objective 2

E 8-2 **Completing Vendor's Page**   Complete a vendor's page in the accounts payable subsidiary ledger given the following information:

June 14, 19XX   Purchased $300 of merchandise on account from Newly Manufacturing. The entry was made in page 5 of the purchases journal.

July 23, 19XX   Purchased $900 of merchandise on account from Newly Manufacturing (page 6 of the purchases journal).

Objective 2

E 8-3 **Recording Freight**   Record the following transaction in a general journal, page 25: A firm received a freight invoice on October 18, 19XX, from Quick Transportation. The terms are n30 and the freight charge is $400.

Objective 3

E 8-4 **Recording Purchases Returns and Allowances**   Record the following transaction in a general journal, page 19: On September 7, 19XX, Tulsa Company returned $600 of defective merchandise previously purchased on account to Portland Distributors. Debit memorandum DM9 is issued to Portland Distributors.

Objective 4

E 8-5 **Recording Other Transactions**   On March 26, 19XX, Florence Tire Supply purchased $2,300 of store supplies (not merchandise inventory) from WHR Company on account. The terms are COD. Record this transaction using (a) T accounts, and then (b) in a general journal, page 47.

Objectives 1 through 4

E 8-6 **Describing Transactions**   Describe the four transactions recorded in the following T accounts:

Office Supplies		Accounts Payable	
(b) 1,900		(d) 200	(a) 3,100
			(b) 1,900
			(c) 400

Purchases		Purchases Returns and Allowances	
(a) 3,100			(d) 200

Freight In	
(c) 400	

Objective 2

E 8-7 **Preparing a Schedule of Accounts Payable**   Prepare a schedule of accounts payable for Robinson Paper Supply given the following vendors and amounts owed: Johnson Limited, $1,100; Tran Enterprises, $2,400; Brinson Company, $4,100; and Michigan Freight, $900. List the vendors alphabetically. The date is December 31, 19XX.

Objective 4

E 8-8 **Recording and Posting Other Transactions**   On January 21, 19XX, a firm purchased a $7,000 copier (not merchandise inventory) from Sanchez Copier Company, terms COD. In your answer, record this transaction in a general journal, page 12, and post to the accounts payable subsidiary ledger and the general ledger. Accounts Payable is account number 205 and Copier is account number 161.

Problems

Objectives 1 and 2

P 8-1 **Recording and Posting Purchases**   Lois Smith is the owner of Smith Plumbing Parts. The firm had the following credit purchases of merchandise during the first half of August 19XX:

DATE	AMOUNT	TERMS	INVOICE NUMBER	VENDOR
August 2	$ 500	n30	498	Zorn Company
August 4	$ 300	1/10, n30	091	Conner Enterprises
August 9	$ 700	2/10, n30	H56	HMC, Inc.
August 11	$1,400	n30	506	Zorn Company
August 12	$ 600	2/10, n30	H61	HMC, Inc.
August 15	$1,700	1/10, n30	098	Conner Enterprises

REQUIRED

1. Record the purchase of merchandise in a purchases journal, page 5.

2. Post to the accounts payable subsidiary ledger. List the vendors alphabetically.

Objectives 1 and 2

P 8-2 **Posting Purchases Transactions**   You are hired as the accountant for Morgan Computer Supply. You find the following purchases journal:

PURCHASES JOURNAL   Page ___6___

Date		Vendor	Invoice Number	Terms	Post Ref.	Amount Purch.(Dr.) A/P (Cr.)
19XX						
Nov.	*1*	*Clayton Company*	*C064*	*2/10, n30*	✓	7 0 0 —
	5	*Whitten Company*	*816*	*1/15, n45*	✓	8 0 0 —
	12	*Rayburn Manufacturing*	*0177*	*n30*	✓	6 0 0 —
	18	*Clayton Company*	*C072*	*2/10, n30*	✓	3 0 0 —
	20	*Rayburn Manufacturing*	*0186*	*n30*	✓	3 4 0 0 —
	24	*Whitten Company*	*829*	*1/15, n45*	✓	1 6 0 0 —
	27	*Clayton Company*	*C081*	*2/10, n30*	✓	9 0 0 —
	30	*Rayburn Manufacturing*	*0193*	*n30*	✓	2 8 0 0 —
						11 1 0 0 —
						(517) (214)

The accountant you replaced recorded the purchases transactions in the purchases journal and included the proper posting references. However, he did not post to the accounts payable subsidiary ledger and the general ledger.

REQUIRED
1. Using the general ledger account numbers below the Amount column, write the account names and account numbers in the general ledger. List Accounts Payable first, followed by Purchases.
2. Post to the accounts payable subsidiary ledger. List the vendors alphabetically.
3. Post to the general ledger.
4. Prepare a schedule of accounts payable.

Objectives 1, 3, and 4

P 8-3

Recording Purchases Returns and Allowances Alvarez Printing Supply had the following credit transactions during the month of January 19XX:

January 2 Purchased $2,900 of merchandise on account from Ramos Company, invoice number R91. Terms are n30.

January 5 Purchased $1,900 of merchandise on credit from Drees Company, invoice number 581. Terms are 1/10, n30.

January 6 Purchased from Yanez Company $1,800 of furniture on account. Terms are n30.

January 7 Returned $400 of inferior merchandise previously purchased January 2 to Ramos Company. Debit memorandum DM87 is issued.

January 12 Received a $100 freight bill from West Coast Transport for the January 5 delivery from Drees Company. Terms are n30.

January 14 Purchased from Drumm Supply $1,900 of store supplies on account. Terms are 1/10, EOM, n30.

January 18 Purchased $2,000 of merchandise on account from Ramos Company, invoice number R98. Terms are n30.

January 21 Purchased $700 of merchandise on credit from Drees Company, invoice number 595. Terms are 1/10, n30.

January 23   Returned $1,600 of damaged merchandise previously purchased January 5 to Drees Company. Debit memorandum DM88 is issued.

January 25   Purchased $1,700 of merchandise on account from Battle Distributors, invoice number 024. Terms are n30.

January 31   Purchased $2,100 of merchandise from Greenwade, Inc. Terms are 2/10, n30. Invoice number is 1637.

REQUIRED

1. Record the purchase of merchandise in a purchases journal, page 10.

2. Record the return of merchandise, purchase of assets other than merchandise, and freight in a general journal, page 19.

Objectives 1 through 4

P 8-4

Comprehensive Chapter Review Problem   Larson Cabinet Supply had the following credit transactions during the month of April 19XX:

April 2   Purchased $4,500 of merchandise on credit from Adams Company, invoice number A047. Terms are 2/10, n30.

April 4   Purchased $7,900 of merchandise on account from Lerman Company, invoice number 342. Terms are 2/10, n30.

April 7   Purchased from Reyna Company $1,800 of merchandise on credit. Terms are n30. The invoice number is 602.

April 8   Received a $550 freight bill from Crosstown Freight for the April 4 delivery from Lerman Company. Terms are 2/10, n30.

April 9   Returned $200 of damaged merchandise previously purchased April 2 to Adams Company. Debit memorandum DM98 is issued.

April 12   Purchased $8,400 of merchandise on credit from Lerman Company, invoice number 358. Terms are 2/10, n30.

April 16   Purchased from Daily Company $800 of office supplies (account number 132) on credit. Terms are 2/10, EOM, n30.

April 17   Purchased $2,900 of merchandise on account from Reyna Company, invoice number 621. Terms are n30.

April 20   Purchased $4,800 of merchandise on credit from Zachery Supply, invoice number 119. Terms are 2/10, n30.

April 21   Received a $350 freight bill from Dartman Delivery for the April 2 delivery from Adams Company. Terms are n30.

April 22   Purchased from Lafoy Company $14,800 of machinery (account number 181) on account. Terms are n30.

April 25   Returned to Reyna Company $400 of inferior merchandise previously purchased April 17. Debit memorandum DM99 is issued.

April 26   Purchased $4,000 of merchandise on credit from Lerman Company, invoice number 373. Terms are 2/10, n30.

April 28   Purchased from Yartosky Company a $13,800 truck (account number 191) on account. Terms are n30.

April 28   Received a $600 freight bill from Fastest Delivery for the April 20 delivery from Zachery Supply. Terms are n30.

April 29   Requested $1,100 allowance for defective merchandise from Lerman Company for the April 26 purchase on credit. Debit memorandum DM100 is issued.

April 30   Purchased $7,900 of merchandise on credit from Bard Company. Terms are 1/10, n30. The invoice number is 0618.

REQUIRED

1. Record the purchase of merchandise in a purchases journal, page 9.

2. Record the return of merchandise, purchase of assets other than merchandise, and freight, in a general journal, page 21. Purchases Returns and Allowances is account number 527, and Freight In is 533.

3. Post to the accounts payable subsidiary ledger. List the vendors alphabetically.

4. Post to the general ledger. Accounts Payable is account number 242, and Purchases is 526.

5. Prepare a schedule of accounts payable.

Checklist of Key Figures

P 8-1	No key figure
P 8-2	(3) Accounts Payable, $11,100
P 8-3	(1) Totals, $11,300
P 8-4	(4) Accounts Payable, $71,400

Answers to Self-Test Questions

1. a   **2.** b   **3.** c   **4.** d   **5.** d

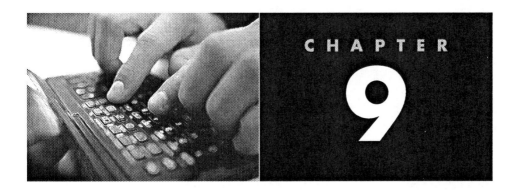

The Cash Receipts and Cash Payments Journals

LEARNING OBJECTIVES

After reading this chapter, discussing the questions, and working the exercises and problems, you will be able to do the following:

1. Understand and use a cash receipts journal

2. Post from a cash receipts journal to a general ledger

3. Post from a cash receipts journal to an accounts receivable subsidiary ledger

4. Understand and use a cash payments journal

5. Post from a cash payments journal to a general ledger

6. Post from a cash payments journal to an accounts payable subsidiary ledger

Earlier we examined the sales and purchases of merchandise on account for United Auto Supply. In this chapter, we will examine both the receipt of cash and the payment of cash.

The Cash Receipts Journal

Objective 1
Understand and use a cash receipts journal.

Let's assume that on October 12, 19XX, United Auto Supply received $1,764 from Emma's Auto Repair. This amount is payment in full for the October 4, 19XX, sale of merchandise on account. The amount is calculated as follows:

October 4, 19XX, Sale Amount	$1,800
Terms 2/10, n30. Discount of 2 percent	× .02
Discount Amount	$ 36

Cash Received = Sale Amount − Discount = $1,800 − $36
= $1,764

Let's use T accounts to illustrate the discount:

Cash		Sales Discounts		Accounts Receivable	
+	−	+	−	+	−
(10/12) 1,764		(10/12) 36			(10/12) 1,800

If United Auto Supply does not use special journals, then the cash received is recorded in a general journal as follows:

GENERAL JOURNAL   Page ___19___

Date		Description	Post Ref.	Debit	Credit
19XX					
Oct.	12	Cash		1764 –	
		Sales Discounts		36 –	
		Accounts Receivable – Emma's Auto Repair			1800 –
		2% Discount			

The cash received is recorded by debiting Cash and Sales Discounts and crediting Accounts Receivable. The actual amount of cash received is debited. **Sales Discounts** is a contra revenue account that reduces Sales and is used to keep track of the discounts a firm gives on sales of merchandise. Sales Discounts has a normal debit balance. Accounts Receivable is credited for the amount of cash received plus any discount.

United Auto Supply does not use a general journal to record the receipt of cash for the following reasons:

1. For each receipt of cash, the accounts used must be written.
2. For each receipt of cash, the accounts used must be posted to the general ledger.

Thus, to save time and effort, and to increase efficiency, the firm uses a cash receipts journal to record the receipt of cash.

A **cash receipts journal** is a special journal used to record cash received from any source. Remember that a special journal is a book of original entry that groups together similar transactions.

Purposes of the Cash Receipts Journal

A cash receipts journal has the following purposes:

1. To record all receipts of cash in one journal, which saves time.
2. To save journalizing space by recording each cash receipt using one line. You may have to use more than one line for certain transactions.
3. The customer's name can be identified easily.
4. The individual account columns (except Other Accounts, which is sometimes called Sundry Accounts) are added, totaled, and posted separately to the general ledger at the end of the accounting period.

Structure of the Cash Receipts Journal

The October 12, 19XX, receipt of cash from Emma's Auto Repair is recorded in a cash receipts journal as shown in Exhibit 9-1.

The cash receipts journal illustrated in Exhibit 9-1 has columns for the Date, Account Credited, Post. Ref., Other Accounts (credit), Accounts Receivable (credit), Sales (credit), Sales Discounts (debit), and Cash (debit). (The Post. Ref. column will be used later.)

EXHIBIT 9-1   Cash Receipts Journal

		Account Credited	Post Ref.	Credits			Debits	
Date				Other Accounts	Accounts Receiv.	Sales	Sales Disc.	Cash
19XX								
Oct.	12	Emma's Auto Repair			1800 –		36 –	1764 –

Posting from the Cash Receipts Journal to the General Ledger

Objective 2
Post from a cash receipts journal to a general ledger.

Two of the purposes of the cash receipts journal are to save time and space. To illustrate this, Exhibit 9-2 shows how the following cash receipts for the month of October for United Auto Supply are recorded and posted:

EXHIBIT 9-2 | Recording and Posting Cash Receipts

CASH RECEIPTS JOURNAL

Page ___10___

Date		Account Credited	Post Ref.	Credits			Debits	
				Other Accounts	Accounts Receiv.	Sales	Sales Disc.	Cash
19XX								
Oct.	3	Cash Sales				9800 –		9800 –
	5	Office Supplies ①	131	600 –				600 –
	8	Notes Payable	221	2100 –				2100 –
	12	Emma's Auto Repair			1800 –		36 –	1764 –
	14	Montana Company			2800 –		56 –	2744 –
	19	Cash Sales				12000 –		12000 –
	25	Lucille Garcia, Capital	301	5000 –				5000 –
	30	Zumwalt Company			1500 –		30 –	1470 –
		②		7700 –	6100 –	21800 –	122 –	35478 –
				(✓)	(111)	(401)	(403)	(101)

③   ④

GENERAL LEDGER ACCOUNTS

Account: *Cash*						Account No. 101	
Date		Item	Post Ref.	Debit	Credit	Balance	
						Debit	Credit
19XX		Previous Bal.				7641 –	
Oct.	31		CR10	35478 –		43119 –	

Account: *Accounts Receivable*						Account No. 111	
Date		Item	Post Ref.	Debit	Credit	Balance	
						Debit	Credit
19XX		Previous Bal.				21322 –	
Oct.	31		CR10		6100 –	15222 –	

Account: *Office Supplies*						Account No. 131	
Date		Item	Post Ref.	Debit	Credit	Balance	
						Debit	Credit
19XX		Previous Bal.				3300 –	
Oct.	5		CR10		① 600 –	2700 –	

(continued)

Ex. 9-2 (continued)

Account: *Notes Payable*							Account No. 221
		Post				Balance	
Date	Item	Ref.	Debit	Credit	Debit	Credit	
19XX	*Previous Bal.*						–0–
Oct. 8		CR10		2100 –		2100 –	

Account: *Lucille Garcia, Capital*							Account No. 301
		Post				Balance	
Date	Item	Ref.	Debit	Credit	Debit	Credit	
19XX	*Previous Bal.*						29100 –
Oct. 25		CR10		5000 –		34100 –	

Account: *Sales*							Account No. 401
		Post				Balance	
Date	Item	Ref.	Debit	Credit	Debit	Credit	
19XX	*Previous Bal.*						19400 –
Oct. 31		CR10		21800 –		41200 –	

Account: *Sales Discounts*							Account No. 403
		Post				Balance	
Date	Item	Ref.	Debit	Credit	Debit	Credit	
19XX	*Previous Bal.*				–0–		
Oct. 31		CR10	122 –		122 –		

October 3   Cash sale of merchandise inventory, $9,800.

October 5   Sold office supplies, which are not merchandise inventory, $600.

October 8   Borrowed $2,100 from the bank. **Notes Payable**, a liability account, is a formal written promise to pay a certain sum of money at a future date. This amount is credited in the Other Accounts credited column because there is no listed column for Notes Payable. This note is to be paid in two years, so it is classified as a *long-term liability* (a liability that is due after one year).

October 12   Received payment in full from Emma's Auto Repair, invoice number 831, less a 2 percent discount. The discount is $36 ($1,800 × .02 = $36). Since this is a full payment, Accounts Receivable is credited for the cash received plus the discount ($1,764 + $36 = $1,800).

October 14   Received payment in full from Montana Company, $2,744, invoice number 832. A 2 percent discount is taken. The discount is $56 ($2,800 × .02 = $56).

October 19   Cash sale of merchandise inventory, $12,000.

October 25   The owner, Lucille Garcia, invested an additional $5,000 in the firm.

October 30   Received $1,470 from Zumwalt Company as payment in full for invoice number 837. A 2 percent discount of $30 ($1,500 × .02 = $30) is taken.

There are four steps for posting from the cash receipts journal to the general ledger, keyed as ①, ②, ③, and ④ in Exhibit 9-2. The posting to Cash is illustrated. The steps are as follows:

①   An amount in the Other Accounts credited column is posted daily or as the transaction occurs. "CR10" is entered in the Post. Ref. column of the general ledger. The general ledger account number is then entered in the Post. Ref. column of the cash receipts journal.

②   The listed columns in the cash receipts journal are totaled and underlined after the final cash receipt is entered for the accounting period. The total is double underlined. These amounts are called *footings*. The debit footings (Cash and Sales Discounts) must equal the credit footings (Other Accounts, Accounts Receivable, and Sales). This process of verifying that the Debit column totals equal the Credit column totals is called **crossfooting**. The column totals are as follows:

COLUMN	DEBIT	CREDIT
Other Accounts		7,700
Accounts Receivable		6,100
Sales		21,800
Sales Discounts	122	
Cash	35,478	
Totals	35,600	35,600

③   The totals are posted to the general ledger. "CR10" is written in the Post. Ref. column of the general ledger to indicate that the posting is from page 10 of the cash receipts journal.

④   After posting the totals to the general ledger accounts, go back to the cash receipts journal and write the account number in parentheses below each column. A check mark in parentheses (✓) is placed below the Other Accounts column to show that the individual amounts have been posted to the general ledger.

Posting to the Accounts Receivable Subsidiary Ledger

Objective 3
Post from a cash receipts journal to an accounts receivable subsidiary ledger.

Any amounts received from previous credit transactions must be posted to the accounts receivable subsidiary ledger. These postings will occur daily or as the cash is received. The appropriate postings to the accounts receivable subsidiary ledger are illustrated in Exhibit 9-3.

EXHIBIT 9-3 Posting to the Accounts Receivable Subsidiary Ledger

CASH RECEIPTS JOURNAL

Page ___10___

Date		Account Credited	Post Ref.	Credits — Other Accounts	Credits — Accounts Receiv.	Sales	Debits — Sales Disc.	Cash
19XX								
Oct.	3	Cash Sales ④				9800 –		9800 –
	5	Office Supplies	131	600 –				600 –
	8	Notes Payable	221	2100 –				2100 –
	12	Emma's Auto Repair ③	✓		1800 –		36 –	1764 –
	14	Montana Company	✓		2800 –		56 –	2744 –
	19	Cash Sales	–			12000 –		12000 –
	25	Lucille Garcia, Capital	301	5000 –				5000 –
	30	Zumwalt Company	✓		1500 –		30 –	1470 –
				7700 –	6100 –	21800 –	122 –	35478 –
				(✓)	(111)	(401)	(403)	(101)

① ACCOUNTS RECEIVABLE SUBSIDIARY LEDGER (partial)

Customer: *Emma's Auto Repair*

Date		Inv. No.	Item	Post Ref.	Debit	Credit	Balance
19XX							
Oct.	4	831		S10	1800 –		1800 –
	12		②	CR10		1800 –	–0–

Customer: *Montana Company*

Date		Inv. No.	Item	Post Ref.	Debit	Credit	Balance
19XX							
Oct.	6	832		S10	2800 –		2800 –
	14			CR10		2800 –	–0–
	22	836		S10	1900 –		1900 –

(continued)

Ex. 9.3 (concluded)

Customer: *Zumwalt Company*

Date		Inv. No.	Item	Post Ref.	Debit	Credit	Balance
19XX							
Oct.	*25*	*837*		*S10*	*1500 –*		*1500 –*
	30			*CR10*		*1500 –*	*–0 –*

There are four steps to follow when posting from the cash receipts journal to the accounts receivable subsidiary ledger, keyed as ①, ②, ③, and ④ in Exhibit 9-3. The posting process is shown for Emma's Auto Repair. Cash receipts from other customers are posted in the same manner. The steps are as follows:

① As cash receipts of previous credit transactions are recorded in the cash receipts journal, they are posted daily or as they occur to the accounts receivable subsidiary ledger.

② "CR10" for cash receipts journal (CR), page 10, is entered in the Post. Ref. column of the customer's accounts receivable subsidiary ledger page after the amount received has been posted from the cash receipts journal.

③ Once the posting has been entered into the customer's accounts receivable subsidiary ledger page, a check mark (✓) is placed in the Post. Ref. column of the cash receipts journal. This signifies that the credit sale amount, including any tax, has been posted to the accounts receivable subsidiary ledger for that customer.

④ If the Post. Ref. column of the cash receipts journal has not been used, a dash (—) is placed in the Post. Ref. column. This occurs whenever a transaction has not been posted to either the general ledger or accounts receivable subsidiary ledger. (An example would be a cash sale of merchandise.)

The Cash Payments Journal

Objective 4
Understand and use a cash payments journal.

On October 9, 19XX, United Auto Supply paid $490 to Boyle Manufacturing for invoice number B6661. This amount is payment in full for the October 1, 19XX, purchase of merchandise on account, less a 2 percent discount. The amount is calculated as follows:

October 1, 19XX, Purchase Amount	$500
Terms 2/10, n30. Discount of 2 percent	$\times .02$
Discount Amount	$ 10

Cash paid = Purchase amount – Discount = $500 – $10 = $490

Let's use T accounts to illustrate the purchases discount:

Accounts Payable		Purchases Discounts		Cash	
–	+	–	+	+	–
(10/9) 500			(10/9) 10		(10/9) 490

If United Auto Supply does not use special journals, then the cash paid is recorded in a general journal as follows:

GENERAL JOURNAL   Page ___19___

Date		Description	Post Ref.	Debit	Credit
19XX					
Oct.	9	Accounts Payable – Boyle Manufacturing		5 0 0 –	
		Purchases Discounts			1 0 –
		Cash			4 9 0 –
		2% Discount			

The cash paid is recorded by debiting Accounts Payable and crediting **Purchases Discounts** and Cash. When a payment is made in full, Accounts Payable is debited for the full, original purchase amount. The actual amount of cash paid is credited. Purchases Discounts is a contra cost of goods sold account that reduces Purchases. This account is used to keep track of the discounts that a firm has taken on purchases of merchandise. Purchases Discounts has a normal credit balance.

United Auto Supply does not use a general journal to record the payment of cash for the following reasons:

1. For each payment of cash, the accounts used must be written.

2. For each payment of cash, the accounts used must be posted to the general ledger.

Thus, a cash payments journal is used to save time and effort, and to increase efficiency. To maintain proper internal control over cash payments, the firm uses a checking account at a bank. Checks (check no.) are prenumbered in consecutive order, and all checks must be accounted for.

A **cash payments journal** is a special journal used to record cash paid for any purpose.

The Structure of the Cash Payments Journal

The October 9, 19XX, payment of cash to Boyle Manufacturing is recorded in a cash payments journal in Exhibit 9-4:

EXHIBIT 9-4 Cash Payments Journal

CASH PAYMENTS JOURNAL   Page ___10___

Date		Chk. No.	Account Debited	Post Ref.	Debits			Credits	
					Other Accounts	Accounts Payable	Purchases	Purch. Disc.	Cash
19XX									
Oct.	9	933	Boyle						
			Manufacturing			5 0 0 –		1 0 –	4 9 0 –

The cash payments journal has columns for the Date, Check No., Account Debited, Post. Ref., Other Accounts (debit), Accounts Payable (debit), Purchases (debit), Purchases Discounts (credit), and Cash (credit). (The Post. Ref. column will be used later.)

Purposes of the Cash Payments Journal

A cash payments journal has the following purposes:

1. To record all payments of cash in one journal, which saves time.
2. To save journalizing space by recording each cash payment using one line. You may have to use more than one line for certain transactions.
3. The vendor's name can be identified easily.
4. The individual account columns (except Other Accounts) are added, totaled, and posted separately to the general ledger at the end of the accounting period.

Posting from the Cash Payments Journal to the General Ledger

Objective 5
Post from a cash payments journal to a general ledger.

United Auto Supply had twenty cash payments during October 19XX. These cash payments are recorded in the cash payments journal and posted to the general ledger in Exhibit 9-5.

October 1	Issued check no. 926 for monthly rent, $1,700.
October 2	Bought merchandise, $2,900, check no. 927.
October 4	Paid utilities bill, $195, check no. 928.
October 5	Paid $270 for freight, check no. 929.
October 5	Paid weekly wages, $2,450, check no. 930.
October 8	The owner, Lucille Garcia, withdrew $1,200 for her personal use, check no. 931.
October 9	Made an error in writing a vendor's name on check no. 932. Voided the check.
October 9	Paid Boyle Manufacturing $490 for invoice no. B6661, check no. 933. A $10 discount is taken.
October 10	Paid for merchandise inventory, $3,800, check no. 934.
October 11	Paid $225 for freight, check no. 935.
October 12	Paid weekly wages, $2,680, check no. 936.
October 15	Received and paid an advertising bill, $190, check no. 937.
October 17	Paid for merchandise inventory, $5,600, check no. 938.
October 19	Paid weekly wages, $2,380, check no. 939.
October 22	Paid $495 for freight, check no. 940.
October 23	Purchased office equipment for $2,500. Issued check no. 941.
October 25	Paid Nguyen Distributors in full, less a 3 percent discount ($1,500 × .03 = $45), check no. 942. Cash paid is $1,455 ($1,500 – $45).
October 26	Paid weekly wages, $2,560, check no. 943.
October 29	Received and paid a freight bill, $710, check no. 944.
October 30	Paid Zamora Warehouse in full, less a 1 percent discount, check no. 945. The invoice no. was 21087. Terms are 1/25, n60. United Auto Supply returned $400 of merchandise on October 29, 19XX. The discount is

EXHIBIT 9-5 Recording and Posting Cash Payments

CASH PAYMENTS JOURNAL

Page ___10___

Date		Chk. No.	Account Debited ①	Post Ref.	Debits			Credits	
					Other Accounts	Accounts Payable	Purchases	Purch. Disc.	Cash
19XX									
Oct.	1	926	Rent Expense	601	1700 –				1700 –
	2	927	Cash Purchase				2900 –		2900 –
	4	928	Utilities Expense	631	195 –				195 –
	5	929	Freight In	516	270 –				270 –
	5	930	Wages Expense	611	2450 –				2450 –
	8	931	Lucille Garcia, Drawing	311	1200 –				1200 –
	9	932	VOID						
	9	933	Boyle Manufacturing			500 –		10 –	490 –
	10	934	Cash Purchases	516			3800 –		3800 –
	11	935	Freight In	611	225 –				225 –
	12	936	Wages Expense		2680 –				2680 –
	15	937	Advertising Expense	621	190 –				190 –
	17	938	Cash Purchases				5600 –		5600 –
	19	939	Wages Expense	611	2380 –				2380 –
	22	940	Freight In	516	495 –				495 –
	23	941	Office Equipment	141	2500 –				2500 –
	25	942	Nguyen Distributors			1500 –		45 –	1455 –
	26	943	Wages Expense	611	2560 –				2560 –
	29	944	Freight In	516	710 –				710 –
	30	945	Zamora Warehouse			1300 –		13 –	1287 –
	31	946	Mehta Manufacturing ②			1900 –		76 –	1824 –
					17555 –	5200 –	12300 –	144 –	34911 –
					(✓)	(201)	(501)	(503)	(101)

③ ④

GENERAL LEDGER ACCOUNTS

Account: Cash							Account No. 101	
		Post Ref.					Balance	
Date		Item		Debit	Credit		Debit	Credit
19XX		Previous Bal.					7641 –	
Oct.	31		CR10	35478 –			43119 –	
	31		CP10		34911 –		8208 –	

Account: Office Equipment							Account No. 141	
		Post Ref.					Balance	
Date		Item		Debit	Credit		Debit	Credit
19XX		Previous Bal.					13000 –	
Oct.	23		CP10	2500 –			15500 –	

(continued)

Ex. 9-5 (continued)

Account: Accounts Payable						Account No. 201
Date	Item	Post Ref.	Debit	Credit	Balance Debit	Balance Credit
19XX	Previous Bal.					14000 –
Oct. 31		CP10	5200 –			8800 –

Account: Lucille Garcia, Drawing						Account No. 311
Date	Item	Post Ref.	Debit	Credit	Balance Debit	Balance Credit
19XX	Previous Bal.				– 0 –	
Oct. 8		CP10	1200 –		1200 –	

Account: Purchases						Account No. 501
Date	Item	Post Ref.	Debit	Credit	Balance Debit	Balance Credit
19XX	Previous Bal.				10800 –	
Oct. 31		CP10	12300 –		23100 –	

Account: Purchase Discounts						Account No. 503
Date	Item	Post Ref.	Debit	Credit	Balance Debit	Balance Credit
19XX	Previous Bal.					– 0 –
Oct. 31		CP10		144 –		144 –

Account: Freight In						Account No. 516
Date	Item	Post Ref.	Debit	Credit	Balance Debit	Balance Credit
19XX	Previous Bal.				300 –	
Oct. 5		CP10	270 –		570 –	
11		CP10	225 –		795 –	
22		CP10	495 –		1290 –	
29		CP10	710 –		2000 –	

(continued)

Ex. 9-5 (concluded)

Account: *Rent Expense*					Account No. *601*	
		Post			Balance	
Date	Item	Ref.	Debit	Credit	Debit	Credit
19XX	*Previous Bal.*				–0–	
Oct. *1*		CP10	1700 –		1700 –	

Account: *Wage Expense*					Account No. 611	
		Post			Balance	
Date	Item	Ref.	Debit	Credit	Debit	Credit
19XX	*Previous Bal.*				–0–	
Oct. *5*		CP10	2450 –		2450 –	
12		CP10	2680 –		5130 –	
19		CP10	2380 –		7510 –	
26		CP10	2560 –		10070 –	

Account: *Advertising Expense*					Account No. *621*	
		Post			Balance	
Date	Item	Ref.	Debit	Credit	Debit	Credit
19XX	*Previous Bal.*				–0–	
Oct. *15*		CP10	190 –		190 –	

Account: *Utilities Expense*					Account No. *631*	
		Post			Balance	
Date	Item	Ref.	Debit	Credit	Debit	Credit
19XX	*Previous Bal.*				–0–	
Oct. *4*		CP10	195 –		195 –	

based on the original purchase amount less the return ($1,700 – $400 = $1,300 × .01 = $13). $1,287 is paid to the vendor ($1,300 – $13).

October 31   Paid Mehta Manufacturing in full, less a 4 percent discount ($1,900 × .04 = $76), check no. 946. The cash paid is the purchase amount less the discount ($1,900 – $76 = $1,824).

There are four steps for posting from the cash payments journal to the general ledger, keyed as ①, ②, ③, and ④ in Exhibit 9-5. The posting to Cash is illustrated. The steps are as follows:

① An amount in the Other Accounts debited column is posted daily or as the transaction occurs. "CP10" is entered in the Post. Ref. column of the general ledger. The general ledger account number is then entered in the Post. Ref. column of the cash payments journal.

② The listed columns in the cash payments journal are totaled and underlined after the final cash payment is entered for the accounting period. The total is double-underlined. You should crossfoot the footings to be sure that total debits equal total credits. The totals are as follows:

COLUMN	DEBIT	CREDIT
Other Accounts	17,555	
Accounts Payable	5,200	
Purchases	12,300	
Purchases Discounts		144
Cash		34,911
Totals	35,055	35,055

③ The totals are posted to the general ledger. "CP10" is written in the Post. Ref. column of the general ledger to indicate that the posting is from page 10 of the cash payments journal.

④ After posting the totals to the general ledger accounts, go back to the cash payments journal and write the account number in parenthesis below each column. A check mark in parentheses (✓) is placed below the Other Accounts column to show that the individual amounts have been posted to the general ledger.

Posting to the Accounts Payable Subsidiary Ledger

Objective 6
Post from a cash payments journal to an accounts payable subsidiary ledger.

When a payment is made on a previous credit transaction, the amount paid is posted to the accounts payable subsidiary ledger. These postings will occur daily (or as the cash is paid). The appropriate postings to the accounts payable subsidiary ledger are illustrated in Exhibit 9-6.

There are four steps to follow when posting from the cash payments journal to the accounts payable subsidiary ledger, keyed as ①, ②, ③, and ④ in Exhibit 9-6. The posting process is shown for Boyle Manufacturing. The cash payments to the other vendors are posted in the same manner. The steps are as follows:

① As cash payments of previous credit transactions are recorded in the cash payments journal, they are posted daily or as they occur to the accounts payable subsidiary ledger.

② "CP10" for cash payments journal (CP), page 10, is entered in the Post. Ref. column of the vendor's accounts payable subsidiary ledger page after the amount paid has been posted from the cash payments journal.

③ Once the posting has been entered into the vendor's accounts payable subsidiary ledger page, a check mark (✓) is placed in the Post. Ref. column of the cash payments journal. This signifies that the cash paid has been posted to the accounts payable subsidiary ledger for that vendor.

④ A dash (—) is placed in any Post. Ref. line in the cash payments journal that has not been used. (An example would be a cash purchase of merchandise.)

EXHIBIT 9-6 Posting to the Accounts Payable Subsidiary Ledger

CASH PAYMENTS JOURNAL   Page ___10___

Date	Chk. No.	Account Debited	Post Ref.	Debits — Other Accounts	Debits — Accounts Payable	Debits — Purchases	Credits — Purch. Disc.	Credits — Cash
19XX								
Oct. 1	926	Rent Expense	601	1700 –				1700 –
2	927	Cash Purchases	– ④			2900 –		2900 –
4	928	Utilities Expense	631	195 –				195 –
5	929	Freight In	516	270 –				270 –
5	930	Wages Expense	611	2450 –				2450 –
8	931	Lucille Garcia, Drawing	311	1200 –				1200 –
9	932	VOID						
9	933	Boyle Manufacturing ③	✓		500 –		10 –	490 –
10	934	Cash Purchases	–			3800 –		3800 –
11	935	Freight In	516	225 –				225 –
12	936	Wages Expense	611	2680 –				2680 –
15	937	Advertising Expense	621	190 –				190 –
17	938	Cash Purchases	–			5600 –		5600 –
19	939	Wages Expense	611	2380 –				2380 –
22	940	Freight In	516	495 –				495 –
23	941	Office Equipment	141	2500 –				2500 –
25	942	Nguyen Distributors	✓		1500 –		45 –	1455 –
26	943	Wages Expense	611	2560 –				2560 –
29	944	Freight In	516	710 –				710 –
30	945	Zamora Warehouse	✓		1300 –		13 –	1287 –
31	946	Mehta Manufacturing	✓		1900 –		76 –	1824 –
				17555 –	5200 –	12300 –	144 –	34911 –
				(✓)	(201)	(501)	(503)	(101)

(continued)

Ex. 9-6 (concluded)

① **ACCOUNTS PAYABLE SUBSIDIARY LEDGER (partial)**

Vendor: *Boyle Manufacturing*

Date		Item	Post Ref.	Debit	Credit	Balance
19XX						
Oct.	1		P10		500 —	500 —
	9	②	CP10	500 —		–0–
	14		P10		1800 —	1800 —

Vendor: *Mehta Manufacturing*

Date		Item	Post Ref.	Debit	Credit	Balance
19XX						
Oct.	28		P10		1900 —	1900 —
	31		CP10	1900 —		–0–

Vendor: *Nguyen Distributors*

Date		Item	Post Ref.	Debit	Credit	Balance
19XX						
Oct.	23		P10		1500 —	1500 —
	25		CP10	1500 —		–0–

Vendor: *Zamora Warehouse*

Date		Item	Post Ref.	Debit	Credit	Balance
19XX						
Oct.	10		P10		1700 —	1700 —
	29		J26	400 —		1300 —
	30		CP10	1300 —		–0–

Chapter Review

1. **Understand and use a cash receipts journal.**
   A cash receipts journal is a special journal used to record cash received from any source. This journal is used to save time and effort, and increase efficiency.

2. **Post from a cash receipts journal to a general ledger.**
   There are four steps for posting from the cash receipts journal to the general ledger.

3. **Post from a cash receipts journal to an accounts receivable subsidiary ledger.**
   Any amounts received from previous credit transactions must be posted to the accounts receivable subsidiary ledger. These postings will occur daily or as the cash is received. There are four steps to follow when posting from the cash receipts journal to the accounts receivable subsidiary ledger.

4. **Understand and use a cash payments journal.**
   A cash payments journal is a special journal used to record cash paid for any purpose. A cash payments journal is used to save time and effort, and increase efficiency.

5. **Post from a cash payments journal to a general ledger.**
   There are four steps for posting from the cash payments journal to the general ledger.

6. **Post from a cash payments journal to an accounts payable subsidiary ledger.**
   When a payment is made on a previous credit transaction, the amount paid is posted to the accounts payable subsidiary ledger. These postings will occur daily or as the cash is paid. There are four steps to follow when posting from the cash payments journal to the accounts payable subsidiary ledger.

Glossary

Cash Payments Journal Special journal used to record cash paid for any purpose

Cash Receipts Journal Special journal used to record cash received from any source

Crossfooting Process of verifying that Debit column totals equal Credit column totals

Notes Payable Formal written promise to pay a certain sum of money at a future date

Purchases Discounts Contra cost of goods sold account that reduces purchases

Sales Discounts Contra revenue account that reduces sales

Self-Test Questions for Review

(Answers are at the end of Chapter 9.)

1. Sales Discounts has a normal _____ balance and is a _____ account.
   a. credit; contra asset
   b. debit; contra revenue
   c. debit; contra asset
   d. credit; contra revenue

2. In the cash receipts journal, Notes Payable is credited in the _____ column.
   a. Sales
   b. Accounts Receivable
   c. Cash
   d. Other Accounts

3. A firm purchased merchandise on account for $1,000, less a 3 percent discount. When paid within the discount period, the amount debited to _____ is _____.

a. Sales; $1,000

b. Purchases Discounts; $30

c. Accounts Payable; $1,000

d. Cash; $970

4. Which of the following accounts will probably have a credit balance after all postings from a cash payments journal?

a. Purchases Discounts

b. Jay Wasserstein, Drawing

c. Purchases

d. Freight In

5. After all postings, a _____ is placed in any Post. Ref. column in the cash payments journal that has not been used.

a. check mark

b. dash

c. general ledger number

d. CP and page number

Practical Review Problem

Objectives 1 and 4

Recording Cash Receipts and Cash Payments Marion Gurski is the owner of Southern Paper Supply. The firm had the following cash receipts and cash payments during the month of October 19XX:

October 1 Received payment in full from Willsey Company, less a 2 percent discount. The original sale was for $10,000.

October 1 Issued check no. 852 for monthly rent, $1,500.

October 3 Borrowed $7,500 from a bank.

October 7 Paid for merchandise inventory, $5,900, check no. 853.

October 10 Cash sale of merchandise, $8,560.

October 12 Paid for freight, $965, check no. 854.

October 13 Received payment in full from Boyer Company, less a 4 percent discount. The original sale was for $7,900.

October 14 Owner withdrew $1,580 for her personal use, check no. 855.

October 15 Paid wages for two weeks, $3,980, check no. 856.

October 18 Made an error in writing a vendor's name on check no. 857. Voided the check.

October 20 Paid McQueen Manufacturing payment in full, less a 3 percent discount, check no. 858. The original purchase was for $8,800.

October 21 Sold all the firm's store supplies, which are not merchandise, $810.

October 23 Purchased office equipment for $910. Issued check no. 859.

October 26 Owner invested an additional $5,500 in the firm.

October 31 Paid wages for two weeks, $3,900, check no. 860.

REQUIRED

Record the transactions in a cash receipts journal, page 1, or a cash payments journal, page 1.

Answer to Practical Review Problem

CASH RECEIPTS JOURNAL

Page _____1_____

Date	Account Credited	Post Ref.	Credits — Other Accounts	Credits — Accounts Receiv.	Credits — Sales	Debits — Sales Disc.	Debits — Cash
19XX							
Oct. 1	Wilsey Company			10000 –		200 –	9800 –
3	Notes Payable		7500 –				7500 –
10	Cash Sales				8560 –		8560 –
13	Boyer Company			7900 –		316 –	7584 –
21	Store Supplies		810 –				810 –
26	Marion Gurski,						
	Capital		5500 –				5500 –
			13810 –	17900 –	8560 –	516 –	39754 –

CASH PAYMENTS JOURNAL

Page _____1_____

Date	Chk. No.	Account Debited	Post Ref.	Debits — Other Accounts	Debits — Accounts Payable	Debits — Purchases	Credits — Purch. Disc.	Credits — Cash
19XX								
Oct. 1	852	Rent Expense		1500 –				1500 –
7	853	Cash Purchases				5900 –		5900 –
12	854	Freight In		965 –				965 –
14	855	Marion Gurski,						
		Drawing		1580 –				1580 –
15	856	Wages Expense		3980 –				3980 –
18	857	VOID						
20	858	McQueen						
		Manufacturing			8800 –		264 –	8536 –
23	859	Office						
		Equipment		910 –				910 –
31	860	Wages Expense		3900 –				3900 –
				12835 –	8800 –	5900 –	264 –	27271 –

Discussion Questions

Q 9-1   What is the sales discounts account? How is a sales discount calculated?

Q 9-2   Give two reasons why a firm would not use a general journal to record the receipt of cash.

Q 9-3   What is a cash receipts journal? Name the four purposes of a cash receipts journal.

Q 9-4   Briefly name the four steps for posting from the cash receipts journal to the general ledger. Also, what is crossfooting?

Q 9-5   Briefly name the four steps for posting from the cash receipts journal to the accounts receivable subsidiary ledger.

Q 9-6   What is the purchases discounts account? How is a purchases discount calculated?

Q 9-7   Name the two reasons why a firm would not use a general journal to record cash payments.

Q 9-8   What is a cash payments journal? Name the four purposes of a cash payments journal.

Q 9-9   How many steps are there for posting from the cash payments journal to the general ledger? Briefly name these steps.

Q 9-10   How many steps are there for posting from the cash payments journal to the accounts payable subsidiary ledger? Briefly name these steps.

Exercises

Objective 1

E 9-1   **Recording Receipts**   Record the following transaction using T accounts: A firm received payment in full from a customer, less a 2 percent discount. The original sale amount was $900.

Objectives 2 and 5

E 9-2   **Identifying Special Journals**   Identify the proper special journal for the following transactions. Use CRJ for the cash receipts journal and CPJ for the cash payments journal.

TRANSACTIONS	JOURNAL (CRJ OR CPJ)
a. Cash sale of merchandise inventory.	_____
b. Paid for monthly rent.	_____
c. Borrowed $1,000 from a bank.	_____
d. Bought merchandise, check no. 518.	_____
e. Received payment in full, less a discount.	_____
f. Paid a vendor in full, less a discount.	_____
g. Received and paid a freight bill.	_____
h. The owner invested an additional $10,000 in the firm.	_____

Objective 4

E 9-3   **Recording Payments**   A firm paid a vendor in full, less a 3 percent discount. The original purchase amount was $3,500. Record this transaction in T account form.

Objective 1

E 9-4   **Recording Receipts**   On May 18, 19XX, Akron Cable Supply received payment in full, less a 4 percent discount from Reginald Simpson. The original sale amount was $6,500. Record this transaction in a general journal, page 13.

Objectives 2 and 5

E 9-5   **Describing Transactions**   Describe the following transactions in your own words:

a. A firm debits Cash and credits Sales in a cash receipts journal.

b. A firm debits Accounts Payable and credits both Cash and Purchases Discounts in a cash payments journal.

c. A firm debits Purchases and credits Cash in a cash payments journal.

d. A firm debits Cash and credits Notes Payable in a cash receipts journal.

e. A firm debits Cash and Sales Discounts and credits Accounts Receivable in a cash receipts journal.

f. A firm debits Rent Expense and credits Cash in a cash payments journal.

Objective 4

E 9-6   Recording Payments   Record the following transaction in a general journal, page 61: On December 13, 19XX, Culver City Sales paid invoice number X304 in full, less a 5 percent discount. Invoice number X304 is from Augusta Metals Company. The original purchase amount was $19,600.

Objectives 2 and 3

E 9-7   Recording and Posting Receipts   A firm had the following cash receipts for the first two days of November 19XX:

November 1   Borrowed $3,000 from a bank.

November 2   Received payment in full from Lim Company, less a 2 percent discount. The original sale amount was $5,000.

In your answer, first open the previous balance in the accounts receivable subsidiary ledger for Lim Company. Second, record the transactions in the cash receipts journal, page 8. Third, post to the general ledger and accounts receivable subsidiary ledger as necessary. Notes Payable is chart-of-accounts number 231.

Objectives 5 and 6

E 9-8   Recording and Posting Payments   Ramirez Sales and Service had the following cash payments for the first three days of February 19XX:

February 1   Paid monthly rent, $1,500, check no. 839.

February 2   Bought merchandise, $900, check no. 840.

February 3   Paid Alaska Company in full, less a 3 percent discount, check no. 841. The original purchase amount was $4,200.

In your answer, first open the previous balance in the accounts payable subsidiary ledger for Alaska Company. Second, record the transactions in the cash payments journal, page 2. Third, post to the general ledger and accounts payable subsidiary ledger as necessary. Rent Expense is chart-of-accounts number 601.

Problems

Objectives 1, 2, and 3

P 9-1   Recording and Posting Receipts   D. W. Lindsey is the owner of Lindsey Office Products. The firm had the following cash receipts during the month of August 19XX:

August 2   Borrowed $3,595 from a bank.

August 5   Cash sale of merchandise, $5,900.

August 9   Received payment in full from Klein Company, less a 2 percent discount. The original sale was for $2,800.

August 12   Sold all the firm's office supplies, which are not merchandise, $235.

August 16   Received payment in full from Zwicker Company, less a 3 percent discount. The original sale was for $6,900.

August 19   Cash sale of merchandise, $4,100.

August 24   The owner invested an additional $3,950 in the firm.

August 27   Of an original sale of $8,900, received payment in full, less a 4 percent discount. The customer was Rey Office Supply.

August 31   Received payment in full from Alavi Company, less a 1 percent discount. The original sale was for $9,100.

The firm had the following partial chart-of-accounts numbers:

Cash	106	D.W. Lindsey, Capital	305
Accounts Receivable	117	Sales	404
Office Supplies	125	Sales Discounts	406
Notes Payable	232		

REQUIRED
1. Open the previous balances in the accounts receivable subsidiary ledger as follows: Alavi Company, $9,100; Klein Company, $2,800; Rey Office Supply, $8,900; Zwicker Company, $6,900. Also, open the previous balances in the Accounts Receivable account, $27,700; and the Office Supplies account, $235. Record the transactions in a cash receipts journal, page 9.
2. Post to the accounts receivable subsidiary ledger.
3. Post to the general ledger.

Objectives 4, 5, and 6

P 9-2   **Recording and Posting Payments**   Murray Fabric Supply is owned by Linda Murray. The firm had the following cash payments during December 19XX:

December 1   Issued check no. 178 for monthly rent, $900.
December 3   Paid for merchandise inventory, $4,890, check no. 179.
December 6   Paid for freight, $370, check no. 180.
December 11   Owner withdrew $3,890 for her personal use, check no. 181.
December 14   Made an error in writing a vendor's name on check no. 182. Voided the check.
December 14   Paid Gentry Manufacturing payment in full, less a 2 percent discount, check no. 183. The original purchase was for $6,700.
December 23   Paid Sauceda Distributing payment in full, less a 3 percent discount, check no. 184. The original purchase was for $10,500.
December 29   Purchased office furniture for $3,710. Issued check no. 185.
December 31   Paid monthly wages, $7,300, check no. 186.

The firm had the following partial chart-of-accounts numbers:

Cash	103	Purchases Discounts	506
Office Furniture	151	Freight In	510
Accounts Payable	204	Rent Expense	609
Linda Murray, Drawing	314	Wages Expense	613
Purchases	503		

REQUIRED
1. Open the previous balances in the accounts payable subsidiary ledger as follows: Gentry Manufacturing, $6,700; Sauceda Distributing, $10,500. Also, open the previous balances in the Cash account, $45,000, and the Accounts Payable account, $17,200. Record the transactions in a cash payments journal, page 5.

2. Post to the accounts payable subsidiary ledger.

3. Post to the general ledger.

Objectives 1, 3, 4, and 6

P 9-3

Recording and Posting Receipts and Payments   Tim O'Grady is the owner of O'Grady Restaurant Supply. The firm had the following cash receipts during March 19XX:

March 1   Received payment in full from Martinez Company, less a 2 percent discount. The original sale was for $8,300.

March 8   Borrowed $7,510 from the bank.

March 11   Cash sale of merchandise, $6,120.

March 15   Received payment in full from Arellano Company, less a 1 percent discount. The original sale was for $3,700.

March 20   Sold all the firm's store supplies, which are not merchandise, $160.

March 24   Received payment in full from Wells Company, less a 3 percent discount. The original sale was for $2,900.

March 27   Cash sale of merchandise, $5,890.

March 30   Owner invested an additional $4,620 in the firm.

March 31   Of an original sale of $5,800, received payment in full, less a 4 percent discount, from Diab Company.

The firm had the following cash payments during March 19XX:

March 1   Issued check no. 302 for monthly rent, $670.

March 4   Paid for merchandise inventory, $1,870, check no. 303.

March 9   Paid for freight, $400, check no. 304.

March 13   Owner withdrew $3,890 for his personal use, check no. 305.

March 18   Made an error in writing a vendor's name on check no. 306. Voided the check.

March 18   Paid Morris Distributors payment in full, less a 2 percent discount, check no. 307. The original purchase was for $4,800.

March 22   Paid a freight bill, $610, check no. 308.

March 24   Paid Yoong Warehouse payment in full, less a 1 percent discount, check no. 309. The original purchase was for $7,000.

March 28   Purchased office equipment for $1,200. Issued check no. 310.

March 31   Paid monthly wages, $8,500, check no. 311.

REQUIRED

1. Open the previous balances in the accounts receivable subsidiary ledger as follows: Arellano Company, $3,700; Diab Company, $5,800; Martinez Company, $8,300; Wells Company, $2,900. Open the previous balances in the accounts payable subsidiary ledger as follows: Morris Distributors, $4,800; Yoong Warehouse, $7,000. Record the transactions in a cash receipts journal, page 7, or a cash payments journal, page 7.

2. Post to the accounts receivable subsidiary ledger or accounts payable subsidiary ledger. Do NOT post to the general ledger.

Objectives 1 through 6

P 9-4

Comprehensive Chapter Review Problem   Jose Raya is the owner of Ready Book Supply. The firm had the following cash receipts and cash payments during the month of April 19XX:

April	1	Received payment in full from Finke Company, less a 2 percent discount. The original sale was for $12,700.
April	1	Issued check no. 908 for monthly rent, $2,470.
April	3	Borrowed $6,250 from a bank.
April	5	Paid for merchandise inventory, $4,670, check no. 909.
April	9	Cash sale of merchandise, $5,890.
April	11	Paid for freight, $710, check no. 910.
April	12	Received payment in full from DeGeorge Company, less a 1 percent discount. The original sale was for $6,800.
April	13	Owner withdrew $2,670 for his personal use, check no. 911.
April	15	Paid wages for two weeks, $3,600, check no. 912.
April	16	Made an error in writing a vendor's name on check no. 913. Voided the check.
April	17	Paid Insley Manufacturing payment in full, less a 2 percent discount, check no. 914. The original purchase was for $4,800.
April	19	Sold all the firm's office supplies, which are not merchandise, $780.
April	20	Paid a freight bill, $800, check no. 915.
April	22	Paid Prejean Distributors payment in full, less a 3 percent discount, check no. 916. The original purchase was for $5,900.
April	23	Purchased office furniture for $870. Issued check no. 917.
April	24	Received payment in full from Supensky Company, less a 4 percent discount. The original sale was for $13,600.
April	25	Cash sale of merchandise, $4,900.
April	26	Owner invested an additional $6,340 in the firm.
April	27	Paid a utilities bill, check no. 918, $140.
April	29	Of an original sale of $8,100, received payment in full, less a 5 percent discount. The customer was Hosan Company.
April	30	Paid wages for two weeks, $3,815, check no. 919.

The firm had the following partial chart-of-accounts numbers:

Cash	102	Sales	404
Accounts Receivable	104	Sales Discounts	407
Office Supplies	125	Purchases	506
Office Furniture	171	Purchases Discounts	511
Accounts Payable	206	Freight In	519
Notes Payable	243	Rent Expense	602
Jose Raya, Capital	311	Wages Expense	604
Jose Raya, Drawing	321	Utilities Expense	623

REQUIRED

1. Open the previous balances in the accounts receivable subsidiary ledger as follows: DeGeorge Company, $6,800; Finke Company, $12,700; Hosan Company, $8,100; Supensky Company, $13,600. Open the previous balances in the accounts payable subsidiary ledger as follows: Insley Manufacturing, $4,800; Prejean Distributors, $5,900. Also, open the previous balances in the Accounts Receivable account, $41,200; Office Supplies account, $780; and Accounts Payable account, $10,700. Record the transactions in a cash receipts journal, page 4; or a cash payments journal, page 5.

2. Post to the accounts receivable subsidiary ledger or accounts payable subsidiary ledger.

3. Post to the general ledger.

Checklist of Key Figures

P 9-1   (1) Cash, $44,770

P 9-2   (1) Cash, $37,811

P 9-3   (1) Cash (Cash Receipts Journal), $44,478

P 9-4   (3) Cash, $33,917

Answers to Self-Test Questions

1. b   **2.** d   **3.** c   **4.** a   **5.** b

Special Journals Review Problem

This review problem will test your knowledge of special journals. The working papers are in your Working Papers Manual. The answer to this review problem will be provided by your instructor.

David Trotter is the sole owner of Trotter Paint Supply. He established the following chart of accounts (only those accounts used in this review problem are listed):

Trotter Paint Supply
Chart of Accounts (partial)

ASSETS (100–199)

101	Cash
111	Accounts Receivable
121	Office Supplies
131	Machinery

LIABILITIES (200–299)

201	Accounts Payable

OWNER'S EQUITY (300–399)

301	David Trotter, Capital
311	David Trotter, Drawing

REVENUES (400–499)

401	Sales
402	Sales Returns and Allowances
403	Sales Discounts

COST OF GOODS SOLD (500–599)

501	Purchases
502	Purchases Returns and Allowances
503	Purchases Discounts
511	Freight In

EXPENSES (600–699)

601	Wages Expense
611	Rent Expense
621	Utilities Expense

Transactions for the month of May 19XX (all sales of merchandise on account have terms of 2/10, n30):

May 1	The owner started the firm by investing $75,090.
May 1	Paid rent for the month, $1,230, check no. 1.
May 1	Hired a secretary.
May 2	Purchased goods for $780. Issued check no. 2.
May 2	Purchased $5,890 of merchandise on credit from Clancy Enterprises. Terms are 2/10, n30, invoice no. 89.
May 3	Sold $2,710 of merchandise to Drake and Associates, invoice no. T001.
May 4	Purchased $4,760 of merchandise on account from Salcedo Manufacturing. Terms are 2/10, n30, invoice no. 683.
May 5	Purchased $1,730 of office supplies on credit from Caldwell Office Supply. Terms are n30.
May 8	Purchased $6,740 of merchandise on credit from Tranh Paint Brokers. Terms are 3/20, n30, invoice no. 764.
May 9	Sold $1,040 of merchandise to Gayle Dickerson, invoice no. T002.
May 10	Cash sale of merchandise, $3,460.
May 10	Received a $490 freight bill from Branigan Freight, terms n30.
May 11	Purchased $15,640 of machinery on credit from Holman Manufacturing. Terms are n30.
May 11	Paid the May 2 credit purchase from Clancy Enterprises in full, less a 2 percent discount. Issued check no. 3.
May 12	Received payment in full, less a 2 percent discount, from Drake and Associates.
May 12	Paid invoice no. 683 (Salcedo Manufacturing) in full, less a 2 percent discount. Issued check no. 4.
May 15	Paid the secretary's two-week wages, $550. Issued check no. 5.
May 16	Received a utilities bill, $340. The utilities company is State Electric. Terms are n30.
May 17	Sold $2,180 of machinery (not merchandise inventory) on credit to Adams and Daughters. Terms are n30.
May 18	Purchased $2,530 of merchandise on credit from Ullman's Supply. Terms are 2/20, n30, invoice no. U561.
May 22	Sold $3,190 of merchandise to Floyd Martinsen, invoice no. T003.
May 23	Cash sale of merchandise, $2,810.
May 24	Floyd Martinsen returned $680 of inferior paint. Credit memorandum CM1 was issued.
May 25	Returned $1,320 of damaged paint to Ullman's Supply. Issued debit memorandum DM1.
May 26	Purchased goods for $1,620. Issued check no. 6.
May 26	Paid Tranh Paint Brokers in full, less a 3 percent discount. Issued check no. 7.
May 29	Received a transportation charge bill from Branigan Freight, $620. Terms are n30.
May 30	Purchased $10,020 of merchandise on credit from Tranh Paint Brokers. Terms are 3/20, n30, invoice no. 798.
May 30	Sold $2,160 of merchandise to Floyd Martinsen, invoice no. T004.
May 31	Paid the secretary's two-week wages, $550. Issued check no. 8.
May 31	The owner withdrew $1,500. Issued check no. 9.

REQUIRED

1. Record the May 19XX transactions in the proper journals (page 1 for all).

2. Post to the subsidiary ledgers and general ledger as necessary.

3. Prepare a trial balance from the general ledger.

4. Prepare a schedule of accounts receivable and compare the balance to the controlling account.

5. Prepare a schedule of accounts payable and compare the balance to the controlling account.

Checklist of Key Figures

(2) Cash, $60,811

(3) Trial Balance Totals, $122,245.20

Cash, Petty Cash, and the Change Fund

LEARNING OBJECTIVES

After reading this chapter, discussing the questions, and working the exercises and problems, you will be able to do the following:

1. Record cash receipts

2. Understand bank transactions

3. Understand and use a petty cash system

4. Understand and use a change fund

A variety of special journals were introduced in earlier chapters, including the sales, purchases, cash receipts, and cash payments journals. Any transaction that could not be entered into these special journals was recorded in the general journal.

In this chapter, we will examine the Cash account for United Auto Supply for October 19XX. A petty cash system and a change fund will also be discussed.

Cash Receipts and Deposits

Objective 1
Record cash receipts.

Many merchandising and other firms use cash registers to record sales. Whenever a sale is made, the salesperson or clerk collects the cash, check, or credit card and gives the customer a receipt. At the same time, another receipt or record of the sale is recorded internally in the cash register itself, usually on a roll of paper or tape. Then, at the end of the day, the tape is removed and compared to the actual amount of cash, checks, and/or credit card slips collected.

Cash Receipts

Sometimes the actual amounts collected do not agree with the cash register tape. This could happen for a variety of reasons; for example, the salesperson or clerk could have recorded the sale incorrectly or an incorrect amount of change might have been given to a customer. If any errors occur, you must account for the difference—all transactions must be in balance; that is, debit(s) must equal credit(s). Normally, the cash register tape prevails and is recorded as the sale amount. So, when there is a difference between the cash register tape (sales) and the actual amounts collected, the account **Cash Short or Over** is used.

Assume that on April 10, 19XX, Owens Company had $1,708 in cash and checks. But the cash register tape total was $1,712. Owens is a service-only business and does not use special journals. The general journal entry is as follows:

GENERAL JOURNAL Page ___4___

Date		Description	Post Ref.	Debit	Credit
19XX					
Apr.	10	Cash		1708 —	
		Cash Short or Over		4 —	
		Sales			1712 —
		Cash Sales			

The $4 debit to Cash Short or Over is necessary to balance the transaction. A debit balance in the Cash Short or Over account signifies a miscellaneous *expense*. Miscellaneous *income* occurs whenever a credit balance exists in the Cash Short or Over account.

Let's look at a similar transaction for a merchandising firm that uses special journals. Silva Products, a merchandising firm, had a cash register tape total of $3,487 on December 29, 19XX. Cash and checks on hand totaled $3,489. The entry in the cash receipts journal is as follows:

CASH RECEIPTS JOURNAL   Page ___7___

| | | | Credits | | | Debits | |
| | Account | Post | Other | Accounts | | Sales | |
Date	Credited	Ref.	Accounts	Receiv.	Sales	Disc.	Cash
19XX							
Dec. 29	*Cash Short or Over*	682	2 –		3 4 8 7 –		3 4 8 9 –

This $2 credit to Cash Short or Over would be classified as miscellaneous income. Silva Products accumulated more cash and checks than could be accounted for on the cash register tape.

Cash and Credit Card Receipts

Lakeside Company, a service-only business, started to use a cash register in March 19XX. At the close of the first day of the month, total collections were $21,480 and the cash register tape was $21,484. Credit card purchases made up $6,000 of the sales, and the firm's bank, Second City Bank, charges 6 percent for credit card deposits. Thus, Lakeside Company receives the cash from the bank less the 6 percent charge. This $360 charge ($6,000 × .06 = $360) is recorded as a debit to Credit Card Expense. The general journal entry is as follows:

GENERAL JOURNAL   Page ___10___

Date	Description	Post Ref.	Debit	Credit
19XX				
Mar. 1	Cash		21 1 2 0 –	
	Credit Card Expense		3 6 0 –	
	Cash Short or Over		4 –	
	Sales			21 4 8 4 –
	Sales for March 1			

Even though sales were $21,484, the firm increased cash by only $21,120. This $364 difference was the result of cash and other collections ($21,484 – $21,480 = $4) plus the credit card expense of $360. Thus Cash is debited for $21,120 [$21,484 – ($4 + $360) = $21,484 – $364 = $21,120].

Bank Transactions

Objective 2
Understand bank transactions.

Most firms use a checking account for payments (checks) and receipts (deposits) of cash. Using a checking account improves the internal control of cash by minimizing the amount of cash on hand. All checks and deposits are entered in the firm's bank, thus providing a safe depository for cash, checks, change, stocks, bonds, and so on.

Signature Cards

A checking account is established by filling out a **signature card** (as illustrated in Exhibit 10-1). This card must be signed by the depositor in exactly the same manner as he or she expects to sign checks. A bank teller can then verify the depositor's signature on a check by comparing it to the signature card.

EXHIBIT 10-1   Signature Card

ACCOUNT TITLE			A/C # 12-34567-8
United Auto Supply		The "Company"	TAXPAYER I.D. # **999-00-9999**

h Savings	h Money Market Checking	h Checking Plus	No. of Required	Date
☒ Checking	h Money Market Savings	Interest	Signatures **1**	Opened **1/1/XX**
h Other_____				

	Specimen Signatures	Authorized Signatures Typed Name
(1)	*Lucille Garcia*	**Lucille Garcia**
(2)	*Hu Le*	**Hu Le**
(3)	_____	_____
(4)	_____	_____
(5)	_____	_____

TO: FIRST CITY NATIONAL BANK OF HOUSTON

The Company is: ____ A Corporation   ____ A Partnership   **X** A Sole Proprietorship

____ Unincorporated Association   ____ Other (Specify) _____

Customer Relationship _____

The Company hereby acknowledges receipt of the Rules which govern this account and agrees to abide by those Rules as stated, or as they may be hereafter amended, and all applicable laws or regulations of the State of Texas or the United States of America.

You are hereby authorized to recognize any **1** of the signatures above in the payment of funds of the Company.

By: *Lucille Garcia*

Title: **Owner**
(Pres., V. Pres., or Treasurer)

The Company hereby acknowledges receipt of the Rules which govern this account and agrees to abide by those Rules as stated, or as they may be hereafter amended, and all applicable laws or regulations of the State of Texas or the United States of America.

Hu Le

Title: **Secretary**

Address **100 Main Street, Houston, Texas 77001**

Mailing Address **Same**

Phone **999-9999**	Ref. Off. _____	Ref. Off. **$25,000.00**
Account Opened By: **Dan Smith Assistant Cashier**		Account Opened By: **Joyce Carr, VP**

Deposit Slips

A **deposit slip** or **deposit ticket** is filled out once all currency, checks, coins, and so on are arranged and endorsed. Currency and coins are usually listed first, followed by checks. Each check should be listed separately, with the appropriate name or company stated. United Auto Supply's October 12, 19XX, deposit is illustrated in Exhibit 10-2.

EXHIBIT 10-2 Deposit Slip

DEPOSIT TICKET				DOLLARS	CENTS
DATE October 12 19 XX		CURRENCY			
Checks and other items are received for deposit subject to the provisions of the Uniform Commercial Code or any applicable collection agreement.		COIN			
	35-1/1130	CHECKS	Emma's Auto Repair	1,764	00
		LIST SINGLY			
		BE SURE EACH ITEM IS ENDORSED			
First City National Bank of Houston P.O. Box 2557 Houston, Texas 77252 FIRST CITY		TOTAL FROM OTHER SIDE			
		TOTAL		1,764	00
UNITED AUTO SUPPLY 100 MAIN ST. Ph 713-999-9999 HOUSTON, TX 77001		USE OTHER SIDE FOR ADDITIONAL LISTING NOT NEGOTIABLE **SAMPLE-VOID** DO NOT CASH!			

⑆000067845⑆ 12345678⑈

Endorsements

A check must be *endorsed* before it can be deposited. The check is signed by the **payee**, who is the person directed to receive the amount written on the face of the check. By endorsing the check, the payee transfers the right to receive the check amount. One type of endorsement is a **blank endorsement**, where the payee simply signs the back of the check. A blank endorsement is payable to anyone who cashes or deposits the check. Most firms, however, use a **restrictive endorsement**, where the payee signs the back of the check and then adds such words as "For deposit only," "Pay to the order of," and so on. This restricts the check to be deposited or cashed to a certain bank or individual. An illustration of these two types of endorsements is shown in Exhibit 10-3.

EXHIBIT 10-3 Examples of Endorsements

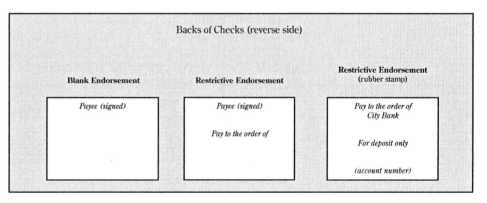

Writing Checks

A **check** directs a bank to pay a certain sum of money to a particular person or firm (payee). All checks should be accounted for in numerical order. Any voided checks should be recorded and listed as VOID.

A check is completed by filling in the date, who the check is to be paid to ("pay to the order of"), and the amount (in figures and words). The check is then signed by the authorized person. United Auto Supply's check number 933 is illustrated in Exhibit 10-4.

EXHIBIT 10-4 Check

UNITED AUTO SUPPLY   0933
100 MAIN ST.   Ph 713-999-9999   Date October 9 ,19 XX
     HOUSTON, TX 77001

PAY
TO THE
ORDER OF___--Boyle Manufacturing--_____ $ | 490.00 |

___Four hundred ninety--------------------------------- DOLLARS

First City National Bank   NOT NEGOTIABLE
    of Houston   **SAMPLE-VOID**
P.O. Box 2557   **F**IRST **CITY**   DO NOT CASH!
Houston, Texas 77252

FOR _____   *Lucille Garcia*_____

⑈000933⑈ ⑆000006784⑈ 123456 78⑈

Bank Statements

Each month, the bank sends a **bank statement** to the depositor (owner of the account) and returns any cancelled checks that have been paid and charged to the depositor's account. The bank statement shows the balance at the beginning of the month, deposits recorded, checks paid, other deposits and payments, and the balance at the end of the month. The bank statement for United Auto Supply for October 31, 19XX, is illustrated in Exhibit 10-5.

General Ledger, Cash Account

The Cash account in the general ledger of United Auto Supply is presented in Exhibit 10-6. The account had an ending balance of $8,208 at October 31, 19XX.

Bank Reconciliation

A **bank reconciliation** is prepared to account for the difference (if any) between the ending balance appearing on the bank statement and the ending balance of Cash in the general ledger. The bank statement (Exhibit 10-5) has an ending balance of $12,623. However, the general ledger shows a balance of $8,208 (Exhibit 10-6). There are a variety of reasons to explain how this discrepancy could occur, some of which follow:

1. **Outstanding Checks:** These are checks issued and recorded by the firm, but not as yet cleared or paid by the bank.

2. **Deposits in Transit:** These are deposits recorded by the firm, but not received by the bank in time to be included on the statement.

3. **Collections:** A firm will often designate a bank to collect certain notes or payments.

4. **Checks with Non-Sufficient Funds (NSF):** Frequently, a firm will unknowingly receive a non-sufficient funds check and deposit it into its bank account. This is a check that is not paid when the firm's bank presents it for payment to the *maker's* (issuer's) bank. The firm's bank will return the check so the firm can collect the amount due. The NSF check must be reclassified from Cash to Accounts Receivable using a bank reconciliation entry.

5. **Interest Earned:** Any interest earned on the checking account must be recorded in the firm's books.

6. **Bank Service Charges:** Banks charge their customers for various services such as handling the firm's account, printing checks, stopping payment on checks, and collections.

EXHIBIT 10-5 Bank Statement

Account Statement

First City National Bank of Houston			Statement Date 10/31/XX
P.O. Box 2557	1001 Main		Page 1
Houston, Texas 77001	PH 713-658-6011		

United Auto Supply
100 Main Street
Houston, Texas 77001
Account 12-34567-8

Previous Balance 9/30/XX	9,645.00
9 Deposits and Other Items	35,578.00
20 Checks and Other Items	32,593.00
Service Charge	7.00
Total Checks and Charges	32,600.00
Ending Balance 10/31/XX	12,623.00

Date Paid	Check Number	Amount	Deposits	Ending Balance
10/01	923	146.00		9,499.00
10/02	924	688.00		8,811.00
10/03	926*	1,700.00	9,800.00	16,911.00
10/05	927	2,900.00	600.00	14,611.00
10/07	929*	270.00		14,341.00
10/09	930	2,450.00	2,100.00	13,991.00
10/13	933*	490.00	1,764.00	15,265.00
10/16	935*	225.00	2,744.00	17,784.00
10/18	934*	3,800.00		13,984.00
10/19	936*	2,608.00		11,376.00
10/22	938*	5,600.00	12,000.00	17,776.00
10/23	939	2,380.00		15,396.00
10/24	940	945.00		14,451.00
10/25	941	2,500.00	5,000.00	16,951.00
10/28	942	1,455.00		15,496.00
10/29	944*	710.00		14,786.00
10/31	946*	1,824.00		
10/31	945*	1,287.00		
10/31			CM 1,500.00	
10/31	SC	7.00		
10/31	RI	600.00		
10/31	DM	15.00	CM 70.00	12,623.00

Codes:	CC	Certified Check	EC	Error Correction
	CM	Credit Memorandum	OD	Overdrawn
	DM	Debit Memorandum	RI	Returned Item
	DC	Deposit Correction	SC	Service Charge

*Check numbers out of sequence

7. Errors: Any error made by either the bank or the firm *must* be corrected. An error made by the firm is usually corrected by a bank reconciliation entry. An error made by the bank is corrected by informing the bank of the error. The bank can then correct the error before the next month's statement is issued.

EXHIBIT 10-6	General Ledger, Cash Account

GENERAL LEDGER ACCOUNTS							
Account: *Cash*						Account No. *101*	
		Post				Balance	
Date	Item	Ref.	Debit	Credit	Debit		Credit
19XX	*Previous Bal.*				7641 –		
Oct. 31		*CR10*	35478 –		43119 –		
31		*CP10*		34911 –	8208 –		

Steps in Preparing the Bank Reconciliation

A bank reconciliation is prepared as follows:

1. Deposits on the bank statement are compared to the deposits recorded in the cash receipts journal or whichever register the firm uses to record deposits. Any deposits recorded in the cash receipts journal—but not on the bank statement—are designated as **Deposits in Transit.**

2. Checks returned with the bank statement should be arranged in numerical order. They should then be compared to the checks listed in the cash payments journal or whichever register the firm uses to record checks. Any checks not returned by the bank should be noted as Outstanding Checks.

3. Any collections, NSF checks, interest earned, and bank service charges listed on the bank statement are compared to the firm's accounting records. For a firm that uses special journals, such as United Auto Supply, this would be the cash receipts and cash payments journals.

4. Any errors, omissions, and/or adjustments that become apparent during the completion of the three previous steps are listed.

Format for a Bank Reconciliation

A format for a bank reconciliation is illustrated in Exhibit 10-7. Any errors or adjustments in the Book Balance section require entries in the general journal to correct the book balance of Cash. Any errors or adjustments in the Bank Balance section do not require entries in the firm's general journal. The bank must be contacted in order to correct these errors.

Bank Reconciliation for United Auto Supply

United Auto Supply received a bank statement (see Exhibit 10-5) for October 31, 19XX, and compared it to the general ledger Cash account (see Exhibit 10-6). To find the difference between these two amounts let's look at the cash receipts journal and cash payments journal for October 19XX (as shown in Exhibit 10-8).

As Hu Le, the accountant for United Auto Supply, prepared the bank reconciliation, she noticed the following adjustments and errors:

1. The October 30, 19XX, deposit of $1,470 did not appear on the bank statement.

2. An outstanding check from the September 19XX bank reconciliation, check number 925, for $1,170 was not returned with the October 31, 19XX, bank statement. Also, four checks issued in October 19XX were outstanding: check number 928, $195; check number 931, $1,200; check number 937, $190; and check number 943, $2,560.

EXHIBIT 10-7 Format for a Bank Reconciliation

Name of Firm
Bank Reconciliation
Date

Bank Balance

Cash Balance per Bank Statement		$ XX
Add: Deposits in Transit	$ XX	
Errors	XX	XX
Subtotal		$ XX
Deduct: Outstanding Checks	$ XX	
Errors	XX	XX
Adjusted Cash Balance per Bank Statement		$ XX

Book Balance

Cash Balance per General Ledger		$ XX
Add: Collections by the Bank	$ XX	
Errors	XX	XX
Subtotal		$ XX
Deduct: Bank Service Charges	$ XX	
Errors	XX	XX
Adjusted Cash Balance per Gereral Ledger		$ XX

EXHIBIT 10-8 Cash Receipts and Cash Payments Journals for United Auto Supply for the Month of October

CASH RECEIPTS JOURNAL Page   10

		Account Credited	Post Ref	Other Accounts	Accounts Receiv.	Sales	Sales Disc.	Cash
Date				Credits			Debits	
19XX								
Oct.	3	Cash Sales	–			9800 –		9800 –
	5	Office Supplies	131	600 –				600 –
	8	Notes Payable	221	2100 –				2100 –
	12	Emma's Auto Repair	✓		1800 –		36 –	1764 –
	14	Montana Company	✓		2800 –		56 –	2744 –
	19	Cash Sales	–			12000 –		12000 –
	25	Lucille Garcia,						
		Capital	301	5000 –				5000 –
	30	Zumwalt Company	✓		1500 –		30 –	1470 –
				7700 –	6100 –	21800 –	122 –	35478 –
				(✓)	(111)	(401)	(403)	(101)

(continued)

Ex. 10-8 (continued)

CASH PAYMENTS JOURNAL Page ____10____

Date	Chk. No.	Account Debited	Post Ref.	Debits Other Accounts	Debits Accounts Payable	Debits Purchases	Credits Purch. Disc.	Credits Cash
19XX								
Oct. 1	926	Rent Expense	601	1700 –				1700 –
2	927	Cash Purchase				2900 –		2900 –
4	928	Utilities Expense	631	195 –				195 –
5	929	Freight In	516	270 –				270 –
5	930	Wages Expense	611	2450 –				2450 –
8	931	Lucille Garcia, Drawing	311	1200 –				1200 –
9	932	VOID						
9	933	Boyle Manufacturing	✓		500 –		10 –	490 –
10	934	Cash Purchases	–			3800 –		3800 –
11	935	Freight In	516	225 –				225 –
12	936	Wages Expense	611	2680 –				2680 –
15	937	Advertising Expense	621	190 –				190 –
17	938	Cash Purchases	–			5600 –		5600 –
19	939	Wages Expense	611	2380 –				2380 –
22	940	Freight In	516	495 –				495 –
23	941	Office Equipment	141	2500 –				2500 –
25	942	Nguyen Distributors	✓		1500 –		45 –	1455 –
26	943	Wages Expense	611	2560 –				2560 –
29	944	Freight In	516	710 –				710 –
30	945	Zamora Warehouse	✓		1300 –		13 –	1287 –
31	946	Mehta Manufacturing	✓		1900 –		76 –	1824 –
				17555 –	5200 –	12300 –	144 –	34911 –
				(✓)	(201)	(501)	(503)	(101)

3. The bank collected $1,500 for United Auto Supply, of which $1,400 is Notes Receivable and $100 is Interest Income. The bank charges a monthly service fee of $7. The deposit made on October 5, 19XX, for $600 was not paid by Duncan Enterprises' bank and was returned as an NSF check. The bank charged United Auto Supply a $15 fee for the returned deposit. The checking account received $70 cash for Interest Income for the month of October 19XX.

4. Check number 936 was incorrectly recorded in the cash payments journal as $2,680. The correct amount was $2,608, which cleared the bank on October 19, 19XX. Check number 940 was also incorrectly recorded in the cash payments journal. The correct amount was $945, which cleared the bank on October 24, 19XX. The incorrect amount written in the cash payments journal was $495.

The completed bank reconciliation is shown in Exhibit 10-9.

EXHIBIT 10-9	Completed Bank Reconciliation

United Auto Supply
Bank Reconciliation
October 31, 19XX

Bank Balance		
Cash Balance per Bank Statement		$12,623 –
Add: Deposits in Transit		1,470 –
Subtotal		$14,093 –
Deduct: Outstanding Checks as Listed:		
Check Number 925	$1,170 –	
Check Number 928	195 –	
Check Number 931	1,200 –	
Check Number 937	190 –	
Check Number 943	2,560 –	5,315 –
Adjusted Cash Balance per Bank Statement		$8,778 –
Book Balance		
Cash Balance per General Ledger		$8,208 –
Add: Collection of Note	$1,400 –	
Collection of Interest on Note	100 –	
Interest on Checking Account	70 –	
Correction of Check Number 936	72 –	1,642 –
Subtotal		$9,850 –
Deduct: Bank Service Charge	$ 7 –	
Returned Check, NSF Check	600 –	
Fee for Returned Check	15 –	
Correction of Check Number 940	450 –	1,072 –
Adjusted Cash Balance per General Ledger		$8,778 –

Bank Reconciliation Entries

Once you are satisfied that the Adjusted Cash Balance per the General Ledger equals the Adjusted Cash Balance per the bank statement you can record bank reconciliation entries in the general journal, not the special journals. There is no actual payment or receipt of cash as there is in the cash payments and cash receipts journals. The Bank Reconciliation general journal entries for United Auto Supply are shown in Exhibit 10-10.

United Auto Supply would attempt to collect $615 ($600 + $15) from Duncan Enterprises to cover both the original receipt and the fee charged by the bank. The $615 should also be posted to the accounts receivable subsidiary ledger for Duncan Enterprises.

General Ledger (Cash) after Bank Reconciliation Entries

The adjusted cash balance of $8,778 would appear on the balance sheet for Cash at October 31, 19XX. Let's look at the Cash account in the general ledger (Exhibit 10-11) after the bank reconciliation entries have been posted.

EXHIBIT 10-10 Bank Reconciliation Entries

GENERAL JOURNAL   Page ___27___

Date		Description	Post Ref.	Debit	Credit
		Bank Reconciliation Entries			
19XX					
Oct.	31	Cash		1500 –	
		Notes Receivable			1400 –
		Interest Income			100 –
		Collection of Note by Bank			
	31	Cash		70 –	
		Interest Income			70 –
		Checking Account Interest			
	31	Cash		72 –	
		Wages Expense			72 –
		Correction of Check Number 936			
	31	Bank Service Expense		7 –	
		Cash			7 –
		Service Charge on Checking Account			
	31	Accounts Receivable – Duncan Enterprises		615 –	
		Cash			615 –
		NSF Check of $600 and $15 Fee by Bank			
	31	Freight In		450 –	
		Cash			450 –
		Correction of Check Number 940			

EXHIBIT 10-11 General Ledger, Cash Account

GENERAL LEDGER ACCOUNTS

Account: *Cash*   Account No. *101*

Date		Item	Post Ref.	Debit	Credit	Balance Debit	Balance Credit
19XX		Previous Bal.				7641 –	
Oct.	31		CR10	35478 –		43119 –	
	31		CP10		34911 –	8208 –	
	31		J27	1500 –		9708 –	
	31		J27	70 –		9778 –	
	31		J27	72 –		9850 –	
	31		J27		7 –	9843 –	
	31		J27		615 –	9228 –	
	31		J27		450 –	8778 –	

The Petty Cash System

Objective 3
Understand and use a petty cash system.

For internal cash control purposes, all payments should be made by check. However, for some small or urgent expenditures, it is not feasible to make all payments by check. Some of these cash payments could include washing the firm's automobile, paying taxi fare, buying a few postage stamps, and so on.

Most firms will set up a **petty cash fund** to pay these small expenditures when it is inconvenient to pay them with a check. A petty cash fund, established for a fixed amount, is referred to as an **imprest system**. (Petty cash is an asset account.)

Establishing the Petty Cash Fund

On November 18, 19XX, Lucille Garcia, the owner of United Auto Supply, decided to establish a petty cash fund for $150, check number 967. She felt that this amount should cover small cash expenditures for an estimated one to two weeks. This transaction would be recorded in the cash payments journal as follows:

CASH PAYMENTS JOURNAL   Page ___11___

| | Chk. | Account | Post | Debits | | | Credits | |
Date	No.	Debited	Ref.	Other Accounts	Accounts Payable	Purchases	Purch. Disc.	Cash
19XX								
Nov. 18	967	Petty Cash	102	150 –				150 –

Petty Cash Disbursements

A **petty cash voucher**, as illustrated in Exhibit 10-12, should be prepared for each expenditure. The custodian of the petty cash fund enters the date, purpose, and amount. The petty cash voucher is signed by the person receiving the payment. For internal control purposes, petty cash vouchers should be prenumbered, and all supporting documentation, such as receipts, should be attached. Lucille Garcia makes Hu Le the custodian of the petty cash fund. In Exhibit 10-12, the first voucher is issued for $2 for washing the firm's automobile.

EXHIBIT 10-12 Prenumbered Petty Cash Voucher

Petty Cash Voucher

Date: November 19, 19XX   No. 001
For: Car Wash
Charge to: Miscellaneous Expense
Amount: $2.00

Frank Rylski
Received by

Petty Cash Reimbursements

The custodian has the responsibility of monitoring the petty cash fund's balance, keeping track of the petty cash vouchers and the cash balance of the fund by means of a **petty cash disbursements record** (as shown in Exhibit 10-13). When the petty cash fund is low(and before it is depleted), it is replenished by a check drawn from the firm's bank account. Each voucher is accounted for, and the disbursements are classified in the appropriate account category. Custodian Hu Le decides to replenish the fund on November 28, 19XX. The fund has a cash balance on hand of $54, and petty cash vouchers 001–004 total $95. The total amount accounted for is thus $149 ($54 + $95).

EXHIBIT 10-13	Petty Cash Disbusements Record

PETTY CASH DISBURSEMENTS RECORD   Page ___1___

Date	Voucher Number	Account Charged	Amount	Fund Balance	Comments
11/18				150.00	Established Fund Check Number 967
11/19	001	Miscellaneous Expense	2.00	148.00	
11/20	002	Office Supplies	26.00	122.00	
11/21	003	Freight In	25.00	97.00	
11/25	004	Postage Expense	42.00	55.00	
11/28				150.00*	Replenished Fund Check Number 989

Petty Cash Reconciliation

The difference of $1 ($150 – $149) is charged to Cash Short or Over. Exhibit 10-14 shows the **petty cash reconciliation** for November 28, 19XX:

EXHIBIT 10-14	Petty Cash Reconciliation

United Auto Supply
Petty Cash Reconciliaion
November 28, 19XX

Beginning Balance, November 18, 19XX			$150 –
Less: Disbursements (vouchers)	$95 –		
Cash on Hand	54 –	149 –	
Difference, Cash Short or Over		$1 –	

*Check number 989 is for $96, which replenishes the fund to $150 (see Exhibit 10-14).

Replenishing the Petty Cash Fund   The entry in the cash payments journal to replenish the petty cash fund would be as follows:

CASH PAYMENTS JOURNAL   Page ___11___

| | | | | | Debits | | | Credits | |
| | Chk. | Account | Post | Other | Accounts | | Purch. | |
Date	No.	Debited	Ref.	Accounts	Payable	Purchases	Disc.	Cash
19XX								
Nov. 28	989	Miscellaneous						
		Expense	691	2 –				
		Office Supplies	131	2 6 –				
		Freight In	516	2 5 –				
		Postage						
		Expense	681	4 2 –				
		Cash Short						
		or Over	682	1 –				9 6 –

Petty Cash Account

The account, Petty Cash, is not debited or credited except in the following situations:

1. The petty cash fund is first established.
2. The amount of the fund's increases. For example, if United Auto Supply increased the size of the fund to $200, a debit is made to Petty Cash for $50 and a credit is made to Cash for $50. This entry in the cash payments journal would be as follows:

CASH PAYMENTS JOURNAL   Page ___12___

| | | | | | Debits | | | Credits | |
| | Chk. | Account | Post | Other | Accounts | | Purch. | |
Date	No.	Debited	Ref.	Accounts	Payable	Purchases	Disc.	Cash
19XX								
Dec. 1	997	Petty Cash	102	5 0 –				5 0 –

3. The amount of the fund's decreases. For example, if United Auto Supply decreased the size of the fund from $150 to $125, a debit is made to Cash for $25 and a credit is made to Petty Cash for $25. This entry in the cash receipts journal would be as follows:

CASH RECEIPTS JOURNAL   Page ___12___

Date		Account Credited	Post Ref.	Credits			Debits	
				Other Accounts	Accounts Receiv.	Sales	Sales Disc.	Cash
19XX								
Dec.	1	Petty Cash	102	2 5 –				2 5 –

4. The petty cash fund is eliminated. In this case, Cash is debited and Petty Cash is credited. If United Auto Supply eliminated the $150 petty cash fund, the entry in the cash receipts journal would be as follows:

CASH RECEIPTS JOURNAL   Page ___12___

Date		Account Credited	Post Ref.	Credits			Debits	
				Other Accounts	Accounts Receiv.	Sales	Sales Disc.	Cash
19XX								
Dec.	1	Petty Cash	102	1 5 0 –				1 5 0 –

The Change Fund

Objective 4
Understand and use a change fund.

At the beginning of this chapter we said that many firms use cash registers to record sales. These firms will establish a **change fund** in the cash register drawer when the following situations occur: (1) there are numerous cash transactions, and (2) to enable the business to make change.

A change fund is a fixed amount of cash that is placed in the cash register drawer. It is used to make change for cash-paying customers. Before establishing the change fund, the firm must first determine the size of the fund and the denominations of coins and bills. For example, a business that establishes a $50 change fund may want $20 of coins and $30 of small bills in its cash register drawer. Let's now examine how a change fund is established.

Establishing the Change Fund

On November 25, 19XX, United Auto Supply decided to establish a $100 change fund. This transaction may be illustrated using T accounts as follows:

Change Fund				Cash	
+	–			+	–
100					100

This transaction would be recorded in the cash payments journal, check number 975, as follows:

CASH PAYMENTS JOURNAL   Page ___11___

Date		Chk. No.	Account Debited	Post Ref.	Debits			Credits	
					Other Accounts	Accounts Payable	Purchases	Purch. Disc.	Cash
19XX									
Nov.	25	975	Change Fund		100 –				100 –

Like the petty cash fund, the account Change Fund will not be debited or credited again unless the firm decided to change the size of the change fund.

Recording Cash Sales

At the end of the business day on November 25, 19XX, United Auto Supply has $410 of cash. The firm's accountant retains the amount of the change fund in convenient denominations, $30 in coins and $70 in small bills (total of $100), and deposits the remainder in a bank. This is determined as follows:

Total cash in cash register drawer	$410
Less: Change fund balance	100
Deposit in bank	$310

This transaction can be shown using T accounts as follows:

Cash			Sales	
+	–		–	+
310				310

The cash received is recorded in the cash receipts journal:

CASH RECEIPTS JOURNAL   Page ___11___

Date		Account Credited	Post Ref.	Credits			Debits	
				Other Accounts	Accounts Receiv.	Sales	Sales Disc.	Cash
19XX								
Nov.	25	Cash Sales				310 –		310 –

Financial Statement Presentation

The Change Fund account is an asset. It is presented on the balance sheet below Cash. The Change Fund account will follow the Petty Cash account if the Petty Cash account balance is larger than the Change Fund account balance. In Exhibit 10-15, Cash, Petty Cash, and Change Fund are shown on a partial balance sheet for United Auto Supply.

EXHIBIT 10-15	Cash, Petty Cash, and Change Fund

United Auto Supply

Balance Sheet (partial)

November 30, 19XX

Assets		
Cash	$10 0 0 0	–
Petty Cash	1 5 0	–
Change Fund	1 0 0	–

Chapter Review

1. **Record cash receipts.**
   Many merchandising and other firms use cash registers to record sales. When there is a difference between the cash register tape (sales) and the actual amounts collected, the account Cash Short or Over is used.

2. **Understand bank transactions.**
   A checking account improves the internal control of cash by minimizing the amount of cash on hand. A checking account is established by filling out a signature card and depositing funds. A bank reconciliation is prepared to account for the difference between the ending balance appearing on the bank statement and the ending balance of Cash in the general ledger.

3. **Understand and use a petty cash system.**
   A petty cash fund can be established to pay small expenditures when it is inconvenient to pay them by check. Petty Cash is an asset account.

4. **Understand and use a change fund.**
   A change fund is a fixed amount of cash that is placed in a cash register drawer. It is established when there are numerous cash transactions and the firm must be able to make change. Like Petty Cash, the account Change Fund is an asset account.

Glossary

Bank Reconciliation Prepared by the depositor to account for the differences between the bank statement balance and the book balance of Cash

Bank Statement Summary of a depositor's Cash account

Blank Endorsement Payee signs the back of the check; payable to anyone who cashes or deposits the check

Cash Short or Over An account that is used to balance an accounting entry

Change Fund A fixed amount of cash that is placed in a cash register drawer

Check An official, preprinted, prenumbered form that directs the maker's bank to pay a specific sum of money to the payee

Deposit Slip Form used to deposit money in a bank account

Depositor Individual or firm that controls or owns a bank account

Deposits in Transit Money that has been deposited in a bank account but is not listed on the current bank statement

Imprest System Petty cash fund established for a fixed amount

Outstanding Checks Checks that have been issued by the depositor, but have not as yet been paid by the bank

Payee Person directed to receive the amount written on the face of a check

Petty Cash Disbursements Record Means of accounting for petty cash payments and reimbursements

Petty Cash Fund Cash account used to pay small expenditures when it is inconvenient to pay them by check

Petty Cash Reconciliation Prepared by the custodian of the petty cash fund to account for disbursements and cash on hand

Petty Cash Voucher Prenumbered form used to record petty cash payments

Restrictive Endorsement Check can only be deposited or cashed by a certain bank or person

Signature Card Form authorizing the appropriate personnel to sign checks for the firm

Self-Test Questions for Review

(Answers are at the end of Chapter 10.)

1. Cash Short or Over is credited in a transaction. This is
   - **a.** a miscellaneous expense.
   - **b.** the cost of goods sold.
   - **c.** an asset.
   - **d.** miscellaneous income.

2. Which of the following is added in the book balance section of a bank reconciliation?
   - **a.** Bank service charges
   - **b.** Outstanding checks
   - **c.** Collections by the bank
   - **d.** Deposits in transit

3. "Collection of Note by Bank" is written as a description for a bank reconciliation entry. _____ is debited.
   - **a.** Cash
   - **b.** Notes Receivable
   - **c.** Interest Income
   - **d.** Accounts Receivable

4. Cash is debited and Petty Cash is credited. This transaction could
   - **a.** establish a change fund.
   - **b.** eliminate a petty cash fund.
   - **c.** increase a petty cash fund.
   - **d.** establish a petty cash fund.

5. Consider the following accounts and account balances (all are normal): Cash, $20,000; Petty Cash, $500; and Change Fund, $700. The balance sheet presentation order is _____ first and _____ third.
   - **a.** Cash; Petty Cash
   - **b.** Petty Cash; Change Fund
   - **c.** Cash; Change Fund
   - **d.** Change Fund; Petty Cash

Practical Review Problem

Objectives 3 and 4

Using a Petty Cash System and Change Fund Goldsmith Paint Supply had the following petty cash, change fund, and cash sales transactions for the week ended April 30, 19XX:

April 26	Established a petty cash fund for $160 (check number 278).
April 27	Established a change fund for $80 (check number 279).
April 27	Cash count, $560.
April 28	Cash count, $430.

April 28	Reimbursed the petty cash fund, check number 280. Cash on hand is $22 and April 27 petty cash vouchers total $136. Voucher 1 ($70) is for store supplies and the remainder is for postage (voucher 2).
April 29	Cash count, $610.
April 30	Increased the petty cash fund to $250, check number 281.
April 30	Cash count, $520.
April 30	Received and reconciled the bank statement. The adjusted Cash balance per the bank statement is $11,070.

REQUIRED

1. Record transactions in the cash payments journal (page 7) or the cash receipts journal (page 4).

2. Prepare a petty cash disbursements record, page 1.

3. Prepare a petty cash reconciliation when the petty cash fund is replenished.

4. Prepare a partial balance sheet on April 30, 19XX, for Cash, Petty Cash, and Change Fund.

Answer to Practical Review Problem

1.   **CASH PAYMENTS JOURNAL**   Page ___7___

Date	Chk. No.	Account Debited	Post Ref.	Other Accounts (Debits)	Accounts Payable (Debits)	Purchases (Debits)	Purch. Disc. (Credits)	Cash (Credits)
19XX								
Apr. 26	278	Petty Cash		160 –				160 –
27	279	Change Fund		80 –				80 –
28	280	Store Supplies		70 –				
		Postage						
		Expense		66 –				
		Cash Short						
		or Over		2 –				138 –
30	281	Petty Cash		90 –				90 –

                        CASH RECEIPTS JOURNAL   Page ___4___

Date	Account Credited	Post Ref.	Other Accounts (Credits)	Accounts Receiv. (Credits)	Sales (Credits)	Sales Disc. (Debits)	Cash (Debits)	
19XX								
Apr. 27	Cash Sales				480 –		480 –	*
28	Cash Sales				350 –		350 –	*
29	Cash Sales				530 –		530 –	*
30	Cash Sales				440 –		440 –	*

*Cash count less change fund.

2. **PETTY CASH DISBURSEMENTS RECORD** Page ____1____

Date	Voucher Number	Account Charged	Amount	Fund Balance	Comments
4/26				160.00	*Established Fund Check*
					Number 278
4/27	1	*Store Supplies*	70.00	90.00	
4/27	2	*Postage Expense*	66.00	24.00	
4/28			**	160.00	*Replenished Fund Check*
					Number 280
4/30				250.00	*Increased Fund Check*
					Number 281

3. **Goldsmith Paint Supply**
Petty Cash Reconciliation
April 28, 19XX

Beginning Balance, April 26, 19XX		$160 –
Less: Disbursements (vouchers)	$136 –	
Cash on Hand	22 –	158 –
Difference, Cash Short or Over		$2 –

4. **Goldsmith Paint Supply**
Balance Sheet (partial)
April 30, 19XX

Assets		
Cash	$11070 –	
Petty Cash	250 –	
Change Fund	80 –	

Discussion Questions

Q 10-1 When is the Cash Short or Over account needed?

Q 10-2 Describe the following in your own words: (a) signature card; (b) deposit slip; (c) check; and (d) bank statement.

Q 10-3 When is a bank reconciliation necessary? What is the purpose of a bank reconciliation?

Q 10-4 Give five reasons for preparing a bank reconciliation.

**Check number 280 is for $138, which replenishes the fund to $160 (see petty cash reconciliation—requirement 3).

Q 10-5   Briefly explain the four steps in preparing a bank reconciliation.

Q 10-6   When are bank reconciliation entries necessary? Name at least four possible bank reconciliation entries that could be journalized in the general journal.

Q 10-7   Why is a petty cash system necessary?

Q 10-8   Briefly describe the process of setting up and replenishing the petty cash fund. When is the account Petty Cash used?

Q 10-9   Name the two situations in which a firm will establish a change fund.

Q 10-10   A firm has a $100 change fund. Cash at the end of a business day totals $270. What is the cash deposit for the day?

Exercises

Objective 1

E 10-1   **Recording Sales**   McCormick Company had total collections of $35,810 for March 19XX. The cash register tape totaled $35,822. A total of $11,500 of the sales were by credit cards, and the firm's bank charges 8 percent for credit card deposits. Prepare a general journal entry to record the March 31, 19XX, sales.

Objective 2

E 10-2   **Preparing a Bank Reconciliation**   Prepare a bank reconciliation for Silberg Company for January 31, 19XX, given the following information:

   a. The cash balance per the general ledger is $9,000.

   b. The cash balance per the bank statement is $10,000.

   c. Interest earned for January 19XX is $50.

   d. Bank service charges are $10.

   e. Outstanding checks total $960.

Objective 1

E 10-3   **Recording Sales**   Bennet Company had a cash register tape of $19,416 and cash and checks on hand of $19,421 on September 30, 19XX. Prepare a general journal entry to record the September sales. Also, prepare an entry in a cash receipts journal to record the sales if the firm used special journals.

Objective 2

E 10-4   **Recording Bank Reconciliation Entries**   Prepare general journal entries to record the following bank reconciliation adjustments, if necessary:

   a. Collection of a note by the bank for $6,500 of which $360 is interest.

   b. A deposit in transit was identified for $1,200.

   c. Four outstanding checks were identified: number A901, $180; number A902, $799; number A908, $1,647; and number A910, $63.

   d. Interest earned for the month is $19.

   e. An NSF check for $700 from Jackowski Company was returned by the bank. The bank charged a $20 fee. The check was for credit purchases.

Objective 3

E 10-5   **Recording Petty Cash Transactions**   Prepare the following entries in a cash payments journal, page 4, for Milligan Company:

   a. On April 14, 19XX, the firm established a petty cash fund for $75, check number 781.

   b. The firm reimbursed the fund on April 18, 19XX, check number 782. Vouchers totaled $68, and cash on hand was $6. All the vouchers were issued for office supplies.

   c. On April 23, 19XX, the firm increased the fund to $125, check number 783.

Objective 2 **E 10-6** **Completing a Bank Reconciliation** Fill in the missing numbers and descriptions for the following bank reconciliation:

BANK BALANCE

Cash Balance per Bank Statement	$1,700
Add: Deposit in Transit	300
Subtotal	$ (a)
Deduct: Outstanding checks	(b)
(c)	$ (d)

BOOK BALANCE

Cash Balance per General Ledger		$ (e)
Add: Collection of Note	$ (f)	
Interest Earned	25	795
Subtotal		$ (g)
Deduct: Bank Service Charge		10
(h)		$1,480

Objective 3 **E 10-7** **Preparing a Petty Cash Reconciliation** Prepare a petty cash reconciliation for Kite Software Supply for February 28, 19XX. Also, prepare an entry in the cash payments journal, page 5, for the reimbursement of the petty cash fund (check number 019) given the following information:

a. The petty cash fund was established on February 4, 19XX, for $165.

b. On February 28, 19XX, cash on hand is $20.

c. The following vouchers were issued: number A19, $22, for Freight In; number A20, $14, for Postage Expense; number A21, $55, for Office Supplies; and number A22, $50, for Miscellaneous Expense.

Objective 4 **E 10-8** **Recording Change Fund Transactions** Consider the following transactions:

a. On November 14, 19XX, Ky Paper Supply establishes a $170 change fund. Record this transaction, first using T accounts and then using a cash payments journal, page 3 (check number 421).

b. At the end of a business day (November 21, 19XX), Ky Paper Supply has $1,260 in cash. Assuming a $170 change fund, record this transaction in a cash receipts journal, page 3.

Problems

Objective 1 **P 10-1** **Recording Deposits** Manning Company's bank fluctuates the rate of credit card percentage charges. The company had the following sales activity for October 19XX:

Date	Cash Register Tape Total	Collection Cash	Collection Credit Card	Collection Total	Credit Card Charge
19XX					
10/3	*$ 12,000*	*$ 11,000*	*$ 1,000*	*$ 12,000*	*6%*
10/11	*74,010*	*67,000*	*7,000*	*74,000*	*10*
10/19	*90,005*	*90,000*	*–0–*	*90,000*	*7*
10/25	*113,616*	*75,610*	*38,000*	*113,610*	*5*
10/30	*49,082*	*40,500*	*8,600*	*49,100*	*8*

REQUIRED

Prepare general journal entries (page 19) to record the deposits.

Objective 2

P 10-2 **Preparing a Bank Reconciliation** The May 19XX bank statement for Hanson's Marine Supply and the May accounting records reveal the following information:

  a. Bank statement balance, $25,890.

  b. Cash account balance, $25,630.

  c. Outstanding checks: number 319, $420; number 331, $190; and number 337, $60.

  d. The May 31, 19XX, deposit of $1,750 did not appear on the bank statement.

  e. The bank collected $1,840 of which $1,800 is Notes Receivable and the remainder is Interest Income.

  f. A deposit made May 14, 19XX, for $780 was not paid by Flannagan Enterprises' bank and was returned as an NSF check. The bank charged a $10 fee for the returned deposit.

  g. Check number 324 cleared the bank correctly for $250. The check was written erroneously for $520 for transportation costs.

  h. Monthly service charge, $20.

  i. Checking account interest income for the month of May, $40.

REQUIRED

1. Prepare a bank reconciliation.

2. Journalize all bank reconciliation entries in the general journal, page 10.

Objectives 3 and 4

P 10-3 **Using a Petty Cash System and Change Fund** Yolanda's Dress Supply had the following petty cash, change fund, and cash sales transactions for the week ended March 31, 19XX:

March 27	Established a petty cash fund for $120 (check number 814).
March 28	Established a change fund for $90 (check number 815).
March 28	Cash count, $1,620.
March 29	Cash count, $1,310.
March 29	Reimbursed the petty cash fund, check number 816. Cash on hand is $36 and March 28 petty cash vouchers total $83. Voucher 1 ($60) is for office supplies and the remainder is for postage (voucher 2).
March 30	Cash count, $1,540.
March 30	Increased the petty cash fund to $200, check number 817.
March 31	Cash count, $1,790.
March 31	Received and reconciled the bank statement. The adjusted Cash balance per the bank statement is $15,630.

REQUIRED

(See Practical Review Problem.)

1. Record transactions in the cash payments journal (page 4) or the cash receipts journal (page 3).

2. Prepare a petty cash disbursements record, page 1.

3. Prepare a petty cash reconciliation when the petty cash fund is replenished.

4. Prepare a partial balance sheet on March 31, 19XX, for Cash, Petty Cash, and Change Fund.

Objective 2

P 10-4 **Comprehensive Bank Reconciliation Problem** Sorensen Company received the following bank statement on January 31, 19XX:

Previous Balance 12/31/XX			3,336.00
5 Deposits and Other Items			5,336.00
6 Checks and Other Items			2,069.00
Service Charge			8.00
Total Checks and Charges			2,077.00
Ending Balance 1/31/XX			6,595.00

Date Paid	Check Number	Amount	Deposits	Ending Balance
1/2			2,150.00	5,486.00
1/4	796	759.00		4,727.00
1/11	797	388.00	513.00	4,852.00
1/19	800*	198.00	1,095.00	5,749.00
1/28	802*	195.00		5,554.00
1/31	SC	8.00		
1/31	RI	513.00		
1/31	DM	16.00		
1/31			CM 1,565.00	
1/31			CM 13.00	6,595.00

Codes:				
CC	Certified Check		EC	Error Correction
CM	Credit Memorandum		OD	Overdrawn
DM	Debit Memorandum		RI	Returned Item
DC	Deposit Correction		SC	Service Charge

*Check numbers out of sequence

Referring to the bank statement: SC 8.00 is a service charge on the checking account; RI 513.00 is an NSF check; DM 16.00 is a fee charged by the bank for the NSF check; CM 1,565.00 is a collection of a note, which includes $115 interest income; and CM 13.00 is checking account interest income.

The Cash account in the general ledger is as follows:

GENERAL LEDGER ACCOUNT						
Account: *Cash*					Account No. *102*	
Date	Item	Post Ref.	Debit	Credit	Balance Debit	Balance Credit
19XX	Previous Bal.				2948 –	
Jan. 31		CR8	4150 –		7098 –	
31		CP9		3171 –	3927 –	

The cash receipts journal is as follows:

CASH RECEIPTS JOURNAL   Page ___8___

Date	Account Credited	Post Ref.	Credits Other Accounts	Accounts Receiv.	Sales	Debits Sales Disc.	Cash
19XX							
Jan. 2	Cash Sales	–			2150 –		2150 –
11	Kay Sawyer	✓		513 –			513 –
19	Cash Sales	–			1095 –		1095 –
31	Larry Caesia	✓		400 –		8 –	392 –
				913 –	3245 –	8 –	4150 –
				(108)	(401)	(403)	(102)

The cash payments journal is as follows:

CASH PAYMENTS JOURNAL   Page ___9___

Date	Chk. No.	Account Debited	Post Ref.	Debits Other Accounts	Accounts Payable	Purchases	Credits Purch. Disc.	Cash
19XX								
Jan. 1	796	Rent Expense	601	795 –				795 –
5	797	Goyle Manufacturing	✓		400 –		12 –	388 –
10	798	VOID						
10	799	Finn Distributors	✓		219 –			219 –
16	800	Advertising Expense	621	198 –				198 –
21	801	Thomas Warehouse	✓		800 –		24 –	776 –
27	802	Cash Purchases	–			195 –		195 –
31	803	Wages Expense	611	600 –				600 –
				1593 –	1419 –	195 –	36 –	3171 –
				(✓)	(202)	(503)	(505)	(102)

Check number 789 for $388 is outstanding from the previous month's bank reconciliation. Check number 796 was incorrectly recorded in the cash payments journal as $795. The check cleared the bank correctly at $759.

REQUIRED

1. Prepare a bank reconciliation.

2. Journalize all bank reconciliation entries in the general journal, page 16.

3. Post the bank reconciliation entries to the cash account in the general ledger (include all previous balances).

Checklist of Key Figures

P 10-1   No key figure

P 10-2   (1) Adjusted Cash Balance, $ 26,970

P 10-3   (3) Cash Short or Over, $1

P 10-4   (1) Adjusted Cash Balance, $5,004

Answers to Self-Test Questions

1. d   **2.** c   **3.** a   **4.** b   **5.** a

11

Adjustments and Worksheets for a Merchandising Firm

LEARNING OBJECTIVES

After reading this chapter, discussing the questions, and working the exercises and problems, you will be able to do the following:

 1. Calculate adjustments including:
a. Merchandise Inventory
b. Deferrals
c. Accruals

2. Prepare a worksheet for a merchandising firm

3. Journalize and post adjusting entries

Earlier we completed the discussion of a service operation or firm, and the accounting records of the service firm were cleared for the next accounting period. Revenues, expenses, Drawing, and Income Summary were closed to Capital. Then, after the closing entries were journalized and posted, a post-closing trial balance was prepared.

In previous chapters we recorded the transactions for United Auto Supply, a merchandising firm. In this chapter we will begin the closing process by preparing adjusting entries and a worksheet. In the next chapter, financial statements will be prepared, along with closing entries and a post-closing trial balance.

Merchandise Inventory Adjustments

Objective 1
Calculate adjustments.

Remember that United Auto Supply uses the *periodic* method to account for merchandise inventory. When using this method, you must count the actual amount of merchandise inventory on hand at the end of the accounting period. This actual amount becomes the *ending balance* of Merchandise Inventory for the accounting period. The beginning balance must therefore be eliminated. So the first adjustment is to eliminate beginning Merchandise. (These adjusting entries will be identified in order by a, b, and so on.)

(a) Beginning Merchandise Inventory   United Auto Supply started the October 19XX accounting period with $8,209 of merchandise inventory. An adjustment is necessary to eliminate Merchandise Inventory for October 19XX.

We will use the Income Summary account when adjusting for Merchandise Inventory because the adjustment is part of the closing process, and the accounting records must be properly set for the next accounting period. When the periodic method is used, Merchandise Inventory must be adjusted to reflect its actual balance at the end of the accounting period. Therefore, the beginning balance of Merchandise Inventory must be closed, and the ending balance must be opened. To illustrate the adjustment for beginning Merchandise Inventory, we'll use T accounts:

Merchandise Inventory		Income Summary	
(10/1) Balance 8,209	(a) 8,209	(a) 8,209	
Balance after closing beginning inventory – 0–		8,209	

This adjustment clears the beginning Merchandise Inventory balance.

(b) Ending Merchandise Inventory   On October 31, 19XX, the end of the accounting period, Frank Rylski counted the auto parts (merchandise inventory) on hand. He determined that $8,285 of inventory was on hand. Because United Auto Supply uses the periodic method of accounting for Merchandise Inventory, we must make an adjustment so this balance can be reflected in the accounting records. Let's use T accounts to illustrate the adjustment for ending Merchandise Inventory:

Merchandise Inventory		Income Summary	
(b) 8,285			(b) 8,285

Merchandise inventory is a balance sheet account, so by making this adjusting entry we will place the correct amount of Merchandise Inventory in the balance sheet. Let's now account for the *deferral* type of adjusting entries for United Auto Supply.

Deferral Adjustments

A deferral is necessary whenever one or both of the following situations occur:

1. Expenses have been paid to apply to future accounting periods.
2. Revenues have been received to apply to future accounting periods.

(c) Office Supplies Adjustment   On October 31, 19XX, United Auto Supply's accountant, Hu Le, counted $2,500 of office supplies on hand at the end of the accounting period. She made the following calculation:

Office, Supplies Available to Be Used	$2,700
Less: October 31, 19XX, Count (Ending Balance)	2,500
Office Supplies Used (Expensed) for the Month	$ 200

To record this adjustment, Office Supplies Expense is debited $200, and Office Supplies is credited $200. Let's use T accounts to illustrate this adjusting entry:

Office Supplies Expense		Office Supplies	
(c) 200			(c) 200

(d) Prepaid Insurance Adjustment   United Auto Supply paid $1,800 for a twelve-month insurance policy on January 1, 19XX. In October 19XX, $150 is allocated as follows:

$1,800 ÷ 12 Months = $150 per Month Expense Allocation

T accounts may be used to show this adjusting entry:

Insurance Expense		Prepaid Insurance	
(d) 150			(d) 150

(e) Depreciation Adjustment: Office Equipment   United Auto Supply uses the straight-line depreciation method where an equal amount of Depreciation Expense is allocated to each accounting period over that asset's useful life. Office equipment costs $15,500 and is estimated to have a $1,100 salvage value at the end of its useful life of four years. In October 19XX, $300 is allocated as follows:

$$\text{Office Equipment Depreciation Expense for October 19XX} = \frac{\$15,500 - \$1,100}{48 \text{ Months}}$$

$$= \frac{\$14,400}{48 \text{ Months}}$$

$$= \$300$$

Using T accounts again to illustrate this adjusting entry:

Depreciation Expense, Office Equipment		Accumulated Depreciation, Office Equipment	
(e) 300			(e) 300

(f) Earned Revenue Adjustment Many firms receive payment for revenues in advance—before the revenues are actually earned. For example, theaters sell season tickets in advance, and magazine subscriptions are paid in advance. On September 1, 19XX, United Auto Supply received $3,000 from Hobbs Car Sales for future sales of merchandise. The entry to record this receipt of cash is as follows:

CASH RECEIPTS JOURNAL   Page ___9___

			Credits			Debits	
Date	Account Credited	Post Ref.	Other Accounts	Accounts Receiv.	Sales	Sales Disc.	Cash
19XX							
Sep. *1*	*Unearned Sales*						
	Revenue	231	3000 –				3000 –

Cash is received and is debited. **Unearned Sales Revenue** is a liability account and is credited. This account indicates that the firm has an obligation to deliver merchandise inventory in the future.

United Auto Supply delivers $1,500 of the merchandise in October 19XX. We'll use T accounts again to demonstrate this adjusting entry:

Unearned Sales Revenue		Sales	
	(10/1 Bal.) 3,000		
(f) 1,500			(f) 1,500
	(10/31 Bal.) 1,500		

Accrual Adjustments

An accrual is necessary whenever one or both of the following situations occur:

1. Expenses are incurred but unrecorded.

2. Revenues are earned but unrecorded.

The accrual adjustment that will be examined for United Auto Supply is for an expense that has been incurred but is not yet recorded.

(g) Wages Expense Adjustment United Auto Supply pays its employees every week on Friday. October 31, 19XX, the last day of the accounting period, was on a Wednesday:

October 19XX

S	M	T	W	T	F	S
	1	2	3	4	5	6
7	8	9	10	11	12	13
14	15	16	17	18	19	20
21	22	23	24	25	26	27
28	29	30	㉛	1	②	

Last Day of Accounting Period ⟶ ㉛   ② ◀—— Payday

If an adjusting entry is not made, then five days (Saturday to Wednesday) of Wages Expense will be entered in the November accounting records. An accrual type of adjusting entry is necessary, since the actual cash payment of wages and salaries will not be made until Friday, November 2, 19XX. Let's use T accounts to demonstrate this adjusting entry:

Wages Expense		Wages Payable	
(g) 1,600			(g) 1,600

The Worksheet

Objective 2
Prepare a worksheet for a merchandising firm.

The trial balance is prepared directly from the general ledger accounts. It is entered on a ten-column worksheet in Exhibit 11-1. (Notice that Merchandise Inventory, a balance sheet account, is included.)

Trial Balance Columns of the Worksheet

In Exhibit 11-1, the trial balance as of October 31, 19XX, before adjustments, is entered on the worksheet. You should add the columns again to be sure that total debits equal total credits before you proceed.

Adjustments Columns of the Worksheet

In Exhibit 11-2, the adjustments prepared earlier in this chapter are entered on the worksheet. Each adjustment is lettered consecutively. Some adjustments may need accounts that have not been used previously in the Trial Balance. These accounts should be listed below the Trial Balance in order of usage. DO NOT try to list these added accounts in chart-of-accounts order because this is unnecessary and, if you have a large number of Adjustments, an error could occur easily.

The two Adjustments columns must be totaled, and total debits must equal total credits before you continue to the Adjusted Trial Balance.

Adjusted Trial Balance Columns

Once the Trial Balance and Adjustments columns are entered and totaled, the Adjusted Trial Balance columns are prepared (see Exhibit 11-3). This step is crucial because an error here will cause the Income Statement and Balance Sheet columns to be incorrect. Those accounts with no adjustments (such as Cash, Sales Discounts, and so on) should be extended to the proper Adjusted Trial Balance column with their balance "as is." Those accounts that have adjustments (such as Prepaid Insurance, Wages Expense, and so on) should be added or subtracted. The resulting balances are extended to the Adjusted Trial Balance. The Adjusted Trial Balance columns are then added, and total debits must equal total credits before you proceed to the next step. At this time it is a good idea to be sure that all account balances are normal; that is, Cash is a debit, Notes Payable is a credit, and so on.

Income Statement and Balance Sheet Columns

In Exhibit 11-4 we will extend the Adjusted Trial Balance account balances to the appropriate Debit or Credit column of the Income Statement or Balance Sheet columns. We have done this before, so you should be familiar with this procedure. However, since we have not prepared a worksheet with Merchandise Inventory, we should examine the steps to account for merchandise inventory on the worksheet:

1. Determine the ending balance of Merchandise Inventory for the accounting period.
2. Enter the adjusting entry for beginning Merchandise Inventory on the worksheet. The beginning Merchandise Inventory balance is debited to Income Summary and credited to Merchandise Inventory. At this time Merchandise Inventory will have a zero balance.

EXHIBIT 11-1 Trial Balance on the Worksheet

United Auto
Work
For the Month Ended

Account	Trial Balance		Adjustments	
	Debit	Credit	Debit	Credit
Cash	8 7 7 8 –			
Accounts Receivable	15 8 3 7 –			
Merchandise Inventory	8 2 0 9 –			
Office Supplies	2 7 0 0 –			
Prepaid Insurance	4 5 0 –			
Office Equipment	15 5 0 0 –			
Accumulated Depreciation, Office Equipment		6 0 0 –		
Accounts Payable		8 8 0 0 –		
Notes Payable (long term)		2 1 0 0 –		
Unearned Sales Revenue		3 0 0 0 –		
Lucille Garcia, Capital		34 1 0 0 –		
Lucille Garcia, Drawing	1 2 0 0 –			
Sales		41 2 0 0 –		
Sales Returns and Allowances	7 8 –			
Sales Discounts	1 2 2 –			
Interest Income		1 7 0 –		
Purchases	23 1 0 0 –			
Purchases Returns and Allowances		4 0 0 –		
Purchases Discounts		1 4 4 –		
Freight In	2 4 5 0 –			
Rent Expense	1 7 0 0 –			
Wages Expense	9 9 9 8 –			
Advertising Expense	1 9 0 –			
Utilities Expense	1 9 5 –			
Bank Service Expense	7 –			
Totals	90 5 1 4 –	90 5 1 4 –		

Supply
sheet
October 31, 19XX

Adjusted Trial Balance		Income Statement		Balance Sheet	
Debit	Credit	Debit	Credit	Debit	Credit

EXHIBIT 11-2	Adjustments Columns on the Worksheet

United Auto
Work
For the Month Ended

Account	Trial Balance		Adjustments	
	Debit	Credit	Debit	Credit
Cash	8 7 7 8 –			
Accounts Receivable	15 8 3 7 –			
Merchandise Inventory	8 2 0 9 –		(b)8 2 8 5 –	(a) 8 2 0 9 –
Office Supplies	2 7 0 0 –			(c) 2 0 0 –
Prepaid Insurance	4 5 0 –			(d) 1 5 0 –
Office Equipment	15 5 0 0 –			
Accumulated Depreciation, Office Equipment		6 0 0 –		(e) 3 0 0 –
Accounts Payable		8 8 0 0 –		
Notes Payable (long term)		2 1 0 0 –		
Unearned Sales Revenue		3 0 0 0 –	(f)1 5 0 0 –	
Lucille Garcia, Capital		34 1 0 0 –		
Lucille Garcia, Drawing	1 2 0 0 –			
Sales		41 2 0 0 –		(f)1 5 0 0 –
Sales Returns and Allowances	7 8 –			
Sales Discounts	1 2 2 –			
Interest Income		1 7 0 –		
Purchases	23 1 0 0 –			
Purchases Returns and Allowances		4 0 0 –		
Purchases Discounts		1 4 4 –		
Freight In	2 4 5 0 –			
Rent Expense	1 7 0 0 –			
Wages Expense	9 9 9 8 –		(g)1 6 0 0 –	
Advertising Expense	1 9 0 –			
Utilities Expense	1 9 5 –			
Bank Service Expense	7 –			
Totals	90 5 1 4 –	90 5 1 4 –		
Income Summary			(a)8 2 0 9 –	(b)8 2 8 5 –
Office Supplies Expense			(c) 2 0 0 –	
Insurance Expense			(d) 1 5 0 –	
Depreciation Expense, Office Equipment			(e) 3 0 0 –	
Wages Payable				(g)1 6 0 0 –
			20 2 4 4 –	20 2 4 4 –

Supply
sheet
October 31, 19XX

Adjusted Trial Balance		Income Statement		Balance Sheet	
Debit	Credit	Debit	Credit	Debit	Credit

EXHIBIT 11-3 Adjusted Trial Balance Columns on the Worksheet

United Auto
Work
For the Month Ended

Account	Trial Balance Debit	Trial Balance Credit	Adjustments Debit	Adjustments Credit
Cash	8778—			
Accounts Receivable	15837—			
Merchandise Inventory	8209—		(b)8285—	(a)8209—
Office Supplies	2700—			(c)200—
Prepaid Insurance	450—			(d)150—
Office Equipment	15500—			
Accumulated Depreciation, Office Equipment		600—		(e)300—
Accounts Payable		8800—		
Notes Payable (long term)		2100—		
Unearned Sales Revenue		3000—	(f)1500—	
Lucille Garcia, Capital		34100—		
Lucille Garcia, Drawing	1200—			
Sales		41200—		(f)1500—
Sales Returns and Allowances	78—			
Sales Discounts	122—			
Interest Income		170—		
Purchases	23100—			
Purchases Returns and Allowances		400—		
Purchases Discounts		144—		
Freight In	2450—			
Rent Expense	1700—			
Wages Expense	9998—		(g)1600—	
Advertising Expense	190—			
Utilities Expense	195—			
Bank Service Expense	7—			
Totals	90514—	90514—		
Income Summary			(a)8209—	(b)8285—
Office Supplies Expense			(c)200—	
Insurance Expense			(d)150—	
Depreciation Expense, Office Equipment			(e)300—	
Wages Payable				(g)1600—
			20244—	20244—

Supply
sheet
October 31, 19XX

Adjusted Trial Balance		Income Statement		Balance Sheet	
Debit	Credit	Debit	Credit	Debit	Credit
8778 –					
15837 –					
8285 –					
2500 –					
300 –					
15500 –					
	900 –				
	8800 –				
	2100 –				
	1500 –				
	34100 –				
1200 –					
	42700 –				
78 –					
122 –					
	170 –				
23100 –					
	400 –				
	144 –				
2450 –					
1700 –					
11598 –					
190 –					
195 –					
7 –					
8209 –	8285 –				
200 –					
150 –					
300 –					
	1600 –				
100699 –	100699 –				

EXHIBIT 11-4   Income Statement and Balance Sheet Columns

United Auto
Work
For the Month Ended

Account	Trial Balance Debit	Trial Balance Credit	Adjustments Debit	Adjustments Credit
Cash	8 7 7 8 –			
Accounts Receivable	15 8 3 7 –			
Merchandise Inventory	8 2 0 9 –		(b)8 2 8 5 –	(a) 8 2 0 9 –
Office Supplies	2 7 0 0 –			(c) 2 0 0 –
Prepaid Insurance	4 5 0 –			(d) 1 5 0 –
Office Equipment	15 5 0 0 –			
Accumulated Depreciation, Office Equipment		6 0 0 –		(e) 3 0 0 –
Accounts Payable		8 8 0 0 –		
Notes Payable (long term)		2 1 0 0 –		
Unearned Sales Revenue		3 0 0 0 –	(f)1 5 0 0 –	
Lucille Garcia, Capital		34 1 0 0 –		
Lucille Garcia, Drawing	1 2 0 0 –			
Sales		41 2 0 0 –		(f)1 5 0 0 –
Sales Returns and Allowances	7 8 –			
Sales Discounts	1 2 2 –			
Interest Income		1 7 0 –		
Purchases	23 1 0 0 –			
Purchases Returns and Allowances		4 0 0 –		
Purchases Discounts		1 4 4 –		
Freight In	2 4 5 0 –			
Rent Expense	1 7 0 0 –			
Wages Expense	9 9 9 8 –		(g)1 6 0 0 –	
Advertising Expense	1 9 0 –			
Utilities Expense	1 9 5 –			
Bank Service Expense	7 –			
Totals	90 5 1 4 –	90 5 1 4 –		
Income Summary			(a)8 2 0 9 –	(b)8 2 8 5 –
Office Supplies Expense			(c) 2 0 0 –	
Insurance Expense			(d) 1 5 0 –	
Depreciation Expense, Office Equipment			(e) 3 0 0 –	
Wages Payable				(g)1 6 0 0 –
			20 2 4 4 –	20 2 4 4 –
Net Income				

Supply
sheet
October 31, 19XX

Adjusted Trial Balance		Income Statement		Balance Sheet	
Debit	Credit	Debit	Credit	Debit	Credit
8778–				8778–	
15837–				15837–	
8285–				8285–	
2500–				2500–	
300–				300–	
15500–				15500–	
	900–				900–
	8800–				8800–
	2100–				2100–
	1500–				1500–
	34100–				34100–
1200–				1200–	
	42700–		42700–		
78–		78–			
122–		122–			
	170–		170–		
23100–		23100–			
	400–		400–		
	144–		144–		
2450–		2450–			
1700–		1700–			
11598–		11598–			
190–		190–			
195–		195–			
7–		7–			
8209–	8285–	8209–	8285–		
200–		200–			
150–		150–			
300–		300–			
	1600–				1600–
100699–	100699–	48299–	51699–	52400–	49000–
		3400–			3400–
		51699–	51699–	52400–	52400–

3. Enter the adjusting entry for ending Merchandise Inventory on the worksheet. The ending Merchandise Inventory balance is debited to Merchandise Inventory and credited to Income Summary.

4. The balances of Merchandise Inventory (second line below Cash) are added and subtracted. The resulting balance is the ending Merchandise Inventory balance for the accounting period. This amount is extended to the Debit column of the Adjusted Trial Balance and Balance Sheet.

5. The Income Summary debit and credit amounts are extended "as is" to the Adjusted Trial Balance and Income Statement columns.

Referring to Exhibit 11-4, the Income Statement and Balance Sheet columns are added and totaled. Net income or net loss places the worksheet in balance.

Finding and Correcting Worksheet Errors

Errors can occur when the worksheet is prepared. Whenever you discover an error, follow these steps:

1. Read the columns to make sure the error was not due to incorrect addition.

2. Be sure that net income or net loss is correct. The net income or net loss should place the worksheet in balance.

3. Check to see if all account balances are normal; that is, Cash has a debit balance, Notes Payable a credit balance, and so on.

4. Check to see if beginning and ending Merchandise Inventory were properly eliminated and restated, respectively.

You MUST correct any errors before you prepare financial statements.

Journalizing and Posting Adjustments

Objective 3
Journalize and post adjusting entries.

Adjusting entries provide a means of placing assets, liabilities, owner's equity, revenue, cost of goods sold, and expense accounts at their proper balances for the accounting period. Adjusting entries are not journalized and posted until the worksheet is complete. This way you can see the "full picture" of how the financial statements will look. By looking at the completed worksheet, you can determine whether or not any additional accounts need to be adjusted. Once you are satisfied with the account balances on the worksheet, you can journalize and post adjusting entries. The adjusting entries are taken directly from the Adjustments columns of the worksheet. The adjusting entries as calculated earlier in this chapter are as follows:

a. Adjust Beginning Inventory.

b. Adjust Ending Inventory.

c. Adjust Office Supplies.

d. Adjust Prepaid Insurance.

e. Adjust Office Equipment.

f. Adjust Unearned Revenue.

g. Adjust Wages Expense.

These seven adjusting entries are journalized in the general journal in Exhibit 11-5 and posted to the general ledger in Exhibit 11-6. Indicate in the general journal and general ledger that these entries and postings are from adjusting entries. In the general journal write "Adjusting Entries" in the Description column before the first adjustment is entered. It is unnecessary to write a description for each adjusting entry since you have indicated that they are adjusting entries. When you post the adjusting entry to the general ledger write "Adjusting" in the Item column. You are then able to distinguish adjusting entries from other entries.

These adjusting entries are posted to the general ledger in Exhibit 11-6, but only those general ledger accounts that are used for this posting process are listed.

EXHIBIT 11-5 Journalizing Adjusting Entries

GENERAL JOURNAL Page 28

Date		Description	Post Ref.	Debit	Credit
		Adjusting Entries			
19XX					
Oct.	31	Income Summary	321	8209 –	
		Merchandise Inventory	121		8209 –
	31	Merchandise Inventory	121	8285 –	
		Income Summary	321		8285 –
	31	Office Supply Expense	641	200 –	
		Office Supplies	131		200 –
	31	Insurance Expense	651	150 –	
		Prepaid Insurance	135		150 –
	31	Depreciation Expense, Office Equipment	661	300 –	
		Accumulated Expense, Office Equipment	142		300 –
	31	Unearned Sales Revenue	231	1500 –	
		Sales	401		1500 –
	31	Wages Expense	611	1600 –	
		Wages Payable	211		1600 –

EXHIBIT 11-6 General Ledger Accounts Used to Post Adjusting Entries

Account: Merchandise Inventory — Account No. 121

Date		Item	Post Ref.	Debit	Credit	Balance Debit	Credit
19XX		Previous Bal.				8209 –	
Oct.	31	Adjusting	J28		8209 –	–0–	
	31	Adjusting	J28	8285 –		8285 –	

Account: Office Supplies — Account No. 131

Date		Item	Post Ref.	Debit	Credit	Balance Debit	Credit
19XX		Previous Bal.				2700 –	
Oct.	31	Adjusting	J28		200 –	2500 –	

(continued)

Ex. 11-6 (continued)

Account: *Prepaid Insurance*					Account No. 135	
		Post			Balance	
Date	Item	Ref.	Debit	Credit	Debit	Credit
19XX	Previous Bal.				450 —	
Oct. 31	Adjusting	J28		150 —	300 —	

Account: *Accumulated Depreciation, Office Equipment*					Account No. 142	
		Post			Balance	
Date	Item	Ref.	Debit	Credit	Debit	Credit
19XX	Previous Bal.					600 —
Oct. 31	Adjusting	J28		300 —		900 —

Account: *Wages Payable*					Account No. 211	
		Post			Balance	
Date	Item	Ref.	Debit	Credit	Debit	Credit
19XX	Previous Bal.					—0—
Oct. 31	Adjusting	J28		1600 —		1600 —

Account: *Unearned Sales Revenue*					Account No. 231	
		Post			Balance	
Date	Item	Ref.	Debit	Credit	Debit	Credit
19XX	Previous Bal.					3000 —
Oct. 31	Adjusting	J28	1500 —			1500 —

Account: *Income Summary*					Account No. 321	
		Post			Balance	
Date	Item	Ref.	Debit	Credit	Debit	Credit
19XX	Previous Bal.				—0—	—0—
Oct. 31	Adjusting	J28	8209 —		8209 —	
31	Adjusting	J28		8285 —		76 —

(continued)

Ex. 11-6 (concluded)

Account: Sales   Account No. 401

Date		Item	Post Ref.	Debit	Credit	Balance Debit	Balance Credit
19XX		Previous Bal.					4 1 2 0 0 —
Oct.	31	Adjusting	J28		1 5 0 0 —		4 2 7 0 0 —

Account: Wages Expenses   Account No. 611

Date		Item	Post Ref.	Debit	Credit	Balance Debit	Balance Credit
19XX		Previous Bal.				9 9 9 8 —	
Oct.	31	Adjusting	J28	1 6 0 0 —		1 1 5 9 8 —	

Account: Office Supply Expense   Account No. 641

Date		Item	Post Ref.	Debit	Credit	Balance Debit	Balance Credit
19XX		Previous Bal.				— 0 —	
Oct.	31	Adjusting	J28	2 0 0 —		2 0 0 —	

Account: Insurance Expense   Account No. 651

Date		Item	Post Ref.	Debit	Credit	Balance Debit	Balance Credit
19XX		Previous Bal.				— 0 —	
Oct.	31	Adjusting	J28	1 5 0 —		1 5 0 —	

Account: Depreciation Expense, Office Equipment   Account No. 661

Date		Item	Post Ref.	Debit	Credit	Balance Debit	Balance Credit
19XX		Previous Bal.				— 0 —	
Oct.	31	Adjusting	J28	3 0 0 —		3 0 0 —	

Chapter Review

1. **Calculate adjustments.**
   When the periodic inventory method is used, you must count the actual amount of merchandise inventory on hand at the end of the accounting period. This actual amount becomes the ending balance of Merchandise Inventory for the accounting period. The beginning balance of Merchandise Inventory must therefore be eliminated.

   Many firms receive payment for revenues in advance, before the revenues are actually earned. This is a "deferral-revenue" type of adjustment.

2. **Prepare a worksheet for a merchandising firm.**
   A worksheet is prepared for a merchandising firm by (a) listing the trial balance on the worksheet, (b) entering the adjustments in the Adjustments columns, (c) extending the Trial Balance columns and the Adjustments columns to the Adjusted Trial Balance columns, and (d) extending the account balances to the appropriate Income Statement and Balance Sheet columns.

3. **Journalize and post adjusting entries.**
   Adjusting entries are NOT journalized and posted until the worksheet is complete. This way you can see the "full picture" of how the financial statements will look. By looking at the completed worksheet, you can determine if any additional accounts need to be adjusted. Once you are satisfied with the account balances on the worksheet, you can journalize and post adjusting entries. The adjusting entries are taken directly from the Adjustments columns of the worksheet.

Glossary

Unearned Sales Revenue Obligation to deliver merchandise inventory in the future; a liability account

Self-Test Questions for Review

(Answers are at the end of Chapter 11.)

1. Which of the following accounts is debited in the adjusting entry to eliminate merchandise inventory?
   a. Merchandise Inventory
   b. Income Summary
   c. Owner, Capital
   d. Accounts Receivable

2. Cash would probably be listed under which of the following columns on a completed ten-column worksheet?
   a. Trial Balance, Credit
   b. Balance Sheet, Credit
   c. Balance Sheet, Debit
   d. Income Statement, Debit

3. The account _____ is credited in the adjusting entry to adjust Unearned Revenue.
   a. Sales
   b. Wages Payable
   c. Income Summary
   d. Unearned Sales Revenue

4. Which of the following is an accrual adjustment?
   a. Adjust Office Supplies
   b. Adjust Prepaid Insurance
   c. Adjust Unearned Revenue
   d. Adjust Wages Expense

5. The account _____ is debited in the adjusting entry to adjust ending Merchandise Inventory.
   a. Owner, Capital
   b. Merchandise Inventory
   c. Income Summary
   d. Accounts Payable

Practical Review Problem

Objective 2

Completing a Worksheet   H. M. Tovar is the owner of Tovar Clothing Store. He had the following partial worksheet.

REQUIRED
1. Using the Trial Balance and Adjusted Trial Balance columns, calculate and place adjusting entries in the Adjustments columns of the worksheet (use the sequence as illustrated in the chapter).
2. Complete the worksheet.

Tovar Clothing Store
Worksheet (partial)
For the Month Ended August 30, 19XX

Account	Trial Balance Debit	Trial Balance Credit	Adjusted Trial Balance Debit	Adjusted Trial Balance Credit
Cash	2518—		2518—	
Merchandise Inventory	1216—		2588—	
Office Supplies	1412—		1268—	
Prepaid Insurance	1800—		1512—	
Furniture	12000—		12000—	
Notes Payable (long-term)		5800—		5800—
Unearned Sales Revenue		3883—		3620—
H. M. Tovar, Capital		9324—		9324—
H. M. Tovar, Drawing	1099—		1099—	
Sales		5969—		6232—
Sales Return and Allowances	217—		217—	
Sales Discounts	64—		64—	
Purchases	3662—		3662—	
Purchases Return and Allowances		126—		126—
Purchases Discounts		98—		98—
Freight In	100—		100—	
Wages Expense	1112—		1390—	
Totals	25200—	25200—		
Income Summary			1216—	2588—
Office Supplies Expense			144—	
Insurance Expense			288—	
Depreciation Expense, Furniture			110—	
Accumulated Depreciation, Furniture				110—
Wages Payable				278—
			28176—	28176—
Net Income				

Answer to Practical Review Problem

1 and 2.

Tovar Clothing
Work
For the Month Ended

Account	Trial Balance		Adjustments	
	Debit	Credit	Debit	Credit
Cash	2518–			
Merchandise Inventory	1216–		(b) 2588–	(a) 1216–
Office Supplies	1412–			(c) 144–
Prepaid Insurance	1800–			(d) 288–
Furniture	12000–			
Notes Payable (long-term)		5800–		
Unearned Sales Revenue		3883–	(f) 263–	
H. M. Tovar, Capital		9324–		
H. M. Tovar, Drawing	1099–			
Sales		5969–		(f) 263–
Sales Return and Allowances	217–			
Sales Discounts	64–			
Purchases	3662–			
Purchases Return and Allowances		126–		
Purchases Discounts		98–		
Freight In	100–			
Wages Expense	1112–		(g) 278–	
Totals	25200–	25200–		
Income Summary			(a) 1216–	(b) 2588–
Office Supplies Expense			(c) 144–	
Insurance Expense			(d) 288–	
Depreciation Expense, Furniture			(e) 110–	
Accumulated Depreciation, Furniture				(e) 110–
Wages Payable				(g) 278–
			4887–	4887–
Net Income				

Discussion Questions

Q 11-1 Briefly explain the necessary adjusting entries that are to close and open Merchandise Inventory.

Q 11-2 Why is Income Summary used to record the opening and closing balances of Merchandise Inventory in an accounting period?

Q 11-3 How are adjustments for beginning and ending Merchandise Inventory entered on the worksheet?

Q 11-4 Explain why the Adjusted Trial Balance columns are necessary to complete a worksheet.

Q 11-5 Name and briefly discuss the three types of adjusting entries explained in this chapter. (Hint: One type is accruals.)

Store

sheet

April 30, 19XX

Adjusted Trial Balance		Income Statement		Balance Sheet	
Debit	Credit	Debit	Credit	Debit	Credit
2 5 1 8 –				2 5 1 8 –	
2 5 8 8 –				2 5 8 8 –	
1 2 6 8 –				1 2 6 8 –	
1 5 1 2 –				1 5 1 2 –	
12 0 0 0 –				12 0 0 0 –	
	5 8 0 0 –				5 8 0 0 –
	3 6 2 0 –				3 6 2 0 –
	9 3 2 4 –				9 3 2 4 –
1 0 9 9 –				1 0 9 9 –	
	6 2 3 2 –		6 2 3 2 –		
2 1 7 –		2 1 7 –			
6 4 –		6 4 –			
3 6 6 2 –		3 6 6 2 –			
	1 2 6 –		1 2 6 –		
	9 8 –		9 8 –		
1 0 0 –		1 0 0 –			
1 3 9 0 –		1 3 9 0 –			
1 2 1 6 –	2 5 8 8 –	1 2 1 6 –	2 5 8 8 –		
1 4 4 –		1 4 4 –			
2 8 8 –		2 8 8 –			
1 1 0 –		1 1 0 –			
	1 1 0 –				1 1 0 –
	2 7 8 –				2 7 8 –
28 1 7 6 –	28 1 7 6 –	7 1 9 1 –	9 0 4 4 –	20 9 8 5 –	19 1 3 2 –
		1 8 5 3 –			1 8 5 3 –
		9 0 4 4 –	9 0 4 4 –	20 9 8 5 –	20 9 8 5 –

Q 11-6   Name the columns used in a worksheet for a merchandising firm, starting with the Trial Balance columns.

Q 11-7   Briefly describe the procedures (steps) in preparing a worksheet, starting with the Trial Balance.

Q 11-8   If you were the accountant for a merchandising firm, which adjusting entries would you probably have at the end of each accounting period?

Q 11-9   Name and briefly discuss the procedures (steps) for finding and correcting worksheet errors.

Q 11-10   Name the five steps to account for Merchandise Inventory on the worksheet.

Exercises

Objective 1   **E 11-1** **Adjusting Merchandise Inventory**   Use T accounts to record the following adjustments: (a) beginning merchandise inventory was $75,000; and (b) ending merchandise inventory is $80,000.

Objective 2   **E 11-2** **Determining Account Placements**   Find the placement (Column, Debit, or Credit) of the following accounts on a completed worksheet for a merchandising firm. Assume adjustments for Merchandise Inventory and Earned Sales Revenue. The first is completed for you.

0. Cash—Trial Balance, Debit; Adjusted Trial Balance, Debit; and Balance Sheet, Debit.

a. Merchandise Inventory.

b. Notes Payable (long-term).

c. Unearned Sales Revenue.

d. Sales.

e. Income Summary.

Objective 3   **E 11-3** **Describing Adjusting Entries**   In your own words, describe the following adjusting entries (in random order) for April 30, 19XX:

GENERAL JOURNAL   Page ____5____

Date		Description	Post Ref.	Debit	Credit
		Adjusting Entries			
19XX					
Oct.	*30*	*Unearned Sales Revenue*	*231*	*6 0 0 –*	
		Sales	*401*		*6 0 0 –*
	30	*Income Summary*	*322*	*3 8 0 0 –*	
		Merchandise Inventory	*129*		*3 8 0 0 –*
	30	*Depreciation Expense, Truck*	*678*	*3 0 0 –*	
		Accumulated Expense, Truck	*146*		*3 0 0 –*
	30	*Wages Expense*	*603*	*1 9 0 0 –*	
		Wages Payable	*222*		*1 9 0 0 –*
	30	*Insurance Expense*	*641*	*2 0 0 –*	
		Prepaid Insurance	*125*		*2 0 0 –*
	30	*Merchandise Inventory*	*129*	*4 9 0 0 –*	
		Income Summary	*322*		*4 9 0 0 –*
	30	*Office Supply Expense*	*666*	*4 0 0 –*	
		Office Supplies	*131*		*4 0 0 –*

Objective 1   **E 11-4** **Adjusting Equipment and Earned Revenue**   Consider the following adjustments for the month ended January 31, 19XX:

a. Equipment costs $18,840 and is estimated to have a $3,000 salvage value at the end of its useful life of six years. Illustrate this adjustment using T accounts. (Use the straight-line method.)

b. On January 3, 19XX, a firm received $3,800 from Parsons, Inc., for future sales of merchandise. During the month, the firm delivers $1,200 of merchandise to Parsons, Inc. In your answer (1) record the receipt of cash in a cash receipts journal, page 4; and (2) illustrate the adjusting entry using T accounts.

Objective 1   **E 11-5** **Illustrating Adjusting Entries** Use T accounts to illustrate the following adjustments:

a. Store Supplies used, $400.

b. Adjust Prepaid Insurance, $100.

c. Depreciation of truck, $200.

d. A total of $700 of previously Unearned Sales Revenue was earned.

e. Accrued Wages Expense, $900.

Objective 2   **E 11-6** **Completing a Worksheet** Complete a worksheet for Clancy Enterprises for August 31, 19XX. Notice that the adjusting entries are included.

Clancy Enterprises
Worksheet (partial)
For the Month Ended August 31, 19XX

Account	Trial Balance Debit	Trial Balance Credit	Adjustments Debit	Adjustments Credit
Cash	3 8 –			
Merchandise Inventory	1 8 –		(b) 2 2 –	(a) 1 8 –
Unearned Sales Revenue		2 1 –	(c) 5 –	
Oliver Clancy, Capital		2 9 –		
Oliver Clancy, Drawing	5 –			
Sales		9 6 –		(c) 5 –
Sales Returns and Allowances	8 –			
Sales Discounts	4 –			
Purchases	6 7 –			
Purchases Returns and Allowances		9 –		
Purchase Discounts		5 –		
Freight In	6 –			
Wages Expense	1 4 –		(d) 3 –	
Totals	1 6 0 –	1 6 0 –		
Income Summary			(a) 1 8 –	(b) 2 2 –
Wages Payable				(d) 3 –

Objective 3   **E 11-7** **Journalizing Adjusting Entries** Record the following adjusting entries in a general journal, page 19, for the month ended June 30, 19XX:

a. Merchandise Inventory on June 1, 19XX, was $9,200.

b. Merchandise Inventory on June 30, 19XX, was $7,900.

c. Office Supplies used during the month, $400.

d. Insurance Expense was $200 for the month.

e. Depreciation of an automobile, $300.

f. Earned $2,100 of previously Unearned Sales Revenue.

g. Wages Expense incurred but not paid, $3,400.

Objective 2   **E 11-8**   **Completing a Worksheet**   Complete the worksheet for Robinson Supply for April 30, 19XX, using the following adjusting entries and Trial Balance:

a. April 1, 19XX, Merchandise Inventory was $18.

b. April 30, 19XX, Merchandise Inventory was $19.

c. Depreciation Expense, Truck, $2.

d. Unearned Sales Revenue of $11 was earned.

e. Wages Expense incurred but not paid, $17.

Robinson Supply
Worksheet (partial)
For the Month Ended August 30, 19XX

	Trial Balance	
Account	Debit	Credit
Cash	44 —	
Accounts Receivable	21 —	
Merchandise Inventory	18 —	
Truck	96 —	
Accumulated Depreciation, Truck		12 —
Unearned Sales Revenue		15 —
G. W. Robinson, Capital		140 —
G. W. Robinson, Drawing	13 —	
Sales		113 —
Sales Returns and Allowances	6 —	
Sales Discounts	3 —	
Purchases	53 —	
Purchases Returns and Allowances		7 —
Purchase Discounts		4 —
Freight In	3 —	
Wages Expense	34 —	
Totals	291 —	291 —

Problems

Objective 2   **P 11-1**   **Completing a Worksheet**   Gunnels Pharmacy, owned by David Gunnels, had the following Trial Balance and Adjustments columns of the worksheet for October 31, 19XX:

Gunnels Pharmacy

Worksheet (partial)

For the Month Ended October 31, 19XX

Account	Trial Balance Debit	Trial Balance Credit	Adjustments Debit	Adjustments Credit
Cash	21900–			
Accounts Receivable	17400–			
Merchandise Inventory	9600–		(b)9800–	(a)9600–
Office Supplies	5700–			(c)2200–
Prepaid Insurance	3800–			(d) 500–
Delivery Truck	26300–			
Accumulated Depreciation, Delivery Truck		5400–		(e) 200–
Accounts Payable		16300–		
Unearned Sales Revenue		2800–	(f)1700–	
David Gunnels, Capital		56000–		
David Gunnels, Drawing	1500–			
Sales		29700–		(f)1700–
Sales Returns and Allowances	1600–			
Purchases	15100–			
Purchases Returns and Allowances		900–		
Freight In	1200–			
Wages Expense	6300–		(g) 800–	
Rent Expense	700–			
Totals	111100–	111100–		
Income Summary			(a)9600–	(b)9800–
Office Supplies Expense			(c)2200–	
Insurance Expense			(d) 500–	
Depreciation Expense, Delivery Truck			(e) 200–	
Wages Payable				(g) 800–
			24800–	24800–

REQUIRED

Complete the worksheet.

Objective 3 **P 11-2 Journalizing and Posting Adjustments** Sawyer Software Supply had the following adjustments and partial chart-of-accounts numbers for the month ended April 30, 19XX. Adjustments:

a. April 1, 19XX, Merchandise Inventory was $5,700.

b. April 30, 19XX, Merchandise Inventory was $6,100.

c. Office Supplies used during the month, $500.

d. Insurance Expense was $100 for the month.

e. Depreciation of office equipment, $200.

f. Unearned Sales Revenue earned during the month was $900.

g. Accrued Wages Expense, $1,900.

Partial chart-of-accounts numbers (previous balances in parentheses):

Merchandise Inventory, 131 ($5,700); Office Supplies, 141 ($3,200); Prepaid Insurance, 145 ($2,100); Accumulated Depreciation, Office Equipment, 152 ($1,200); Wages Payable, 211 ($-0-); Unearned Sales Revenue, 241 ($4,600); Income Summary, 331 ($-0-); Sales, 401 ($21,300); Wages Expense, 621 ($3,900); Office Supplies Expense, 651 ($-0-); Insurance Expense, 661 ($-0-); and Depreciation Expense, Office Equipment, 671 ($-0-).

REQUIRED

1. Enter the account names, account numbers, and previous balances in the general ledger.

2. Journalize the adjusting entries in the general journal, page 21.

3. Post the adjusting entries to the general ledger.

Objectives 2 and 3   **P 11-3**   **Completing a Worksheet and Journalizing Adjustments**   Howard Flowers, the owner of Flowers Music Store, had the following partial worksheet:

Flowers Music Store

Worksheet (partial)

For the Month Ended March 31, 19XX

Account	Trial Balance Debit	Trial Balance Credit	Adjusted Trial Balance Debit	Adjusted Trial Balance Credit
Cash	5050—		5050—	
Accounts Receivable	1250—		1250—	
Merchandise Inventory	3940—		4890—	
Office Supplies	1980—		960—	
Prepaid Insurance	950—		760—	
Computer	17500—		17500—	
Accumulated Depreciation, Computer		750—		1000—
Accounts Payable		3480—		3480—
Unearned Sales Revenue		1280—		520—
Howard Flowers, Capital		24720—		24720—
Howard Flowers, Drawing	890—		890—	
Sales		12890—		13650—
Sales Discounts	280—		280—	
Purchases	7630—		7630—	
Purchases Discounts		380—		380—
Freight In	580—		580—	
Wages Expense	2890—		3630—	
Rent Expense	560—		560—	
Totals	43500—	43500—		
Income Summary			3940—	4890—
Office Supplies Expense			1020—	
Insurance Expense			190—	
Depreciation Expense, Computer			250—	
Wages Payable				740—
			49380—	49380—
Net Income				

REQUIRED

1. Using the Trial Balance and Adjusted Trial Balance columns, calculate and place adjusting entries in the Adjustments columns of the worksheet (use the sequence as illustrated in the chapter). See the Practical Review Problem if you need help.

2. Complete the worksheet.

3. Journalize the adjusting entries in the general journal, page 26. DO NOT post to the general ledger.

Objectives 1, 2, and 3

P 11-4

Comprehensive Chapter Review Problem   Elaine Dixon owns Midwest Card Store. She had the following Trial Balance columns of the worksheet and adjusting entries for January 31, 19XX:

Midwest Card Store

Worksheet (partial)

For the Month Ended January 31, 19XX

Account	Trial Balance	
	Debit	Credit
Cash	14045 –	
Accounts Receivable	2781 –	
Merchandise Inventory	6999 –	
Office Supplies	1612 –	
Prepaid Insurance	2567 –	
Equipment	17000 –	
Accumulated Depreciation, Equipment		1500 –
Accounts Payable		1003 –
Unearned Sales Revenue		5770 –
Elaine Dixon, Capital		35397 –
Elaine Dixon, Drawing	1200 –	
Sales		13453 –
Sales Returns and Allowances	335 –	
Sales Discounts	421 –	
Interest Income		1813 –
Purchases	9073 –	
Purchases Returns and Allowances		666 –
Purchase Discounts		954 –
Freight In	299 –	
Wages Expense	3899 –	
Advertising Expense	325 –	
Totals	60556 –	60556 –

Adjusting entries:

a. Merchandise Inventory for January 1, 19XX, $6,999.

b. Merchandise Inventory for January 31, was $8,452.

c. An actual count of office supplies on January 31, 19XX, revealed $789 on hand.

d. A total of $77 of Prepaid Insurance was used during the month.

e. Equipment cost $17,000 and will have a useful life of ten years; the salvage value is $2,000; and the straight-line method of depreciation is used.

f. A total of $609 of Unearned Sales Revenue was earned during the month.

g. Accrued Wages Expense, $700.

The chart-of-accounts numbers (partial) are as follows: 112, Merchandise Inventory; 125, Office Supplies; 134, Prepaid Insurance; 146, Accumulated Depreciation, Equipment; 208, Wages Payable; 214, Unearned Sales Revenue; 324, Income Summary; 405, Sales; 605, Wages Expense; 631, Office Supplies Expense; 641, Insurance Expense; 651, Depreciation Expense, Equipment.

REQUIRED
1. Complete the worksheet.
2. Journalize the adjusting entries in a general journal, page 36.
3. From the Trial Balance columns on the worksheet, open the previous account balances in the general ledger (include account names and numbers). Post the adjusting entries to the general ledger.

Checklist of Key Figures

P 11-1   Net Income, $3,900

P 11-2   No key figure

P 11-3   (2) Net Income, $840

P 11-4   (1) Net Income, $2,871

Answers to Self-Test Questions

1. b   2. c   3. a   4. d   5. b

Financial Statements and Closing Entries for a Merchandising Firm

Earlier we began the closing process for United Auto Supply by adjusting Merchandise Inventory. In this chapter we will finish the closing process by preparing closing entries and a post-closing trial balance. Financial statements will be prepared and analyzed to measure performance and to state the firm's financial position. You will also have the option of using *reversing entries* for certain adjusting entries.

EXHIBIT 12-1 Income Statement and Balance Sheet Columns of the Worksheet

United Auto Supply
Worksheet
For the Month Ended October 31, 19XX

Account	Income Statement Debit	Income Statement Credit	Balance Sheet Debit	Balance Sheet Credit
Cash			8 7 7 8 —	
Accounts Receivable			15 8 3 7 —	
Merchandise Inventory			8 2 8 5 —	
Office Supplies			2 5 0 0 —	
Prepaid Insurance			3 0 0 —	
Office Equipment			15 5 0 0 —	
Accumulated Depreciation, Office Equipment				9 0 0 —
Accounts Payable				8 8 0 0 —
Notes Payable (long term)				2 1 0 0 —
Unearned Sales Revenue				1 5 0 0 —
Lucille Garcia, Capital				34 1 0 0 —
Lucille Garcia, Drawing			1 2 0 0 —	
Sales		42 7 0 0 —		
Sales Returns and Allowances	7 8 —			
Sales Discounts	1 2 2 —			
Interest Income		1 7 0 —		
Purchases	23 1 0 0 —			
Purchases Returns and Allowances		4 0 0 —		
Purchases Discounts		1 4 4 —		
Freight In	2 4 5 0 —			
Rent Expense	1 7 0 0 —			
Wage Expense	11 5 9 8 —			
Advertising Expense	1 9 0 —			
Utilities Expense	1 9 5 —			
Bank Service Expense	7 —			
Totals				
Income Summary	8 2 0 9 —	8 2 8 5 —		
Office Supplies Expense	2 0 0 —			
Insurance Expense	1 5 0 —			
Depreciation Expense, Office Equipment	3 0 0 —			
Wages Payable				1 6 0 0 —
	48 2 9 9 —	51 6 9 9 —	52 4 0 0 —	49 0 0 0 —
Net Income	3 4 0 0 —			3 4 0 0 —
	51 6 9 9 —	51 6 9 9 —	52 4 0 0 —	52 4 0 0 —

(continued)

Ex. 12-1 (concluded)

GENERAL LEDGER ACCOUNT								
Account: *Lucille Garcia, Capital*							Account No. *301*	
		Post					Balance	
Date	Item	Ref.	Debit	Credit			Debit	Credit
19XX	Previous Bal.							2 9 1 0 0 –
Oct. 25		CR10		5 0 0 0 –				3 4 1 0 0 –

Preparing Financial Statements

Objective 1
Prepare financial statements.

Previously we completed the worksheet for United Auto Supply for the month ended October 31, 19XX. To help us prepare financial statements, the Income Statement and Balance Sheet columns of this worksheet are illustrated in Exhibit 12-1. Included in Exhibit 12-1 is the owner's Capital account in the general ledger. The first financial statement that we will prepare is the income statement. We will then prepare the statement of owner's equity, followed by the balance sheet.

The Income Statement

We are now ready to prepare a **detailed income statement**, so called because each unique part is stated separately. For example, revenues are either classified as a part of Sales or listed under the caption "Other Revenue." Costs and expenses are separated into two categories: Cost of Goods Sold or Operating Expenses. Let's examine each part of the detailed income statement.

Revenues from Sales   For a merchandising firm, the revenues section of the income statement will be different than one for a service-type firm in three ways:

1. Revenues for a merchandising firm consist of sales of resalable merchandise versus service revenues for a service firm.
2. Sales Returns and Allowances and Sales Discounts must be subtracted from Sales, if appropriate, to arrive at Net (final) Sales.
3. Any other type of revenue earned—other than sales of merchandise inventory—must be listed under "Other Revenue" at the end of the income statement. This is because Cost of Goods Sold is subtracted from Net Sales to arrive at the gross profit on sales. This proper matching of revenues (Net Sales) and costs (Cost of Goods Sold) is consistent with the Matching Principle. Remember that with the Matching Principle we wanted to get a proper matching of the appropriate revenues and the associated costs or expenses.

Using the Income Statement columns in Exhibit 12-1, the Revenue from Sales section for United Auto Supply for October 19XX is as follows:

United Auto Supply
Income Statement (partial)
For the Month Ended October 31, 19XX

Revenue from Sales				
Sales			$42 7 0 0 –	
Less: Sales Returns and Allowances	$ 7 8 –			
Sales Discounts	1 2 2 –	2 0 0 –		
Net Sales				$42 5 0 0 –

The two contra accounts, Sales Returns and Allowances and Sales Discounts, are summed. They are then subtracted from Sales to arrive at the final or Net Sales amount.

Cost of Goods Sold   The Cost of Goods Sold section of the income statement is used by a merchandising firm to comply with the Matching Principle. Remember that the Matching Principle requires that the associated costs be allocated or matched to the revenues for an accounting period. Therefore Cost of Goods Sold represents the cost of the merchandise sold in the accounting period. The format to arrive at Cost of Goods Sold is as follows:

Cost of Goods Sold			
Merchandise Inventory, Beginning Date		$XX	
Purchases	$XX		
Less: Purchases Returns and Allowances	XX		
Purchases Discounts	XX		
Net Purchases		XX	
Freight In		XX	
Cost of Goods Available for Sale			$XX
Less: Merchandise Inventory, Ending Date			XX
Cost of Goods Sold			$XX

As you can see, in the Cost of Goods Sold format, four amount columns are used. Starting from the right is Cost of Goods Sold, determined by subtracting the amount of Merchandise Inventory on hand at the end of the accounting period from the total amount of Cost of Goods Available for Sale. The Cost of Goods Available for Sale is either sold (Cost of Goods Sold) or unsold (Merchandise Inventory, Ending Date).

Cost of Goods Available for Sale is calculated by adding the beginning Merchandise Inventory, Net Purchases, and Freight In. Net Purchases results from subtracting the two contra accounts, Purchases Returns and Allowances and Purchases Discounts, from Purchases.

This detailed listing of the Cost of Goods Sold section should enable the reader to go into as much depth as necessary. One person may only want to examine the total of Cost of Goods Sold whereas another may want to see Net Purchases. The income statement provides an uncluttered and informative form for the reader.

Using the Income Statement columns in Exhibit 12-1, the Cost of Goods Sold section of the income statement for United Auto Supply can be prepared. On October 31, 19XX, the end of the accounting period, Frank Rylski counted the auto parts (Merchandise Inventory). He determined that $8,285 of inventory was on hand. This is the ending

Merchandise Inventory for this accounting period, and it will be the beginning Merchandise Inventory for the next accounting period. This section of the income statement for October 19XX is prepared as follows:

United Auto Supply
Income Statement (partial)
For the Month Ended October 31, 19XX

Cost of Goods Sold				
Merchandise Inventory, October 1		$8 2 0 9 –		
Purchases	$23 1 0 0 –			
Less: Purchases Returns and Allowances	4 0 0 –			
Purchases Discounts	1 4 4 –			
Net Purchases		22 5 5 6 –		
Freight In		2 4 5 0 –		
Cost of Goods Available for Sale			$33 2 1 5 –	
Less: Merchandise Inventory, October 31			8 2 8 5 –	
Cost of Goods Sold				$24 9 3 0 –

A detailed income statement for United Auto Supply is completed in Exhibit 12-2.

Gross Profit on Sales   Subtracting Cost of Goods Sold from Net Sales on the income statement yields **Gross Profit on Sales** (see Exhibit 12-2). This balance represents the profit from sales after the appropriate cost of those sales has been applied. This balance is very important because a firm must sell its merchandise at a price that is high enough to cover the cost of sales (Cost of Goods Sold) and operating expenses. However, the firm's merchandise must also be competitively priced.

Operating Expenses   Expenses that occur in the normal course of business are called *Operating Expenses*. These are needed to conduct everyday business activities. The Operating Expenses for United Auto Supply (see Exhibit 12-2) total $14,340.

Income from Operations   Total Operating Expenses are subtracted from Gross Profit on Sales to arrive at **Income from Operations** (see Exhibit 12-2). This amount represents the profit or loss from normal business activities, that is, what the firm is primarily in business for.

Other Revenue   Any other types of revenues for a merchandising firm (such as interest income, dividend income, revenues from performing services, and so on) are included under **Other Revenue.** For example, a grocery store is in business to sell food, but this store would also most likely have interest income from checking and savings accounts, dividend income from stock investments, and so on. These transactions are not part of the normal course of business—food sales—but occur as a result of being in business and making various decisions. The firm would therefore separate these revenue accounts out from grocery sales. United Auto Supply had interest income from its bank checking account and a note. This $170 is listed under Other Revenue.

EXHIBIT 12-2   Completed Detailed Income Statement

United Auto Supply
Income Statement
For the Month Ended October 31, 19XX

Revenue from Sales				
Sales			$42 700 —	
Less: Sales Returns and Allowances		$ 78 —		
Sales Discounts		1 22 —	2 00 —	
Net Sales				$42 500 —
Cost of Goods Sold				
Merchandise Inventory, October 1		$8 209 —		
Purchases	$23 100 —			
Less: Purchases Returns and Allowances	4 00 —			
Purchases Discounts	1 44 —			
Net Purchases		22 556 —		
Freight In		2 450 —		
Cost of Goods Available for Sale			$33 215 —	
Less: Merchandise Inventory October 31			8 285 —	
Cost of Goods Sold				24 930 —
Gross Profit on Sales				$17 570 —
Operating Expenses				
Rent Expense			$1 700 —	
Wages Expense			11 598 —	
Advertising Expense			1 90 —	
Utilities Expense			1 95 —	
Bank Service Expense			7 —	
Office Supplies Expense			2 00 —	
Insurance Expense			1 50 —	
Depreciation Expense, Office Equipment			3 00 —	
Total Operating Expenses				14 340 —
Income from Operations				$3 230 —
Other Revenue				
Interest Income				1 70 —
Net Income				$3 400 —

Net Income   Net income is determined by adding Other Revenue and Income from Operations. In Exhibit 12-2, we see that Net Income for United Auto Supply is $3,400.

The Statement of Owner's Equity

We will use the Balance Sheet columns of the worksheet and the owner's Capital account in the general ledger to prepare the statement of owner's equity. Exhibit 12-3 shows a statement of owner's equity for United Auto Supply:

EXHIBIT 12-3 Statement of Owner's Equity

<table>
<tr><td colspan="2" align="center">**United Auto Supply**</td></tr>
<tr><td colspan="2" align="center">**Statement of Owner's Equity**</td></tr>
<tr><td colspan="2" align="center">**For the Month Ended October 31, 19XX**</td></tr>
<tr><td>*Lucille Garcia, Capital, October 31*</td><td>$29|1|0|0| –</td></tr>
<tr><td>*Add: Net Income for October*</td><td>3|4|0|0| –</td></tr>
<tr><td>*Additional Investment*</td><td>5|0|0|0| –</td></tr>
<tr><td>*Subtotal*</td><td>$37|5|0|0| –</td></tr>
<tr><td>*Less: Lucille Garcia, Drawing*</td><td>1|2|0|0| –</td></tr>
<tr><td>*Lucille Garcia, Capital, October 31*</td><td>$36|3|0|0| –</td></tr>
</table>

The Balance Sheet

A balance sheet can be prepared after the income statement and statement of owner's equity. We will use the Balance Sheet columns in Exhibit 12-1 and the Statement of Owner's Equity to prepare the balance sheet. The balance sheet prepared in Exhibit 12-4 is called a **classified balance sheet** because it separates (or classifies) various accounts. The assets of the firm are divided into two categories: Current Assets, and Property, Plant, and Equipment. Three other asset categories—Investments, Intangible Assets, and Other Assets—are also commonly used but are not applicable to United Auto Supply at this time. Liabilities are separated into two categories: Current and Long-term.

Assets

Current Assets   Considered to be the most liquid assets, **Current Assets** will be realized into cash within the normal cycle of a business, which is generally twelve months. Current Assets are listed in order of their *liquidity*, that is, their convertibility into cash. Cash would obviously be listed first. Accounts Receivable is usually realized (cash collected) within a month or a few months. Merchandise Inventory would be sold for cash or on account. Office Supplies and Prepaid Expenses are considered to be Current Assets because cash is paid to buy these assets, which will be used up (consumed) within the normal cycle of a business.

Investments   If applicable, **Investments** would be listed next. Investments are long-term assets that will not be used by the firm within the normal cycle of business. Some examples would include land held for future use, equipment not used in the business, and so on.

EXHIBIT 12-4   Classified Balance Sheet

United Auto Supply
Balance Sheet
October 31, 19XX

Assets			
Current Assets			
Cash	$8 7 8 –		
Accounts Receivable	15 8 3 7 –		
Merchandise Inventory	8 2 8 5 –		
Office Supplies	2 5 0 0 –		
Prepaid Insurance	3 0 0 –		
Total Current Assets		$35 7 0 0 –	
Property, Plant, and Equipment			
Office Equipment	$15 5 0 0 –		
Less: Accumulated Depreciation	9 0 0 –	14 6 0 0 –	
Total Assets		$50 3 0 0 –	
Liabilities			
Current Liabilities			
Accounts Payable	$8 8 0 0 –		
Wages Payable	1 6 0 0 –		
Unearned Sales Revenue	1 5 0 0 –		
Total Current Liabilities		$11 9 0 0 –	
Long-Term Liabilities			
Notes Payable		2 1 0 0 –	
Total Liabilities		$14 0 0 0 –	
Owner's Equity			
Lucille Garcia, Capital		36 3 0 0 –	
Total Liabilities and Owner's Equity		$50 3 0 0 –	

Property, Plant, and Equipment   Under this heading you would find long-term assets that are used in the continuing operations of the firm. Accumulated Depreciation is placed below each depreciable asset to present the book value of that asset. Office Equipment, in Exhibit 12-4, would have a book value of $14,600 ($15,500 – $900).

Intangible Assets   Following Property, Plant, and Equipment are **Intangible Assets**. These are long-term assets that have a value but do not have any physical substance. The value is based on the privileges or rights that belong to the owner. Some examples would include patents, copyrights, and trademarks.

Other Assets   If applicable, **Other Assets** would be listed next. This category would include any assets that cannot be placed under the first four categories. United Auto

Supply does not need this category because all its assets can be classified using the established categories.

Liabilities

Current Liabilities   Obligations or debts that are due to be paid by United Auto Supply to others within the normal **cycle of business** (one year) of a business are called **Current Liabilities**. Accounts Payable, Wages Payable, and Unearned Sales Revenue are some examples.

Long-Term Liabilities   Obligations or debts that are due to be paid in more than one year, or the normal cycle, are called **Long-Term Liabilities**. Some examples would include Notes Payable (long-term), Mortgages Payable, and Bonds Payable.

Analyzing Financial Statements

Objective 2
Analyze financial statements.

The preparation of the Detailed Income Statement and Classified Balance Sheet will help us analyze the financial statements of United Auto Supply. Financial statements must be analyzed to determine whether certain relationships or trends are favorable or unfavorable. We will look at three types of analysis: working capital, current ratio, and profit margin.

Working Capital

Working Capital is the amount by which current assets exceed current liabilities. United Auto Supply's working capital would be as follows:

Current Assets	$35,700
Less: Current Liabilities	11,900
Working Capital	$23,800

This indicates that the firm is able to pay its current obligations with current assets and still have $23,800 remaining.

Current Ratio

Another way of stating working capital is by the **current ratio,** which is current assets divided by current liabilities:

$$\text{Current Ratio} = \frac{\text{Current Assets}}{\text{Current Liabilities}}$$

For United Auto Supply this would be as follows:

$$\text{Current Ratio} = \frac{\$35,700}{\$11,900} = 3 \text{ times}$$

This indicates that the firm would be able to pay its current obligations or debts three (3) times with current assets.

Profit Margin

The **profit margin** is determined by dividing net income by net sales:

$$\text{Profit Margin} = \frac{\text{Net Income}}{\text{Net Sales}}$$

This ratio shows the percentage of profit from net sales. For United Auto Supply this would be as follows:

$$\text{Profit Margin} = \frac{\$3,400}{\$42,500} = .08 = 8\%$$

This indicates that net income is 8 percent of net sales, or 8 cents of every net sales dollar is realized in net income.

Converting Decimals to Percents

To convert a decimal number to a percent, move the decimal point two places to the right and add the percent sign. For example, .04 is converted to 4%, .12 could be converted to 12%, .25 to 25%, and so on.

Closing Entries

Objective 3
Prepare and journalize closing entries.

We prepared closing entries earlier for a service-type firm. In this chapter we will prepare closing entries for the merchandising firm, United Auto Supply. We will again prepare the same four closing entries. However, we now have additional *nominal* accounts that must be cleared at the end of the accounting period, such as Sales Discounts, Purchases Returns and Allowances, and so on. Thus, to include these additional accounts, we will clear all temporary accounts with credit balances in the first closing entry. Those temporary or nominal accounts with debit balances will be cleared in the second closing entry. Income Summary is closed to Capital in the third closing entry, and Drawing is cleared to Capital in the fourth.

(1) Close Revenues and Other Credits to Income Summary   For a merchandising firm, the first closing entry clears all revenue accounts and any other credit balances (nominal accounts only) to Income Summary. The first closing entry for United Auto Supply would be as follows:

GENERAL JOURNAL   Page ___29___

Date		Description	Post Ref.	Debit	Credit
		Closing Entries			
19XX					
Oct.	31	Sales		42 7 0 0 –	
		Interest Income		1 7 0 –	
		Purchases Returns and Allowances		4 0 0 –	
		Purchases Discounts		1 4 4 –	
		Income Summary			43 4 1 4 –

(2) Close Expenses and Other Debits to Income Summary The second closing entry for a merchandising firm clears all expense accounts and any other debit balances (nominal accounts only) to Income Summary. The second closing entry for United Auto Supply would be as follows:

	31	Income Summary		40 0 9 0	—			
		Sales Returns and Allowances				7 8	—	
		Sales Discounts				1 2 2	—	
		Purchases				23 1 0 0	—	
		Freight In				2 4 5 0	—	
		Rent Expense				1 7 0 0	—	
		Wages Expense				11 5 9 8	—	
		Advertising Expense				1 9 0	—	
		Utilities Expense				1 9 5	—	
		Bank Service Expense				7	—	
		Office Supplies Expense				2 0 0	—	
		Insurance Expense				1 5 0	—	
		Depreciation Expense, Office Equipment				3 0 0	—	

(3) Close Income Summary to Capital You should post the first two closing entries to the Income Summary account before journalizing the third closing entry. The resulting balance confirms the net income or net loss for the accounting period.

The third closing entry is to clear the Income Summary account to the owner's Capital account. Let's use a T account to illustrate the activity in the Income Summary account after the adjusting entry for Merchandise Inventory and the two preceding closing entries:

Income Summary			
(10/31) Adjusting Entry (beginning Merchandise Inventory)	8,209		
		8,285	(10/31) Adjusting Entry (ending Merchandise Inventory)
		43,414	(10/31) Closing Entry (clear credits)
(10/31) Closing Entry (clear debits)	40,090		
		3,400	Balance to be cleared to owner's Capital

United Auto Supply had a Net Income of $3,400 for October 19XX, which corresponds to the balance of the Income Summary account. The third closing entry for United Auto Supply would be as follows:

	31	Income Summary		3 4 0 0	—			
		Lucille Garcia, Capital				3 4 0 0	—	

Once again, let's use a T account to illustrate the activity in the Income Summary account after the third closing entry is posted:

Income Summary			
(10/31) Adjusting Entry (beginning Merchandise Inventory)	8,209		
		8,285	(10/31) Adjusting Entry (ending Merchandise Inventory)
		43,414	(10/31) Closing Entry (clear credits)
(10/31) Closing Entry (clear debits)	40,090		
(10/31) Closing Entry (clear Income Summary)	3,400		
(10/31) Final Balance	–0–	–0–	

Now, let's use a T account to illustrate the activity in the owner's Capital account after the third closing entry is posted:

Lucille Garcia, Capital		
	34,100	(10/25) Previous Balance
	3,400	(10/31) Third closing entry posted
	37,500	(10/31) Balance after third closing entry

(4) Close Drawing to Capital   The owner's Drawing account is cleared in the last closing entry by debiting the owner's Capital account and crediting the owner's Drawing account. The fourth and final closing entry for United Auto Supply is as follows:

	31	Lucille Garcia, Capital		1 2 0 0 –	
		Lucille Garcia, Drawing			1 2 0 0 –

Using a T account once again, we'll demonstrate the activity in the owner's Capital account after the fourth closing entry is posted:

Lucille Garcia, Capital		
	34,100	(10/25) Previous Balance
	3,400	(10/31) Third closing entry posted
(10/31) Fourth closing entry posted 1,200		
	36,300	(10/31) Final Balance

The Post-Closing Trial Balance

Objective 4

Prepare a post-closing trial balance.

An accountant may be very confident that all appropriate closing entries have been properly journalized and posted. But to ensure that the accounting records, in particular the general ledger, are ready for the start of the next accounting period, a **post-closing trial balance** must be prepared. The post-closing trial balance for a merchandising firm has the following purposes:

1. All nominal accounts are closed
2. Total debits equal total credits
3. All account balances are normal
4. Ending Merchandise Inventory is correct

The post-closing trial balance for a merchandising firm is very similar to the post-closing trial balance prepared for a service-type firm. The general ledger accounts are listed in chart-of-accounts' order. Any account that has a zero balance is not listed. The post-closing trial balance for United Auto Supply at the end of the accounting period, October 19XX, is shown in Exhibit 12-5.

Now that the post-closing trial balance has been prepared, let's see if the four purposes have been met. First, we can see that no nominal accounts are listed. This indicates that all nominal accounts have zero balances. Next, we see that total debits equal total credits. Then, looking at the accounts and account balances, we see that all account balances are normal; that is, Accounts Receivable has a debit balance, Accounts Payable a credit balance, and so on. Finally, we see that ending Merchandise Inventory has the correct balance. The accounting records are therefore properly set for the next accounting period. You should always thoroughly examine the accounting records to be sure that all journal entries, postings, descriptions, and so on are correct before you go on to the next accounting period.

EXHIBIT 12-5 Post-Closing Trial Balance

United Auto Supply
Post-Closing Trial Balance
October 31, 19XX

Accounts	Debit	Credit
Cash	8 778 —	
Accounts Receivable	15 837 —	
Merchandise Inventory	8 285 —	
Office Supplies	2 500 —	
Prepaid Insurance	300 —	
Office Equipment	15 500 —	
Accumulated Depreciation, Office Equipment		900 —
Accounts Payable		8 800 —
Wages Payable		1 600 —
Notes Payable (long-term)		2 100 —
Unearned Sales Revenue		1 500 —
Lucille Garcia, Capital		36 300 —
Totals	51 200 —	51 200 —

Reversing Entries

Objective 5
Prepare and journalize reversing entries (optional).

Some adjusting entries made in the previous accounting period may be reversed at the beginning of the current accounting period. A **reversing entry** reverses or "turns around" a previous adjusting entry.

Reversing entries have the following purposes:

1. To facilitate recording revenues in the proper accounting period
2. To facilitate recording expenses in the proper accounting period
3. To ensure that transactions are recorded in a smooth and routine manner between two accounting periods

Since the accounting records for United Auto Supply are now closed, the current accounting period is November 19XX. Reversing entries are not necessary or required. These are merely another tool you may employ to make your work as an accountant easier and to reduce the possibility of errors.

Let's follow the process in Exhibit 12-6 for the use of reversing entries. In this example we will assume that a $961 Wages Expense adjustment was recorded May 31, 19XX. A total of $1,200 Cash will be paid June 5, 19XX. A total of $239 Wages Expense is to be allocated to June, and $961 to May.

EXHIBIT 12-6 Reversing Entry: Thought and Procedure Process

REVERSING ENTRY PROCESS						
				Effect on Accounts		
General Journal Entry			**Wages Expense**		**Wages Payable**	
			+	–	–	+
Adjusting	Dr.	Cr.				
(5/31) Wages Expense	*961*		*961*			
Wages Payable		*961*				*961*
Closing						
(5/31) Income Summary	*961*					
Wages Expense		*961*		*961*		
Account Balance after Closing Entry			*–0–*			*961*
Reversing						
(6/1) Wages Payable	*961*				*961*	
Wages Expense		*961*		*961*		
Account Balance after Reversing Entry				*961(a)*		*–0–(b)*
Payment of Cash						
(6/5) Wages Expense	*1,200*		*1,200*			
Cash		*1,200*				
Account Balance after Payment Entry			*(c)239*			*–0–*

(a) Because this balance is not normal, it will remind you that another entry must be made to bring the account balance back to normal.

(b) There is no liability for the new accounting period.

(c) Cash paid for Wages Expense is apportioned to the correct accounting period. Total cash paid of $1,200 for Wages Expense (debit) minus May Wages Expense of $961 (credit) equals June Wages Expense of $239. Or, $1,200 debit minus $961 credit equals a $239 debit balance.

T accounts are used to show the account balances after each entry is made. The "+" indicates that the account has increased. Remember that the plus side is the normal side. The "–" indicates that the account has decreased. An account with a minus balance is not considered to be normal.

Any adjustment (adjusting entry) that will not be realized into cash paid or received in the following accounting period should not be reversed. Therefore, the *deferral* type of adjusting entry would not be reversed. An *accrual* type of adjusting entry may be reversed depending on whether cash is to be received or paid in the next accounting period following the one in which the adjusting entry is made.

Remember that if you do not use reversing entries then you must go back and look in the accounting records to see, in this example, how much of the $1,200 Wages Expense is to be allocated to June 19XX. This may not appear to be a problem. But imagine working with the accounting records if you were an accountant employed by a large firm with numerous transactions and many employees. This review could then be quite difficult and time consuming.

Chapter Review

1. **Prepare financial statements.**
   The Income Statement and Balance Sheet columns of the worksheet were used to prepare financial statements. The financial statements were prepared in this order: (a) income statement, (b) statement of owner's equity, and (c) balance sheet.

2. **Analyze financial statements.**
   Financial statements are analyzed to determine whether certain relationships or trends are favorable or unfavorable. The types of analysis that were examined in this chapter include (a) working capital, (b) current ratio, and (c) profit margin.

3. **Prepare and journalize closing entries.**
   All temporary accounts with credit balances are cleared in the first closing entry. Those temporary or nominal accounts with debit balances are closed in the second closing entry. Income Summary is cleared to Capital in the third closing entry. Finally, Drawing is closed to Capital in the fourth closing entry.

4. **Prepare a post-closing trial balance.**
   A post-closing trial balance is prepared to ensure that the accounting records, in particular the general ledger, are ready for the start of the next accounting period.

5. **Prepare and journalize reversing entries (optional).**
   A reversing entry reverses or "turns around" a previous adjusting entry. Reversing entries are another tool an accountant may use to make his or her work easier and to reduce errors.

Glossary

Classified Balance Sheet Balance sheet that separates each unique category of accounts

Current Assets Assets that are realized into cash within the normal cycle of a business

Current Liabilities Obligations or debts that are due to others within the normal cycle of a business

Current Ratio Current Assets divided by Current Liabilities

Detailed Income Statement An income statement that separates each unique category of accounts

Gross Profit on Sales Net Sales minus Cost of Goods Sold

Income from Operations Gross Profit on Sales minus Total Operating Expenses

Intangible Assets Valuable long-term assets having no physical substance

Investments Long-term assets that will not be used in the normal cycle of a business

Long-Term Liabilities Obligations or debts that are due to others in more than one year

Normal Course of Business The main profit-making or business activity or activities of a firm

Normal Cycle of Business One year (12 months) for most firms

Other Assets Any asset that cannot be categorized into the four major categories of assets

Profit Margin Net Income divided by Net sales

Property, Plant, and Equipment Long-term assets used in the continuing operations of a business

Reversing Entry Turns around a previous adjusting entry

Working Capital Current Assets minus Current Liabilities

Self-Test Questions for Review

(Answers are at the end of Chapter 12.)

1. On a detailed income statement, Interest Income is included with
   a. Revenue from Sales.   **b.** Cost of Goods Sold.
   c. Operating Expenses.   **d.** Other Revenue.

2. Which of the following categories immediately follows Property, Plant, and Equipment on a classified balance sheet?
   a. Current Assets   **b.** Intangible Assets
   c. Investments   **d.** Other Assets

3. _____ is subtracted to find working capital.
   a. Current Liabilities   **b.** Net Income
   c. Current Assets   **d.** Net Sales

4. Close Income Summary to Capital is the _____ closing entry.
   a. first   **b.** second
   c. third   **d.** fourth

5. Assuming all balances are normal, which of the following accounts could be found in the credit column on a post-closing trial balance?
   a. Accounts Receivable   **b.** Merchandise Inventory
   c. Income Summary   **d.** Unearned Sales Revenue

Practical Review Problem

Objectives 3 and 4

Journalizing Closing Entries and Preparing a Post-Closing Trial Balance Frances Carter is the accountant for Lewistown Furniture Store. She finds the following accounts and account balances (all are normal) before closing entries at July 31, 19XX:

Cash	$34,870
Accounts Receivable	19,320
Merchandise Inventory	29,130
Office Supplies	4,650
Prepaid Insurance	3,240
Office Equipment	46,780
Accumulated Depreciation, Office Equipment	6,900
Accounts Payable	16,310
Notes Payable (long-term)	5,430
Unearned Sales Revenue	7,120
Felix Franks, Capital	94,120
Felix Franks, Drawing	1,460
Sales	46,690
Sales Returns and Allowances	2,360
Sales Discounts	1,050
Interest Income	340
Purchases	22,130
Purchases Returns and Allowances	1,810
Purchases Discounts	520
Freight In	3,090
Rent Expense	1,580
Wages Expense	13,420
Advertising Expense	870
Utilities Expense	230
Bank Service Expense	20
Income Summary	2,540 (credit)
Office Supplies Expense	710
Insurance Expense	250
Depreciation Expense, Office Equipment	300
Wages Payable	3,680

REQUIRED
1. Journalize the closing entries in a general journal, page 35.
2. Prepare a post-closing trial balance.

Answer to Practical Review Problem

1. **GENERAL JOURNAL** Page ___35___

Date		Description	Post Ref.	Debit	Credit
		Closing Entries			
19XX					
July	31	Sales		46 6 9 0 –	
		Interest Income		3 4 0 –	
		Purchase Returns and Allowances		1 8 1 0 –	
		Purchase Discounts		5 2 0 –	
		Income Summary			49 3 6 0 –
	31	Income Summary		46 0 1 0 –	
		Sales Returns and Allowances			2 3 6 0 –
		Sales Discounts			1 0 5 0 –
		Purchases			22 1 3 0 –
		Freight In			3 0 9 0 –
		Rent Expense			1 5 8 0 –
		Wages Expense			13 4 2 0 –
		Advertising Expense			8 7 0 –
		Utilities Expense			2 3 0 –
		Bank Service Expense			2 0 –
		Office Supplies Expense			7 1 0 –
		Insurance Expense			2 5 0 –
		Depreciation Expense, Office Equipment			3 0 0 –
	31	Income Summary		5 8 9 0 –	
		Felix Franks, Capital			5 8 9 0 –
	31	Felix Franks, Capital		1 4 6 0 –	
		Felix Franks, Drawing			1 4 6 0 –

2.

Lewiston Furniture Store				
Post-Closing Trial Balance				
July 31, 19XX				
Accounts	Debit	Credit	
Cash	34 8 7 0 –		
Accounts Receivable	19 3 2 0 –		
Merchandise Inventory	29 1 3 0 –		
Office Supplies	4 6 5 0 –		
Prepaid Insurance	3 2 4 0 –		
Office Equipment	46 7 8 0 –		
Accumulated Depreciation, Office Equipment		6 9 0 0 –	
Accounts Payable		16 3 1 0 –	
Wages Payable		3 6 8 0 –	
Notes Payable (long-term)		5 4 3 0 –	
Unearned Sales Revenue		7 1 2 0 –	
Felix Franks, Capital		98 5 5 0 –	*
Totals	137 9 9 0 –	137 9 9 0 –	

* $94,120 + $5,890 – $1,460 = $98,550

Discussion Questions

Q 12-1   Briefly describe a detailed income statement.

Q 12-2   In which two categories are costs and expenses separated in a detailed income statement?

Q 12-3   Briefly describe a classified balance sheet.

Q 12-4   Explain how assets and liability accounts are categorized in a classified balance sheet.

Q 12-5   Why must a post-closing trial balance be prepared for a merchandising firm as well as a for service-type firm?

Q 12-6   Name and give the formulas for the three analyses described in this chapter.

Q 12-7   Explain the first closing entry for a merchandising firm. Identify, in your answer, some accounts that you would expect to find in this entry.

Q 12-8   Explain the second closing entry for a merchandising firm. Identify, in your answer, some accounts that you would expect to find in this entry.

Q 12-9   Explain the third and fourth closing entries for a merchandising firm. Name the accounts that you would most likely find in these two entries.

Q 12-10
(optional)   What type of adjusting entries can be reversed for a merchandising firm? What type cannot be reversed? Explain your answers.

Exercises

Objective 1   **E 12-1   Completing an Income Statement**   Fill in the missing amounts in the following detailed income statement. [Hint: (b) is $400 – $300 = $100.]

Barfield Equipment Sales
Income Statement
For the Month Ended November 30, 19XX

Revenues from Sales			
Sales		$ (a)	
Less: Sales Returns and Allowances	$ 300		
Sales Discounts	(b)	400	
Net Sales			$8,900
Cost of Goods Sold			
Merchandise Inventory, November 1		$3,100	
Purchases	$5,700		
Less: Purchases Returns and Allowances	500		
Purchases Discounts	200		
Net Purchases		(c)	
Freight In		$ 100	
Cost of Goods Available for Sale		$ (d)	
Less: Merchandise Inventory, November 30		$3,600	
Cost of Goods Sold			(e)
Gross Profit on Sales			$ (f)
Operating Expenses			
Wages Expense		$1,900	
Depreciation Expense, Truck		200	
Total Operating Expenses			$ (g)
Income from Operations			$ (h)
Other Revenue			
Interest Income			$ 800
Net Income			$3,000

Objective 2

E 12-2 Analyzing Financial Statements   Determine (a) working capital, (b) current ratio, and (c) profit margin given the following information: Net Sales, $34,600; Current Assets, $89,400; Net Income, $5,190; and Current Liabilities, $29,800.

Objective 1

E 12-3 Completing a Balance Sheet   Fill in the missing amounts in the following classified balance sheet. [Hint: (b) is $16,800 –$16,000 = $800]:

Mendoza Sales
Balance Sheet
January 31, 19XX

Assets

Current Assets		
Cash	$ (a)	
Accounts Receivable	$ 2,450	
Merchandise Inventory	4,860	
Prepaid Insurance	2,530	
Total Current Assets		$18,110
Property, Plant, and Equipment		
Truck	$16,800	
Less: Accumulated Depreciation	(b)	16,000
Total Assets		$ (c)

Liabilities

Current Liabilities		
Wages Payable	$3,660	
Unearned Sales Revenue	990	
Total Current Liabilities		$ (d)
Long-Term Liabilities		
Notes Payable		$12,770
Total Liabilities		$ (e)

Owner's Equity

Hector Mendoza, Capital	$ (f)
Total Liabilities and Owner's Equity	$ (g)

Objective 3 **E 12-4 Completing Closing Entries** Complete the following closing entries:

GENERAL JOURNAL   Page ___29___

Date		Description	Post Ref.	Debit	Credit
		Closing Entries			
19XX					
Apr.	30	*Sales*		22 6 0 0 —	
		Interest Income		1 1 0 0 —	
		Purchase Returns and Allowances		9 0 0 —	
		Purchase Discounts		2 0 0 —	
		(a)			*(b)* —
	30	*(c)*		*(d)* —	
		Sales Returns and Allowances			1 4 0 0 —
		Sales Discounts			8 0 0 —
		Purchases			11 8 0 0 —
		Freight In			4 0 0 —
		Wages Expense			4 8 0 0 —
		Depreciation Expense, Store Equipment			3 0 0 —
	30	*(e)*		8 2 0 0 —	
		Gayle Gilder, Capital			8 2 0 0 —
	30	*(f)*		7 0 0 —	
		(g)			7 0 0 —

Objective 1 **E 12-5 Preparing an Income Statement** Prepare a Detailed Income Statement given the Income Statement columns from the worksheet for Ramsey Company (p. 12-22).

Objective 4 **E 12-6 Completing a Post-Closing Trial Balance** Complete the post-closing trial balance on August 31, 19XX, for Kelso's Magazine Stand (p. 12-22).

Ramsey Company
Worksheet
For the Month Ended October 31, 19XX

Account	Income Statement Debit	Income Statement Credit
Sales		14 0 4 0 –
Sales Returns and Allowances	6 1 0 –	
Sales Discounts	8 8 0 –	
Interest Income		4 3 0 –
Purchases	7 8 5 0 –	
Purchases Returns and Allowances		4 5 0 –
Purchases Discounts		1 9 0 –
Freight In	4 2 0 –	
Wages Expense	2 8 8 0 –	
Telephone Expense	4 4 0 –	
Income Summary	4 3 3 0 –	5 3 8 0 –
Depreciation Expense, Machinery	3 3 0 –	
	17 7 4 0 –	20 4 9 0 –
Net Income	2 7 5 0 –	
	20 4 9 0 –	20 4 9 0 –

(a)

(b)

(c)

(d)   (e)   (f)

Account	Debit	Credit
Cash	13 9 0 0 –	
Accounts Receivable	16 1 0 0 –	
Merchandise Inventory	12 7 0 0 –	
Wages Payable		4 8 0 0 –
Unearned Sales Revenue		2 7 0 0 –
Doris Kelso, Capital		(g) –
Totals	(h) –	(i) –

Objective 3

E 12-7 Journalizing Closing Entries The accountant for Lopez Sports Supply finds the following selected accounts and account balances (all are normal) for the month ended February 28, 19XX:

L. T. Lopez, Capital, $45,670; L. T. Lopez, Drawing, $2,010; Income Summary, $2,560 credit balance; Sales, $31,940; Sales Returns and Allowances, $280; Sales Discounts, $190; Interest Income, $1,360; Purchases, $19,530; Purchases Returns and Allowances, $1,710; Purchases Discounts, $230; Freight In, $1,650; Rent Expense, $1,350; Wages Expense, $9,770; Advertising Expense, $340.

Journalize the closing entries in the general journal, page 17, as follows: Close revenues and other credits, close expenses and other debits, close Income Summary (include the previous credit balance), and close drawing.

Objective 5
(Optional)

E 12-8 **Journalizing Reversing Entries** A $1,950 Wages Expense adjustment was recorded December 31, 19XX. A total of $4,180 cash will be paid January 4, 19XX. Record the following entries in a general journal:

a. December 31, 19XX, adjusting entry

b. December 31, 19XX, closing entry (for Wages Expense)

c. January 1, 19XX, reversing entry

d. January 4, 19XX, payment of cash

Problems

Objective 1

P 12-1 **Preparing Financial Statements** Lori Hayes owns and operates Hayes Equipment Sales. She invested $1,000 during the month, which is included in the owner's Capital account on the worksheet. Lori had the following worksheet (partial) for June 30, 19XX:

Hayes Equipment Sales
Worksheet
For the Month Ended June 30, 19XX

Account	Income Statement Debit	Income Statement Credit	Balance Sheet Debit	Balance Sheet Credit
Cash			9 700 –	
Accounts Receivable			12 300 –	
Merchandise Inventory			8 700 –	
Truck			21 600 –	
Accumulated Depreciation, Truck				800 –
Notes Payable (long-term)				14 700 –
Unearned Sales Revenue				2 900 –
Lori Hayes, Capital				32 500 –
Lori Hayes, Drawing			2 100 –	
Sales		13 200 –		
Sales Return and Allowances	300 –			
Sales Discounts	400 –			
Interest Income		600 –		
Purchases	6 700 –			
Purchases Return and Allowances		700 –		
Purchases Discounts		100 –		
Freight In	200 –			
Rent Expense	900 –			
Wages Expense	3 500 –			
Telephone Expense	500 –			
Income Summary	8 900 –	8 700 –		
Depreciation Expense, Truck	100 –			
Wages Payable				1 700 –
	21 500 –	23 300 –	54 400 –	52 600 –
Net Income	1 800 –			1 800 –
	23 300 –	23 300 –	54 400 –	54 400 –

REQUIRED

1. Prepare financial statements including (a) detailed income statement, (b) statement of owner's equity, and (c) classified balance sheet.

Objectives 3 and 4

P 12-2 **Journalizing Closing Entries and Preparing a Post-Closing Trial Balance** Billy Simmons is the accountant for North Central Apparel Store. He finds the following accounts and account balances (all are normal) before closing entries at December 31, 19XX:

Cash	$25,120
Accounts Receivable	8,350
Merchandise Inventory	18,430
Office Supplies	3,890
Prepaid Insurance	2,160
Office Equipment	35,240
Accumulated Depreciation, Office Equipment	5,500
Accounts Payable	7,280
Notes Payable (long-term)	4,210
Unearned Sales Revenue	5,090
Mary Konacek, Capital	65,720
Mary Konacek, Drawing	930
Sales	30,240
Sales Returns and Allowances	720
Sales Discounts	810
Interest Income	290
Purchases	13,620
Purchases Returns and Allowances	730
Purchases Discounts	240
Freight In	1,670
Rent Expense	1,850
Wages Expense	6,790
Advertising Expense	540
Utilities Expense	290
Bank Service Expense	10
Income Summary	1,060 (credit)
Office Supplies Expense	580
Insurance Expense	150
Depreciation Expense, Office Equipment	500
Wages Payable	1,290

REQUIRED

1. Journalize the closing entries in a general journal, page 22.

2. Prepare a post-closing trial balance. See the Practical Review Problem if you need help.

Objectives 1 and 2

P 12-3 **Preparing and Analyzing Financial Statements** Rudy Luna owns and operates Northern Furniture Sales. He invested $2,980 during the month, which is included in the owner's Capital account on the worksheet. Rudy had the following worksheet (partial) for August 31, 19XX:

REQUIRED
1. Prepare financial statements including the (a) detailed income statement, (b) statement of owner's equity, and (c) classified balance sheet.
2. Analyze financial statements by calculating (a) working capital, (b) current ratio, and (c) profit margin.

Northern Furniture Sales

Worksheet

For the Month Ended August 31, 19XX

Account	Income Statement Debit	Income Statement Credit	Balance Sheet Debit	Balance Sheet Credit
Cash			12 89 0 –	
Accounts Receivable			9 67 0 –	
Merchandise Inventory			14 89 0 –	
Prepaid Insurance			3 45 0 –	
Automobile			18 78 0 –	
Accumulated Depreciation, Automobile				2 38 0 –
Accounts Payable				13 56 0 –
Notes Payable (long-term)				9 45 0 –
Unearned Sales Revenue				1 22 0 –
Rudy Luna, Capital				26 08 0 –
Rudy Luna, Drawing			3 57 0 –	
Sales		33 55 0 –		
Sales Returns and Allowances	5 2 0 –			
Sales Discounts	4 3 0 –			
Interest Income		6 3 0 –		
Purchases	18 16 0 –			
Purchases Returns and Allowances		7 1 0 –		
Purchases Discounts		2 8 0 –		
Freight In	1 34 0 –			
Rent Expense	1 28 0 –			
Wages Expense	9 34 0 –			
Utilities Expense	1 2 0 –			
Income Summary	13 56 0 –	14 89 0 –		
Insurance Expense	1 9 0 –			
Depreciation Expense, Automobile	2 3 0 –			
Wages Payable				5 67 0 –
	45 17 0 –	50 06 0 –	63 25 0 –	58 36 0 –
Net Income	4 89 0 –			4 89 0 –
	50 06 0 –	50 06 0 –	63 25 0 –	63 25 0 –

Objectives 1 through 5

P 12-4 **Comprehensive Chapter Review Problem** Brown's Health Store is owned and operated by Shirley Brown. She invested $1,380 during the month, which is included in the owner's Capital account. The following accounts and account balances (all are normal) were taken from the Income Statement and Balance Sheet columns of her completed worksheet for the month ended October 31, 19XX:

Cash, $9,712; Accounts Receivable, $11,782; Merchandise Inventory, $18,091; Prepaid Insurance, $1,488; Office Equipment, $35,891; Accumulated Depreciation, Office Equipment, $3,480; Accounts Payable, $4,453; Notes Payable (long-term), $18,715; Unearned Sales Revenue, $4,672; Shirley Brown, Capital, $36,423; Shirley Brown, Drawing, $2,168; Sales, $35,458; Sales Returns and Allowances, $561; Sales Discounts, $782; Interest Income, $892; Purchases, $14,570; Purchases Returns and Allowances, $781; Purchases Discounts, $452; Freight In, $987; Rent Expense, $1,515; Wages Expense, $9,561; Advertising Expense, $782; Income Summary, $19,564 debit and $18,091 credit; Wages Payable, $4,566; Insurance Expense, $181; and Depreciation Expense, Office Equipment, $348.

REQUIRED
1. Prepare financial statements including (a) detailed income statement, (b) statement of owner's equity, and (c) classified balance sheet.
2. Analyze financial statements by calculating (a) working capital, (b) current ratio, and (c) profit margin.
3. Prepare and journalize (page 42) closing entries. DO NOT post to the general ledger.
4. Prepare a post-closing trial balance.
5. (Optional) Prepare and journalize (page 43) the reversing entry for Wages Payable on November 1, 19XX. DO NOT post to the general ledger.
6. The firm paid wages on November 6, 19XX, $6,019. Record this transaction in a general journal, page 43. DO NOT post to the general ledger.

Checklist of Key Figures

P12-1 Net Income, $1,800
P12-2 (2) Totals, 93,190
P12-3 (1) Net Income, $4,890
P12-4 (1) Net Income, $6,823

Answers to Self-Test Questions

1. d　　2. b　　3. a　　4. c　　5. d

Payroll: Employee Earnings and Deductions

LEARNING OBJECTIVES

After reading this chapter, discussing the questions, and working the exercises and problems, you will be able to do the following:

1. Understand employee payroll accounting

2. Calculate gross and net pay

3. Prepare an employee compensation record and a payroll register

In this chapter we'll examine payroll. Payroll is a major expense for most firms. In fact, in many service businesses, such as law, accounting, banking, and brokerage, payroll costs represent half or more of operating expenses.

Employee Payroll Accounting

Objective 1
Understand employee payroll accounting.

Payroll accounting has three objectives:

1. To compute the amount of wages or salaries due employees
2. To pay the wages or salaries promptly
3. To complete various government reports

We will examine the first two in this chapter.

The Employer/Employee Relationship   An **employer** is a person or firm who hires an **employee** to perform designated tasks or services. The employer usually provides the place of work for the employee and usually has the right to hire, fire, and control the work of the employee.

An **independent contractor** is in business for him- or herself; examples are attorneys, dentists, and certified public accountants. An independent contractor is hired by a person or firm to perform designated services. However, the person or firm does not have the right to control or supervise the independent contractor. Other examples include medical doctors and photographers.

Hourly Wages and Salaries   **Wages** are the earnings of employees who are paid on an hourly or piecework basis. A few examples of this type of worker are automobile assembly line workers, machinists, and steelworkers. **Salaries** are the earnings of employees who are paid on a monthly or annual basis. Some examples of this type of worker are teachers, store managers, and police officers.

Payroll Tax Laws

Certain laws passed by the U.S. Congress affect the amount a person is paid. Three of the major payroll-related laws are the Fair Labor Standards Act, the Federal Insurance Contributions Act, and the Sixteenth Amendment to the Constitution.

Fair Labor Standards Act   The **Fair Labor Standards Act (FLSA)**, commonly known as the Federal Wage and Hour Law, was established in 1938. It is administered by the Wage and Hour Division of the U.S. Department of Labor. This act states that **overtime pay** is required for all hours worked in excess of forty during a workweek. For any hours over forty, the required overtime pay is equal to time and one-half (1.5) the employee's regular hourly rate of pay.

For example, assume that Donna Newhart's regular rate of pay is $10.10 per hour. Her overtime rate would be $10.10 times 1.5, which is $15.15 per hour.

Federal Insurance Contributions Act   The **Federal Insurance Contributions Act (FICA)**, commonly known as the Social Security Act, was enacted in 1935. This act, with all its amendments, provides for a federal system of old age, survivors, disability, and hospital insurance. This hospital (or health) insurance is known as Medicare. Both the employee and employer contribute equal amounts to this fund. We will assume in this chapter a Social Security tax rate of 6.2 percent of the first $68,400 in earnings for each employee. The Medicare tax rate is 1.45 percent with no maximum of earnings. Thus an employee and employer could each contribute the following maximum taxes:

      ▪ Social Security tax: $4,240.80 maximum ($68,400 × .062)

      ▪ Medicare tax: No maximum—all earnings are subject to the Medicare tax

If an employee is paid more than $68,400, no additional Social Security taxes are withheld; however, all earnings would be subject to Medicare taxes.

For example, assume that Fran Harris had year-to-date earnings of $41,500. Her Social Security tax is $2,573 ($41,500 × .062) and her Medicare tax is $601.75 ($41,500 × .0145). Fran's employer would contribute an equal amount.

Sixteenth Amendment On March 1, 1913, the **Sixteenth Amendment** to the Constitution was enacted to allow income (earnings) to be taxed by the federal government. Until 1943 employees paid the amount due at the end of the year. But with the passage of the **Current Tax Payment Act of 1943** employers were required to withhold federal income taxes from the wages and salaries paid to their employees on a "pay-as-you-go" basis.

Calculating the Gross Payroll

Objective 2
Calculate gross and net pay.

The total amount earned by all employees before deductions is called the *gross payroll* or *gross pay*. The gross payroll involves the earnings of those employees paid on an hourly and piecework basis (wages) and those paid on a monthly or annual basis (salary). Let's first calculate the gross pay of an hourly worker for United Auto Supply for the week ended January 31, 19XX.

Wage Earners Carl Moore is an hourly worker who is paid $10.50 per hour. United Auto Supply pays time and one-half for hours worked in excess of forty for the week. He works forty-two hours during the week, so his gross pay is calculated as follows:

	40 Hours at Straight Time	40 × $10.50 = $420.00
	2 Hours Overtime	2 × 15.75 = 31.50
Total	42 Hours	$451.50

The $15.75 overtime rate is calculated by multiplying the regular hourly rate times one and one-half ($10.50 × 1.5 = $15.75).

Overtime is calculated for a specific workweek only, even if an employee is paid every two weeks. For example, if an employee worked thirty-seven hours one week and forty-four hours the next, the four hours in the second week would be considered overtime. The weeks are not averaged together.

Salaried Earners Hu Le, the accountant for United Auto Supply, is a salaried employee who is paid $27,300 per year. The gross earnings per pay period are computed as follows:

PAY PERIOD	NUMBER OF PAY PERIODS IN A YEAR	GROSS PAY PER PERIOD
Monthly	12 months	$27,300 ÷ 12 = $2,275
Bi-weekly	26 weeks	$27,300 ÷ 26 = $1,050
Weekly	52 weeks	$27,300 ÷ 52 = $525

Piece Rate Some employees are paid on a unit-of-production basis called *piece rate*. For example, Larry Hayes, a factory worker, is paid $0.26 for each unit produced. If he produces 1,340 units, then his pay is $348.40 (1,340 units × $0.26).

Commission Many salespeople are paid on a *commission* basis. For example, Sarah McNutt, a lumber salesperson, is paid 4 percent of her sales. She sells $11,762 of lumber, so her pay is $470.48 ($11,762 × .04).

Calculating Net Pay

An employee does not usually receive his or her gross (total) earnings as **net pay**. Net pay is the actual cash amount that an employee receives in the form of a paycheck. The difference is due to deductions applied to the employee's gross pay. These deductions may be voluntary (such as charitable contributions, savings bonds, life insurance, and so on), or they could be involuntary (such as Social Security tax, Medicare tax, federal income tax, state income tax, and so on).

The largest deduction for most employees is their estimated liability for federal income tax. Since March 1, 1913, income has been taxed by the federal government. Employers are required to withhold federal income taxes from the wages and salaries paid their employees on a "pay-as-you-go" basis. This amount is then forwarded to the Internal Revenue Service. Exhibit 13-1 shows a withholding table for married employees who are paid weekly. This withholding table is found in *Circular E, Employer's Tax*

EXHIBIT 13-1 Circular E: Married Persons—Weekly Payroll

If the wages are—		And the number of withholding allowances claimed is—										
At least	But less than	0	1	2	3	4	5	6	7	8	9	10
		The amount of income tax to be withheld is—										
$0	$125	0	0	0	0	0	0	0	0	0	0	0
125	130	1	0	0	0	0	0	0	0	0	0	0
130	135	1	0	0	0	0	0	0	0	0	0	0
135	140	2	0	0	0	0	0	0	0	0	0	0
140	145	3	0	0	0	0	0	0	0	0	0	0
145	150	4	0	0	0	0	0	0	0	0	0	0
150	155	4	0	0	0	0	0	0	0	0	0	0
155	160	5	0	0	0	0	0	0	0	0	0	0
160	165	6	0	0	0	0	0	0	0	0	0	0
165	170	7	0	0	0	0	0	0	0	0	0	0
170	175	7	0	0	0	0	0	0	0	0	0	0
175	180	8	0	0	0	0	0	0	0	0	0	0
180	185	9	1	0	0	0	0	0	0	0	0	0
185	190	10	2	0	0	0	0	0	0	0	0	0
190	195	10	2	0	0	0	0	0	0	0	0	0
195	200	11	3	0	0	0	0	0	0	0	0	0
200	210	12	4	0	0	0	0	0	0	0	0	0
210	220	14	6	0	0	0	0	0	0	0	0	0
220	230	15	7	0	0	0	0	0	0	0	0	0
230	240	17	9	1	0	0	0	0	0	0	0	0
240	250	18	10	3	0	0	0	0	0	0	0	0
250	260	20	12	4	0	0	0	0	0	0	0	0
260	270	21	13	6	0	0	0	0	0	0	0	0
270	280	23	15	7	0	0	0	0	0	0	0	0
280	290	24	16	9	1	0	0	0	0	0	0	0
290	300	26	18	10	2	0	0	0	0	0	0	0
300	310	27	19	12	4	0	0	0	0	0	0	0
310	320	29	21	13	5	0	0	0	0	0	0	0
320	330	30	22	15	7	0	0	0	0	0	0	0
330	340	32	24	16	8	0	0	0	0	0	0	0
340	350	33	25	18	10	2	0	0	0	0	0	0
350	360	35	27	19	11	3	0	0	0	0	0	0
360	370	36	28	21	13	5	0	0	0	0	0	0
370	380	38	30	22	14	6	0	0	0	0	0	0
380	390	39	31	24	16	8	0	0	0	0	0	0
390	400	41	33	25	17	9	2	0	0	0	0	0
400	410	42	34	27	19	11	3	0	0	0	0	0
410	420	44	36	28	20	12	5	0	0	0	0	0
420	430	45	37	30	22	14	6	0	0	0	0	0
430	440	47	39	31	23	15	8	0	0	0	0	0
440	450	48	40	33	25	17	9	1	0	0	0	0
450	460	50	42	34	26	18	11	3	0	0	0	0
460	470	51	43	36	28	20	12	4	0	0	0	0
470	480	53	45	37	29	21	14	6	0	0	0	0
480	490	54	46	39	31	23	15	8	0	0	0	0
490	500	56	48	40	32	24	17	9	1	0	0	0
500	510	57	49	42	34	26	18	10	3	0	0	0
510	520	59	51	43	35	27	20	12	4	0	0	0
520	530	60	52	45	37	29	21	13	6	0	0	0
530	540	62	54	46	38	30	23	15	7	0	0	0
540	550	63	55	48	40	32	24	16	9	1	0	0
550	560	65	57	49	41	33	26	18	10	2	0	0
560	570	66	58	51	43	35	27	19	12	4	0	0
570	580	68	60	52	44	36	29	21	13	5	0	0
580	590	69	61	54	46	38	30	22	15	7	0	0
590	600	71	63	55	47	39	32	24	16	8	1	0
600	610	72	64	57	49	41	33	25	18	10	2	0
610	620	74	66	58	50	42	35	27	19	11	4	0
620	630	75	67	60	52	44	36	28	21	13	5	0
630	640	77	69	61	53	45	38	30	22	14	7	0
640	650	78	70	63	55	47	39	31	24	16	8	0
650	660	80	72	64	56	48	41	33	25	17	10	2
660	670	81	73	66	58	50	42	34	27	19	11	3
670	680	83	75	67	59	51	44	36	28	20	13	5
680	690	84	76	69	61	53	45	37	30	22	14	6
690	700	86	78	70	62	54	47	39	31	23	16	8
700	710	87	79	72	64	56	48	40	33	25	17	9
710	720	89	81	73	65	57	50	42	34	26	19	11
720	730	90	82	75	67	59	51	43	36	28	20	12
730	740	92	84	76	68	60	53	45	37	29	22	14

Guide, which is obtained from the IRS. This guide tells employers about their tax responsibilities to their employees.

Hu Le is married and claims four withholding allowances (dependents). Her weekly pay is $525. Therefore, the federal income tax to be withheld by United Auto Supply for Hu is $29 (see Exhibit 13-1). This $29 is determined by finding the wages in the left-hand column (525) and then matching that with the withholding allowances at the top (4). Her $525 falls between the "At least" $520 "But less than" $530, so the rate is $29. To know how much federal income tax to withhold from an employee's salary or wages, the employer should have a **Form W-4, Employee's Withholding Allowance Certificate**, on file for each employee. The amount to be withheld is determined by the employee's gross wages or salary and the information submitted by the employee on Form W-4 (see Exhibit 13-2). This information includes the employee's marital status, the number of withholding allowances claimed, the employee's request to have additional tax withheld, and the employee's claim to exemption from withholdings.

If the wages are—		And the number of withholding allowances claimed is—										
At least	But less than	0	1	2	3	4	5	6	7	8	9	10
		The amount of income tax to be withheld is—										
$740	$750	93	85	78	70	62	54	46	39	31	23	15
750	760	95	87	79	71	63	56	48	40	32	25	17
760	770	96	88	81	73	65	57	49	42	34	26	18
770	780	98	90	82	74	66	59	51	43	35	28	20
780	790	99	91	84	76	68	60	52	45	37	29	21
790	800	101	93	85	77	69	62	54	46	38	31	23
800	810	102	94	87	79	71	63	55	48	40	32	24
810	820	104	96	88	80	72	65	57	49	41	34	26
820	830	105	97	90	82	74	66	58	51	43	35	27
830	840	107	99	91	83	75	68	60	52	44	37	29
840	850	108	100	93	85	77	69	61	54	46	38	30
850	860	110	102	94	86	78	71	63	55	47	40	32
860	870	111	103	96	88	80	72	64	57	49	41	33
870	880	113	105	97	89	81	74	66	58	50	43	35
880	890	114	106	99	91	83	75	67	60	52	44	36
890	900	116	108	100	92	84	77	69	61	53	46	38
900	910	118	109	102	94	86	78	70	63	55	47	39
910	920	121	111	103	95	87	80	72	64	56	49	41
920	930	124	112	105	97	89	81	73	66	58	50	42
930	940	126	114	106	98	90	83	75	67	59	52	44
940	950	129	115	108	100	92	84	76	69	61	53	45
950	960	132	117	109	101	93	86	78	70	62	55	47
960	970	135	120	111	103	95	87	79	72	64	56	48
970	980	138	123	112	104	96	89	81	73	65	58	50
980	990	140	126	114	106	98	90	82	75	67	59	51
990	1,000	143	129	115	107	99	92	84	76	68	61	53
1,000	1,010	146	131	117	109	101	93	85	78	70	62	54
1,010	1,020	149	134	120	110	102	95	87	79	71	64	56
1,020	1,030	152	137	122	112	104	96	88	81	73	65	57
1,030	1,040	154	140	125	113	105	98	90	82	74	67	59
1,040	1,050	157	143	128	115	107	99	91	84	76	68	60
1,050	1,060	160	145	131	116	108	101	93	85	77	70	62
1,060	1,070	163	148	134	119	110	102	94	87	79	71	63
1,070	1,080	166	151	136	122	111	104	96	88	80	73	65
1,080	1,090	168	154	139	125	113	105	97	90	82	74	66
1,090	1,100	171	157	142	128	114	107	99	91	83	76	68
1,100	1,110	174	159	145	130	116	108	100	93	85	77	69
1,110	1,120	177	162	148	133	119	110	102	94	86	79	71
1,120	1,130	180	165	150	136	121	111	103	96	88	80	72
1,130	1,140	182	168	153	139	124	113	105	97	89	82	74
1,140	1,150	185	171	156	142	127	114	106	99	91	83	75
1,150	1,160	188	173	159	144	130	116	108	100	92	85	77
1,160	1,170	191	176	162	147	133	118	109	102	94	86	78
1,170	1,180	194	179	164	150	135	121	111	103	95	88	80
1,180	1,190	196	182	167	153	138	124	112	105	97	89	81
1,190	1,200	199	185	170	156	141	126	114	106	98	91	83
1,200	1,210	202	187	173	158	144	129	115	108	100	92	84
1,210	1,220	205	190	176	161	147	132	117	109	101	94	86
1,220	1,230	208	193	178	164	149	135	120	111	103	95	87
1,230	1,240	210	196	181	167	152	138	123	112	104	97	89
1,240	1,250	213	199	184	170	155	140	126	114	106	98	90
1,250	1,260	216	201	187	172	158	143	129	115	107	100	92
1,260	1,270	219	204	190	175	161	146	131	117	109	101	93
1,270	1,280	222	207	192	178	163	149	134	120	110	103	95
1,280	1,290	224	210	195	181	166	152	137	123	112	104	96
1,290	1,300	227	213	198	184	169	154	140	125	113	106	98
1,300	1,310	230	215	201	186	172	157	143	128	115	107	99
1,310	1,320	233	218	204	189	175	160	145	131	116	109	101
1,320	1,330	236	221	206	192	177	163	148	134	119	110	102
1,330	1,340	238	224	209	195	180	166	151	137	122	112	104
1,340	1,350	241	227	212	198	183	168	154	139	125	113	105
1,350	1,360	244	229	215	200	186	171	157	142	128	115	107
1,360	1,370	247	232	218	203	189	174	159	145	130	116	108
1,370	1,380	250	235	220	206	191	177	162	148	133	119	110
1,380	1,390	252	238	223	209	194	180	165	151	136	121	111

EXHIBIT 13-2 W-4: Employee's Withholding Allowance Certificate

Form **W-4** Department of the Treasury Internal Revenue Service	**Employee's Withholding Allowance Certificate** ▶ For Privacy Act and Paperwork Reduction Act Notice, see page 2.		OMB No. 1545-0010
1 Type or print your first name and middle initial **Hu**	Last name **Le**		2 Your social security number **400 00 0000**
Home address (number and street or rural route) **12 G Avenue**	3 ☐ Single ☒ Married ☐ Married, but withhold at higher Single rate. Note: If married, but legally separated, or spouse is a nonresident alien, check the Single box.		
City or town, state, and ZIP code **Houston, Texas 77002**	4 If your last name differs from that on your social security card, check here and call 1-800-772-1213 for a new card . . . . . ▶ ☐		

5	Total number of allowances you are claiming (from line H above or from the worksheets on page 2 if they apply) .	**5**	**4**
6	Additional amount, if any, you want withheld from each paycheck	**6**	$ **-0-**
7	I claim exemption from withholding for 19XX and I certify that I meet BOTH of the following conditions for exemption:		

● Last year I had a right to a refund of ALL Federal income tax withheld because I had NO tax liability AND
● This year I expect a refund of ALL Federal income tax withheld because I expect to have NO tax liability.
If you meet both conditions, enter "EXEMPT" here . . . . ▶ **7**

Under penalties of perjury, I certify that I am entitled to the number of withholding allowances claimed on this certificate or entitled to claim exempt status.

Employee's signature ▶ *Hu Le*   Date ▶ **February 1** , 19 **XX**

8 Employer's name and address (Employer: Complete 8 and 10 only if sending to the IRS)	9 Office code (optional)	10 Employer identification number

Cat. No. 10220Q

Hu Le's take-home or net pay for the week ended December 31, 19XX, is computed as follows:

Gross Earnings (Pay)		$525.00
Less Deductions:		
Social Security Tax ($525 × .062)	$32.55	
Medicare Tax ($525 × .0145)	7.61*	
Federal Income Tax	29.00	
Total Deductions		69.16
Net (Take-Home) Pay		$455.84

*Rounded to the cent. See "Rounding to the Cent."

Rounding to the Cent

There are three steps to follow when rounding to the cent (two places). First, identify the digit to be rounded, which is the cent (two places to the right of the decimal point). Second, if the digit to the right of the cent is 5 or more, increase the cent by one. If 4 or less, the cent is not changed. And third, change all of the digits to the right of the cent to zeros. For example, $12.689 is rounded to $12.69, $6.9954 is rounded to $7.00, $547.01462 is rounded to $547.01, and so on.

Payroll Deductions An employee may have deductions other than the ones listed previously. A *deduction* is an amount that reduces an employee's take-home or net pay. Some of these deductions may include the following:

1. State income tax

2. City income tax

3. Purchase of U.S. savings bonds

4. Union dues

5. Life insurance premiums

6. Contributions to charities
7. Loan payments to a company credit union
8. Savings through a company credit union

Employee Compensation Records

Objective 3

Prepare an employee compensation record and a payroll register.

An employer must keep a record of earnings and withholdings for each employee. United Auto Supply would have an **employee compensation record** for each employee. The one for Hu Le is shown in Exhibit 13-3.

EXHIBIT 13-3 | Employee Compensation Record

Employee Compensation Record

Employee's Name _____ Hu Le _____   Social Security No. ____ 400-00-0000 ____

Address ___ 12 G Avenue ___   Male ___ Female _X_   Weekly Pay Rate _$525.00_

____ Houston, Texas 77002 ____   Married _X_ Single ___   Hourly Equivalent _$13.13_

Date of Birth _April 5, 1952_   Withholding Allowances _4_

Position _Accountant_   Date of Employment ___ February 1, 19XX ___

Date Employment Ended _____

Pay Period Ending	Total Hours	Earnings			Deductions				Net Pay	Cumulative Gross Earnings
		Regular	Overtime	Total	Social Sec. Tax	Medicare Tax	Federal Income Tax	Total Deductions		
12/10	40	525.00	0.00	525.00	32.55	7.61	29.00	69.16	455.84	24,675.00
12/17	40	525.00	0.00	525.00	32.55	7.61	29.00	69.16	455.84	25,200.00
12/24	40	525.00	0.00	525.00	32.55	7.61	29.00	69.16	455.84	25,725.00
12/31	40	525.00	0.00	525.00	32.55	7.61	29.00	69.16	455.84	26,250.00

Payroll Registers

The employer also prepares a **payroll register** for each payroll period, which summarizes the payroll for *all* employees. The payroll register is prepared using each employee's compensation record. Exhibit 13-4 shows a payroll register for United Auto Supply for the week ended December 31, 19XX.

Completing the Payroll Register

There are nine steps to follow when completing the payroll register. The steps are keyed to Exhibit 13-4 as follows:

① Use one line for each employee for each payroll period.

② Calculate Total Earnings for each employee, including any overtime pay. Total the Earnings columns.

③ Verify that Regular Earnings and Overtime Earnings equal Total Earnings as follows:

Total Regular Earnings	$2,153.00
Total Overtime Earnings	95.40
Total Earnings	$2,248.40

④ Determine the Deductions for each employee.

⑤ Total the Deductions columns.

⑥ Verify that the Deductions columns equal the Total Deductions column as follows:

Total Social Security Tax	$139.40
Total Medicare Tax	32.60
Total Federal Income Tax	186.00
Total Deductions	$358.00

⑦ Calculate the Net Pay for each employee by subtracting the employee's Total Deductions from the employee's Total Earnings. Total the Net Pay column.

⑧ Verify that Total Deductions subtracted from Total Earnings equals Total Net Pay as follows:

Total Earnings	$2,248.40
Less: Total Deductions	358.00
Total Net Pay	$1,890.40

⑨ Record the distribution.

EXHIBIT 13-4 Payroll Register

Payroll Register

For the Week Ended December 31, 19XX

Employee	Total Hours	Earnings ② Regular	Overtime	Total	Deductions ④ Social Sec. Tax	Medicare Tax	Federal Income Tax	Total Deductions	⑦ Net Pay	Distribution Wage Expense
Le, H. ①	40	525.00	0.00	525.00	32.55	7.61	29.00	69.16	455.84	525.00
Moore, C.	42	420.00	31.50	451.50	27.99	6.55	34.00	68.54	382.96	451.50
Rylski, F.	40	640.00	0.00	640.00	39.68	9.28	70.00	118.96	521.04	640.00
Vega, B.	43	568.00	63.90	631.90	39.18	9.16	53.00	101.34	530.56	631.90
Totals ③		2,153.00	95.40	2,248.40	139.40	32.60	186.00	358.00	1,890.40	2,248.40
					⑤	⑥			⑧	⑨

Recording the Payroll

The payroll entry is recorded in the general journal using the information from the payroll register. Since payroll calculations are usually made before paychecks are distributed to employees, the accountant credits Wages Payable rather than Cash. Using the information from the payroll register in Exhibit 13-4, the payroll entry is journalized in Exhibit 13-5.

EXHIBIT 13-5 | Payroll Entry

GENERAL JOURNAL Page ___40___

Date		Description	Post Ref.	Debit	Credit
19XX					
Dec.	31	Wages Expense ①		2 2 4 8 40	
		Social Security Tax Payable			1 3 9 40
		② Medicare Tax Payable			3 2 60
		Federal Income Tax Payable			1 8 6 —
		③ Wages Payable			1 8 9 0 40
		Employee's Payroll for the Week Ended December 31, 19XX			

There are three steps to follow when preparing the payroll entry from the payroll register. These steps are keyed in Exhibit 13-5. The amounts are taken from the payroll register (Exhibit 13-4). For United Auto Supply, the steps are as follows:

① The Total Earnings from the payroll register is listed as Wages Expense in the payroll entry. This amount is debited.

② Each of the Deductions is credited in the payroll entry. The Deductions represent liabilities that must be paid at a later date to the appropriate authorities.

③ The Total Net Pay amount in the payroll register is recorded as Wages Payable in the payroll entry. This amount is a liability and is credited. Wages Payable (Net Pay) is the total amount the employees will receive in cash for this payroll period. Remember that employees have deductions withheld, thus reducing the amount of money they will actually receive.

Payroll Checking Accounts

Many firms maintain a special payroll checking account at a bank. The purposes for this account are as follows:

1. Payroll checks can be issued separately from other check payments, such as rent expense, purchases of merchandise, and so on. This makes it easier for many firms with a large number of employees to reconcile bank checking accounts.

2. Only the Total Net Pay amount is deposited in the special payroll checking account, thus providing greater internal control over Cash. The special payroll checking account should have a zero balance after all payroll checks have cleared the bank.

3. Only a few employees, such as the payroll accountant, will know the amount of money other employees are paid. Thus, by having a special payroll checking account, there is more privacy.

To deposit the necessary funds (money) to pay employees with a special payroll checking account, the following cash payment is made (using T accounts):

Wages Payable		Cash	
1,890.40			1,890.40

Individual checks are then written to the employees from the special payroll checking account. Once the checks have been issued and clear the bank, the special payroll checking account has a zero balance.

Chapter Review

1. **Understand employee payroll accounting.**
   Payroll accounting has three objectives: (a) to compute wages or salaries due employees, (b) to pay wages or salaries promptly, and (c) to complete various government reports. Some of the important payroll tax laws include the Fair Labor Standards Act, the Federal Insurance Contributions Act, and the Sixteenth Amendment.

2. **Calculate gross and net pay.**
   Gross payroll is the total amount earned by all employees. Net pay is calculated by subtracting deductions from the gross pay. Some deductions may include Social Security tax, Federal income tax, state income tax, city income tax, union dues, and so on.

3. **Prepare an employee compensation record and a payroll register.**
   An employee compensation record is used to keep track of earnings and withholdings for each employee. The employer prepares a payroll register for each payroll period summarizing the payroll for all employees. The payroll register is prepared by using each employee's compensation record.

Glossary

Circular E, Employer's Tax Guide Government-published guide that tells employers about their tax responsibilities to their employees

Current Tax Payment Act of 1943 Requires employers to withhold federal income taxes from the wages and salaries paid their employees on a "pay-as-you-go" basis

Employee Person hired by an employer to perform services subject to the control and supervision of the employer

Employee Compensation Record Record of earnings and withholdings for each employee

Employer Person or firm who hires an employee to perform designated services

Employer's Withholding Allowance Certificate (Form W-4) Form filled out by the employee regarding dependents and marital status; this determines how much income tax is to be withheld

Fair Labor Standards Act (FLSA) Act requiring overtime pay for all hours worked in excess of forty during a workweek

Federal Insurance Contributions Act Act providing for a federal system of old age, survivors, disability, and hospital insurance. Both the employee and employer contribute equal amounts

Gross Pay Employee's total earnings before deductions

Independent Contractor Hired by a person or firm to perform designated services; the person or firm does not have the right to control and supervise the independent contractor. Examples include CPAs and attorneys.

Net Pay Gross pay less deductions

Overtime Pay Premium paid to employees for hours worked in excess of forty during a workweek

Payroll Register Record prepared by the employer for each payroll period summarizing the payroll for all employees

Salaries (Salary) Earnings of employees who are paid on a monthly or annual basis

Sixteenth Amendment Enacted to allow income to be taxed by the federal government

Wages Earnings of employees who are paid on an hourly or piecework basis

Self-Test Questions for Review

(Answers are at the end of Chapter 13.)

1. Which of the following, enacted on March 1, 1913, pertains to taxes?
   a. Fair Labor Standards Act   **b.** Social Security Act
   c. Sixteenth Amendment   **d.** Current Tax Payment Act

2. A person is paid 5 percent of her sales. This is an example of
   a. a commission.   **b.** piecework.
   c. wages.   **d.** a salary.

3. The Medicare tax rate used in the chapter is _____ for the employee and _____ for the employer.
   a. 1.45 percent; none   **b.** none; 1.45 percent
   c. 1.45 percent; 1.25 percent   **d.** 1.45 percent; 1.45 percent

4. "Record the distribution" is step _____ of completing the payroll register.
   a. 3   **b.** 5
   c. 1   **d.** 9

5. _____ is debited and _____ is credited when depositing money in a special payroll checking account.
   a. Cash; Wages Expense   **b.** Wages Payable; Cash
   c. Cash; Wages Payable   **d.** Accounts Payable; Cash

Practical Review Problem

Objective 3

Completing Employee Compensation Records Saunders Fuel Supply has two employees. To complete the employee compensation records for Maria D'Amico and Fred Walters (both are married) for the week ended October 23, 19XX, this information was collected:

	MARIA D'AMICO	FRED WALTERS
SOCIAL SECURITY NUMBERS	111-11-0000	222-22-0000
ADDRESSES	195 Canal Modesto, California 95354	401 Santa Ana Ave. Modesto, California 95350
WEEKLY OR HOURLY PAY RATE	$710/week	$10.60/hour
WITHHOLDING ALLOWANCES	2	4
CUMULATIVE GROSS EARNINGS (INCLUDING THIS PAY PERIOD)	$31,950	$19,060
POSITION	Office Manager	Bookkeeper
EMPLOYMENT DATE	February 2, 19XX	March 9, 19XX
BIRTH DATE	April 6, 1948	July 18, 1951
OVERTIME EARNINGS	$-0-	6 hours

Other Payroll Data:

a. For each employee the Social Security tax is 6.2 percent of the first $68,400 of earnings; the Medicare tax is 1.45 percent with no maximum.

b. Use Exhibit 13-1 to determine federal income taxes.

c. The firm pays overtime pay at time and one-half (1.5) for any hours worked in excess of forty per workweek.

REQUIRED

Complete an employee compensation record for each employee. Round all amounts to the cent. For purposes of simplicity, assume that there is no state or city income tax.

Answer to Practical Review Problem

Employee Compensation Record

Employee's Name _____Maria D'Amico_____   Social Security No. _____111-11-0000_____ ①

Address __195 Canal__   Male ___ Female _X_   Weekly Pay Rate _$710.00_

_____Modesto, California 95354_____   Married _X_ Single ___   Hourly Equivalent _$17.75_

Date of Birth __April 6, 1948__   Withholding Allowances _2_

Position __Office Manager__   Date of Employment __February 2, 19XX__

Date Employment Ended _____

Pay Period Ending	Total Hours	Earnings			Deductions				Net Pay	Cumulative Gross Earnings
		Regular	Overtime	Total	Social Sec. Tax	Medicare Tax	Federal Income Tax	Total Deductions		
10/23	40	710.00	0.00	710.00	44.02	10.30	73.00	127.32	582.68	31,950.00

Employee Compensation Record

Employee's Name _____Fred Walters_____   Social Security No. ___222-22-0000___

Address ___401 Santa Ana___   Male _X_ Female ___   Weekly Pay Rate _$424.00_ ②

_____Modesto, California 95350_____   Married _X_ Single ___   Hourly Equivalent _$10.60_

Date of Birth _July 18, 1951_   Withholding Allowances _4_

Position _Bookkeeper_   Date of Employment __March 9, 19XX__

          Date Employment Ended _____

| Pay Period Ending | Total Hours | Earnings | | | Deductions | | | | Net Pay | Cumulative Gross Earnings |
		Regular	Overtime	Total	Social Sec. Tax	Medicare Tax	Federal Income Tax	Total Deduc-tions		
10/23	46	424.00	95.40 ③	519.40	32.20 ④	7.53	27.00	66.73	452.67	19,060.00

① $710 ÷ 40 = $17.75.

② $10.60 × 40 = $424.

③ $10.60 × 1.5 = $15.90 × 6 = $95.40.

④ Example of rounding: $519.40 × .062 = $32.2028 = $32.20 rounded to the cent.

Discussion Questions

Q 13-1 What are the three objectives of payroll accounting?

Q 13-2 Identify and briefly explain the major payroll laws.

Q 13-3 In your own words, explain the reason(s) for paying employees time and a half. Is this beneficial for both the employee and employer? Explain why or why not.

Q 13-4 How is net pay calculated? Could gross pay ever equal net pay?

Q 13-5 What is the purpose of an employee compensation record and a payroll register? Are they related? If yes, explain how.

Q 13-6 List at least five payroll deductions.

Q 13-7 List the steps in completing the payroll register.

Q 13-8 List the steps to follow when preparing the payroll entry from the payroll register.

Q 13-9 From their paychecks, what is the largest deduction for most employees? What type of deductions do you have or have you had from *your* paycheck?

Q 13-10 List the three reasons why a firm would have a special payroll checking account.

Exercises

Objective 2   **E 13-1** **Categorizing Deductions** Categorize the following deductions as voluntary (V) or involuntary (I):

a. Social Security tax   **b.** Savings bonds

c. Life insurance   **d.** State income tax

e. Charitable contributions   **f.** Federal income tax

g. Savings through a company credit union   **h.** Medicare tax

Objective 2

E 13-2 Calculating Gross Pay Calculate the gross pay for the following employees:

a. D. Bui is paid time and a half for all hours over forty. She works forty-five hours during a workweek, and her regular pay is $10 per hour.

b. F. Young is paid weekly. His gross earnings for the year (52 weeks) are $21,320.

c. J. Rojas is paid 5 percent of her sales. She sells $10,740.

Objective 3

E 13-3 Completing an Employee Compensation Record Complete an employee compensation record using the following information: The employee is Jack Allbright, his Social Security number is 500-00-0000. Jack's address is 7100 South Phillips, Chicago, Illinois 60649. He is single and has zero withholding allowances. He was employed as an accountant for the firm on March 7, 19XX, at a weekly (40 hours) rate of $600. For the pay period ending June 7, 19XX, Jack worked 40 hours with no overtime hours. His Social Security tax is $37.20, Medicare tax is $8.70, and federal income tax is $72. Jack was born June 16, 1960. His cumulative gross earnings are $6,000 (as of June 7, 19XX). For purposes of simplicity, assume that there is no state or city income tax.

Objective 1

E 13-4 Calculating Social Security and Medicare Taxes Kelso Sales and Service uses the following rates: Social Security tax, 6.2 percent of the first $68,400 of earnings; and Medicare tax, 1.45 percent with no maximum of earnings. Using this information, calculate Social Security and Medicare taxes for the following employees:

a. Jeremy Paulsen has weekly wages of $1,200 (all wages subject to Social Security and Medicare taxes).

b. Helen Neuman has year-to-date earnings of $71,000 before the current month's salary of $7,000.

Objective 2

E 13-5 Determining Federal Income Taxes Use Exhibit 13-1 to determine the federal income taxes for the following employees (all are married):

a. K. Parker has weekly wages of $805 and claims 3 withholding allowances.

b. R. Pacetti has weekly wages of $978 and claims 2 withholding allowances.

c. A. Schmidt has weekly wages of $460 and claims 0 withholding allowances.

Objective 3

E 13-6 Completing a Payroll Register Complete the following payroll register:

Payroll Register
For the Week Ended April 18, 19XX

Employee	Total Hours	Regular	Overtime	Total	Social Sec. Tax	Medicare Tax	Federal Income Tax	Total Deductions	Net Pay	Wage Expense
Bond, I.	40	700.00	0.00	(a)	43.40	10.15	40.00	(b)	(c)	(d)
Jacks, L.	46	600.00	135.00	(e)	45.57	10.66	68.00	(f)	(g)	(h)
Stone, A.	48	400.00	120.00	(i)	32.24	7.54	45.00	(j)	(k)	(l)
Totals		(m)	(n)	(o)	(p)	(q)	(r)	(s)	(t)	(u)

Objective 2 **E 13-7** **Calculating Net Pay** Assume the following employee payroll tax rates: Social Security tax, 6.2 percent of the first $68,400 of earnings; and Medicare tax, 1.45 percent with no maximum of earnings. Using this information, calculate the net pay (use Exhibit 13-1 for federal income taxes) for the following employees:

a. Yolanda Flores is married and claims 4 withholding allowances. Her weekly pay is $715 (all subject to Social Security and Medicare taxes).

b. D. J. Lewis has savings bonds ($25), and medical insurance ($30) withheld from her weekly pay. She is married and her weekly pay is $820 (all subject to Social Security and Medicare taxes). D. J. claims 5 withholding allowances.

Objective 3 **E 13-8** **Recording Payroll and Depositing Funds** Wagner Company had the following employee payroll amounts for the week ended February 9, 19XX: Total earnings, $12,000; Social Security tax withheld, $744; federal income tax withheld, $3,100; and Medicare tax withheld, $174. In your answer, (a) record this payroll transaction in a general journal, page 19; and (b) deposit the necessary funds in a special payroll checking account, using T accounts.

Problems

Objective 2 **P 13-1** **Calculating Gross Pay and Social Security and Medicare Taxes** Consider the following four employees:

a. Vera Darnell is a salaried employee who earns $29,380 per year (52 weeks). All of her weekly salary is subject to Social Security and Medicare taxes.

b. Roger Weston is an hourly worker who is paid $11.50 per hour. His firm pays time and one-half for hours worked in excess of forty for the week. He works fifty hours during the week. All wages are subject to Social Security and Medicare taxes.

c. Juan Morales is a factory worker who is paid $0.35 for each unit produced. He produces 1,200 units during a week, and all his pay is subject to Social Security and Medicare taxes.

d. Before this pay period, Mai Wilson had year-to-date earnings of $69,000. She is a carpet salesperson who is paid 6 percent of her sales. She sells $21,700 during a week.

REQUIRED
(If necessary, round to the cent.)
1. Calculate the weekly gross pay for each employee.
2. Calculate the Social Security, if any, and Medicare taxes for each employee. Assume the Social Security tax is 6.2 percent of the first $68,400 of earnings and Medicare tax is 1.45 percent with no maximum of earnings.

Objective 3 **P 13-2** **Completing Employee Compensation Records** Graber Marine Supply has two employees. The following information was collected to complete the employee compensation records for Marilyn Adams and George Potosky (both are married) for the week ended August 17, 19XX:

	MARILYN ADAMS	GEORGE POTOSKY
SOCIAL SECURITY NUMBERS	233-00-3333	255-00-5555
ADDRESSES	610 Third Avenue Cleveland, Ohio 44112	19001 Day Street Cleveland, Ohio 44129
WEEKLY OR HOURLY PAY RATE	$580/week	$11.80/hour
WITHHOLDING ALLOWANCES	4	3
CUMULATIVE GROSS EARNINGS (INCLUDING THIS PAY PERIOD)	$8,120	$12,880
POSITION	Bookkeeper	Driver
EMPLOYMENT DATE	May 13, 19XX	March 5, 19XX
BIRTH DATE	June 12, 1954	April 7, 1956
OVERTIME EARNINGS	$–0–	4 hours

Other Payroll Data:

a. For each employee the Social Security tax is 6.2 percent of the first $68,400 of earnings and the Medicare tax is 1.45 percent with no maximum.

b. Use Exhibit 13-1 to determine federal income taxes.

c. The firm pays overtime pay at time and one-half (1.5) for any hours worked in excess of forty per workweek.

REQUIRED

Complete an employee compensation record for each employee. Round all amounts to the cent. See the Practical Review Problem if you need help. For purposes of simplicity, assume that there is no state or city income tax.

Objective 3   P 13-3   **Preparing a Payroll Register and Recording Payroll**   Morganstein Computer Supply has four employees. The firm's accountant accumulated employee's payroll data from the employee compensation records (by employee) for the week ended November 15, 19XX as follows:

a. Alex Pitts has regular earnings of $416.00 and overtime earnings of $62.40. His deductions are Social Security tax, $29.66; federal income tax, $37.00; and Medicare tax, $6.94. He worked 44 hours during the week.

b. Fran Clark worked 42 hours during the week. Her deductions are federal income tax, $25.00; Social Security tax, $21.33; and Medicare tax, $4.99. Her overtime earnings were $24.00, and her regular earnings were $320.00.

c. Oscar Vargas is a salaried employee who worked 40 hours during the week at $695.00. He had $10.08 deducted for Medicare tax, $43.09 for Social Security tax, and $62.00 for federal income tax.

d. I. H. Tran had the following deductions: Medicare tax, $7.66; federal income tax, $37.00; and Social Security tax, $32.74. She is an employee who receives a salary of $528.00. She worked 40 hours during the week.

REQUIRED

1. Prepare a payroll register. List employees in alphabetical order, by last name. Use the first letter of the employee's first name. Calculate total earnings, total deductions, and net pay for each employee. Total the appropriate columns. All earnings are distributed as Wages Expense.

2. Record the employee's payroll in a general journal, page 56.

Objectives 1   P 13-4   **Comprehensive Chapter Review Problem**   Gallagher Beverage Supply has two
2, and 3   employees: Floyd Givens and Nancy Ruiz. Floyd's Social Security number is 299-00-0000.

Floyd's address is 1390 Lake Street, Rochester, New York 14615. He is married and has two withholding allowances. Floyd was born December 5, 1932, and is employed as a bookkeeper. He was employed April 2, 19XX, at a weekly (40 hours) rate of $715. For the pay period ending August 13, 19XX, Floyd worked 40 hours with no overtime hours. His cumulative gross earnings are $13,585 (as of August 13, 19XX). Nancy's address is 150 Walnut Drive, Rochester, New York 14608. Her cumulative gross earnings are $29,640 (as of August 13, 19XX). She was employed February 9, 19XX, at an hourly rate of $22.80. For the pay period ending August 13, 19XX, Nancy worked 43 hours (3 overtime hours). Nancy's Social Security number is 199-00-0000. She is married and has three withholding allowances. Nancy was born September 1, 1952. She is employed as a driver.

REQUIRED

1. Complete an employee's compensation record for each employee for the week ended August 13, 19XX. Calculate the Social Security and Medicare taxes for each employee. Assume the Social Security tax is 6.2 percent of the first $68,400 of earnings and Medicare tax is 1.45 percent with no maximum of earnings. Using Exhibit 13-1, determine the federal income tax for each employee. Round all amounts to the cent. For purposes of simplicity, assume that there is no state or city income tax.

2. Using the information in 1, prepare a payroll register (list employees alphabetically).

3. Prepare a general journal entry, page 43, to record the employee's payroll.

4. Using T accounts, make the necessary deposit in a special payroll checking account.

Checklist of Key Figures

P 13-1 (1a) $565.00

P 13-2 Adams Net Pay, $497.63

P 13-3 (1) Net Pay, $1,727.91

P 13-4 (2) Net Pay, $1,414.28

Answers to Self-Test Questions

1. c   **2.** a   **3.** d   **4.** d   **5.** b

Payroll: Employer's Taxes and Reports

LEARNING OBJECTIVES

After reading this chapter, discussing the questions, and working the exercises and problems, you will be able to do the following:

1. Understand and compute employer's payroll taxes

2. Prepare Form 941

3. Prepare Form 940-EZ

4. Record the payment of payroll liabilities

5. Calculate and record worker's compensation insurance

Employers are responsible for collecting payroll taxes and then remitting those taxes to the proper tax authorities. Earlier we saw that payroll taxes and other deductions were withheld from employees' pay. In this chapter we will examine the *employer's* payroll taxes. We will also look at how these payroll taxes are deposited and reported.

Applications for Employer Identification Numbers

Objective 1
Understand and compute employer's payroll taxes.

An application for an employer identification number must be filed by every employer of one or more persons. The application is completed on **Form SS-4**, which is available at any IRS or Social Security Office. The employer identification number (EIN) must be included on all correspondence, forms, and returns submitted to the IRS relating to payroll taxes.

Employer's Payroll Taxes

In order to compute the employer's payroll taxes, the payroll register must be expanded. This is shown in Exhibit 14-1, where three columns are added: Year-to-Date Earnings, Social Security Taxable Earnings, and Federal (FUTA) and State (SUTA) Unemployment Taxable Earnings. A separate column for Medicare tax is not necessary under the Taxable Earnings column. Remember, ALL earnings are taxable for Medicare tax purposes.

Year-to-Date Earnings

Referring to Exhibit 14-1, the Year-to-Date Earnings column represents the total earnings of the employee up to and including this (the current) payroll period. This amount becomes the basis for computing the employer's payroll taxes.

EXHIBIT 14-1 | Expanded Payroll Register

Payroll Register
For the Week Ended   December 31, 19XX

Employee	Total Hours	Earnings Regular	Earnings Over-time	Earnings Total	Deductions Social Sec. Tax	Deductions Medi-care Tax	Deductions Federal Income Tax	Deductions Total Deduc-tions	Net Pay	Distribution Wage Expense	Year-To-Date Earnings	Taxable Earnings Social Security	Taxable Earnings FUTA/SUTA ①
Le, H.	40	525.00	0.00	525.00	32.55	7.61	29.00	69.16	455.84	525.00	26,250.00	525.00	② 0.00
Moore, C.	42	420.00	31.50	451.50	27.99	6.55	34.00	68.54	382.96	451.50	7,000.00	451.50	451.50
Rylski, F.	40	640.00	0.00	640.00	39.68	9.28	70.00	118.96	521.04	640.00	7,340.00	640.00	③ 300.00
Vega, B.	43	568.00	63.90	631.90	39.18	9.16	53.00	101.34	530.56	631.90	32,180.00	631.90	② 0.00
Totals		2,153.00	95.40	2,248.40	139.40	32.60	186.00	358.00	1,890.40	2,248.40	72,770.00	2,248.40	751.50

① FUTA/SUTA is an abbreviation for federal unemployment tax, and state unemployment tax.

② Over $7,000 limit.

③ ($7,340 – $640 = $6,700. $7,000 limit – $6,700 = $300 taxable earnings.)

FICA (Social Security) Tax

We will assume that the employer must pay the same Social Security and Medicare taxes as the employee. In this textbook we are using the following rates: Social Security tax, 6.2 percent of the first $68,400 of earnings for a calendar year (January 1 to December 31); and Medicare tax, 1.45 percent with no maximum for the calendar year. Remember, payroll taxes are based on a calendar year, not a fiscal year. (The employer's Social Security and Medicare taxes, as well as the federal income tax, are reported to the IRS on Form 941, which we will examine later.)

United Auto Supply paid $139.40 of Social Security taxes for the week ended December 31, 19XX ($2,248.40 × .062). The employee's contribution was also $139.40.

Using T accounts, the entry to record the employer's portion of the Social Security tax is as follows:

Payroll Tax Expense			Social Security Tax Payable	
+	−		−	+
(12/31) 139.40				(12/31) 139.40

The employer had $32.60 of Medicare taxes ($2,248.40 × .0145); employees contribute an equal amount. We can use T accounts to illustrate the employer's share:

Payroll Tax Expense			Medicare Tax Payable	
+	−		−	+
(12/31) 32.60				(12/31) 32.60

Federal and State Unemployment Taxes

The **Federal Unemployment Tax Act (FUTA)** allows the state and federal government to cooperate in establishing and administering an unemployment tax program. This program provides unemployment compensation to workers who have lost their jobs. Each state creates its own employment insurance system, whereas the federal government approves state's laws and pays the administrative costs of each state's program.

Under this dual system, the employer is first subject to a tax levied by the state. This tax then becomes a credit against a separate federal tax. (A firm could be exempt from the state tax but would still have to pay the federal tax.) The federal unemployment tax is reported on **Employer's Annual Federal Unemployment (FUTA) Tax Return (Form 940-EZ)**. This form covers one calendar year and is due January 31 of the following year.

We will assume that the maximum amount of wages subject to Federal Unemployment (FUTA) tax is $7,000 and that the FUTA tax rate is 6.2 percent. We will also assume that the credit against the FUTA tax for payments to state unemployment funds is a maximum of 5.4 percent. Thus the net federal unemployment tax could be 0.8 percent (.008) assuming a state unemployment rate of 5.4 percent (6.2% − 5.4% = 0.8%). United Auto Supply pays state unemployment taxes of 5.4 percent and federal unemployment taxes of 0.8 percent. These taxes are paid only by the employer and are NOT deducted from wages paid to employees.

Calculating the Federal Unemployment Tax

Assuming a rate of 0.8 percent (.008) and taxable earnings of $751.50 (see Exhibit 14-1), the federal unemployment tax is calculated as follows:

$$\$751.50 \times .008 = \$6.01$$

As shown in Exhibit 14-1, Hu Le and Bernita Vega have already earned more than $7,000, so any additional earnings are NOT subject to federal unemployment taxes. Using T accounts, this tax is recorded as follows:

```
                                              Federal Unemployment
        Payroll Tax Expense                      Tax Payable
        +    |    −                           −    |    +
  (12/31)  6.01 |                                  | (12/31)  6.01
```

Calculating State Unemployment Tax

Assuming a rate of 5.4 percent (.054) and taxable wages of $751.50 (see Exhibit 14-1), the state unemployment tax is calculated as follows:

$$$751.50 \times .054 = $40.58$$

As shown in Exhibit 14-1, some of the employees have already earned more than $7,000, so any additional earnings are not subject to state unemployment taxes. Using T accounts, this tax is recorded as follows:

```
                                              State Unemployment
        Payroll Tax Expense                      Tax Payable
        +    |    −                           −    |    +
  (12/31)  40.58 |                                 | (12/31)  40.58
```

Recording the Employer's Payroll Taxes

The employer's payroll taxes for the four people we have just discussed would be recorded together in the accounting records, using a general journal. Since United Auto Supply pays its employees weekly, this payroll tax entry is also made weekly. Of course, the amounts will most likely change because total earnings and the earnings subject to unemployment taxes change.

GENERAL JOURNAL Page ___40___

Date		Description	Post Ref.	Debit	Credit
19XX					
Dec.	31	Payroll Tax Expense		218 59	
		Social Security Tax Payable			139 40
		Medicare Tax Payable			32 60
		Federal Unemployment Tax Payable			6 01
		State Unemployment Tax Payable			40 58
		Employee's Payroll Taxes for the Week Ended			
		December 31, 19XX			

Form 941

Objective 2
Prepare Form 941.

An employer who is required to withhold federal income taxes and/or Social Security and Medicare taxes must file a return reporting the amounts withheld. Normally, **Employer's Quarterly Federal Tax Return (Form 941)** is used for this purpose.

When to File

Form 941 is due no later than the last day of the month after each quarter ends:

QUARTERS	ENDING DATE	DUE DATE*
January, February, March	March 31	April 30
April, May, June	June 30	July 31
July, August, September	September 30	October 31
October, November, December	December 31	January 31

If an employer deposits all taxes when due for a quarter, the employer is allowed an additional 10 days after the above due dates to file Form 941.

When Deposits Are Due

The amount of taxes that a firm owes determines the frequency of deposits. These taxes are owed when the wages are paid, not when the payroll period ends. The following rules indicate when deposits are due.

There are two deposit schedules (monthly or semiweekly) and two exceptions (the $500 rule and the $100,000 rule). An employer's deposit schedule for a calendar year is determined from the total taxes reported on Form 941 in a four-quarter lookback period—July 1 through June 30. For example, the lookback period for calendar year 19X7 is the six-month or two-quarter periods in the two preceding years:

19X6 (last year)—January 1 to March 31 and April 1 to June 30

19X5 (year before 19X6)—July 1 to September 30 and October 1 to December 31

The monthly deposit schedule rule is followed if an employer reports $50,000 or less in employment taxes for the lookback period. All employment taxes must be deposited by the fifteenth day of the following month. A new employer is considered to be a monthly depositor for the first year of business, unless the new employer falls under the $100,000 next-day deposit rule exception (see rule exception below).

The semiweekly deposit schedule rule is followed if employment taxes are greater than $50,000 for the lookback period. Under the semiweekly rule, employment taxes withheld on payments made on Wednesday, Thursday, and/or Friday must be deposited by the following Wednesday. Amounts accumulated on payments made on Saturday, Sunday, Monday, and/or Tuesday must be deposited by the following Friday.

The $500 rule is used if an employer accumulates less than a $500 tax liability during a quarter. Under this special rule, the employment taxes are deposited by the end of the month following the quarter. Or an employer can remit the taxes when mailing Form 941.

The $100,000 next-day deposit rule is used when the total accumulated payroll tax reaches $100,000 on any day during a deposit period. The amount must be deposited by the next banking day, whether the employer is a monthly or semiweekly depositor.

How to Make Deposits

An employer must deposit income tax withheld and both the employer and employee Social Security and Medicare taxes with an authorized financial institution or a Federal Reserve Bank or branch. Exhibit 14-2 illustrates **Form 8109-B, Federal Tax Deposit Coupon**, which must be included with each deposit to indicate the type of tax being deposited. Some employers make deposits electronically. The Electronic Federal Tax Payment System (EFTPS) must be used to make electronic deposits. This topic is beyond the scope of this textbook and will be covered in a more advanced accounting and/or payroll course.

---

*If the due date for a return falls on a Saturday, Sunday, or legal holiday, the due date is the next regular workday.

EXHIBIT 14-2 | Form 8109-B

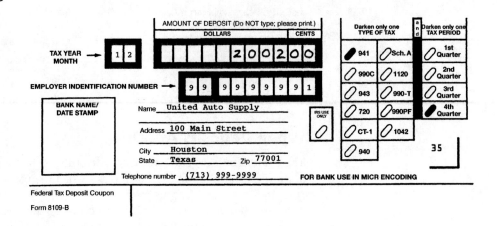

Federal Tax Deposit Coupon
Form 8109-B

Completing Form 941

United Auto Supply completed Form 941 for the quarter ended December 31, 19XX (see Exhibit 14-3).

In the heading, the trade name is United Auto Supply. The address is 100 Main Street, Houston, Texas 77001. The quarter ended December 31, 19XX, and the employer identification number is 99-9999991.

A description of the process for completing Form 941 is as follows:

LINE 2	Enter the total of all wages paid, tips reported, and other compensation paid to employees. The total for October through December 19XX is $26,000.
LINE 3	Enter the income tax withheld. United Auto Supply withheld $2,232.
LINE 5	The firm had no adjustments, so the amount withheld is $2,232.
LINE 6a	Enter the total wages subject to Social Security taxes paid to employees during the quarter. This amount is $26,000 multiplied by 12.4 percent, which equals $3,224. This is the total of both the employee's and employer's Social Security taxes.
LINE 7a	Use this line to report all wages and tips subject to the Medicare portion of Social Security: $26,000 is multiplied by 2.9 percent, which equals $754. Remember, the 2.9 percent is the total of both the employee's and employer's Medicare taxes (1.45 percent each).
LINE 8	This is the total of lines 6b, 6d, and 7b, which is $3,978.
LINE 10	The firm had no adjustments, so the total is $3,978.
LINE 11	Lines 5 and 10 are added. The firm's total taxes are $6,210.
LINE 13	The net taxes are $6,210.
LINE 14	Enter the total deposits for the quarter including any overpayment applied from the previous quarter. United Auto Supply deposited the correct amount of $6,210.
LINE 15	The balance due is zero.
LINE 17	This section is a summary of the employer's tax liability. If line 13 is less than $500, the employer does not need to complete line 17. We will assume that United Auto Supply is a monthly depositor (check second box). Remember, a firm is a monthly depositor if the amount of employment taxes during the lookback period is not more than $50,000. Also remember that the lookback period is defined as the four consecutive quarters ending on June 30 of the prior year.

EXHIBIT 14-3 Form 941

Form **941** Employer's Quarterly Federal Tax Return

Department of the Treasury
Internal Revenue Service (O)

▶ See separate instructions for information on completing this return.
Please type or print.

Enter state code for state in which deposits were made ONLY if different from state in address to the right ▶ (see page 3 of instructions).

Name (as distinguished from trade name)	Date quarter ended		OMB No. 1545-0029
	December 31, 19XX		T
Trade name, if any	Employer identification number		FF
United Auto Supply	99-9999991		FD
Address (number and street)	City, state, and ZIP code		FP
100 Main Street	Houston, TX 77001		I
			T

If address is different from prior return, check here ▶

IRS Use

1 1 1 1 1 1 1 1 1   2   3 3 3 3 3 3 3   4 4 4   5 5 5
6   7   8 8 8 8 8 8 8   9 9 9 9   10 10 10 10 10 10 10 10 10

If you do not have to file returns in the future, check here ▶ ☐ and enter date final wages paid ▶
If you are a seasonal employer, see **Seasonal employers** on page 1 of the instructions and check here ▶

1	Number of employees in the pay period that includes March 12th . ▶	**1**		
2	Total wages and tips, plus other compensation	**2**	26,000	00
3	Total income tax withheld from wages, tips, and sick pay	**3**	2,232	00
4	Adjustment of withheld income tax for preceding quarters of calendar year	**4**		
5	Adjusted total of income tax withheld (line 3 as adjusted by line 4—see instructions) . . .	**5**	2,232	00
6	Taxable social security wages	6a	26,000	00	× 12.4% (.124) =	**6b**	3,224	00
	Taxable social security tips	6c			× 12.4% (.124) =	**6d**		
7	Taxable Medicare wages and tips . . .	7a	26,000	00	× 2.9% (.029) =	**7b**	754	00
8	Total social security and Medicare taxes (add lines 6b, 6d, and 7b). Check here if wages are not subject to social security and/or Medicare tax . . . . ▶ ☐	**8**	3,978	00
9	Adjustment of social security and Medicare taxes (see instructions for required explanation) Sick Pay $_____ ± Fractions of Cents $_____ ± Other $_____ =	**9**		
10	Adjusted total of social security and Medicare taxes (line 8 as adjusted by line 9—see instructions)	**10**	3,978	00
11	**Total taxes** (add lines 5 and 10)	**11**	6,210	00
12	Advance earned income credit (EIC) payments made to employees	**12**		
13	Net taxes (subtract line 12 from line 11). **This should equal line 17, column (d) below (or line D of Schedule B (Form 941))**	**13**	6,210	00
14	Total deposits for quarter, including overpayment applied from a prior quarter	**14**	6,210	00
15	Balance due (subtract line 14 from line 13). See instructions	**15**	0	00
16	Overpayment, if line 14 is more than line 13, enter excess here ▶ $_____ and check if to be: ☐ Applied to next return **OR** ☐ Refunded.			

● **All filers:** If line 13 is less than $500, you need not complete line 17 or Schedule B (Form 941).
● **Semiweekly schedule depositors:** Complete Schedule B (Form 941) and check here . . . . ▶ ☐
● **Monthly schedule depositors:** Complete line 17, columns (a) through (d), and check here . . . . ▶ ☒

17	Monthly Summary of Federal Tax Liability. Do not complete if you were a semiweekly schedule depositor.			
	(a) First month liability	**(b)** Second month liability	**(c)** Third month liability	**(d)** Total liability for quarter
	2,107	2,101	2,002	6,210

Sign Here

Under penalties of perjury, I declare that I have examined this return, including accompanying schedules and statements, and to the best of my knowledge and belief, it is true, correct, and complete.

Signature ▶ *Lucille Garcia*   Print Your Name and Title ▶ Lucille Garcia Owner   Date ▶ 12/31/XX

Form 940-EZ

Objective 3
Prepare Form 940-EZ.

Depositing the Tax

FUTA Amount to Deposit For deposit purposes, FUTA tax is figured quarterly. A firm determines its FUTA tax for each of the first three quarters by multiplying by .008 that part of the first $7,000 paid to each employee during the quarter. For the fourth quarter, the amount is the total FUTA tax for the year minus the first three quarters of the year.

Employers Required to Deposit (More than $100 for a Quarter) If the FUTA tax for any of the calendar year quarters is over $100 (including any undeposited

EXHIBIT 14-4 | Form 940-EZ

Form **940-EZ**	**Employer's Annual Federal Unemployment (FUTA) Tax Return**	OMB No. 1545-1110

Department of the Treasury
Internal Revenue Service (O)

		T	
Name (as distinguished from trade name)	Calendar year 19XX	FF	
		FD	
Trade name, if any		FP	
United Auto SUpply		I	
Address and ZIP code	Employer identification number	T	
100 Main Street Houston, TX 77001	99 : 9999991		

Follow the chart under Who May Use Form 940-EZ on page 2. If you cannot use Form 940-EZ, you must use Form 940 instead.

A Enter the amount of contributions paid to your state unemployment fund. (See instructions for line A on page 4.)▶ $ .... 1,512 | 00

B (1) Enter the name of the state where you have to pay contributions . . . . ▶ Texas
(2) Enter your state reporting number as shown on state unemployment tax return ▶ 99999

If you will not have to file returns in the future, check here (see Who must file on page 2) and complete and sign the return . . . . . ▶ ☐
If this is an Amended Return, check here . . . . ▶ ☐

Part I Taxable Wages and FUTA Tax

1	Total payments (including payments shown on lines 2 and 3) during the calendar year for services of employees	**1**		72,770	00
			Amount paid		
2	Exempt payments. (Explain all exempt payments, attaching additional sheets if necessary.) ▶	**2**			
3	Payments for services of more than $7,000. Enter only amounts over the first $7,000 paid to each employee. Do not include any exempt payments from line 2. Do not use your state wage limitation. The $7,000 amount is the Federal wage base. Your state wage base may be different	**3**	44,770	00	
4	Total exempt payments (add lines 2 and 3)	**4**		44,770	00
5	**Total taxable wages** (subtract line 4 from line 1) . . . . ▶	**5**		28,000	00
6	FUTA tax. Multiply the wages on line 5 by .008 and enter here. (If the result is over $100, also complete Part II.) .	**6**		224	00
7	Total FUTA tax deposited for the year, including any overpayment applied from a prior year (from your records) .	**7**		224	00
8	Amount you owe (subtract line 7 from line 6). This should be $100 or less. Pay to "Internal Revenue Service." ▶	**8**		0	00
9	Overpayment (subtract line 6 from line 7). Check if it is to be: ☐ Applied to next return or ☐ Refunded ▶	**9**			

Part II Record of Quarterly Federal Unemployment Tax Liability (Do not include state liability.) Complete only if line 6 is over $100.

Quarter	First (Jan. 1 – Mar. 31)	Second (Apr. 1 – June 30)	Third (July 1 – Sept. 30)	Fourth (Oct. 1 – Dec. 31)	Total for year
Liability for quarter	79.00	67.00	48.00	30.00	224.00

Under penalties of perjury, I declare that I have examined this return, including accompanying schedules and statements, and, to the best of my knowledge and belief, it is true, correct, and complete, and that no part of any payment made to a state unemployment fund claimed as a credit was, or is to be, deducted from the payments to employees.

Signature ▶ *Lucille Garcia* Title (Owner, etc.) ▶ Owner Date ▶ 1/31/XX

amount from any earlier quarter), the FUTA tax must be deposited by the last day of the first month after the quarter ends. For example, for the quarter that ends on December 31 (October–December) the due date is January 31.

Employers Required to Deposit (Less than $100 for a Quarter, But More than $100 for the Year) If the FUTA tax for any of the calendar year quarters is $100 or less (including any undeposited amount from any earlier quarter), the tax may be carried over to the next quarter. If the FUTA tax for the fourth quarter (plus any undeposited amount from any earlier quarter) is over $100, the entire amount must be deposited by the due date of Form 940.

Employers Not Required to Deposit (Less than $100 for the Year) If the total FUTA tax for the year is $100 or less, the employer has two options: pay the FUTA tax with Form 940 or make a deposit.

When to File The due date of Form 940 is January 31. However, if all FUTA taxes were deposited when due, an employer may file Form 940 on or before February 10.

Deposits are made by electronic funds transfer (EFTPS) or in an authorized financial institution using a federal tax deposit (FTD) coupon. Form 8109, Federal Tax Deposit Coupon Book, is sent to the employer automatically after he or she has applied for an employer identification number (see Exhibit 14-2).

Completing Form 940-EZ   United Auto Supply completed Form 940-EZ (Exhibit 14-4) for the 19XX calendar year on January 31, 19XX. The heading includes the trade name, address, and employer identification number. For Question A the firm paid $1,512 to the state unemployment fund. The state is Texas (Question B1), and the state reporting number is 99999 (Question B2).

A firm can use Form 940-EZ if three conditions are met: (1) unemployment contributions are paid to only one state, (2) all state unemployment contributions are paid by January 31, and (3) all wages that were taxable for FUTA tax are also taxable for the state's unemployment tax. If any or all of these three conditions are not met, a firm would have to use Form 940 instead. We will assume that United Auto Supply meets the three conditions and can use Form 940-EZ.

Here is the process of completing Form 940-EZ (this form has changed from time to time):

Part I Computation of Taxable Wages

LINE 1	Enter the total payments made to employees during the calendar year, even if they are not taxable. The firm paid $72,770.
LINE 3	Enter the total amounts of more than $7,000 that were paid to each employee. The excess was $44,770 ($72,770 – $28,000; [$28,000 is $7,000 times four employees]).
LINE 4	The total exempt payments are $44,770.
LINE 5	The firm had $28,000 in taxable wages ($72,770 – $44,770).
LINE 6	The total FUTA tax is $224. This is determined by multiplying line 5 ($28,000) times .008.
LINE 7	The firm deposited $224.00 for the year.
LINE 8	The balance due is zero.

Part II Record of Quarterly Federal Unemployment Tax Liability   This part must be completed if the total tax (Part I, line 6) is over $100. Remember that the liability for the fourth quarter is the total tax (Part I, line 6) minus the liability for the first three quarters of the year. The firm had the following liabilities for the first through fourth quarters: $79, $67, $48, and $30, for a total of $224.

The Payment of Payroll Liabilities

Objective 4
Record the payment of payroll liabilities.

Social Security, Medicare, and federal income taxes must be computed and filed on Form 941 (see Exhibit 14-3). We assumed that United Auto Supply if a monthly depositor. Remember, a firm is a monthly depositor if the amount of employment taxes during the lookback period is not more than $50,000. Also remember that the lookback period is defined as the four consecutive quarters ending on June 30 of the prior year. Therefore, the Social Security tax (employer and employee), Medicare tax (employer and employee), and federal income tax (employee only) must be deposited by the fifteenth day of the following month. United Auto Supply debits (a) payroll liabilities and credits Cash for $2,002 (see Exhibits 14-2 and 14-3) when the deposit is made.

Payments for the employer's (b) state and (c) federal unemployment tax liabilities were made on January 31, 19XX, for the quarter ended December 31, 19XX. The firm pays $202.50 ($3,750 × 5.4 percent) to the State Unemployment Commission of Texas. The firm pays the federal unemployment taxes of $30 ($3,750 × .8 percent) to the Federal Reserve Bank.

Using T accounts, the payments are recorded and paid as follows:

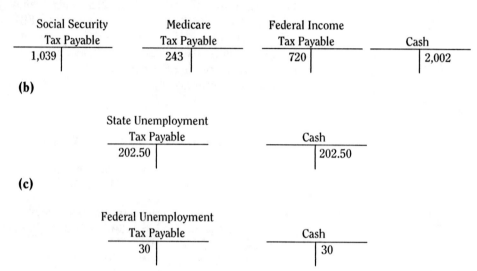

(a)

Social Security Tax Payable	Medicare Tax Payable	Federal Income Tax Payable	Cash
1,039	243	720	2,002

(b)

State Unemployment Tax Payable	Cash
202.50	202.50

(c)

Federal Unemployment Tax Payable	Cash
30	30

Let's assume that a firm deducted and collected $552 in medical insurance payments from its employees for a calendar year. A few weeks after the end of the year, this amount was paid to an insurance company. We can illustrate this payment using T accounts as follows:

Medical Insurance Payable	Cash
552	552

Form W-2

The employer must give copies B and C of **Form W-2, Wage and Tax Statement**, to each employee. Hu Le's Form W-2, as illustrated in Exhibit 14-5, shows (a) total wages and other compensation paid; (b) amounts deducted for income tax; (c) amounts deducted for social security and Medicare taxes; and other disclosures, if applicable. The employer must give each employee the statement by January 31 following the end of the calendar year covered. If the employment ends before the close of the year, the employee may request the form earlier. In this case, the employer must give the employee the statement within thirty days of the employee's written request, if the thirty-day period ends before January.

Form W-3

Each year, the employer must file **Form W-3, Transmittal of Income and Tax Statements**, to transmit Copy A of Forms W-2 to the Social Security Administration. Form W-3, as shown in Exhibit 14-6, and Copy A of Forms W-2 must be filed by the last day of

| EXHIBIT 14-5 | Form W-2: Wage and Tax Statement, Copy B |

a Control number	22222	Void ☐	For Official Use Only ▶ OMB No. 1545-0008	
b Employer's identification number 99-9999991			1 Wages, tips, other compensation 26,250.00	2 Federal income tax withheld 2,250.00
c Employer's name, address, and ZIP code United Auto Supply 100 Main Street Houston, Texas 77001			3 Social security wages 26,250.00	4 Social security tax withheld 1,627.50
			5 Medicare wages and tips 26,250.00	6 Medicare tax withheld 380.63
			7 Social security tips	8 Allocated tips
d Employee's social security number 400-00-0000			9 Advance EIC payment	10 Dependent care benefits
e Employee's name (first, middle initial, last) Hu Le 12 G Avenue Houston, Texas 77002			11 Nonqualified plans	12 Benefits included in box 1
			13 See Instrs. for box 13	14 Other
f Employee's address and ZIP code			15 Statutory employee ☐ Deceased ☐ Pension plan ☐ Legal rep. ☐ Hshld. emp. ☐ Subtotal ☐ Deferred compensation ☐	
16 State Employer's state I.D. No.	17 State wages, tips, etc.	18 State income tax	19 Locality name 20 Local wages, tips, etc.	21 Local income tax

Cat. No. 10134D   Department of the Treasury—Internal Revenue Service

Form W-2 **Wage and Tax Statement**

Copy A For Social Security Administration

For Paperwork Reduction Act Notice, see separate instructions.

February after the calendar year for which the Forms W-2 are prepared. The Social Security Administration will process these forms and relay the income tax data from these forms to the Internal Revenue Service.

Worker's Compensation Insurance

Objective 5
Calculate and record worker's compensation insurance.

Employees and their dependents are protected against losses due to on-the-job injury or death by **worker's compensation insurance**. The employer pays the premium in advance, based on the estimated payroll for the year. The insurance premiums are usually stated in terms of each $100 of weekly wages paid to employees. Most states require employers to provide the insurance through plans administered by the state or through private insurance agencies approved by the state. Premium rates vary among the types of jobs and the firm's historical number of accidents.

At United Auto Supply, there are two different grades (types) of work: office clerical and sales. At the beginning of the year, the firm's accountant estimated the annual premium as follows:

GRADE OF WORK	ESTIMATED PAYROLL	RATE PER HUNDRED	PREMIUM
Office Clerical	$30,000	.13	$ 39.00*
Sales	$40,000	.70	280.00**
Total Estimated Premium			$319.00

*$30,000 × .0013 = $39.00.
**$40,000 × .007 = $280.00.

EXHIBIT 14-6	Form W-3: Transmittal of Income and Tax Statements

DO NOT STAPLE

a Control number	33333	For Official Use Only ▶ OMB No. 1545-0008		

b		941	Military	943		1 Wages, tips, other compensation	2 Federal income tax withheld
	Kind of Payer	XX □	□	□		72,770.00	9,411.00
		CT-1 □	Hshld. □	Medicare govt. emp. □		3 Social security wages 72,770.00	4 Social security tax withheld 4,511.74

c Total number of statements 4	d Establishment number --	5 Medicare wages and tips 72,770.00	6 Medicare tax withheld 1,055.17

e Employer's identification number 99-9999991	7 Social security tips --	8 Allocated tips --

f Employer's name United Auto Supply 100 Main Street Houston, Texas 77001	9 Advance EIC payments --	10 Dependent care benefits --
	11 Nonqualified plans --	12 Deferred compensation --
	13	
	14	

g Employer's address and ZIP code		
h Other EIN used this year --	15 Income tax withheld by third-party payer --	
i Employer's state I.D. No. --		

Under penalties of perjury, I declare that I have examined this return and accompanying documents, and, to the best of my knowledge and belief, they are true, correct, and complete.

Signature ▶ Lucille Garcia   Title ▶ **Owner**   Date ▶ 1/31/XX
Telephone number (713) 999-9999

Using T accounts, the amount paid at the beginning of the year was recorded as follows:

Prepaid Insurance		Cash	
319			319

At the end of the year, the accountant analyzed the payroll data for the year. The actual payroll for the year is as follows:

GRADE OF WORK	ACTUAL PAYROLL	RATE PER HUNDRED	PREMIUM
Office Clerical	$32,500	.13	$ 42.25
Sales	$40,750	.70	285.25
Total Actual Premium			$327.50
Less: Estimated Premium Paid January 1			319.00
Balance of Premium Due			$ 8.50

Using T accounts, the additional balance of the premium ($8.50) is paid as follows:

Insurance Expense		Cash	
8.50			8.50

If the firm had overpaid its insurance obligation then it would be due a refund.

Chapter Review

1. **Understand and compute employer's payroll taxes.**
   Employers are responsible for collecting payroll taxes and then remitting the taxes to the proper tax authorities. The payroll register must be expanded to include the employer's payroll taxes.

2. **Prepare Form 941.**
   An employer that is required to withhold federal income taxes and/or Social Security and Medicare taxes must file a return reporting the amounts withheld. Normally, Form 941, Employer's Quarterly Federal Tax Return, is used for this purpose.

3. **Prepare Form 940-EZ.**
   The Employer's Annual Federal Unemployment (FUTA) Tax Return (Form 940-EZ) is used to report the amount of unemployment taxes owed and paid.

4. **Record the payment of payroll liabilities.**
   The employer is responsible for paying payroll liabilities to the appropriate authorities. The employer must give copies B and C of Form W-2, Wage and Tax Statement, to each employee. Each year, the employer must file Form W-3, Transmittal of Income and Tax Statements, to transmit Copy A of Forms W-2 to the Social Security Administration.

5. **Calculate and record worker's compensation insurance.**
   Worker's compensation insurance protects employees and their dependents against on-the-job losses due to injury or death. The employer pays the premium in advance, based on the estimated payroll for the year. Most states require employers to provide worker's compensation insurance through plans administered by the state or through private insurance agencies approved by the state.

Glossary

Employer's Annual Federal Unemployment (FUTA) Tax Return (Form 940-EZ) Form to fill out and file that states the amount of federal unemployment taxes owed and paid

Employer's Quarterly Federal Tax Return (Form 941) Form that reports amounts withheld for federal income taxes and/or Social Security and Medicare taxes and the employer's matching Social Security and Medicare taxes

Federal Tax Deposit Coupon (Form 8109-B) Form used to indicate the type of tax being deposited; it must be included with each income tax and Social Security tax deposit

Federal Unemployment Tax Act (FUTA) Act that provides for the state and federal government to cooperate in establishing and administering an unemployment tax program

Form SS-4 Used to apply for an employer identification number (EIN)

Form W-2 Called the Wage and Tax Statement, this shows wages paid, income tax deductions, Social Security tax deductions, and other disclosures, if applicable

Form W-3 Used to transmit Copy A of Forms W-2 to the Social Security Administration

State Unemployment Tax (SUTA) Tax paid by the employer to comply with the federal government in establishing and administering the unemployment tax program

Worker's Compensation Insurance Protects employees and their dependents against on-the-job losses due to injury or death

Self-Test Questions for Review

(Answers are at the end of Chapter 14.)

1. Sue contributes $1,000 for Social Security taxes. Her employer will contribute
   a. exactly $1,000.
   b. more than $1,000.
   c. less than $1,000.
   d. exactly $2,000.

2. The federal unemployment tax rate used in this chapter is
   a. 5.4 percent.
   b. 8.0 percent.
   c. 0.8 percent.
   d. 0.54 percent.

3. A description for a transaction reads "Employer's Payroll Taxes for the Week Ended May 21, 19XX." The account debited for this transaction is
   a. Wages Payable
   b. Payroll Tax Expense.
   c. Wages Expense.
   d. Cash.

4. Form 941 is due by April 19XX. This due date pertains to the quarter ended
   a. December.
   b. June.
   c. September.
   d. March.

5. _____ is debited and _____ is credited when paying for worker's compensation insurance at the beginning of the year.
   a. Prepaid Insurance; Cash
   b. Cash; Prepaid Insurance
   c. Cash; Insurance Expense
   d. Insurance Expense; Cash

Practical Review Problem

Objective 5

Calculating and Recording Worker's Compensation Insurance The accountant for Smythe Company accumulated the following data for worker's compensation insurance for the year ended December 31, 19XX:

a. The company has five different grades (types) of work:

GRADE OF WORK	RATE PER HUNDRED	ESTIMATED PAYROLL
Office Clerical	.12	$76,000
Office Sales	.15	27,000
Outside Sales	.60	48,000
Drivers	1.20	31,000
Manufacturing	1.40	59,000

b. The actual payroll for the year is as follows:

GRADE OF WORK	RATE PER HUNDRED	ACTUAL PAYROLL
Office Clerical	.12	$81,300
Office Sales	.15	22,800
Outside Sales	.60	49,300
Drivers	1.20	30,900
Manufacturing	1.40	59,100

REQUIRED
1. Calculate the estimated premium.
2. Using T accounts, record the payment on January 1, 19XX, to Johnson Insurance Agency.
3. Calculate the actual premium.
4. Using T accounts, record the payment of the additional premium on December 31, 19XX, to Johnson Insurance Agency.

Answer to Practical Review Problem

1. Calculate the estimated premium.

Grade of Work	Estimated Payroll	Rate per Hundred	Premium
Office Clerical	*$76,000*	*.12*	*$ 91.20*
Office Sales	*27,000*	*.15*	*40.50*
Outside Sales	*48,000*	*.60*	*288.00*
Drivers	*31,000*	*1.20*	*372.00*
Manufacturing	*59,000*	*1.40*	*826.00*
Total Estimated Payroll			*$1,617.70*

2. Record the payment on January 1, 19XX.

Prepaid Insurance		Cash	
1,617.70			1,617.70

3. Calculate the actual premium.

Grade of Work	Actual Payroll	Rate per Hundred	Premium
Office Clerical	*$81,300*	*.12*	*$ 97.56*
Office Sales	*22,800*	*.15*	*34.20*
Outside Sales	*49,300*	*.60*	*295.80*
Drivers	*30,900*	*1.20*	*370.80*
Manufacturing	*59,100*	*1.40*	*827.40*
Total Actual Payroll			*$1,625.76*
Less: Estimated Premium Paid January 1			*1,617.70*
Balance of Premium Due			*$ 8.06*

4. Record the payment of the additional premium on December 31, 19XX.

Insurance Expense		Cash	
8.06			8.06

Discussion Questions

Q 14-1 Briefly explain what Form SS-4 is used for.

Q 14-2 Briefly explain the provisions of the Federal Unemployment Tax Act.

Q 14-3 For what is Form 941 used? What time period does it cover? When is it due?

Q 14-4 For what is Form 940-EZ used? What time period does it cover? When is it due?

Q 14-5 Briefly explain what Form 8109-B is used for.

Q 14-6 For deposit purposes, when is FUTA tax figured? Where are deposits made?

Q 14-7 Name the accounts that are debited or credited for the following payroll payments: (a) payment of Social Security, Medicare, and federal income taxes; (b) payment of state and federal unemployment taxes; and (c) payment of medical insurance.

Q 14-8 What is the purpose of Forms W-2 and W-3?

Q 14-9 What is the purpose of worker's compensation insurance? How is it administered? By whom is it administered?

Q 14-10 How do the premium rates for worker's compensation insurance vary? List at least two different grades (types) of work.

Exercises

Objective 1

E 14-1 Calculating and Recording Payroll Taxes Record each of the following payroll taxes separately using T accounts:

PAYROLL TAX	TAXABLE EARNINGS	RATE (%)
Social Security	$61,200	6.20
Medicare	61,200	1.45
Federal Unemployment Tax	37,800	0.80
State Unemployment Tax	37,800	5.40

Objective 2

E 14-2 Determining Form 941 Filings and Deposits Determine (a) the ending date of the quarter, (b) the due date of Form 941 for that quarter, and (c) when the Form 941 taxes must be deposited given the following situation: Garrison Lumber Supply is a monthly depositor and Form 941 is prepared for the quarter that begins in January.

Objective 3

E 14-3 Completing Form 940-EZ Referring to Form 940-EZ in Exhibit 14-4, fill in the blanks for Gomex Oil Tool Services: Part I, line 1, $200,000; line 3, $120,000; line 4, (a); line 5, (b); and line 6, (c).

Objective 4

E 14-4 Paying Payroll Liabilities Use T accounts to record the payment of the following payroll taxes and deductions during 19XX:

TAX OR DEDUCTION	DATE PAID	AMOUNT
Social Security Tax	April 14	$4,960
Medicare Tax	April 14	1,160
Federal Income Tax	April 14	9,370
State Unemployment Tax	April 30	4,320
Federal Unemployment Tax	April 30	640

In addition, record a payment of $967 for life insurance using T accounts.

Objective 5   **E 14-5** **Calculating Worker's Compensation Insurance** Calculate the premium:

GRADE OF WORK	RATE PER HUNDRED	ESTIMATED PAYROLL
Office Clerical	.11	$15,000
Office Sales	.18	18,000
Manufacturing	1.20	34,000
Drivers	1.10	27,000

Objective 1   **E 14-6** **Recording Payroll Taxes** Record the following payroll taxes in a general journal, page 74, for the week ending March 12, 19XX:

PAYROLL TAX	TAXABLE EARNINGS	RATE (%)
Social Security	$122,400	6.20
Medicare	122,400	1.45
Federal Unemployment Tax	75,600	0.80
State Unemployment Tax	75,600	5.40

Objective 2   **E 14-7** **Determining Form 941 Deposits** Referring to Form 941 in Exhibit 14-3, determine when the deposit is due for the following business firms:

FIRM	TYPE OF DEPOSITOR
a. Chen Window Supply	Monthly
b. Powell Computer Services	Semiweekly (taxes withheld on Friday)
c. Herrea Department Store	Semiweekly (taxes withheld on Tuesday)

Objective 5   **E 14-8** **Recording Worker's Compensation Insurance** On January 1, 19XX, Mancuso Feed Supply estimated that its worker's compensation insurance premium for the year was $870. At the end of the year, on December 31, 19XX, the firm calculated the actual premium of $930. From this information, (a) record the estimated premium using T accounts, (b) calculate the balance of premium due, and (c) record the additional premium using T accounts.

Problems

Objective 1   **P 14-1** **Calculating and Recording Payroll Taxes** Logan Plastic Supply had the following payroll taxes during the second week of October 19XX:

WEEK ENDING	PAYROLL TAX	TAXABLE EARNINGS	RATE (%)
October 14	Social Security	$225,400	6.20
October 14	Medicare	225,400	1.45
October 14	Federal Unemployment Tax	127,800	0.80
October 14	State Unemployment Tax	127,800	5.40

REQUIRED
1. In T account form, calculate the payroll taxes for the week separately.
2. Prepare general journal entries to record the payroll at the end of the week (use the information in 1).

Objective 2   **P 14-2** **Preparing Form 941** The accountant for Springtime Video Store located at 2400 Monterey Road, San Jose, California 95111, is accumulating the necessary data to complete Form 941 for the quarter ended December 31, 19XX. The employer's identification number is 44-4444441. The data for lines 2 through 17 are as follows:

Total wages subject to withholding, $35,000; total income tax withheld from wages, $3,200; taxable Social Security and Medicare wages paid, $35,000.

The data for the record of federal tax liability are as follows (monthly depositor):

■ First month, $3,059; second month, $2,421; third month, $3,075.

The owner, Joyce Parsons, signs the form December 31, 19XX.

REQUIRED
Complete Form 941.

Objective 3

P 14-3 **Preparing Form 940-EZ** John Emerson is the accountant for Pembrook Clothing Store. The firm's address is 650 First Street, Minneapolis, Minnesota 55403, and the employer's identification number is 00-2345678. John accumulated the following data to complete Form 940-EZ for the year ended December 31, 19XX:

■ Questions—The firm listed $2,268 for question A

■ The state where contributions are paid is Minnesota, the reporting number is 432-876

■ Part I—Total payments, $96,800; payments for services of more than $7,000, $54,800

■ Part II—First quarter, $171; second quarter, $102; third quarter, $42; and fourth quarter, $21

The owner, Mariano Reyes, signs the form January 31, 19XX.

REQUIRED
Complete Form 940-EZ.

Objective 5

P 14-4 **Calculating and Recording Worker's Compensation Insurance** The accountant for Fulton Company accumulated the following data for worker's compensation insurance for the year ended December 31, 19XX:

a. The company has five different grades (types) of work:

GRADE OF WORK	RATE PER HUNDRED	ESTIMATED PAYROLL
Office Clerical	.16	$123,000
Office Sales	.18	165,000
Outside Sales	.80	218,000
Drivers	1.30	98,000
Production	1.50	146,000

b. The actual payroll for the year is as follows:

GRADE OF WORK	RATE PER HUNDRED	ACTUAL PAYROLL
Office Clerical	.16	$125,700
Office Sales	.18	171,800
Outside Sales	.80	214,670
Drivers	1.30	99,690
Production	1.50	148,580

REQUIRED
1. Calculate the estimated premium.
2. Using T accounts, record the payment on January 1, 19XX, to Robbins Insurance Agency.
3. Calculate the actual premium.

4. Using T accounts, record the payment of the additional premium on December 31, 19XX, to Robbins Insurance Agency.

Checklist of Key Figures

P 14-1   (2.) Payroll Tax Expense, $25,166.70
P 14-2   Line 8, $5,355
P 14-3   Part I, Line 5, $42,000
P 14-4   (2) Cash, $5,701.80

Answers to Self-Test Questions

1. a   **2.** c   **3.** b   **4.** d   **5.** a

Payroll Review Problem

This review problem will test your knowledge of payroll. The working papers are in your *Working Papers* manual. The answer to this review problem will be provided by your instructor.

Denise Smithfield is the payroll accountant for Liberty Plumbing Supply. She reviews the following general payroll information:

- The owner of Liberty Plumbing Supply is Gayle Parker
- The firm is located at 3794 Las Olas, El Paso, Texas 79951
- State unemployment taxes are 5.4 percent of the first $7,000 of taxable income for each employee
- The employer's identification number is 88-0945121
- Social Security tax is 6.2 percent of the first $68,400 of earnings for each employee; Medicare tax is 1.45 percent for each employee with no maximum; both employer and employee pay the same amount
- Federal unemployment taxes are 0.8 percent of the first $7,000 of taxable income for each employee
- Liberty Plumbing Supply uses a special payroll checking account

Denise accumulates the following data from a completed payroll register for the week ended June 30, 19XX:

- The firm has five employees
- For the week, regular earnings were $1,700; overtime earnings were $300
- All earnings are taxable for Social Security and Medicare tax purposes
- Federal income tax deductions total $295
- $1,000 of earnings are taxable for both federal and state unemployment taxes

Denise also reviews payroll information for the quarter that ends June 30, 19XX, and finds (Form 941):

- Total wages subject to withholding total $30,000
- Total income tax withheld from wages total $3,750
- Taxable Social Security and Medicare wages paid total $30,000

The data for the record of federal tax liability is (Form 941) as follows:

■ First month, $2,967; second month, $2,382; third month, $2,991

The owner signs Form 941 on July 31, 19XX.

REQUIRED
1. Record the employee's and the employer's payroll in a general journal, page 18, for the week ended June 30, 19XX.
2. Make the necessary deposit in a special payroll checking account to pay employees. Use T accounts.
3. Complete Form 941 for the quarter ended June 30, 19XX (assume monthly depositor).

Index

WORKING PAPERS
to accompany

Introduction to College Accounting

FOURTH EDITION

Gregory W. Bischoff

Houston Community College

Harcourt Brace Custom Publishers

Fort Worth   Philadelphia   San Diego   New York   Orlando   Austin   San Antonio
Toronto   Montreal   London   Sydney   Tokyo

ISBN: 0-03-044737-2

Address for Orders
Harcourt Brace Custom Publishers, 6277 Sea Harbor Drive, Orlando, FL 32887-6777
1-800-782-4479

Address for Editorial Correspondence
Harcourt Brace Custom Publishers, 301 Commerce Street, Suite 3700, Fort Worth, TX 76102

Web site Address
http://www.hbcollege.com

Printed in the United States of America

8 9 0 1 2 3 4 5 6 7   795   9 8 7 6 5 4 3 2 1

Harcourt Brace Custom Publishers

Name _____

Section _____ Date _____

E 1-1

a. _____

b. _____

c. _____

E 1-2

a. _____

b. _____

E 1-3

(a) _____

(b) _____

(c) _____

E 1-4

(a) _____

(b) _____

(c) _____

(d) _____

E 1-5

a. _____

b. _____

c. _____

d. _____

E 1-6

a. _____

b. _____

c. _____

E 1-7

(a) _____

(b) _____

(c) _____

Name _____

Section _____ Date _____

Name _____

Section _____ Date _____

a. Increased: _____

   Decreased: _____

b. Increased: _____

   Decreased: _____

c. Increased: _____

   Decreased: _____

d. Increased: _____

   Decreased: _____

e. Increased: _____

   Decreased: _____

Name _____   **P 1-2**

Section _____ Date _____

1 and 2.

								=	Liabilities	+	Owner's Equity
	Cash	+	Office Equip.	+	Office Supp.	+	Library	=	Accounts Payable	+	Capital
a.											
b.								=			
Bal.											
c.								=			
Bal.											
d.								=			
Bal.											
e.								=			
Bal.											
f.								=			
Bal.											

3.   Left Side   Right Side

Account	Final Balance	Account	Final Balance
Cash	+	Accounts Payable	+
Office Equipment	+	, Capital	+
Office Supplies	+		
Library	+		
Left Side Totals		Right Side Totals	

1 and 2.

	Cash	+	Office Equip.	+	Office Supp.	+	Library	=	Accounts Payable	+	Capital
			Assets					=	Liabilities	+	Owner's Equity
a.											
b.	_____							=	_____		_____
Bal.											
c.	_____							=	_____		_____
Bal.											
d.	_____							=	_____		_____
Bal.											
e.	_____							=	_____		_____
Bal.											
f.	_____							=	_____		_____
Bal.											

3.   Left Side   Right Side

Account	Final Balance	Account	Final Balance
Cash	+	Accounts Payable	+
Office Equipment	+	, Capital	+
Office Supplies	+		
Library	+ _____		_____
Left Side Totals		Right Side Totals	

Name _____

Section _____ Date _____

4. _____
   _____
   _____

a.   Account Debited: _____

     Account Credited: _____

b.   Account Debited: _____

     Account Credited: _____

E 2-2

a.

b.

c.

d.

e.

Name _____

Section _____ Date _____

E 2-3

a. _____
b. _____
c. _____
d. _____
e. _____
f. _____
g. _____
h. _____
i. _____

E 2-4

a. _____
b. _____
c. _____
d. _____
e. _____
f. _____
g. _____
h. _____

E 2-5

a. _____
b. _____
c. _____
d. _____
e. _____
f. _____
g. _____
h. _____
i. _____
j. _____
k. _____
l. _____
m. _____
n. _____

a.

b.

c.

d.

e.

f.

E 2-7

Assets	=	Liabilities	+	Owner's Equity	+	Revenues	–	Expenses

Name _____

Section _____ Date _____

E 2-8

(a) _____
_____
_____

(b) _____
_____
_____

Name _____

Section _____ Date _____

1 and 2.

Date		Account	
_____.	Account Debited:	_____	
	Account Credited:	_____	
_____.	Account Debited:	_____	
	Account Credited:	_____	
_____.	Account Debited:	_____	
	Account Credited:	_____	
_____.	Account Debited:	_____	
	Account Credited:	_____	
_____.	Account Debited:	_____	
	Account Credited:	_____	
_____.	Account Debited:	_____	
	Account Credited:	_____	
_____.	Account Debited:	_____	
	Account Credited:	_____	

Name _____

Section _____ Date _____

a.

b.

c.

d.

e.

f.

g.

h.

i.

Name _____

Section _____ Date _____

1.

a.

b.

c.

d.

e.

f.

g.

h.

i.

j.

k.

1.

m.

2.

Assets	=	Liabilities	+	Owner's Equity	+	Revenues	–	Expenses

3. _____
_____
_____

Accounts	Debit	Credit

4. _____
_____
_____

a. _____
b. _____
c. _____

E 3-2

a. _____
b. _____
c. _____
d. _____
e. _____
_____

E 3-3

a.

b.

c.

d.

Name _____

Section _____ Date _____

E 3-4

GENERAL JOURNAL

Page ___1___

Date	Description	Post. Ref.	Debit	Credit

GENERAL LEDGER ACCOUNTS

								Account No.		
Account:										
		Post.					Balance			
Date	Item	Ref.	Debit		Credit		Debit		Credit	

								Account No.		
Account:										
		Post.					Balance			
Date	Item	Ref.	Debit		Credit		Debit		Credit	

								Account No.		
Account:										
		Post.					Balance			
Date	Item	Ref.	Debit		Credit		Debit		Credit	

								Account No.		
Account:										
		Post.					Balance			
Date	Item	Ref.	Debit		Credit		Debit		Credit	

								Account No.		
Account:										
		Post.					Balance			
Date	Item	Ref.	Debit		Credit		Debit		Credit	

Account:							Account No.	
		Post.					Balance	
Date	Item	Ref.	Debit		Credit		Debit	Credit

Account:							Account No.	
		Post.					Balance	
Date	Item	Ref.	Debit		Credit		Debit	Credit

Account:							Account No.	
		Post.					Balance	
Date	Item	Ref.	Debit		Credit		Debit	Credit

Account:							Account No.	
		Post.					Balance	
Date	Item	Ref.	Debit		Credit		Debit	Credit

Name _____

Section _____ Date _____

a. _____

b. _____

c. _____

d. _____

e. _____

f. _____

g. _____

h. _____

i. _____

j. _____

k. _____

GENERAL JOURNAL

Page _____

	Date	Description	Post. Ref.	Debit	Credit
a.					
b.					
c.					

Accounts	Debit	Credit

GENERAL JOURNAL

Page _____

Date	Description	Post. Ref.	Debit	Credit

Name _____

Section _____ Date _____

GENERAL JOURNAL   Page _____

Date	Description	Post. Ref.	Debit	Credit

1 and 2.

GENERAL LEDGER ACCOUNTS						
Account:					Account No.	
		Post.			Balance	
Date	Item	Ref.	Debit	Credit	Debit	Credit

Account:					Account No.	
		Post.			Balance	
Date	Item	Ref.	Debit	Credit	Debit	Credit

Account:					Account No.	
		Post.			Balance	
Date	Item	Ref.	Debit	Credit	Debit	Credit

Account:					Account No.	
		Post.			Balance	
Date	Item	Ref.	Debit	Credit	Debit	Credit

Account:					Account No.	
		Post.			Balance	
Date	Item	Ref.	Debit	Credit	Debit	Credit

1 and 2. *(continued)*

Account:							Account No.	
		Post.					Balance	
Date	Item	Ref.	Debit	Credit			Debit	Credit

Account:							Account No.	
		Post.					Balance	
Date	Item	Ref.	Debit	Credit			Debit	Credit

Account:							Account No.	
		Post.					Balance	
Date	Item	Ref.	Debit	Credit			Debit	Credit

Name _____

Section _____ Date _____

P 3-3

Accounts	Debit	Credit

1.   **GENERAL JOURNAL**   Page _____

Date		Description	Post. Ref.	Debit	Credit

Name _____

Section _____ Date _____

Name _____

Section _____ Date _____

Name _____

Section _____ Date _____

P 3-4

2/6

1.   **GENERAL JOURNAL**   Page _____

Date	Description	Post. Ref.	Debit	Credit

Name _____

Section _____ Date _____

2.

GENERAL LEDGER ACCOUNTS								
Account:						Account No.	
Date	Item	Post. Ref.	Debit	Credit	Balance Debit	Credit	

Account:					Account No.
Date	Item	Post. Ref.	Debit	Credit	Balance Debit	Credit

Account:					Account No.
Date	Item	Post. Ref.	Debit	Credit	Balance Debit	Credit

Account:					Account No.
Date	Item	Post. Ref.	Debit	Credit	Balance Debit	Credit

2.

Account:							Account No.	
Date	Item	Post. Ref.	Debit	Credit	Balance Debit		Credit	

GENERAL LEDGER ACCOUNTS

Account:							Account No.	
Date	Item	Post. Ref.	Debit	Credit	Balance Debit		Credit	

Account:							Account No.	
Date	Item	Post. Ref.	Debit	Credit	Balance Debit		Credit	

Account:							Account No.	
Date	Item	Post. Ref.	Debit	Credit	Balance Debit		Credit	

2. *(continued)*

Account:						Account No.	
		Post.				Balance	
Date	Item	Ref.	Debit	Credit	Debit	Credit	

Account:						Account No.	
		Post.				Balance	
Date	Item	Ref.	Debit	Credit	Debit	Credit	

Account:						Account No.	
		Post.				Balance	
Date	Item	Ref.	Debit	Credit	Debit	Credit	

Account:						Account No.	
		Post.				Balance	
Date	Item	Ref.	Debit	Credit	Debit	Credit	

Account:						Account No.	
		Post.				Balance	
Date	Item	Ref.	Debit	Credit	Debit	Credit	

3. _____
_____
_____

Accounts	Debit	Credit

E 4-2

E 4-3

a. _____

b. _____

c. _____

E 4-5

E 4-6

_____
_____
_____

Account	Trial Balance		Adjustments	
	Debit	Credit	Debit	Credit

_____
_____
_____

Adjusted Trial Balance		Income Statement		Balance Sheet	
Debit	Credit	Debit	Credit	Debit	Credit

_____

_____

_____

Account	Trial Balance		Adjustments	
	Debit	Credit	Debit	Credit

Adjusted Trial Balance		Income Statement		Balance Sheet	
Debit	Credit	Debit	Credit	Debit	Credit

Name _____

Section _____ Date _____

1. a. _____ $ _____

_____

_____ $ _____

_____

_____ $ _____

b.

c.

d.

2. _____

1.

2. _____
_____
_____
_____

Account	Trial Balance		Adjustments	
	Debit	Credit	Debit	Credit

_____
_____
_____
_____

Adjusted Trial Balance		Income Statement		Balance Sheet	
Debit	Credit	Debit	Credit	Debit	Credit

1.

2. _____
_____
_____
_____

Account	Trial Balance		Adjustments	
	Debit	Credit	Debit	Credit

Adjusted Trial Balance		Income Statement		Balance Sheet	
Debit	Credit	Debit	Credit	Debit	Credit

1.

2. _____
_____
_____

Account	Trial Balance		Adjustments	
	Debit	Credit	Debit	Credit

Name _____

Section _____ Date _____

Adjusted Trial Balance		Income Statement		Balance Sheet	
Debit	Credit	Debit	Credit	Debit	Credit

Name _____

Section _____ Date _____

a. _____
   _____
   _____

b. _____

c. _____
   _____

d. _____

e. _____
   _____
   _____

a. _____

b. _____

c. _____

d. _____

e. _____

f. _____

g. _____

h. _____

i _____

a. _____

b. _____

c. _____

d. _____

e. _____

f. _____

g. _____

h. _____

i _____

j. _____

Name _____

Section _____ Date _____

E 5-4

a. _____
b. _____
c. _____
d. _____

E 5-5

a. _____
b. _____
c. _____
d. _____
e. _____
f. _____
g. _____
h. _____
i _____
j. _____
k. _____
l. _____
m._____
n. _____

Name _____

Section _____ Date _____

GENERAL JOURNAL   Page ___3___

Date		Description	Post. Ref.	Debit	Credit

E 5-7

GENERAL JOURNAL   Page _____

Date		Description	Post. Ref.	Debit	Credit

GENERAL LEDGER ACCOUNTS

Account: _____   Account No. _____

					Balance	
Date	Item	Post. Ref.	Debit	Credit	Debit	Credit

Account: _____   Account No. _____

					Balance	
Date	Item	Post. Ref.	Debit	Credit	Debit	Credit

Account: _____   Account No. _____

					Balance	
Date	Item	Post. Ref.	Debit	Credit	Debit	Credit

Account:							Account No.	
		Post.				Balance		
Date	Item	Ref.	Debit	Credit	Debit		Credit	

Account:							Account No.	
		Post.				Balance		
Date	Item	Ref.	Debit	Credit	Debit		Credit	

Account:							Account No.	
		Post.				Balance		
Date	Item	Ref.	Debit	Credit	Debit		Credit	

Account:							Account No.	
		Post.				Balance		
Date	Item	Ref.	Debit	Credit	Debit		Credit	

Account:							Account No.	
		Post.				Balance		
Date	Item	Ref.	Debit	Credit	Debit		Credit	

2.   **GENERAL JOURNAL**   Page _____

Date	Description	Post. Ref.	Debit	Credit

1 and 3.

GENERAL LEDGER ACCOUNTS

Account: Account No.

Date	Item	Post. Ref.	Debit	Credit	Balance Debit	Balance Credit

Account: Account No.

Date	Item	Post. Ref.	Debit	Credit	Balance Debit	Balance Credit

Account: Account No.

Date	Item	Post. Ref.	Debit	Credit	Balance Debit	Balance Credit

continued

1 and 3. (*continued*)

Account:						Account No.	
		Post.			Balance		
Date	Item	Ref.	Debit	Credit	Debit	Credit	

Account:						Account No.	
		Post.			Balance		
Date	Item	Ref.	Debit	Credit	Debit	Credit	

Account:						Account No.	
		Post.			Balance		
Date	Item	Ref.	Debit	Credit	Debit	Credit	

Account:						Account No.	
		Post.			Balance		
Date	Item	Ref.	Debit	Credit	Debit	Credit	

Account:						Account No.	
		Post.			Balance		
Date	Item	Ref.	Debit	Credit	Debit	Credit	

1. _____
_____
_____

3.   **GENERAL JOURNAL**   Page _____

Date	Description	Post. Ref.	Debit	Credit

2 and 4.

GENERAL LEDGER ACCOUNTS						
Account:						Account No.
		Post.			Balance	
Date	Item	Ref.	Debit	Credit	Debit	Credit

Account:						Account No.
		Post.			Balance	
Date	Item	Ref.	Debit	Credit	Debit	Credit

Account:						Account No.
		Post.			Balance	
Date	Item	Ref.	Debit	Credit	Debit	Credit

Account:						Account No.
		Post.			Balance	
Date	Item	Ref.	Debit	Credit	Debit	Credit

Account:						Account No.
		Post.			Balance	
Date	Item	Ref.	Debit	Credit	Debit	Credit

2 and 4.

Account:								Account No.
		Post.				Balance		
Date	Item	Ref.	Debit	Credit	Debit		Credit	

Account:								Account No.
		Post.				Balance		
Date	Item	Ref.	Debit	Credit	Debit		Credit	

Account:								Account No.
		Post.				Balance		
Date	Item	Ref.	Debit	Credit	Debit		Credit	

Name _____

Section _____ Date _____

1.

(a)

(b)

(c)

(d)

Name _____

Section _____ Date _____

2. _____

_____

_____

Account	Trial Balance		Adjustments	
	Debit	Credit	Debit	Credit

_____
_____
_____

Adjusted Trial Balance		Income Statement		Balance Sheet	
Debit	Credit	Debit	Credit	Debit	Credit

3. _____
_____
_____

3. _____

_____

_____

4.   **GENERAL JOURNAL**   Page _____

Date		Description	Post. Ref.	Debit	Credit

5.

GENERAL LEDGER ACCOUNTS

Account:						Account No.	
Date	Item	Post Ref.	Debit	Credit	Balance		
					Debit	Credit	

Account:						Account No.	
Date	Item	Post Ref.	Debit	Credit	Balance		
					Debit	Credit	

Account:		Post	Debit	Credit	Account No.	
					Balance	
Date	Item	Ref.	Debit	Credit	Debit	Credit

Account:		Post	Debit	Credit	Account No.	
					Balance	
Date	Item	Ref.	Debit	Credit	Debit	Credit

Account:		Post	Debit	Credit	Account No.	
					Balance	
Date	Item	Ref.	Debit	Credit	Debit	Credit

Account:		Post	Debit	Credit	Account No.	
					Balance	
Date	Item	Ref.	Debit	Credit	Debit	Credit

continued

5. *(continued)*

Account:						Account No.	
		Post				Balance	
Date	Item	Ref.	Debit	Credit	Debit		Credit

Account:						Account No.	
		Post				Balance	
Date	Item	Ref.	Debit	Credit	Debit		Credit

Name _____

Section _____ Date _____

E 6-1

Nominal: _____

_____

_____

_____

_____

Real: _____

_____

_____

_____

E 6-2

_____

_____

_____

E 6-3

a. _____   b. _____

c. _____   d. _____

e. _____   f. _____

g. _____   h. _____

i. _____   j. _____

k. _____   l. _____

m. _____   n. _____

E 6-4

(a) _____

(b) _____

(c) _____

E 6-5

(a) _____

(b) _____

(c) _____

E 6-6

(a) _____

(b)

GENERAL JOURNAL

Page ___10___

Date		Description	Post. Ref.	Debit	Credit

E 6-7

GENERAL JOURNAL

Page _____

Date		Description	Post. Ref.	Debit	Credit

Name _____

Section _____ Date _____

Accounts	Debit	Credit

GENERAL JOURNAL

Page _____

Date	Description	Post. Ref.	Debit	Credit

1 and 2.

GENERAL LEDGER ACCOUNTS						
Account:					Account No.	
		Post.			Balance	
Date	Item	Ref.	Debit	Credit	Debit	Credit

Account:					Account No.	
		Post.			Balance	
Date	Item	Ref.	Debit	Credit	Debit	Credit

Account:					Account No.	
		Post.			Balance	
Date	Item	Ref.	Debit	Credit	Debit	Credit

Account:					Account No.	
		Post.			Balance	
Date	Item	Ref.	Debit	Credit	Debit	Credit

Account:					Account No.	
		Post.			Balance	
Date	Item	Ref.	Debit	Credit	Debit	Credit

1 and 2.

Account:						Account No.	
		Post.			Balance		
Date	Item	Ref.	Debit	Credit	Debit	Credit	

Account:						Account No.	
		Post.			Balance		
Date	Item	Ref.	Debit	Credit	Debit	Credit	

Account:						Account No.	
		Post.			Balance		
Date	Item	Ref.	Debit	Credit	Debit	Credit	

Account:						Account No.	
		Post.			Balance		
Date	Item	Ref.	Debit	Credit	Debit	Credit	

Account:						Account No.	
		Post.			Balance		
Date	Item	Ref.	Debit	Credit	Debit	Credit	

Account:						Account No.	
		Post.			Balance		
Date	Item	Ref.	Debit	Credit	Debit	Credit	

1   **GENERAL JOURNAL**   **Page** _____

Date	Description	Post. Ref.	Debit	Credit

2. _____

_____

Accounts	Debit	Credit

1   GENERAL JOURNAL   **Page** _____

Date	Description	Post. Ref.	Debit	Credit

2.

GENERAL LEDGER ACCOUNTS							
Account:						Account No.	
						Balance	
Date	Item	Post. Ref.	Debit	Credit		Debit	Credit

continued

2. *(continued)*

Account:									Account No.			
		Post.							Balance			
Date	Item	Ref.	Debit			Credit			Debit		Credit	

Account:									Account No.			
		Post.							Balance			
Date	Item	Ref.	Debit			Credit			Debit		Credit	

Account:									Account No.			
		Post.							Balance			
Date	Item	Ref.	Debit			Credit			Debit		Credit	

Account:									Account No.			
		Post.							Balance			
Date	Item	Ref.	Debit			Credit			Debit		Credit	

Name _____

Section _____ Date _____

2.

Account:					Account No.	
		Post.			Balance	
Date	Item	Ref.	Debit	Credit	Debit	Credit

Account:					Account No.	
		Post.			Balance	
Date	Item	Ref.	Debit	Credit	Debit	Credit

Account:					Account No.	
		Post.			Balance	
Date	Item	Ref.	Debit	Credit	Debit	Credit

Account:					Account No.	
		Post.			Balance	
Date	Item	Ref.	Debit	Credit	Debit	Credit

Account:					Account No.	
		Post.			Balance	
Date	Item	Ref.	Debit	Credit	Debit	Credit

2. *(continued)*

Account:							Account No.	
		Post.				Balance		
Date	Item	Ref.	Debit	Credit	Debit		Credit	

Account:							Account No.	
		Post.				Balance		
Date	Item	Ref.	Debit	Credit	Debit		Credit	

Account:							Account No.	
		Post.				Balance		
Date	Item	Ref.	Debit	Credit	Debit		Credit	

3. _____
_____
_____

Accounts	Debit	Credit

GENERAL JOURNAL   Page ___1___

Date	Description	Post. Ref.	Debit	Credit

continued

GENERAL JOURNAL   Page ____2____

Date	Description	Post. Ref.	Debit	Credit

GENERAL JOURNAL   Page ___3___

Date	Description	Post. Ref.	Debit	Credit

continued

GENERAL JOURNAL   Page ___4___

Date	Description	Post. Ref.	Debit	Credit

GENERAL JOURNAL   Page ___5___

Date	Description	Post. Ref.	Debit	Credit

continued

GENERAL JOURNAL   Page ___6___

Date	Description	Post. Ref.	Debit	Credit

GENERAL LEDGER ACCOUNTS

Account:						Account No.	
Date	Item	Post. Ref.	Debit	Credit	Balance		
					Debit	Credit	

Account:						Account No.	
Date	Item	Post. Ref.	Debit	Credit	Balance		
					Debit	Credit	

continued

Account:						Account No.	
		Post.				Balance	
Date	Item	Ref.	Debit	Credit	Debit		Credit

Account:						Account No.	
		Post.				Balance	
Date	Item	Ref.	Debit	Credit	Debit		Credit

Account:						Account No.	
		Post.				Balance	
Date	Item	Ref.	Debit	Credit	Debit		Credit

Account:						Account No.	
		Post.				Balance	
Date	Item	Ref.	Debit	Credit	Debit		Credit

Account:						Account No.	
		Post.				Balance	
Date	Item	Ref.	Debit	Credit	Debit	Credit	

Account:						Account No.	
		Post.				Balance	
Date	Item	Ref.	Debit	Credit	Debit	Credit	

Account:						Account No.	
		Post.				Balance	
Date	Item	Ref.	Debit	Credit	Debit	Credit	

continued

Name _____

Section _____ Date _____

Account:						Account No.	
		Post.			Balance		
Date	Item	Ref.	Debit	Credit	Debit	Credit	

Account:						Account No.	
		Post.			Balance		
Date	Item	Ref.	Debit	Credit	Debit	Credit	

Account:						Account No.	
		Post.			Balance		
Date	Item	Ref.	Debit	Credit	Debit	Credit	

Name _____

Section _____ Date _____

Accounting Cycle
Practical Review Problem

11/20

Account:								Account No.	
		Post.					Balance		
Date	Item	Ref.	Debit		Credit		Debit		Credit

Account:								Account No.	
		Post.					Balance		
Date	Item	Ref.	Debit		Credit		Debit		Credit

Account:								Account No.	
		Post.					Balance		
Date	Item	Ref.	Debit		Credit		Debit		Credit

continued

Account:							Account No.	
		Post.				Balance		
Date	Item	Ref.	Debit	Credit	Debit		Credit	

Account:							Account No.	
		Post.				Balance		
Date	Item	Ref.	Debit	Credit	Debit		Credit	

Account:							Account No.	
		Post.					Balance	
Date	Item	Ref.	Debit	Credit		Debit		Credit

Account:							Account No.	
		Post.					Balance	
Date	Item	Ref.	Debit	Credit		Debit		Credit

Account:							Account No.	
		Post.					Balance	
Date	Item	Ref.	Debit	Credit		Debit		Credit

continued

Account:						Account No.	
		Post.				Balance	
Date	Item	Ref.	Debit	Credit	Debit	Credit	

Account:						Account No.	
		Post.				Balance	
Date	Item	Ref.	Debit	Credit	Debit	Credit	

Account:						Account No.	
		Post.				Balance	
Date	Item	Ref.	Debit	Credit	Debit	Credit	

Account:						Account No.	
		Post.				Balance	
Date	Item	Ref.	Debit	Credit	Debit	Credit	

_____
_____
_____

Account	Trial Balance		Adjustments	
	Debit	Credit	Debit	Credit

_____
_____
_____

Adjusted Trial Balance		Income Statement		Balance Sheet	
Debit	Credit	Debit	Credit	Debit	Credit

continued

continued

Name _____

Section _____ Date _____

**Accounting Cycle
Practical Review Problem**

20/20

_____
_____
_____

Accounts	Debit	Credit

E 7-1

(a) **GENERAL JOURNAL** Page _____

Date	Description	Post. Ref.	Debit	Credit

(b) **SALES JOURNAL** Page _____

Date	Customer	Invoice Number	Terms	Post Ref.	Amount A/R (Dr.) Sales (Cr.)

E 7-2

ACCOUNTS RECEIVABLE SUBSIDIARY LEDGER

Customer:

Date	Inv. No.	Item	Post Ref.	Debit	Credit	Balance
			—			

E 7-3

GENERAL JOURNAL Page _____

Date	Description	Post. Ref.	Debit	Credit

E 7-5

(a) _____

(b) _____

(c) _____

E 7-6

(a) _____   _____   _____

(b)

SALES JOURNAL   Page _____

Date	Customer	Invoice Number	Terms	Post. Ref.	Debit Accounts Receivable	Credits Sales Tax Payable	Sales

E 7-7

a. _____

b. _____

c. _____

d. _____

e. _____

f. _____

GENERAL JOURNAL

Page _____

Date	Description	Post. Ref.	Debit	Credit

GENERAL LEDGER ACCOUNTS

Account: _____ Account No. _____

Date	Item	Post. Ref.	Debit	Credit	Balance Debit	Balance Credit

Account: _____ Account No. _____

Date	Item	Post. Ref.	Debit	Credit	Balance Debit	Balance Credit

ACCOUNTS RECEIVABLE SUBSIDIARY LEDGER

Customer:

Date	Inv. No.	Item	Post Ref.	Debit	Credit	Balance

1.   **SALES JOURNAL**   Page _____

Date	Customer	Invoice Number	Terms	Post Ref.	Amount A/R (Dr.) Sales (Cr.)

2.   **ACCOUNTS RECEIVABLE SUBSIDIARY LEDGER**

Customer:

Date	Inv. No.	Item	Post Ref.	Debit	Credit	Balance
			−			

Customer:

Date	Inv. No.	Item	Post Ref.	Debit	Credit	Balance

Customer:

Date	Inv. No.	Item	Post Ref.	Debit	Credit	Balance

2. **ACCOUNTS RECEIVABLE SUBSIDIARY LEDGER**

Customer:

Date	Inv. No.	Item	Post Ref.	Debit	Credit	Balance
			–			

Customer:

Date	Inv. No.	Item	Post Ref.	Debit	Credit	Balance

Customer:

Date	Inv. No.	Item	Post Ref.	Debit	Credit	Balance

1 and 3.

GENERAL LEDGER ACCOUNTS

Account:					Account No.	
Date	Item	Post. Ref.	Debit	Credit	Balance Debit	Balance Credit

Account:					Account No.	
Date	Item	Post. Ref.	Debit	Credit	Balance Debit	Balance Credit

Name _____

Section _____ Date _____

4. _____
_____
_____

Customer			Amount Owed	

Name _____

Section _____ Date _____

1.   **SALES JOURNAL**   Page _____

Date	Customer	Invoice Number	Terms	Post Ref.	Amount A/R (Dr.) Sales (Cr.)

2.   **GENERAL JOURNAL**   Page _____

Date	Description	Post. Ref.	Debit	Credit

Name _____

Section _____ Date _____

1.   SALES JOURNAL   Page _____

Date	Customer	Invoice Number	Terms	Post Ref.	Amount A/R (Dr.) Sales (Cr.)

2.   GENERAL JOURNAL   Page _____

Date	Description	Post. Ref.	Debit	Credit

3.   **ACCOUNTS RECEIVABLE SUBSIDIARY LEDGER**

Customer:

Date	Inv. No.	Item	Post Ref.	Debit	Credit	Balance
			—			

Customer:

Date	Inv. No.	Item	Post Ref.	Debit	Credit	Balance

Customer:

Date	Inv. No.	Item	Post Ref.	Debit	Credit	Balance

Customer:

Date	Inv. No.	Item	Post Ref.	Debit	Credit	Balance

Customer:

Date	Inv. No.	Item	Post Ref.	Debit	Credit	Balance

continued

3. *(continued)*
Customer:

Date	Inv. No.	Item	Post Ref.	Debit	Credit	Balance
			−			

Customer:

Date	Inv. No.	Item	Post Ref.	Debit	Credit	Balance

Customer:

Date	Inv. No.	Item	Post Ref.	Debit	Credit	Balance

Customer:

Date	Inv. No.	Item	Post Ref.	Debit	Credit	Balance

Customer:

Date	Inv. No.	Item	Post Ref.	Debit	Credit	Balance

4.

	**GENERAL LEDGER ACCOUNTS**

Account:					Account No.		
		Post.				Balance	
Date	Item	Ref.	Debit	Credit	Debit	Credit	

Account:					Account No.		
		Post.				Balance	
Date	Item	Ref.	Debit	Credit	Debit	Credit	

Account:					Account No.		
		Post.				Balance	
Date	Item	Ref.	Debit	Credit	Debit	Credit	

Account:					Account No.		
		Post.				Balance	
Date	Item	Ref.	Debit	Credit	Debit	Credit	

continued

4. *(continued)*

Date	Item	Post. Ref.	Debit	Credit	Balance Debit	Balance Credit
Account:					Account No.	

Date	Item	Post. Ref.	Debit	Credit	Balance Debit	Balance Credit
Account:					Account No.	

5. _____
_____
_____

Customer	Amount Owed	

(a)   **GENERAL JOURNAL**   Page _____

Date	Description	Post. Ref.	Debit	Credit

(b)   **PURCHASES JOURNAL**   Page _____

Date	Vendor	Invoice Number	Terms	Post Ref.	Amount Purch. (Dr.) A/P (Cr.)

E 8-2

ACCOUNTS PAYABLE SUBSIDIARY LEDGER

Vendor:

Date	Inv. No.	Item	Post Ref.	Debit	Credit	Balance
			—			

E 8-3

GENERAL JOURNAL   Page _____

Date	Description	Post. Ref.	Debit	Credit

GENERAL JOURNAL   Page _____

Date		Description	Post. Ref.	Debit	Credit

E 8-5

(a)

(b)

GENERAL JOURNAL   Page _____

Date		Description	Post. Ref.	Debit	Credit

E 8-6

(a) _____

_____

(b) _____

_____

(c) _____

_____

(d) _____

_____

Name _____

Section _____ Date _____

_____
_____
_____

Vendor				Amount Owed	

GENERAL JOURNAL   Page _____

Date	Description	Post. Ref.	Debit	Credit

GENERAL LEDGER ACCOUNTS

Account: _____   Account No. _____

Date	Item	Post. Ref.	Debit	Credit	Balance Debit	Credit

Account: _____   Account No. _____

Date	Item	Post. Ref.	Debit	Credit	Balance Debit	Credit

ACCOUNTS PAYABLE SUBSIDIARY LEDGER

Vendor:

Date	Inv. No.	Item	Post Ref.	Debit	Credit	Balance
			—			

1. **PURCHASES JOURNAL** Page _____

Date		Vendor	Invoice Number	Terms	Post Ref.	Amount Purch. (Dr.) A/P (Cr.)

2. **ACCOUNTS PAYABLE SUBSIDIARY LEDGER**

Vendor:

Date	Inv. No.	Item	Post Ref.	Debit	Credit	Balance
			–			

Vendor:

Date	Inv. No.	Item	Post Ref.	Debit	Credit	Balance
			–			

Vendor:

Date	Inv. No.	Item	Post Ref.	Debit	Credit	Balance
			–			

2.   ACCOUNTS PAYABLE SUBSIDIARY LEDGER

Vendor:

Date	Inv. No.	Item	Post Ref.	Debit	Credit	Balance
			–			

Vendor:

Date	Inv. No.	Item	Post Ref.	Debit	Credit	Balance

Vendor:

Date	Inv. No.	Item	Post Ref.	Debit	Credit	Balance

1 and 3.

GENERAL LEDGER ACCOUNTS

Account:					Account No.	
Date	Item	Post Ref.	Debit	Credit	Balance Debit	Balance Credit

Account:					Account No.	
Date	Item	Post Ref.	Debit	Credit	Balance Debit	Balance Credit

4. _____

_____

_____

_____

Vendor								Amount Owed				

1.   PURCHASES JOURNAL   Page _____

Date		Vendor	Invoice Number	Terms	Post Ref.	Amount Purch. (Dr.) A/P(Cr.)				

2.   GENERAL JOURNAL   Page _____

Date		Description	Post. Ref.	Debit					Credit				

1.   **PURCHASES JOURNAL**   Page _____

Date		Vendor	Invoice Number	Terms	Post Ref.	Amount Purch. (Dr.) A/P(Cr.)					

2.   **GENERAL JOURNAL**   Page _____

Date	Description	Post. Ref.	Debit	Credit

3. ### ACCOUNTS PAYABLE SUBSIDIARY LEDGER

Vendor:

Date	Inv. No.	Item	Post Ref.	Debit	Credit	Balance
			–			

Vendor:

Date	Inv. No.	Item	Post Ref.	Debit	Credit	Balance
			–			

Vendor:

Date	Inv. No.	Item	Post Ref.	Debit	Credit	Balance
			–			

Vendor:

Date	Inv. No.	Item	Post Ref.	Debit	Credit	Balance
			–			

Vendor:

Date	Inv. No.	Item	Post Ref.	Debit	Credit	Balance
			–			

continued

3. *(continued)*

Vendor:

Date	Inv. No.	Item	Post Ref.	Debit	Credit	Balance
			—			

Vendor:

Date	Inv. No.	Item	Post Ref.	Debit	Credit	Balance
			—			

Vendor:

Date	Inv. No.	Item	Post Ref.	Debit	Credit	Balance
			—			

Vendor:

Date	Inv. No.	Item	Post Ref.	Debit	Credit	Balance
			—			

Vendor:

Date	Inv. No.	Item	Post Ref.	Debit	Credit	Balance
			—			

3.

Vendor:

Date	Inv. No.	Item	Post Ref.	Debit	Credit	Balance
			–			

4.

GENERAL LEDGER ACCOUNTS							
Account:						Account No.	
		Post. Ref.				Balance	
Date	Item		Debit	Credit	Debit	Credit	

Account:					Account No.	
		Post. Ref.			Balance	
Date	Item		Debit	Credit	Debit	Credit

Account:					Account No.	
		Post. Ref.			Balance	
Date	Item		Debit	Credit	Debit	Credit

continued

4. *(continued)*

Account:							Account No.	
		Post.					Balance	
Date	Item	Ref.	Debit	Credit		Debit	Credit	

Account:							Account No.	
		Post.					Balance	
Date	Item	Ref.	Debit	Credit		Debit	Credit	

Account:							Account No.	
		Post.					Balance	
Date	Item	Ref.	Debit	Credit		Debit	Credit	

Account:							Account No.	
		Post.					Balance	
Date	Item	Ref.	Debit	Credit		Debit	Credit	

continued

Name _____

Section _____ Date _____

5. _____

_____

Vendor			Amount Owed

E 9-1

E 9-2

a. _____   b. _____   c. _____   d. _____

e. _____   f. _____   g. _____   h. _____

E 9-3

E 9-4

GENERAL JOURNAL

Page _____

Date	Description	Post. Ref.	Debit	Credit

E 9-5

a. _____

b. _____

c. _____

d. _____

e. _____

f. _____

Name _____

Section _____ Date _____

GENERAL JOURNAL

Page _____

Date	Description	Post. Ref.	Debit	Credit

CASH RECEIPTS JOURNAL

Page _____

Date	Account Credited	Post Ref	Credits Other Accounts	Credits Accounts Receiv.	Sales	Debits Sales Disc.	Debits Cash
					—		

GENERAL LEDGER ACCOUNTS

Account: _____   Account No. _____

Date	Item	Post. Ref.	Debit	Credit	Balance Debit	Balance Credit

ACCOUNTS RECEIVABLE SUBSIDIARY LEDGER

Customer: _____

Date	Inv. No.	Item	Post Ref.	Debit	Credit	Balance
			—			

Name _____

Section _____ Date _____

CASH PAYMENTS JOURNAL

Page_____

				Debits			Credits	
Date	Ck. No.	Account Debited	Post Ref	Other Accounts	Accounts Payable	Purchases	Purch. Disc.	Cash
							–	

GENERAL LEDGER ACCOUNTS

Account:					Account No.		
Date	Item	Post. Ref.	Debit	Credit	Balance		
					Debit	Credit	

ACCOUNTS PAYABLE SUBSIDIARY LEDGER

Vendor:

Date	Inv. No.	Item	Post Ref.	Debit	Credit	Balance
			–			

1.   **CASH RECEIPTS JOURNAL**   **Page_____**

			Credits			Debits	
Date	Account Credited	Post Ref	Other Accounts	Accounts Receiv.	Sales	Sales Disc.	Cash
						—	

2.   **ACCOUNTS RECEIVABLE SUBSIDIARY LEDGER**

Customer:

Date	Inv. No.	Item	Post Ref.	Debit	Credit	Balance
			—			

Customer:

Date	Inv. No.	Item	Post Ref.	Debit	Credit	Balance
			—			

Customer:

Date	Inv. No.	Item	Post Ref.	Debit	Credit	Balance
			—			

continued

2. *(continued)*

Customer:

Date	Inv. No.	Item	Post Ref.	Debit	Credit	Balance
			—			

3.

GENERAL LEDGER ACCOUNTS

Account:					Account No.	
		Post. Ref.			Balance	
Date	Item		Debit	Credit	Debit	Credit

Account:					Account No.	
		Post. Ref.			Balance	
Date	Item		Debit	Credit	Debit	Credit

Account:					Account No.	
		Post. Ref.			Balance	
Date	Item		Debit	Credit	Debit	Credit

Account:					Account No.	
		Post. Ref.			Balance	
Date	Item		Debit	Credit	Debit	Credit

3.

Account:							Account No.	
			Post.				Balance	
Date	Item		Ref.	Debit	Credit	Debit	Credit	

Account:							Account No.	
			Post.				Balance	
Date	Item		Ref.	Debit	Credit	Debit	Credit	

Account:							Account No.	
			Post.				Balance	
Date	Item		Ref.	Debit	Credit	Debit	Credit	

3. (*continued*)

Account:							Account No.	
		Post.				Balance		
Date	Item	Ref.	Debit	Credit	Debit		Credit	

Account:							Account No.	
		Post.				Balance		
Date	Item	Ref.	Debit	Credit	Debit		Credit	

Account:							Account No.	
		Post.				Balance		
Date	Item	Ref.	Debit	Credit	Debit		Credit	

Account:							Account No.	
		Post.				Balance		
Date	Item	Ref.	Debit	Credit	Debit		Credit	

Name _____

Section _____ Date _____

1.   **CASH RECEIPTS JOURNAL**   Page_____

Date	Account Credited	Post Ref	Credits			Debits	
			Other Accounts	Accounts Receiv.	Sales	Sales Disc.	Cash

CASH PAYMENTS JOURNAL   Page_____

Date	Ck. No.	Account Debited	Post Ref	Debits			Credits	
				Other Accounts	Accounts Payable	Purchases	Purch. Disc.	Cash

2.   **ACCOUNTS RECEIVABLE SUBSIDIARY LEDGER**

Customer:

Date	Inv. No.	Item	Post Ref.	Debit	Credit	Balance
			–			

Customer:

Date	Inv. No.	Item	Post Ref.	Debit	Credit	Balance
			–			

Customer:

Date	Inv. No.	Item	Post Ref.	Debit	Credit	Balance
			–			

Customer:

Date	Inv. No.	Item	Post Ref.	Debit	Credit	Balance
			–			

2.   **ACCOUNTS PAYABLE SUBSIDIARY LEDGER**

Vendor:

Date	Inv. No.	Item	Post Ref.	Debit	Credit	Balance
			–			

Vendor:

Date	Inv. No.	Item	Post Ref.	Debit	Credit	Balance
			–			

Name _____

Section _____ Date _____

1.   **CASH RECEIPTS JOURNAL**   Page_____

Date	Account Credited	Post Ref	Credits			Debits	
			Other Accounts	Accounts Receiv.	Sales	Sales Disc.	Cash

1.   **CASH PAYMENTS JOURNAL**   Page_____

Date	Ck. No.	Account Debited	Post Ref	Debits			Credits	
				Other Accounts	Accounts Payable	Purchases	Purch. Disc.	Cash

2.   **ACCOUNTS RECEIVABLE SUBSIDIARY LEDGER**

Customer:

Date	Inv. No.	Item	Post Ref.	Debit	Credit	Balance

Customer:

Date	Inv. No.	Item	Post Ref.	Debit	Credit	Balance

continued

2. *(continued)*

Customer: _____

Date	Inv. No.	Item	Post Ref.	Debit	Credit	Balance
			–			

Customer: _____

Date	Inv. No.	Item	Post Ref.	Debit	Credit	Balance
			–			

ACCOUNTS PAYABLE SUBSIDIARY LEDGER

Vendor: _____

Date	Inv. No.	Item	Post Ref.	Debit	Credit	Balance
			–			

Vendor: _____

Date	Inv. No.	Item	Post Ref.	Debit	Credit	Balance
			–			

3.

GENERAL LEDGER ACCOUNTS						
Account:					Account No.	
		Post.			Balance	
Date	Item	Ref.	Debit	Credit	Debit	Credit

Account:					Account No.	
		Post.			Balance	
Date	Item	Ref.	Debit	Credit	Debit	Credit

Account:					Account No.	
		Post.			Balance	
Date	Item	Ref.	Debit	Credit	Debit	Credit

Account:					Account No.	
		Post.			Balance	
Date	Item	Ref.	Debit	Credit	Debit	Credit

Account:					Account No.	
		Post.			Balance	
Date	Item	Ref.	Debit	Credit	Debit	Credit

continued

3. *(continued)*

Account:						Account No.	
		Post.				Balance	
Date	Item	Ref.	Debit	Credit	Debit	Credit	

Account:						Account No.	
		Post.				Balance	
Date	Item	Ref.	Debit	Credit	Debit	Credit	

Account:						Account No.	
		Post.				Balance	
Date	Item	Ref.	Debit	Credit	Debit	Credit	

Account:						Account No.	
		Post.				Balance	
Date	Item	Ref.	Debit	Credit	Debit	Credit	

Account:						Account No.	
		Post.				Balance	
Date	Item	Ref.	Debit	Credit	Debit	Credit	

Account:						Account No.	
		Post.				Balance	
Date	Item	Ref.	Debit	Credit	Debit	Credit	

3.

Account:						Account No.	
		Post.			Balance		
Date	Item	Ref.	Debit	Credit	Debit	Credit	

Account:						Account No.	
		Post.			Balance		
Date	Item	Ref.	Debit	Credit	Debit	Credit	

Account:						Account No.	
		Post.			Balance		
Date	Item	Ref.	Debit	Credit	Debit	Credit	

Account:						Account No.	
		Post.			Balance		
Date	Item	Ref.	Debit	Credit	Debit	Credit	

Account:						Account No.	
		Post.			Balance		
Date	Item	Ref.	Debit	Credit	Debit	Credit	

Name _____

Section _____ Date _____

Special Journals Review Problem

1/11

1.   **SALES JOURNAL**   Page ___1___

Date		Customer	Invoice Number	Terms	Post Ref.	Amount A/R (Dr.) Sales (Cr.)				

PURCHASES JOURNAL   Page ___1___

Date		Vendor	Invoice Number	Terms	Post Ref.	Amount Purch. (Dr.) A/P(Cr.)				

1.   CASH RECEIPTS JOURNAL   Page____1____

Date	Account Credited	Post Ref	Credits			Debits	
			Other Accounts	Accounts Receiv.	Sales	Sales Disc.	Cash

CASH PAYMENTS JOURNAL   Page____1____

Date	Ck. No.	Account Debited	Post Ref	Debits			Credits	
				Other Accounts	Accounts Payable	Purchases	Purch. Disc.	Cash

continued

1. *(continued)*

Date	Description	Post. Ref.	Debit	Credit

Name _____

Section _____ Date _____

Special Journals Review Problem

2.

GENERAL LEDGER ACCOUNTS						
Account:					Account No.	
Date	Item	Post. Ref.	Debit	Credit	Balance	
					Debit	Credit

Account:					Account No.	
Date	Item	Post. Ref.	Debit	Credit	Balance	
					Debit	Credit

Account:					Account No.	
Date	Item	Post. Ref.	Debit	Credit	Balance	
					Debit	Credit

Account:					Account No.	
Date	Item	Post. Ref.	Debit	Credit	Balance	
					Debit	Credit

2. (*continued*)

Account:						Account No.	
		Post.				Balance	
Date	Item	Ref.	Debit	Credit	Debit	Credit	

Account:						Account No.	
		Post.				Balance	
Date	Item	Ref.	Debit	Credit	Debit	Credit	

Account:						Account No.	
		Post.				Balance	
Date	Item	Ref.	Debit	Credit	Debit	Credit	

Account:						Account No.	
		Post.				Balance	
Date	Item	Ref.	Debit	Credit	Debit	Credit	

2.

Account:					Account No.	
		Post.			Balance	
Date	Item	Ref.	Debit	Credit	Debit	Credit

Account:					Account No.	
		Post.			Balance	
Date	Item	Ref.	Debit	Credit	Debit	Credit

Account:					Account No.	
		Post.			Balance	
Date	Item	Ref.	Debit	Credit	Debit	Credit

Account:					Account No.	
		Post.			Balance	
Date	Item	Ref.	Debit	Credit	Debit	Credit

Account:					Account No.	
		Post.			Balance	
Date	Item	Ref.	Debit	Credit	Debit	Credit

continued

2. *(continued)*

Account:						Account No.	
		Post.			Balance		
Date	Item	Ref.	Debit	Credit	Debit	Credit	

Account:						Account No.	
		Post.			Balance		
Date	Item	Ref.	Debit	Credit	Debit	Credit	

Account:						Account No.	
		Post.			Balance		
Date	Item	Ref.	Debit	Credit	Debit	Credit	

Account:						Account No.	
		Post.			Balance		
Date	Item	Ref.	Debit	Credit	Debit	Credit	

2.   **ACCOUNTS RECEIVABLE SUBSIDIARY LEDGER**

Customer:

Date	Inv. No.	Item	Post Ref.	Debit	Credit	Balance
			–			

Customer:

Date	Inv. No.	Item	Post Ref.	Debit	Credit	Balance
			–			

Customer:

Date	Inv. No.	Item	Post Ref.	Debit	Credit	Balance
			–			

Customer:

Date	Inv. No.	Item	Post Ref.	Debit	Credit	Balance

ACCOUNTS PAYABLE SUBSIDIARY LEDGER

Vendor:

Date	Inv. No.	Item	Post Ref.	Debit	Credit	Balance
			–			

continued

2. *(continued)*

Vendor:

Date	Inv. No.	Item	Post Ref.	Debit	Credit	Balance
			−			

Vendor:

Date	Inv. No.	Item	Post Ref.	Debit	Credit	Balance
			−			

Vendor:

Date	Inv. No.	Item	Post Ref.	Debit	Credit	Balance
			−			

Vendor:

Date	Inv. No.	Item	Post Ref.	Debit	Credit	Balance
			−			

Vendor:

Date	Inv. No.	Item	Post Ref.	Debit	Credit	Balance
			−			

2.

Vendor: _____

Date	Inv. No.	Item	Post Ref.	Debit	Credit	Balance
			–			

Vendor: _____

Date	Inv. No.	Item	Post Ref.	Debit	Credit	Balance
			–			

3. _____

Accounts	Debit	Credit

4. _____
_____
_____

Customer								Amount Owed					

5. _____
_____
_____

Vendor								Amount Owed					

GENERAL JOURNAL

Page _____

Date	Description	Post. Ref.	Debit	Credit

E 10-2

_____

_____

_____

GENERAL JOURNAL

Page _____

Date	Description	Post. Ref.	Debit	Credit

CASH RECEIPTS JOURNAL

Page _____

Date	Account Credited	Post Ref	Credits			Debits	
			Other Accounts	Accounts Receiv.	Sales	Sales Disc.	Cash

GENERAL JOURNAL

Page _____

Date	Description	Post. Ref.	Debit	Credit
	Bank Reconciliation Entries			

Name _____

Section _____ Date _____

1.   **CASH PAYMENTS JOURNAL**   Page_____

Date	Ck. No.	Account Debited	Post Ref	Debits			Credits	
				Other Accounts	Accounts Payable	Purchases	Purch. Disc.	Cash

E 10-6

(a) _____

_____

(b) _____

_____

(c) _____

_____

(d) _____

_____

(e) _____

_____

(f) _____

_____

(g) _____

_____

(h) _____

_____

1.   **CASH PAYMENTS JOURNAL**   Page_____

Date	Ck. No.	Account Debited	Post Ref	Debits			Credits	
				Other Accounts	Accounts Payable	Purchases	Purch. Disc.	Cash

a. _____   _____

1. <center>**CASH PAYMENTS JOURNAL**</center>   Page_____

Date	Ck. No.	Account Debited	Post Ref	Debits			Credits	
				Other Accounts	Accounts Payable	Purchases	Purch. Disc.	Cash

b. <center>**CASH RECEIPTS JOURNAL**</center>   Page_____

Date	Account Credited	Post Ref	Credits			Debits	
			Other Accounts	Accounts Receiv.	Sales	Sales Disc.	Cash

Name _____

Section _____ Date _____

GENERAL JOURNAL

Page _____

Date	Description	Post. Ref.	Debit	Credit

1. _____
_____
_____

2.   **GENERAL JOURNAL**   Page _____

Date		Description	Post. Ref.	Debit						Credit					
		Bank Reconciliation Entries													

Name _____

Section _____ Date _____

1. **CASH PAYMENTS JOURNAL** Page_____

Date	Ck. No.	Account Debited	Post Ref	Debits			Credits	
				Other Accounts	Accounts Payable	Purchases	Purch. Disc.	Cash

CASH RECEIPTS JOURNAL Page_____

Date	Account Credited	Post Ref	Credits			Debits	
			Other Accounts	Accounts Receiv.	Sales	Sales Disc.	Cash

2. **PETTY CASH DISBURSEMENTS RECORD** Page_____

Date	Voucher Number	Account Charged	Amount	Fund Balance	Comments

3. _____

4. _____

1. _____
_____
_____

2.   **GENERAL JOURNAL**   **Page** _____

Date	Description	Post. Ref.	Debit	Credit

3.

GENERAL LEDGER ACCOUNTS						
Account:					Account No.	
		Post.			Balance	
Date	Item	Ref.	Debit	Credit	Debit	Credit

a.

b.

a. _____

_____

b. _____

_____

c. _____

_____

d. _____

_____

e. _____

_____

E 11-3

a. _____
_____

b. _____
_____

c. _____
_____

d. _____
_____

e. _____
_____

f. _____
_____

g. _____
_____

E 11-4

a. Calculations:

b. (a)   **CASH RECEIPTS JOURNAL**   **Page_____**

Date	Account Credited	Post Ref	Credits			Debits	
			Other Accounts	Accounts Receiv.	Sales	Sales Disc.	Cash

(b)

Name _____

Section _____ Date _____

a.

b.

c.

d.

e.

_____

_____

_____

Account	Trial Balance		Adjustments	
	Debit	Credit	Debit	Credit

_____
_____
_____

Adjusted Trial Balance		Income Statement		Balance Sheet	
Debit	Credit	Debit	Credit	Debit	Credit

GENERAL JOURNAL   Page _____

Date	Description	Post. Ref.	Debit	Credit

_____

_____

_____

Account	Trial Balance		Adjustments	
	Debit	Credit	Debit	Credit

_____
_____
_____

Adjusted Trial Balance		Income Statement		Balance Sheet	
Debit	Credit	Debit	Credit	Debit	Credit

_____
_____
_____

Account	Trial Balance		Adjustments	
	Debit	Credit	Debit	Credit

_____
_____
_____

Adjusted Trial Balance		Income Statement		Balance Sheet	
Debit	Credit	Debit	Credit	Debit	Credit

GENERAL JOURNAL   **Page** _____

Date		Description	Post. Ref.	Debit	Credit

1 and 3.

GENERAL LEDGER ACCOUNTS						
Account:					Account No.	
		Post.			Balance	
Date	Item	Ref.	Debit	Credit	Debit	Credit

Account:					Account No.	
		Post.			Balance	
Date	Item	Ref.	Debit	Credit	Debit	Credit

Account:					Account No.	
		Post.			Balance	
Date	Item	Ref.	Debit	Credit	Debit	Credit

Account:					Account No.	
		Post.			Balance	
Date	Item	Ref.	Debit	Credit	Debit	Credit

continued

1 and 3. (*continued*)

Account:								Account No.	
		Post.						Balance	
Date	Item	Ref.	Debit		Credit		Debit		Credit

Account:								Account No.	
		Post.						Balance	
Date	Item	Ref.	Debit		Credit		Debit		Credit

GENERAL LEDGER ACCOUNTS									
Account:								Account No.	
		Post.						Balance	
Date	Item	Ref.	Debit		Credit		Debit		Credit

Account:								Account No.	
		Post.						Balance	
Date	Item	Ref.	Debit		Credit		Debit		Credit

Account:								Account No.	
		Post.						Balance	
Date	Item	Ref.	Debit		Credit		Debit		Credit

1 and 3.

Account:								Account No.	
		Post.					Balance		
Date	Item	Ref.	Debit		Credit		Debit		Credit

Account:								Account No.	
		Post.					Balance		
Date	Item	Ref.	Debit		Credit		Debit		Credit

Account:								Account No.	
		Post.					Balance		
Date	Item	Ref.	Debit		Credit		Debit		Credit

1 and 2 _____
_____
_____

Account	Trial Balance		Adjustments	
	Debit	Credit	Debit	Credit

_____
_____
_____

Adjusted Trial Balance		Income Statement		Balance Sheet	
Debit	Credit	Debit	Credit	Debit	Credit

3. GENERAL JOURNAL Page _____

Date		Description	Post. Ref.	Debit	Credit

1. _____
_____
_____

Account	Trial Balance		Adjustments	
	Debit	Credit	Debit	Credit

_____
_____
_____

Adjusted Trial Balance		Income Statement		Balance Sheet	
Debit	Credit	Debit	Credit	Debit	Credit

2.   **GENERAL JOURNAL**   **Page** _____

Date	Description	Post. Ref.	Debit	Credit

3.

GENERAL LEDGER ACCOUNTS						
Account:					Account No.	
Date	Item	Post. Ref.	Debit	Credit	Balance Debit	Balance Credit

3.

Account:						Account No.	
		Post.			Balance		
Date	Item	Ref.	Debit	Credit	Debit	Credit	

Account:						Account No.	
		Post.			Balance		
Date	Item	Ref.	Debit	Credit	Debit	Credit	

Account:						Account No.	
		Post.			Balance		
Date	Item	Ref.	Debit	Credit	Debit	Credit	

Account:						Account No.	
		Post.			Balance		
Date	Item	Ref.	Debit	Credit	Debit	Credit	

Account:						Account No.	
		Post.			Balance		
Date	Item	Ref.	Debit	Credit	Debit	Credit	

continued

3. *(continued)*

Account:							Account No.	
		Post.				Balance		
Date	Item	Ref.	Debit	Credit	Debit		Credit	

Account:							Account No.	
		Post.				Balance		
Date	Item	Ref.	Debit	Credit	Debit		Credit	

Account:							Account No.	
		Post.				Balance		
Date	Item	Ref.	Debit	Credit	Debit		Credit	

Account:							Account No.	
		Post.				Balance		
Date	Item	Ref.	Debit	Credit	Debit		Credit	

Account:							Account No.	
		Post.				Balance		
Date	Item	Ref.	Debit	Credit	Debit		Credit	

Account:							Account No.	
		Post.				Balance		
Date	Item	Ref.	Debit	Credit	Debit		Credit	

Name _____

Section _____ Date _____

E 12-1

(a) _____

(b) _____

(c) _____

(d) _____

(e) _____

(f) _____

(g) _____

(h) _____

E 12-2

(a) _____

(b)

(c)

E 12-3

(a) _____

(b) _____

(c) _____

(d) _____

(e) _____

(f) _____

(g) _____

E 12-4

(a) _____

(b) _____

(c) _____

(d) _____

(e) _____

(f) _____

(g) _____

Name _____

Section _____ Date _____

(a) _____

(b) _____

(c) _____

(d) _____

(e) _____

(f) _____

(g) _____

(h) _____

(i) _____

E 12-7

GENERAL JOURNAL   **Page** _____

Date	Description	Post. Ref.	Debit	Credit

GENERAL JOURNAL   Page _____

Date	Description	Post. Ref.	Debit	Credit
	Adjusting Entries			

Date	Description	Post. Ref.	Debit	Credit
	Closing Entries			

Date	Description	Post. Ref.	Debit	Credit
	Reversing Entries			

Date	Description	Post. Ref.	Debit	Credit
	Payment			

_____
_____
_____

1.   **GENERAL JOURNAL**   **Page** _____

Date		Description	Post. Ref.	Debit	Credit

2. _____
_____
_____

Accounts	Debit	Credit

1. _____
_____
_____
_____

Name _____

Section _____ Date _____

1. _____
_____
_____

continued

1. *(continued)*

2.

(a)

(b)

(c)

Name _____

Section _____ Date _____

1/6

1. _____

1. _____

_____

_____

continued

1. *(continued)*

2.

(a)

(b)

(c)

3.

GENERAL JOURNAL

Page _____

Date		Description	Post. Ref.	Debit	Credit

4. _____
_____
_____

Accounts	Debit	Credit

5 and 6. **GENERAL JOURNAL** Page _____

Date	Description	Post. Ref.	Debit	Credit

Name _____

Section _____ Date _____

a.____   b.____   c.____   d.____
e.____   f.____   g.____   h.____

Name _____

Section _____ Date _____

Employee Compensation Record

Employee's Name _____ Social Security No. _____

Address _____ Male ___   Female ___   Weekly Pay Rate _____

_____ Married ___   Single ___   Hourly Equivalent _____

Date of Birth _____ Withholding Allowances ___

Position _____ Date of Employment _____

Date Employment Ended _____

| Pay Period Ending | Total Hours | Earnings | | | Deductions | | | | Net Pay | Cumulative Gross Earnings |
		Regular	Overtime	Total	Social Sec. Tax	Medicare Tax	Federal Income Tax	Total Deduc- tions		

E 13-4

E 13-6

a._____   b._____   c._____   d._____
e._____   f._____   g._____   h._____
i._____   j._____   k._____   l._____
m._____   n._____   o._____   p._____
q._____   r._____   s._____   t._____
u._____

(a)   **GENERAL JOURNAL**   **Page _____**

Date	Description	Post. Ref.	Debit	Credit

(b)

Name _____

Section _____ Date _____

Employee Compensation Record

Employee's Name _____   Social Security No. _____

Address _____   Male ___   Female ___   Weekly Pay Rate _____

_____   Married ___   Single ___   Hourly Equivalent _____

Date of Birth _____   Withholding Allowances ___

Position _____   Date of Employment _____

Date Employment Ended _____

Pay Period Ending	Total Hours	Earnings			Deductions				Net Pay	Cumulative Gross Earnings
		Regular	Overtime	Total	Social Sec. Tax	Medicare Tax	Federal Income Tax	Total Deduc- tions		

Employee Compensation Record

Employee's Name _____   Social Security No. _____

Address _____   Male ___   Female ___   Weekly Pay Rate _____

_____   Married ___   Single ___   Hourly Equivalent _____

Date of Birth _____   Withholding Allowances ___

Position _____   Date of Employment _____

Date Employment Ended _____

Pay Period Ending	Total Hours	Earnings			Deductions				Net Pay	Cumulative Gross Earnings
		Regular	Overtime	Total	Social Sec. Tax	Medicare Tax	Federal Income Tax	Total Deduc- tions		

1.

		Earnings			Deductions					Distribution
					Payroll Register					
				For the Week Ended _____						
Employee	Total Hours	Regular	Overtime	Total	Social Security Tax	Medicare Tax	Federal Income Tax	Total Deduc- tions	Net Pay	Wage Expense

2. **GENERAL JOURNAL** Page _____

Date	Description	Post. Ref.	Debit	Credit

Employee Compensation Record

Employee's Name _____ Social Security No. _____

Address _____ Male ___ Female ___ Weekly Pay Rate _____

_____ Married ___ Single ___ Hourly Equivalent _____

Date of Birth _____ Withholding Allowances ___

Position _____ Date of Employment _____

Date Employment Ended _____

Pay Period Ending	Total Hours	Earnings			Deductions				Net Pay	Cumulative Gross Earnings
		Regular	Overtime	Total	Social Sec. Tax	Medicare Tax	Federal Income Tax	Total Deduc- tions		

Employee Compensation Record

Employee's Name _____ Social Security No. _____

Address _____ Male ___ Female ___ Weekly Pay Rate _____

_____ Married ___ Single ___ Hourly Equivalent _____

Date of Birth _____ Withholding Allowances ___

Position _____ Date of Employment _____

Date Employment Ended _____

Pay Period Ending	Total Hours	Earnings			Deductions				Net Pay	Cumulative Gross Earnings
		Regular	Overtime	Total	Social Sec. Tax	Medicare Tax	Federal Income Tax	Total Deduc- tions		

2.

			Payroll Register								
			For the Week Ended _____								

Employee	Total Hours	Earnings			Deductions				Net Pay	Distribution
		Regular	Overtime	Total	Social Security Tax	Medicare Tax	Federal Income Tax	Total Deduc-tions		Wage Expense

3. **GENERAL JOURNAL** Page _____

Date	Description	Post. Ref.	Debit	Credit

4.

a. _____
b. _____
c. _____

a. _____
b. _____
c. _____

Name _____

Section _____ Date _____

GRADE OF WORK	ESTIMATED PAYROLL	RATE PER HUNDRED	PREMIUM

GENERAL JOURNAL   Page _____

Date		Description	Post. Ref.	Debit	Credit

E 14-7

a. _____

_____

b. _____

_____

c. _____

_____

Name _____

Section _____ Date _____

a.

b. _____

c.

1. Second Week.

Date	Description	Post. Ref.	Debit	Credit

GENERAL JOURNAL

Page _____

Date	Description	Post. Ref.	Debit	Credit

Form 941

Department of the Treasury
Internal Revenue Service (O)

Employer's Quarterly Federal Tax Return
▶ See separate instructions for information on completing this return.
Please type or print.

OMB No. 1545-0029

T	
FF	
FD	
FP	
I	
T	

Enter state code for state in which deposits were made ONLY if different from state in address to the right ▶ ☐ (see page 3 of instructions).

Name (as distinguished from trade name)   Date quarter ended

Trade name, if any   Employer identification number

Address (number and street)   City, state, and ZIP code

If address is different from prior return, check here ▶ ☐

IRS Use

1 1	1 1 1 1	1 1 1 1	2	3 3 3 3 3 3	4 4 4	5 5 5
6	7	8 8 8 8 8 8 8		9 9 9 9 9	10 10 10 10 10 10 10 10 10 10	

If you do not have to file returns in the future, check here ▶ ☐ and enter date final wages paid ▶

If you are a seasonal employer, see **Seasonal employers** on page 1 of the instructions and check here ▶ ☐

1	Number of employees in the pay period that includes March 12th . ▶ 1	
2	Total wages and tips, plus other compensation	**2**
3	Total income tax withheld from wages, tips, and sick pay	**3**
4	Adjustment of withheld income tax for preceding quarters of calendar year	**4**
5	Adjusted total of income tax withheld (line 3 as adjusted by line 4—see instructions) . . .	**5**
6	Taxable social security wages	**6a** _____ × 12.4% (.124) = **6b**
	Taxable social security tips	**6c** _____ × 12.4% (.124) = **6d**
7	Taxable Medicare wages and tips . . .	**7a** _____ × 2.9% (.029) = **7b**
8	Total social security and Medicare taxes (add lines 6b, 6d, and 7b). Check here if wages are not subject to social security and/or Medicare tax . . . . ▶ ☐	**8**
9	Adjustment of social security and Medicare taxes (see instructions for required explanation) Sick Pay $ _____ ± Fractions of Cents $ _____ ± Other $ _____ =	**9**
10	Adjusted total of social security and Medicare taxes (line 8 as adjusted by line 9—see instructions)	**10**
11	**Total taxes** (add lines 5 and 10)	**11**
12	Advance earned income credit (EIC) payments made to employees	**12**
13	Net taxes (subtract line 12 from line 11). **This should equal line 17, column (d) below (or line D of Schedule B (Form 941))**	**13**
14	Total deposits for quarter, including overpayment applied from a prior quarter	**14**
15	**Balance due** (subtract line 14 from line 13). See instructions	**15**
16	**Overpayment,** if line 14 is more than line 13, enter excess here ▶ $ _____	

and check if to be: ☐ Applied to next return **OR** ☐ Refunded.

● **All filers:** If line 13 is less than $500, you need not complete line 17 or Schedule B (Form 941).

● **Semiweekly schedule depositors:** Complete Schedule B (Form 941) and check here . . . . ▶ ☐

● **Monthly schedule depositors:** Complete line 17, columns (a) through (d), and check here . . . . ▶ ☐

17	Monthly Summary of Federal Tax Liability. Do not complete if you were a semiweekly schedule depositor.		
(a) First month liability	**(b)** Second month liability	**(c)** Third month liability	**(d)** Total liability for quarter

Sign Here

Under penalties of perjury, I declare that I have examined this return, including accompanying schedules and statements, and to the best of my knowledge and belief, it is true, correct, and complete.

Signature ▶   Print Your Name and Title ▶   Date ▶

For Privacy Act and Paperwork Reduction Act Notice, see page 4 of separate instructions.   Cat. No. 17001Z   Form **941**

Form **940-EZ**

Department of the Treasury
Internal Revenue Service   (O)

**Employer's Annual Federal
Unemployment (FUTA) Tax Return**

▶ For Paperwork Reduction Act Notice, see page 4.

OMB No. 1545-1110

T	
FF	
FD	
FP	
I	
T	

Name (as distinguished from trade name)   Calendar year

Trade name, if any

Address and ZIP code   Employer identification number

Follow the chart under Who May Use Form 940-EZ on page 2. If you cannot use Form 940-EZ, you must use Form 940 instead.

A Enter the amount of contributions paid to your state unemployment fund. (See instructions for line A on page 4.)▶ $ ....

B (1) Enter the name of the state where you have to pay contributions   . . . . ▶ ....
    (2) Enter your state reporting number as shown on state unemployment tax return ▶

If you will not have to file returns in the future, check here (see Who must file on page 2) and complete and sign the return   . . . . . ▶ ☐

If this is an Amended Return, check here   . . . . ▶ ☐

Part I   **Taxable Wages and FUTA Tax**

		Amount paid		
1	Total payments (including payments shown on lines 2 and 3) during the calendar year for services of employees	**1**		
2	Exempt payments. (Explain all exempt payments, attaching additional sheets if necessary.) ▶	**2**		
3	Payments for services of more than $7,000. Enter only amounts over the first $7,000 paid to each employee. Do not include any exempt payments from line 2. Do not use your state wage limitation. The $7,000 amount is the Federal wage base. Your state wage base may be different	**3**		
4	Total exempt payments (add lines 2 and 3)		**4**	
5	**Total taxable wages** (subtract line 4 from line 1) . . . . ▶		**5**	
6	**FUTA tax.** Multiply the wages on line 5 by .008 and enter here. (If the result is over $100, also complete Part II.)		**6**	
7	Total FUTA tax deposited for the year, including any overpayment applied from a prior year (from your records)		**7**	
8	**Amount you owe** (subtract line 7 from line 6). This should be $100 or less. Pay to "Internal Revenue Service." ▶		**8**	
9	Overpayment (subtract line 6 from line 7). Check if it is to be: ☐ **Applied to next return or** ☐ **Refunded** ▶		**9**	

Part II   **Record of Quarterly Federal Unemployment Tax Liability** (Do not include state liability.) Complete only if line 6 is over $100.

Quarter	First (Jan. 1 – Mar. 31)	Second (Apr. 1 – June 30)	Third (July 1 – Sept. 30)	Fourth (Oct. 1 – Dec. 31)	Total for year
Liability for quarter					

Under penalties of perjury, I declare that I have examined this return, including accompanying schedules and statements, and, to the best of my knowledge and belief, it is true, correct, and complete, and that no part of any payment made to a state unemployment fund claimed as a credit was, or is to be, deducted from the payments to employees.

Signature ▶   Title (Owner, etc.) ▶   Date ▶

Name _____

Section _____ Date _____

P 14-4

1/2

1.

2.

3.

4.

1.   **GENERAL JOURNAL**   **Page** _____

Date		Description	Post. Ref.	Debit	Credit

2.

Form **941**

Department of the Treasury
Internal Revenue Service   (O)

Employer's Quarterly Federal Tax Return

▶ See separate instructions for information on completing this return.

Please type or print.

OMB No. 1545-0029

Enter state code for state in which deposits were made ONLY if different from state in address to the right ▶ ⬚

(see page 3 of instructions).

Name (as distinguished from trade name)	Date quarter ended
Trade name, if any	Employer identification number
Address (number and street)	City, state, and ZIP code

T	
FF	
FD	
FP	
I	
T	

If address is different from prior return, check here ▶ ⬚

IRS Use

1 1 1 1 1 1 1 1 1   2   3 3 3 3 3 3 3   4 4 4   5 5 5

6   7   8 8 8 8 8 8 8 8   9 9 9 9 9   10 10 10 10 10 10 10 10 10 10

If you do not have to file returns in the future, check here ▶ ⬚   and enter date final wages paid ▶

If you are a seasonal employer, see **Seasonal employers** on page 1 of the instructions and check here ▶

1	Number of employees in the pay period that includes March 12th . ▶	1	
2	Total wages and tips, plus other compensation	**2**	
3	Total income tax withheld from wages, tips, and sick pay	**3**	
4	Adjustment of withheld income tax for preceding quarters of calendar year	**4**	
5	Adjusted total of income tax withheld (line 3 as adjusted by line 4—see instructions) . . .	**5**	

6	Taxable social security wages	**6a**		× 12.4% (.124) =	**6b**	
	Taxable social security tips	**6c**		× 12.4% (.124) =	**6d**	
7	Taxable Medicare wages and tips . . .	**7a**		× 2.9% (.029) =	**7b**	

8	Total social security and Medicare taxes (add lines 6b, 6d, and 7b). Check here if wages are not subject to social security and/or Medicare tax . . . . ▶ ⬚	**8**	
9	Adjustment of social security and Medicare taxes (see instructions for required explanation) Sick Pay $ _____ ± Fractions of Cents $ _____ ± Other $ _____ =	**9**	
10	Adjusted total of social security and Medicare taxes (line 8 as adjusted by line 9—see instructions)	**10**	
11	**Total taxes** (add lines 5 and 10)	**11**	
12	Advance earned income credit (EIC) payments made to employees	**12**	
13	Net taxes (subtract line 12 from line 11). **This should equal line 17, column (d) below (or line D of Schedule B (Form 941))**	**13**	
14	Total deposits for quarter, including overpayment applied from a prior quarter	**14**	
15	**Balance due** (subtract line 14 from line 13). See instructions	**15**	

16 **Overpayment,** if line 14 is more than line 13, enter excess here ▶ $ _____

and check if to be: ⬚ Applied to next return   **OR**   ⬚ Refunded.

● **All filers:** If line 13 is less than $500, you need not complete line 17 or Schedule B (Form 941).

● **Semiweekly schedule depositors:** Complete Schedule B (Form 941) and check here . . . . ▶ ⬚

● **Monthly schedule depositors:** Complete line 17, columns (a) through (d), and check here . . . . ▶ ⬚

17   Monthly Summary of Federal Tax Liability. Do not complete if you were a semiweekly schedule depositor.

(a) First month liability	(b) Second month liability	(c) Third month liability	(d) Total liability for quarter

Sign Here

Under penalties of perjury, I declare that I have examined this return, including accompanying schedules and statements, and to the best of my knowledge and belief, it is true, correct, and complete.

Signature ▶ _____   Print Your Name and Title ▶ _____   Date ▶ _____

For Privacy Act and Paperwork Reduction Act Notice, see page 4 of separate instructions.   Cat. No. 17001Z   Form **941**